"Sunday Coming"

"Sunday Coming"
Black Baseball in Virginia
SECOND EDITION

Darrell J. Howard

McFarland & Company, Inc., Publishers
Jefferson, North Carolina

Library of Congress Cataloging-in-Publication Data

Names: Howard, Darrell J., 1967– author.
Title: "Sunday coming" : Black baseball in Virginia / Darrell J. Howard.
Description: Second edition. | Jefferson, North Carolina : McFarland & Company, Inc., Publishers, 2025 | Includes bibliographical references and index.
Identifiers: LCCN 2025000575 | ISBN 9781476696157 (paperback : acid free paper) ♾
ISBN 9781476654553 (ebook)
Subjects: LCSH: Negro leagues—Virginia—History. | Baseball players—Virginia—Biography. | African American baseball players—Virginia—Biography.
Classification: LCC GV875.A1 N69 2025 | DDC 796.357/64/089960730755—dc23/eng/20250117
LC record available at https://lccn.loc.gov/2025000575

ISBN (print) 978-1-4766-9615-7
ISBN (ebook) 978-1-4766-5455-3

© 2025 Darrell J. Howard. All rights reserved

No part of this book may be reproduced or transmitted in any form or by any means, electronic or mechanical, including photocopying or recording, or by any information storage and retrieval system, without permission in writing from the publisher.

Front cover image: Arlington White Sox, circa 1930s
(Center for Local History, Arlington Public Library)

Printed in the United States of America

*McFarland & Company, Inc., Publishers
Box 611, Jefferson, North Carolina 28640
www.mcfarlandpub.com*

For Mom, Dad and Cranston,
and to the black baseball teams of Virginia

Acknowledgments

The author would like to offer special thanks and gratitude to Robert Anthony, Zann Nelson, Alan G. Johnson, H.B. Awkard, Janet Rogers, James Madison's Montpelier, the Orange County African American Historical Society, the Lucy F. Simms School, the Roanoke Public Library, the Shenandoah Valley Black Heritage Project and Special Collections at the University of Virginia.

Contents

Acknowledgments	vi
Preface	1
Introduction	3
I. Pete Hill, a Legacy Nearly Lost (by Zann Nelson)	7
II. Top of the Order, 1930–1940	19
III. Heart of the Order, 1940–1950	38
IV. Uncrowned Champions, 1950–1960	64
V. Bases Loaded, 1960–1970	104
VI. Bottom of the Order, 1970–1980	152
VII. Race Against Time	188
VIII. Game Over: Vacant Sandlots	198
Appendix 1: Norfolk Journal and Guide *Baseball Directory*	207
Appendix 2: Leagues and Teams	209
Appendix 3: Virginia Player Register	214
Chapter Notes	221
Bibliography	225
Index	227

Preface

"*Sunday Coming*": *Black Baseball in Virginia* was inspired by childhood memories of weekend baseball games in the 1970s. Black baseball in Virginia is a part of my family's history, and I grew up approximately 400 feet from home plate of one of the last black baseball teams—the Ivy Virginia Eagles. When I began my research, I envisioned a book of moderate proportions, not knowing that what occurred within walking distance from my parents' front yard happened all over Virginia for several decades. From the first interview to the last, it was the stories and the spirit of the remaining ballplayers that defined the importance of the project.

The second edition remains consistent with the structure of the first, with more player-related perspectives and fact-based findings. All except a few of the former ballplayers interviewed in the first edition are gone, but their stories—and now, in the pages that follow, those of others—remain. In the years since the first edition was published, I have fielded questions from around the Mid-Atlantic; in my attempts to answer them, I've added author's notes throughout, not merely to introduce material but to lend greater context to time periods, people and places.

Introduction

> The league we were in you had to produce; or they would send you home! We knew there were lots of black guys in the cotton patches in the South and other places that could play just as good as we could play. It was just a lucky few that was given the chance.
> —*Riley Stewart, Negro League Chicago American Giants*
> *(quoted in Ken Burns'* Baseball*)*

Sunday Coming is the story of black baseball in Virginia, written with the aid of a few remaining facts, and recreated through the words of the men who played, and whose spirited memories speak volumes for their love of baseball in a bygone era. The phrase "black baseball" is used to differentiate play in the sandlots from that in the professional Negro leagues that existed between 1920 and 1950.

From Winchester to Tidewater and Danville to Fairfax, black baseball was the longest-running form of entertainment and recreation in the black communities of the Old Dominion. For those able to recall the enduring tradition, it is one of the most talked about and treasured topics. For five decades Virginia's black teams played their form of Negro League baseball in rural pastures, cleared-out forested properties, city parks and—for a fortunate few—minor league stadiums.

The characters and humble facilities mirrored the essence of what evolved into the professional Negro Leagues. It was the same fast-paced play and showmanship, complemented by descriptive nicknames such as "Preacher" and "Rooster."

Black baseball in Virginia was family and community baseball through Jim Crow segregation, the civil rights movement and the early stages of integration. Nearly every community statewide had at least one black baseball team between 1930 and 1970. The ball team carried the banner of the community, so that communities became synonymous with the baseball team and the families who filled out the team.

The players were mechanics, truck drivers, loggers, and shipyard workers, men who worked hard and played harder. They came to evening practices dressed in their work clothes and wearing boots bearing the burdens of a day's labor, but when they put on their ball caps and their gloves, and worked the baseball around talking it up to one another, all thoughts were on the big weekend game, who they were playing and where it was to be played. They played baseball and they loved it.

Jim Dowell, Covesville Tigers & Astros:

We used to work hard, hauling pinewood logs, hay, everything. And we were ready to play that ball on Saturday and Sunday. We'd talk about that ball all through the week. I guess we made our work easy, because we were working hard and talking about playing ball.

The players loved baseball for the sport and competition, without the expensive promotion, sponsorship, gratuitous pay and reward. There were no clinics, no coaches—just a resolve and will to perfect their skills. Game results turned into stories, not statistics, that got better over time.

Their baseball was news, whether you followed it in Virginia's black press or by word of mouth. Down at the barbershop and in the sawmills, black baseball fans talked about which community had the best pitcher and best hitter. After church on Sunday, visitors asked around about the local ball team, voluntarily talking up their own, saying, "we have a good team; maybe your team would like to play our community." Many fans were as memorable as any of the ball teams. They were devoted, and followed their home team; but also, notably, they learned something about black communities two hours away, and often they had something to share about their home community. Baseball was another form of networking in the black community.

Going to a ballgame in Virginia was akin to celebrating the 4th of July every weekend.

Kenny Diggs, 1970s Avon Virginia A's:

When we went to play Wilmington, everybody had a meeting place, and my aunts and everybody in every car that you went to had at least four or five chickens in it, coolers full of sodas and beers. You were picnicking, everything. If you lost you would go home with a full stomach—you would enjoy your day.

Behind the competition and entertainment was the collective effort and cooperation to keep the event going. Black baseball in Virginia worked, because the teams worked together to make the event happen. There was an importance to participating and playing baseball.

Mel Perrow, 1970s Shipman Virginia Angels, Massies Mill Cubs:

If we only have two pitchers and the other team is eating them up, then it was nothing for one of the guys playing somewhere else, say right field, to come in and catch. And then the catcher would pitch, and the pitcher would play somewhere else. We had to switch guys around, but most guys were multi-talented, and most of us had to play several positions because we didn't have enough backup especially if you're only carrying 13 players. Most of them liked playing so they would do anything to stay in the game.

Some played and performed like professional ballplayers; others were just happy to be a part of the team and contribute their best. The mediocre players and the poor teams that struggled along were an important piece to keeping the tradition going decade after decade. Black baseball's demise in the Commonwealth passed like the short summer season. There is not just one significant reason the tradition faded but a list of factors that loomed larger with the evolving times. Parks and fields

Armstead Hill, former site of the Ivy Eagles' field (photograph courtesy Jon Glassberg).

where black baseball occurred were closed and renamed without references to teams that made the area popular. Rural diamonds were developed or plowed over.

Sunday Coming documents an exultant time period in Virginia's African American subculture while honoring the tradition of baseball in America.

The first edition of this book began chronologically in the year 1930, not at random but because coverage of the teams and games appeared consistently in print by that point, produced by a great number of African American newspapers and periodicals. However, black baseball nationwide was thriving at least thirty years prior with professional teams—the Negro National League and Negro Southern League, for instance, having formed in 1920—and regional black traveling teams playing amateur and sandlot ball. In my own hometown the Charlottesville Tigers preceded the heyday of the famed Kelly's All-Stars playing traveling teams in the teens from Richmond, Virginia; West Virginia; and Pennsylvania. The Tigers played against the Manhattan Giants from Lynchburg, the Brooklyn Slides of Richmond and the Hot Springs Homestead Giants. Baseball promoter Charlie Jones bridged the ballplaying eras between managing the Charlottesville Tigers and a handful of other town teams in the teens and 1920s before his final run with Kelly's All-Stars of the 1930s. Jones, a courier for the town newspaper, was a small-town Rube Foster with an eye for athletic talent and promotion. The Tigers in this post–Reconstruction Jim Crow–era were nonetheless chronicled as a hometown favorite receiving regular press in the *Charlottesville Daily Progress* and playing a number of their games on Lambeth Field on the University of Virginia grounds. They entertained and played during special summer celebrations with the mayor of the era documented as being present and throwing out the first pitch. White baseball fans were encouraged to turn out and cheer on the Tigers. The Brooklyn Slides became the Richmond Giants in the 1920s, producing pitcher Chauncey "Rats" Henderson who went on to play for the Atlantic City Bacharach Giants, Eastern Colored League Pennant winners in 1926 and 1927.

Thus, it is appropriate to adjust the timeline for this second edition and lend perspective to celebrated Virginia native and black baseball legend Pete Hill, whose career exploits were well documented beyond the Blue Ridge Mountains.

I

Pete Hill, a Legacy Nearly Lost

BY ZANN NELSON*

Introduction by Darrell J. Howard

John Preston "Pete" Hill grew up playing baseball on the sandlots around late 19th-century Pittsburgh, Pennsylvania. The diamond sport was already a favored pastime along the Allegheny but youths like Pete were further inspired by the exposure to some of the best Negro League teams in the history of the game.

Hill's home state produced a record number of legendary Negro League teams and players: the Homestead Grays, Pittsburgh Crawfords, and Hilldales from Darby, Pennsylvania, to name a few. He first played professionally at age nineteen for the Pittsburgh Keystones, finding his footing as a fleet outfielder and rapidly developing hitter. A year later during a barnstorming matchup against Negro League powerhouse the Cuban X Giants, Hill left town on their roster. After two seasons with the Giants, Hill's batting average and reputation were on the rise, and by 1903 his exploits had garnered the interest of Andrew "Rube" Foster, one of the most revered baseball minds in the history of the game. From 1903 to 1919 Rube Foster kept Pete Hill on the roster; this included his squads the Leland Giants, Philadelphia Giants and Chicago American Giants.

Regardless of the destination or barnstorming stops on the East or West Coast, Pete Hill was known for his strong-armed accurate throws from the outfield and power at the plate. He played with Negro League greats Smokey Joe Williams, "Home Run" Johnson, and John Henry "Pop" Lloyd. It is documented that Hill reached base safely in 115 out of 116 straight games. The Major League record is fifty-six games.

Pete Hill and Rube Foster developed a bond akin to father and son in those years and as Hill matured and faced the end of his playing days Foster often left the running and daily business of the team to Pete Hill during his absences, everything from managing to bookkeeping.

---

*Culpeper, Virginia, native Zann Nelson is a researcher, writer, public speaker and advocate as well as the creator of the Right the Record program, which seeks to raise awareness of the African American history and heritage of Culpeper,.

At the end of his career, he was the player-manager of the famed Detroit Stars who conquered his mentor's Chicago American Giants for the championship in 1919, and from there he managed the fledgling Baltimore Black Sox. Baltimore, his last stop in professional baseball, allowed Pete Hill to groom up-and-coming Negro League great third baseman Jud "Boojum" Wilson. Wilson, like Pete Hill, hailed originally from Virginia in the county adjacent to Culpeper, Fauquier, and after a brief military service he was discovered by the Baltimore Black Sox on the Washington, D.C., sandlots. Ironically, Pete Hill and Jud Wilson would later be inducted into the Major League Baseball Hall of Fame in the same year, 2006, on the Negro League ballot.

Hill retired from baseball after the 1925 season, but he was a restless traveling man who had been on the road for more than thirty years, so he moved back and forth between the big Midwestern cities of Detroit and Chicago and Western New York's Buffalo. It is documented that at various intervals after retirement from baseball he found employment with the Ford Motor Company and then the railroad.

During these lost years tracking the movements of Pete Hill, an early-century Negro League all-star team was created based on input from former managers and players. Hill was touted by Homestead Grays owner Cumberland Posey as one of the most consistent hitters of all time in 1944. Pete Hill, who was now in his sixties and still exhibiting the truth that baseball was in his blood, formed a semipro black ball team, the Buffalo Red Caps.

Whether this was for enjoyment, for recreation, or for taking on the role of mentor—as Rube Foster had done for him long ago, it is not known. After 1947 and the Major League additions of Jackie Robinson and Larry Doby, the viable settings for Negro League baseball were ending.

Did Pete Hill, with his wealth of playing experience and managing acumen, have plans for the Red Caps in a professional setting?

With the rest of Pete Hill's Hall of Fame story is Culpeper County, Virginia, native and guest author and researcher Zann Nelson:

> In July of 2006, a man named Joseph Preston "Pete" Hill, born in Pittsburgh, Pennsylvania, in 1880 was inducted into the Baseball Hall of Fame in Cooperstown, New York. Among numerous accolades, Pete was called "one of the greatest line-drive hitters of his era."
>
> Despite an extraordinary career, spanning a quarter of a century playing ball for the Negro Leagues as an outfielder, Pete's induction lacked fanfare and the expected "hometown-hero" press.
>
> There are numerous halls of fame, but none as prestigious as Cooperstown. Having one's bronzed image and accompanying stats selected for inclusion alongside other baseball greats is truly a lifetime accomplishment, the Pulitzer Prize of baseball.
>
> As with many players, the selection was made long after Pete's death in 1951;

nonetheless, there was a distinct absence of fans. More important, there was not a single chest-pounding, proud-as-punch family member present.

His induction ceremony was witnessed only by strangers present to share the glory of some other inductee. The few die-hard aficionados who recognized his achievements, despite knowing little of his personal life, were more than a little puzzled and began to ask questions.

Their research was extremely thorough and led to a remarkable discovery: the man inducted in 2006 indeed was "Pete" Hill, but his real name was John, not Joseph; his birthdate was not 1880; and he was not born in Pittsburgh, Pennsylvania.

Brad Horn, Sr., director of communications and education at the National Baseball Hall of Fame and Museum,

John Preston "Pete" Hill (artist Becky Parish)

commented, "As an historical institution, providing the most accurate information is paramount to our responsibility as an education center."

States and communities lust after the claim of birthing and raising a world-class baseball player. For example, Virginia claims only four of the 289 baseball Hall of Famers; they hail from Remington, Culpeper, Richmond and Norfolk.

By the summer of 2009, exhaustive research suggested that Pete Hill would become Virginia's fifth Hall of Famer and the county of Culpeper just might be able to claim a second one.

The question: Was "Pete" Hill born in Culpeper County, Virginia? The challenge: If so, can it be proven?

By August of 2009 the path to the truth of Pete Hill's personal life, including his correct name, birthplace and birthdate, was well worn by at least a half dozen baseball historians. This was my first foray into the vast world of baseball history, and I was duly impressed by the depth of commitment and the array of interested persons. Among them was an anesthesiologist from Chicago; a college professor from Buffalo, New York; a Negro League historian from Kansas City; and the well-known baseball blogger Gary Ashwill; each was equally taunted by the "Mystery of Pete Hill."

Documentation obtained from newspaper articles, ships' passenger lists, World War I and World War II draft registrations, census records (1900, 1910, 1920, and 1930), a Social Security application and a death certificate all confirmed the following:

PETE'S OFFICIAL NAME: John Preston Hill
BIRTHPLACE: Virginia
BIRTH YEAR: The day is always listed as October 12; the year varied between 1882 and 1884 with 1882 the most consistent
MOTHER: Elizabeth "Lizzie" Seals Hill, born about 1857 in Virginia
FATHER: "Ike" Hill, listed by name in only one document with no further information. All census records list Pete's father as born in Virginia
GRANDMOTHER: Mary Frances Seals, born about 1835 in Virginia; died in 1912 in Rapidan, Culpeper County, Virginia
SIBLINGS: Jerome Bryant Hill and Walter Vaughn Hill, born about 1879 and 1881 in Rapidan, Virginia
PETE'S RESIDENCES:
1900: living with mother, stepfather and two brothers in Pittsburgh, Pennsylvania
1910: living with wife Gertrude in Chicago, Illinois
1920: living with wife Gertrude and 11-year-old son Kenneth in Chicago, Illinois
1930: living single in Buffalo, New York, listed as divorced
MARRIAGE: Between 1906 and 1907 married to Gertrude Lawson
CHILDREN: Kenneth P. Hill, b. 1-21-1909 in Chicago, Illinois, d. 12-06-2001 in Gary, Indiana
OCCUPATIONS: Baseball player, 1899–1924 (1920 census, ship's passenger manifest); railroad porter, 1930–1951 (death certificate)
DEATH: December 19, 1951, Buffalo, New York

The data collected from more than a dozen official documents is substantial with no glaring discrepancies. John Preston Hill, born October 12, 1882, in Virginia was indeed the same Pete Hill inducted into the baseball Hall of Fame in 2006.

But what of Pete's roots, his family, his hometown? The details of his personal heritage were yet to be discovered. It became clear that corroborating evidence was required. But could it be found?

The task would be extensive; it would necessitate a chain of additional records including deeds, wills, and marriage, death and birth reports. Personal interviews, photographs and field surveys of homes and gravesites would hopefully finalize the conclusions. The hunt was on!

The illustrious baseball career of John Preston "Pete" Hill is now and forever a matter of legendary record in the Hall of Fame in Cooperstown, New York. However, to historians and family members alike, his personal stats are equally important.

Research has proven irrefutably that he was born in Virginia. But Virginia is a vast state; was Pete born on a farm, in a city, at the seashore or in the mountains? A birthplace often provides the single thread imbued with color, character and strength that connects the generations.

Pete Hill's Social Security application recorded Rapidan, Virginia, as his birthplace. However, on one other document, another location was named. In 1916, while Hill was returning from the winter baseball season in Cuba aboard the SS *Chalmette*, the passenger manifest listed his birthplace as Buena Vista, Virginia.

Rather than confusing the issue, the seemingly insignificant factoid lends more credence to the theory that Pete was born in the village of Buena, near Rapidan, in Culpeper County, Virginia.

Rapidan, Virginia

In the southeastern corner of Culpeper County, the Rapidan River acts as boundary between the counties of Orange and Culpeper. In 1853, Rapid Ann Station, so named for the river that skirted the streets of the tiny village, was established on the Culpeper County side to support the Orange and Alexandria Railroad. A post office was approved in 1854 and continues to serve residents along both banks of the river.

The Orange and Alexandria (O & A) Railroad with its four depots in Culpeper County would bring untold commercial opportunities to the Southern agrarian populace until its presence became a sought-after commodity during the American Civil War.

In 1872, the O & A merged with at least two other rail lines, changed its name to the Virginia Midland Railroad Company and initiated connecting service to Georgetown (Washington, D.C.) and all points north. The steel roadways became the pathways to the true fruits of freedom and the beginnings of the Great Migration from the farm to the factory.

Buena or Buena Vista, Virginia

There are two localities in Virginia known by the name of Buena Vista, one near the town of Lexington and the other in King and Queen County, but neither is remotely close to Rapidan, Virginia.

There is, however, a little community known as "Buena" located in Culpeper County, Virginia, and situated approximately two miles north of the village of Rapidan and directly across from mile marker #76 on the rail line.

Unlike most rural hamlets of the period whose businesses were owned and operated by whites despite a largely black customer base, Buena was completely segregated. The businesses were all black owned and operated.

A post office at Buena was not established until 1892, but when it did open, Robert Murray, an African American, was named the first postmaster.

Why Was Buena Not Listed as the Birthplace?

Prior to state- and/or county-mandated recordkeeping, individuals identified their residence with the nearest post office. Until 1892, even if one was born, lived or died in the village of Buena, all reports would have registered the event as having occurred in Rapidan, Virginia.

Perhaps while on that ship in 1916, knowing there was now a post office in Buena, Pete listed the tiny hamlet as his actual place of birth. Most likely, the word Vista was added arbitrarily by someone else, assuming that the more common name was intended.

Logic and facts lead to only one conclusion: the reference to "Rapidan, Virginia," on the official documents is the very same Rapidan area of Culpeper County, Virginia.

Furthermore, at the time of Pete Hill's birth, had there been a post office closer to his home, certainly the name given for the birthplace would have been Buena, Virginia.

Riding the Rails from Rural Rapidan to Pittsburgh Possibilities

How does a young black boy from the impoverished rural regions of backwater Virginia, struggling with the new culture of the Emancipated South, find his way to the baseball fields of Pittsburgh, Pennsylvania?

It was a metamorphosis: from the Underground Railroad to the real deal, the steel rails of the "iron horse."

In 1863, an estimated 93 percent of African Americans lived in the slave-holding Southern states. In 1900, an estimated 90 percent remained, but by 1930, the African American population in the South had decreased by 40 percent.

Scholars place the first Great Migration of African Americans—those that would flee their homeland in the South for the "promised land" of the North—occurring between the years 1910 and 1940.

The Culpeper Exodus

In Culpeper and the surrounding area, the migration started much earlier; travelers bound for a new life headed most frequently for the steel mills of

Pittsburgh, Pennsylvania. The 1880 census reveals vast numbers of African Americans who had been born in Virginia resided in Pittsburgh.

Blacks from Culpeper began to flee in the 1870s. Why earlier than many others? Their flight to a better life was facilitated by the Orange and Alexandria Railroad built in 1851–1853.

The tracks were laid through the outlying fields of the county, fields that were less than fertile and would become pockets for black settlements. Placed on these tracks were four stations: Brandy, Culpeper, Mitchells and Rapidan. One can envision the burgeoning network of communication.

The Motivation:

Poverty, lack of work, racial violence, Jim Crow Laws of segregation and discrimination and educational opportunities

The News:

Tales of the "promised land" traveled by word of mouth and the distribution of black-owned and -operated newspapers such as the *Pittsburgh Courier* and the *Chicago Defender* along the path of the rail line.

The word was circulated among the community and centered in the church. Family members who had already made the journey were the best source of information.

Baseball Hall of Famer and most likely the son of former slaves, John Preston "Pete" Hill, born in the village of Buena, Culpeper County, Virginia, in 1882, lived his entire adult life north of the Mason-Dixon Line.

He played ball not for the fame, but like so many of the early players, he was driven by a genuine love of the game. When he could no longer play competitively, he managed the team. Then with some irony, his later life brought him back to the very same mechanism that gave him his first opportunity: the railroad.

Though there is no evidence that Pete ever returned to his homeplace, it is doubtful that he forgot it. Many of his friends and relatives had also relocated to Pittsburgh, but Buena was still home and staying in touch with grandparents, aunts, uncles and cousins was a family mandate.

Time tends to eradicate records; letters are destroyed and contact information lost. Pete's induction into the Hall of Fame has rekindled the fires of family connections and a desire to reestablish ancestral roots.

~ ~ ~ ~

The primary source of data for non–property-owning residents is Federal census records. However, there is a 10-year gap from census to census in which many life changing events can occur.

Despite these circumstances, significant facts have been discovered proving that the Seals and Hill families lived for decades in the area of Buena/Rapidan in Culpeper County, Virginia.

Roots of a Migration

The Seals

The 1880 census record has the Seals family living in Orange County, Virginia, across the Rapidan River from the village of Buena. Listed in the household were parents Edward and Mary Francis and children Ella, Lizzie, Annie, Mollie, Maria, Emily and James.

To date, no marriage record has been found for Pete's mother, Lizzie Seals. Was the marriage performed in another county? Did she never marry the father of the three boys or was it simply unrecorded? The answers to those questions may remain uncertain. However, a death record in the Culpeper County Courthouse could provide a clue.

A single line in the record book states that on November 3, 1887, a 30-year-old colored male, whose surname was Hill, died. There was no given name and no cause of death.

Perhaps this was Pete's father and with his death came the impetus for Lizzie to relocate. Family history reports that Lizzie arrived in Pittsburgh, Pennsylvania, with Jerome, Walter and John about 1889.

The Hills

William and Betty Hill of Madison County, Virginia, settled in the Buena area as early as 1870. Migrating with them were numerous sons and daughters, including Robert, born in 1851.

Historical maps, oral histories and field surveys reveal a network of roads that crisscrossed Cedar Mountain between the White Oak Church area on Route 15 and the heart of Buena. It was along these now-abandoned cart paths on the slopes of the mountain that the Hills established their homeplace and began their life of freedom.

On the mountain side, one can still find the simple artifacts of a life long since abandoned. A stone foundation, the artwork of a hand-dug and stone-lined well, and a fence-enclosed graveyard remain as ghosts declaring, "We were here!"

Did Lizzie Seals live here with her sister and brother-in-law? Was Pete's birth an event at one of the evident homesteads? Did he spend his early childhood on the mountainside above Buena?

During his lifetime, Robert H. Hill married three times (the second time to Pete's aunt Ella), fathered several children and acquired a considerable amount of wealth.

Despite the new findings, it was unclear which of the Hill men was the father of Pete and his brothers—that is, until death certificates were uncovered for Pete's two brothers. They confirmed their birth in Rapidan, Virginia, and the name of their father, Reuben W. Hill.

The economy in post–Civil War Virginia was dour even for those with opportunity, education, and hope. The plight of the freedman was bleak beyond comprehension. Members of this population were faced with a haunting decision: "Do I stay on the land of my father or do I strike out for an unknown and unwelcoming world?"

Pete's father Reuben and his uncle Abraham followed Andrew's lead and in 1880 also relocated to West Virginia to work fpr the C&O. Interestingly, records indicate that the men would come and go between Culpeper and West Virginia.

Abraham would eventually move to Boston, Massachusetts, where he purchased a home and raised a family of five.

Reuben chose a different path, dividing his time throughout the 1880s between Cedar Mountain and the steel rails of West Virginia. He would father three sons from his union with Lizzie Seals and dedicate his life to God. Continuing to hunger for work, Reuben headed for the coal fields of West Virginia, returning home periodically to pastor a small church in the village of Rapidan.

An ordained minister, the Rev. Reuben W. Hill became the pastor of Mt. Calvary Baptist Church in Princeton, West Virginia, and preached there until his death on January 22, 1936.

~ ~ ~ ~

All records to this point in the investigation substantiated the argument that John Preston "Pete" Hill was the Negro League player posthumously inducted into the National Baseball Hall of Fame and that the true facts were his given name was John (not Joseph), and he was born in Culpeper County, Virginia (not Pittsburgh, Pennsylvania). But would the prestigious Hall of Fame be willing to change the records?

When approached, the museum executives cited the documentation that had been presented previously and asked that I supply similar material for the counter-argument. Being aware of the need to prove theories, I knew that they were not doubting the existence of a baseball-playing Pete Hill from Culpeper. What I was tasked to prove was that this fellow from Culpeper was the very same one they inducted posthumously. They cautioned me that a change might take years to prove and implement.

Undaunted, I set out to showcase all the facts, documentation, and paperwork. With each piece I connected the dots that would always lead back to their inductee. In February of 2010 I sent the paperwork and held my breath while their own research department double checked all the documents and sources. By June they declared that Pete's given name and place of birth listed at the HOF were inaccurate, stating that it was the most thorough research they had seen.

The Hall of Fame accelerated its process, and on what would have been Pete's 128th birthday, October 12, 2010, Pete Hill Day was hosted in Cooperstown, New York. One might have called it a pilgrimage as it certainly felt like one. Cooperstown is an out-of-the-way place not easily accessed. The residents fondly state, "six months out of the year it is difficult, but the other six, it is an impossible destination."

However, it was early October, the weather crisply pleasant and the fall leaves at the height of their glory. Visitors were arriving from faraway places to revel in "Pete Hill Day at the National Baseball Hall of Fame."

The months and months of research had been confirmed and the leadership at the HOF had ordered a new plaque for Pete correcting his given name from Joseph (as inducted) to John, the one given him by his parents. They also corrected his place of birth, erroneously recorded there as Pittsburgh, Pennsylvania, substituting the actual homeplace of the Hill and Seals family in Buena, Culpeper County, VA.

People came from Los Angeles, Pittsburgh, Boston, Cleveland, Chicago, and, of course, Culpeper: family, friends, and ardent researchers. It felt every bit as exhilarating as winning the World Series.

I often laugh when I imagine the scene of the 2006 induction ceremony where there were no Pete Hill family members or hardcore baseball fans present to celebrate his life achievements. But at Pete Hill Day, it was an entirely different story! Everyone from fans to family, researchers inside and outside of the HOF, and even large numbers of unknowing strangers witnessed the correction to the record of his personal life and family heritage.

Jeff Idelson, president of the Hall of Fame, opened the ceremony in the plaque gallery with a detailed accounting of Pete's baseball career and closed with a personal commitment to historic accuracy.

The actual installation of the new plaque was accompanied by quiet emotional reflection rather than boisterous fanfare and was quickly followed by media interviews, flashing cameras and congratulations all around.

The individual and collective spirit of triumph was flowing freely, and the festivities continued during a small private reception hosted by the Hall of Fame.

The final event of the day was a panel discussion held in the Bullpen Theater about Negro and Pre–Negro League baseball, Pete Hill and the research that had brought everyone together for this most memorable occasion.

It was impossible to prioritize the moments throughout the day by their level of meaningfulness. It was no small privilege for me to sit with Jim Gates, director of the Hall of Fame library, and Eric Strohl, Sr., director of museum exhibits and collections, as we presented our separate yet collaborative work on bringing the human story to baseball, that of John Preston "Pete" Hill. But far more poignant was the significance of the day for Pete's family.

His nephew, Ron Hill, expressed it clearly: "Knowing that my uncle came to Pittsburgh as a young boy from Virginia, only 20 years removed from slavery, and grew to become a great ball player gave me a personal sense of family pride. More importantly, I could point out to my own children that anything is possible no matter where you come from in life [and] you can succeed. I could give them an example in their own uncle. Thanks, Uncle Pete."

~ ~ ~ ~

The event at Cooperstown was splendid. Only one part of the puzzle remained a mystery: Where was Pete Hill buried?

It had been 59 years since his death. The search had never lacked dedication or diligence. Many had engaged in the hunt for Hill's burial site, but perhaps none more diligently than Dr. Jeremy Krock, a pediatric anesthesiologist from Peoria, Illinois, and founder of the Negro Leagues Grave Marker Project. Hill's death certificate provided a wealth of data, including a statement that the body had been shipped to Chicago for burial, but there the trail ran cold.

Funeral homes are not required to keep records indefinitely and storage certainly becomes an issue. After some time, Hill's records, perhaps containing the needed clues such as who received the body in Chicago, were destroyed.

Pete's son Kenneth Hill was alive when his father died and was a member of a small Catholic congregation in Gary, Indiana, not far from the city of Chicago. In 2009 the local priest was contacted but to no avail.

The records of the most obvious cemeteries in the Chicago area were examined, particularly those where other baseball greats were laid to rest. There was no gravesite for John Preston "Pete" Hill.

Hope was making it exist. The consensus was that Pete's gravesite was one of those obliterated by an outrageous act of greed and immorality. It had been discovered that sections of burial grounds in a Chicago cemetery had been ravaged. The grounds were dug, the bodies removed, and the plots resold. It is not clear what became of the remains of those unfortunate souls, but it was the consensus that Pete Hill was a victim of this heinous crime.

However, the recent celebrations at the National Baseball Hall of Fame and the resurgence of Pete Hill's story caused Dr. Krock to begin to speculate once again on the mystery of Hill's final resting place. One evening after watching the movie *Cadillac Records*, the story of Chicago's Chess Records label, Krock got an idea.

"I started searching on the Internet to see where these great blues players are buried," Krock said. "Most are in the places we have been: Burr Oak, Restvale, Lincoln, Mount Glenwood, etc. One of the main characters, Little Walter, was buried in a Roman Catholic cemetery, [so] I decided to refocus our attention on some other less obvious cemeteries."

John Preston "Pete" Hill was discovered in an unmarked grave at Holy Sepulchre Cemetery in Alsip, Illinois, about ten miles southwest of Chicago. Hill's son, the late Kenneth Hill, had purchased three plots in Alsip's Holy Sepulchre Cemetery, but only his father is buried there.

Highway marker, Buena, Virginia (History.com).

The Negro Leagues Grave Marker Project in collaboration with the Hill family placed a lovely marker at the gravesite. Ron Hill of Pittsburgh, the most vocal advocate of chronicling the heritage of his ancestor, said, "Now, his family can finally rest in peace."

Addendum: In addition to the corrections at the Hall of Fame, the City of Pittsburgh and the State of Virginia passed resolutions in commemoration of John Preston "Pete" Hill; the Virginia Department of Historic Resources and the Virginia Department of Transportation erected a marker to him at Cedar Grove Baptist Church in Buena, Virginia; and the County of Culpeper placed an interpretative marker documenting his life at the Little League baseball field.

On August 13, 2022, an estimated 100 Hill family members from far and wide traveled to Culpeper to witness the addition of Pete Hill's portrait to the walls of the Culpeper County Circuit Court. His is the first and, for now, the only representative of the African American community in Culpeper. But as Judge Dale Durer said, "Culpeper County's greatest outfielder and hitter shall be displayed in the Culpeper County Circuit Court. May his presence make our union a little more perfect and inspire all in its presence."*

Biographical Encyclopedia of The Negro Baseball Leagues, Riley, James, pp. 381, 382.

II

Top of the Order, 1930–1940

Central Virginia has a long and rich history of black baseball but none as celebrated as Kelly's All-Stars of Charlottesville, Virginia. James, Harry and Raleigh Kelly lived on the outskirts of Charlottesville in an area known as "Kelly Town," part of the Rugby Road neighborhoods today. The brothers first formed the ball club in the nineteen twenties as an outlet for recreation amongst family and friends, and saw it slowly evolve into a stellar baseball unit recognized from West Virginia to Washington, D.C. Washington Park located on Preston Avenue was the town's first black recreational park and home field to the Kelly team in the early '30s; it still exists today. On many Saturday and Sunday afternoons black baseball fans gathered on Preston Avenue to watch the Kelly team take on the Clifton Forge C & O Nine, West Virginia Yellow Jackets, Gordonsville Bacharachs, and Covington Red Sox.

The team was managed by Charles Jones, a tough-minded baseball man who lauded the accomplishments of his players in the local white press, and never hesitated to scold them when they lost a few games too many.

"I'll bench the whole line-up and bring in some high school players if they don't get down to the business of winning," Jones told the *Charlottesville Daily Progress* in 1937. This critical outburst came in response to three consecutive losses suffered by his All-Stars. It was not uncommon for Jones to bring in a standout player from anywhere in the region to ensure the business of his Kelly team winning.

The Charlottesville newspaper referred to Jones as a colored baseball mogul, and he used his gamesmanship and knack for promotion to make the Kelly team's exploits news. Shortly after Jones took over the reign of the team in the early '30s the All-Stars made Winecellar Field inside Charlottesville their new home. Given that Winecellar Field was also home to at least two other white teams in the town it was indeed a major accomplishment further highlighting Jones' influence. Leroy Kelly was the team's booking manager and promoted the All-Stars' progress in the Washington, D.C., *Afro-American*, a valuable way of advertising that led to the expansion of the Kelly team's schedule.[1] The Kelly team was one of two featured black semi-pro teams in the town of Charlottesville, the other being the Charlottesville Elks. Though well-staffed and convincing in their appearance the Elks lacked the prowess of Jones' All-Stars, and he often loaned out a few of his finest to shore up the Elks' lineup against a stronger opponent.[2]

Standing (l-r): Levi Kelly, Harry Kelly, Leroy Kelly, Manager Charlie Jones, Louis Tolliver, James Kelly, Raleigh Kelly, Arthur Banks, Walker Kelly, Robert Glover. Seated (l-r): Bud Cabell, Dan Reaves, Chuck Chisholm, Tom Jones.

Like many Negro League and black semipro teams of the era the Kelly lineup was multifaceted. Practically every team member was capable of playing more than one position. Harry Kelly was an outfielder and relief pitcher; Bud Cabell played catcher and second base.

Robert "Slick" Glover was one of the best outfielders in the region, but also played an excellent shortstop position.

Willie Lewis started almost anywhere he was needed on the diamond. Charles Jones shifted the lineup around according to the opposition, and his charges were both swift and brawny.

At six feet four inches and two hundred forty pounds, outfielder James Kelly was Jones' most dangerous offensive weapon.

Windows, water towers, and occasionally railroad cars were all in fair territory when James Kelly brought the bat around. He resembled Negro League slugger Mule Suttles and produced at the plate in the same manner as the legendary Newark Eagle first baseman.

Defensively, Charley Yancey and Arthur Banks were two of the best pitchers in the region. Yancey pitched a no-hit no-run ball game in 1937, and left-handed fireballer Banks was known to record 15 strikeout performances at will. Either man could have been the number one starter for almost any other team, but on the All-Stars they both ranked behind the man called "Red."

He was called "Ace" Tolliver in the press, and friends and fans were partial to calling him "Dirty Red" because of light skin that the sun turned a reddish brown. By either moniker, Lewis Tolliver was one of the most effective pitchers in the state of Virginia. It was commonplace for Tolliver to record double digit strikeouts, win or lose against the best hitters on the semipro circuit. Using a multiple array of off-speed fastballs, and a high-velocity overhand curve, the favored "drop" ball so popular in black baseball, Tolliver toppled the competition like tenpins.

He was a plasterer by trade, and after weekend outings on the pitching mound he was known to front a local blues band as a singer.

The stylish ace recorded a scattered tally of 200 strikeouts between 1935 and 1938 with his highest single game total holding at 19 against a Culpeper Virginia ball team, and then again in a 5–1 defeat of a Baltimore club in 1937.[3] "Red" had a command and presence on the mound unmatched, typically staring in at the batter with a rueful grin that predicted the outcome of the pitch before it ever reached home plate. Taking careful consideration of the schedule and travel of the Kelly team in the '30s, it is a mystery how Lewis Tolliver failed to attract the attention of a Negro League ball club.

In 1935 the All-Stars began putting together impressive win streaks. They earned their reputation as top diamond men not by winning close games, but running opposing nines off the diamond by wide margins and shutouts. When any team gave the Kellys a close game, it was news. The Civilian Conservation Corps or CCC founded by President Franklin D. Roosevelt in the '30s taught trades and prepared black and white youth of America for the labor force. Athletics were also a mandatory part of the CCC experience and some of the best young baseball talent could be found amongst the ranks of the corps. Kelly's All-Stars dropped one game on record to a CCC ball club when they hosted a scrappy squad from a Fredericksburg camp in 1935. Despite a thrilling 17 strikeout performance by Lewis Tolliver the All-Stars were edged 4–3 thanks in part to a 10-strikeout showing by a young CCC pitcher with the last name Boze.

Charles Jones promptly scheduled a return game the following week and this time his All-Stars came out on top 12–9 with Tolliver again recording 17 strikeouts and young Boze on the losing end this time with 11.[4]

The Kelly team might have complemented their dominance with a couple of undefeated seasons were it not for their regional rivalries against Nelson County's Massies Mill Giants, and the Orange Black Sox of Orange, Virginia. The Massies Mill Giants were made up of the Giles, Ligon, and Vaughn families. Team owner Fulton Ligon owned a saw mill, a country store and a dance hall in the town of Massies Mill. The ball team worked in the mill by day and practiced baseball in the evenings. Many local residents showed up just to watch the Giants practice. The most popular player on Ligon's razor-sharp nine was a young show-stopping first baseman named Alex Giles.

Giles scooped up balls while executing splits, and when the bases were empty caught throws from shortstop with his ball cap. He had a long and storied tour in central Virginia's black baseball circuit, and was later referred to respectfully as "old man Giles." Tales of Alex Giles' mastery at first base remained the talk of black Virginia baseball for decades. The Giants had their own mound stars in John "Buster" Giles, Wallace Giles, Roger Giles, and later Alex and Ben Vaughn.

The burly six-foot-plus mill workers were a force to be reckoned with and only the most steely-nerved batters reached first base against Giants pitchers. Buster Giles caught the attention of the Negro League Homestead Grays and had a roster place for the taking, but had to decline because his family needed him more at home. His next career highlight appears to be a doubleheader pitched against a traveling black semipro team from Florida in the forties.

Buster Giles teamed up with another ace from Bedford, Virginia, known only as Smokey Joe. Giles lost the opener 5–4, but Smokey Joe pitched a 2–0 shutout victory in the second contest helping Massies Mill secure a split with their out-of-town guest. Buster Giles was at his best when contested by the Kellys' "Red" Tolliver. When the Nelson County ace met his match in "Red," it was the popping sound of the ball striking leather and not wood that echoed around the park. Massies Mill usually arrived in Charlottesville on the back of Fulton Ligon's flatbed logging truck and the hype whipped through the crowd. "There's Buster Giles, he's pitching against Red!" "Brother you're going to see a ballgame today!"[5]

By 1937 the Kellys versus Massies Mill rivalry had reached such proportions that the Giants joined forces with another Nelson County foe, the Shipman Spiders, to tame the Charlottesville nine. Jones added a left-handed pitcher and a hard-hitting outfielder to his own lineup. Results of the encounter were not published.[6] Orange matched up with the Kelly team perhaps better than anyone, often finding a way to confound Jones' All-Stars. Gus Ellis, the Sneads, and the Robinsons played a similar schedule and though they never blew out the Kelly squad, they somehow managed to jump on the Charlottesvillians and make them stay down for the win.[7] The Culpeper Athletic Club always gave the All-Stars a good game but most often came up short. Culpeper's dominance was still a few years down the road in the '30s. Due to inconsistent data it is difficult to verify how close the winning percentages might have been between the Kellys, Massies Mill and the Orange Black Sox.

All three played an identical traveling schedule that matched them against skillful black semipro clubs in and out of Virginia. Matchups within the trio appear to have been even throughout the '30s.

Nineteen thirty-six was a peak season for the All-Stars and by October the team had won nineteen of twenty-one starts. Both Losses came at the hands of Massies Mill and Orange. To complete their winning campaign the Kelly team had to face off against the strong Sperryville Yellow Jackets of Northern Virginia, and then face off against their nemesis, Massies Mill, for the third time during the season after losing 2–1 and winning 2–0.[8] As evidenced by a *Daily Progress* news article the following season, the Kelly team hurdled both Sperryville and Massies Mill on the way to an all-time best 26–2 record. The *Progress* deemed Jones' nine mythical state champions.

Mythical champs was appropriate since the Kellys were not part of a sanctioned league and did not compete against semipro teams in Richmond or Tidewater. Richmond appeared on the Kelly schedule in 1937. In their only recorded encounter the Kellys handed the Richmond City champion Capital City Elks a 6–1 defeat in 1937. Big James Kelly had a home run and three triples.[9] There was a scheduled matchup against a team of Richmond All-Stars in August 1936, but, due to missing results, it is only guesswork that the Kellys triumphed.[10]

The All-Stars stumbled out of the gate in 1937 leading up to Jones' fire-starting quote in the *Daily Progress*. They stalled at the worst possible time when their competition was about to reach another level. The Niles A.C. of Washington had come to Charlottesville and claimed a 2–0 victory. The loss proved to be a tune-up before the Kellys faced Maryland's renowned Myrtle Athletic Club.

In 1936 the Myrtle squad won 37 of 45 games played that included sweeps through North and South Carolina.[11] Charles Jones shuffled the pitching rotation and started Banks and Yancey over star Tolliver whom he used as a closer. Despite the strategy employed by Jones the Marylander's outfit scored consecutive victories of 4–2, 3–2, 1–0, and 2–0 over the All-Stars, defeating both Tolliver and Banks in 1937. At first it appeared that the level of baseball played in the District was slightly over the heads of the Kelly squad. But the Kellys finally caught up with the Myrtle Nine in October '37 when Charley Yancey displayed his brilliant 1–0 no-hitter. Neither club was satisfied to end the season's rivalry with the Kellys' spoiler, and two more games were scheduled to follow.[12] In August '37 the All-Stars were scheduled to play Front Royal, one of northwest Virginia's best black teams. The Front Royal nine sported a 24–4 record to the Kellys' 22–6 mark.[13]

In 1938 Jones booked a game with an all-star team from Meadow, Maryland, comprised of black and white players. Since Jim Crow Laws varied in all parts of the South it is not known whether the contest was permitted. Blacks and whites were forbidden to engage in any activities within the confines of a publicly maintained facility.[14] There was no further mention of matchups against Washington, D.C., semipros, but Jones' men shut down a Warrenton, Virginia, nine 8–2 in a June 1938 encounter.[15] The last publicized triumph credited to the Kelly team was in 1939 when they won a 13–11 barnburner over the young and up and coming Dupont Grays, an industrial aggregation from Waynesboro, Virginia. James Kelly was five for five and Lewis Tolliver struck out 15 Grays batters.[16]

Kelly's All-Stars continued their run into the early 1940s. World War II broke up the original lineup but a few of the original All-Stars that included a now aged but competitive Red Tolliver formed a new squad that often included Morgan State all–American Bob Smith and central Virginia pitching legend Early Dowell. The new team again traveled to West Virginia, Maryland, and Washington, D.C., and at home took on traveling semipro teams. This last formation of the Kelly team dissolved during the mid-fifties, setting the standard for a new generation of Charlottesville baseball players.

How good were Kelly's All-Stars? They were exceptional ball players, and had a manager whose resources primed the All-Stars for playing competitive baseball beyond a recreational level. The pitching rotation led by Red Tolliver was often unhittable, despite the fact that these working men may have only managed 2 to 3 days of practice. They had multipositional players, and a manager bent on winning. So the Kellys were as good as they needed to be in many situations. In their era of play they easily shook up the top ten black ball clubs, and with a few additions made a strong run at the top five black Virginia teams from 1930 to 1940.

In Richmond, Virginia, black baseball first made headlines in the Roaring Twenties with the success of the Richmond Giants, the first recorded black semiprofessional team in Virginia's capital city. The listing of the Giants team in the annals of Negro League research would indicate that the Giants were a competitive traveling club. Richmond native Arthur "Rats" Henderson was an ace pitcher for the Giants of 1922 and 1923. Henderson along with teammate Robert "Eggie" Clarke both made their way to the professional Negro League after 1923.

Clarke, a versatile catcher and infielder, enjoyed a long career playing for the Baltimore Black Sox, New York Black Yankees, and Baltimore Elite Giants. He also served stints as a manager during his time in the big leagues. Rats Henderson's first stop in the big leagues was Atlantic City, New Jersey, and the Bacharach Giants. As the story goes, Henderson defeated the Bacharachs who were in the midst of an early season barnstorming tour. The Bacharachs did not leave town without Rats Henderson.[17]

Henderson was considered one of the best curve-ball pitchers of the '20s, and Cumberland Posey, owner of the Homestead Grays, named the stout right-hander as a starting pitcher on his 1924 all-star team.[18]

Pitching back-to-back games in the 1926 Negro League world series for the Bacharach Giants, Henderson lost game 6 against the Chicago American Giants and Negro League pitching great Willie Foster 5–4. Undaunted, he bounced back in game 7 versus George Harney and pitched a shutout 3–0.

Incredibly, Henderson received the call again in game 9, his worst outing, as Chicago proceeded to shut down Henderson and Atlantic City 13–0. Though the Bacharach Giants lost the ten-game series to Chicago, Henderson distinguished himself with a shutout and a 1.45 ERA.[19] After posting a 19 wins 7 losses record in 1927 Henderson began experiencing arm trouble the following season. Not a surprise considering his workhorse mound appearances. Still he posted a 13–2 record before injury forced him to the bench. Rats Henderson's strong right arm never came back after 1928 and he spent the last few years making sporadic appearances with the Detroit Stars.

Richmond's most celebrated black baseball alum was a short bowlegged infielder from Churchill on Richmond's south side named Raymond Dandridge. For all of his physical peculiarities there was no denying Ray Dandridge's abilities on the ballfield. The only way to get a hit by Dandridge was to line it high above his head because he was sure to make a play on anything down on the infield. He was an all-star at third base, but excelled anywhere the team needed him.

Dandridge was playing for a Richmond team called the Paramount All-Stars in 1933 when the team matched up against the barnstorming Negro League Detroit Stars.

During the contest Stars manager "Candy" Jim Taylor saw what every baseball fan would see for the next eighteen years of Dandridge's Hall of Fame career—a consummate fielder who could do anything he desired at the bat. The next day Ray Dandridge left Richmond for Detroit and the rest was baseball history.

At age 36 after sixteen seasons in the Negro Leagues Dandridge was called up to the Minneapolis Millers of the minor league American Association in 1949. He led the league batting .362, and the following season batted .311 to win the MVP. Fans black and white hoped Dandridge would receive the call to the major league arena, but it was not to be and Ray Dandridge retired in 1951.

He is the only black baseball hall of famer from the Commonwealth of Virginia.[20]

Aside from the accomplishments of Ray Dandridge and the long-forgotten Paramount All-Stars, Richmond's black baseball picture remains murky, with references to a Richmond Panthers semipro team.[21] Touring Negro League teams made Richmond a stopover as they progressed south. It was the Capital City Elks baseball team known as "the pride of Richmond" that created an association between black baseball and the capital city in the Depression era '30s. The Elks played an independent or barnstorming schedule in Virginia and the Carolinas until 1940 in their only season of league play. It appears that the 1934 baseball season may have been the team's best as they were listed as City Champions of Richmond in the Baltimore *Afro American*.[22]

The Elks Lodge located on bustling Second Street in the heart of black Richmond was a grand structure conjuring up images of the Taj Mahal, further adding to the ambience of the Second Street corridor.

Elks baseball teams of the late 1930s and 1940s were good but never great. In theory they were probably as good as any team in the Mid-Atlantic region. Unfortunately this was all in theory because in reality the Elks had a tendency to pendulum from brilliance to agonizingly subpar play. To their credit Elks teams always showed up to compete, never shying away from high caliber baseball teams.

In a 1946 baseball tilt the Elks were last-minute stand-ins for the Montgomery Alabama Dodgers who were scheduled to take on the Negro Southern League Atlanta Black Crackers. The game was never close as Atlanta ran Richmond ragged 16–2, but the Elks gamely played the contest out to save the evening gate.[23] The Banks family made up the cornerstone of the ball team. Second and third baseman

Norman Banks' glove work earned him a wartime spot on the Newark Eagles roster in 1945. He might have remained in the northeast a little longer were it not for poor performances at the plate.

North Carolinian Roy Debran played the first half of his 1940 baseball season with the New York Black Yankees batting .333 in limited appearances. Perhaps making his way home to Durham, a stay in Richmond and a chance meeting landed Debran with the Elks for the remainder of the 1940 baseball season. A full-time outfielder, Debran was also known to make mound appearances as a relief pitcher in the semipros.

Debran appears in Negro American Association news clippings throughout post–World War II black baseball for the Durham Black Sox where he was a teammate of Durham's black baseball legend Lamb Barbee.

Historic Mayo Island was the premier locale for baseball in 1930s Richmond. Local baseball fans witnessed the hitting displays of Babe Ruth and Lou Gehrig during Yankee spring exhibition games on the isle.

The historic Richmond park was the home of the Richmond Colts, a white ball club playing in an Eastern professional league in the twenties (a minor league). The Colts played on the island through 1941, but by all accounts the park was accessible to the top-ranked black semipro teams in Richmond City (Elks, Boosters, Hilldales).

When Mayo Island (or later Richmond Stadium) was not available black teams played on the sandlots of Churchill and Fulton in the predominantly black south end of the city. In 1932 the Richmond Boosters club sponsored an athletic program with baseball as the first of many recreational activities.

Three years later a team of players formerly known as the Albemarle All-Stars began play as the B.B. Boosters and a five-year run as one of the best teams in Virginia.

The Boosters provided the first hint of their rise to prominence by defeating the 1934 city champion Elks 5–3 in a July 1935 encounter.[24] By 1935 the Boosters were playing several games a week and traveling to play matchups in North Carolina and West Virginia.

"Slim" Jim Elam, Eulie Hall, and Junius Matthews made up the pitching rotation and were largely responsible for the Boosters' winning seasons.

Tall Eulie Hall was a sure bet to reach double-digit strikeouts in almost any contest, and Junius Matthews set a city record striking out 18 men in a 10–9 loss to the Ashland Virginia Tigers in June 1939.[25] Jim Elam is the only known Boosters player to receive a call up to the Negro Leagues. Elam's height, blazing speed and confounding curveball pitches kept batters off balance in Virginia, and earned him a spot on the 1943 Newark Eagles roster. Military service during World War II cut short Elam's professional career.[26]

The Boosters lineup did not feature power hitting but timely hitting. Rarely was an opportunity missed to move a runner around the base path.

Thornton, the Boosters regular catcher, and first baseman Hackett were clutch performers in the batting order. By 1940 the B.B. Boosters roster included players from the Carolinas as well as Richmond City. Winning seasons drew the best in semipro black baseball to the Old Dominion to play the Boosters. They were pitted against the Brooklyn Royal Giants under former Negro League first baseman Dave "Showboat" Thomas in 1940, and also played the white House of David Bearded 9.

Bordering Richmond, a number of small communities and towns held good black baseball teams looking for an opportunity to play the city boys. These teams played a local schedule but they were competitive and especially hard to beat on their own sandlot fields.

There were the Emporia Virginia Eagles, Chesterfield Hornets, Page Semipros, Yellow Tavern All-Stars, and Petersburg Red Sox. In Williamsburg the Black Sox were one of the better independent ball teams between Richmond and Tidewater. Not much is known about the team, first called the Lackawanna Black Sox, or the extent of their playing schedule, but throughout the thirties and forties, Williamsburg fared well on the regional circuit.

The Black Sox home field was listed as Treasure Island Park, and Robert Bartlett was the listed manager in a 1941 baseball directory. Williamsburg matched up against the Boosters, and Newport News.

The Giants of Newport News were especially unkind to the Williamsburg nine, trouncing the Black Sox by lopsided scores in nearly every meeting.[27] At the start of the 1941 season Williamsburg bolted out of the gate winning seven of their first eight contests. In a July doubleheader Suffolk's Aces suffered one of their few defeats of the season at the hands of Williamsburg losing a 4–3 decision.[28]

In 1939, the year several black teams from Virginia participated in league play, the B.B. Boosters became members of the Richmond City County League along with their nemesis from the peninsula, the Tidewater Giants. Leading up to the '39 season the Giants were undeniably the best black team in Virginia. However, in 1939 and 1940 Newport News began to lose its edge over many local and regional foes.

The league carried eleven teams with four junior and seven senior teams classified as A and AA. Both divisions competed on Saturdays and Sundays playing a twenty-four game schedule from early May through September. Joining the Boosters and Giants were the Richmond Cardinals referred to in the press as the Price Athletic Club, Ashland Tigers, Richmond Royal Giants, Pearson's All-Stars of Alexandria, and the Franklin Co. Elks. Pearson's All-Stars of Alexandria traveled one to two hours to compete in the league as did the Franklin Elks. The Suffolk Aces joined the league roster for the second half as the third Tidewater team.[29]

The Ashland Tigers' hopes rested on the shoulders of Lester Jackson. Jackson was a Negro League prospect beginning in the late '30s with the Newark Eagles as an outfielder, and next seeing action patrolling the outfield for the New York Black Yankees in 1940 and 1941.[30] Jackson began the '39 season with the Boston Royal Giants and then came home to manage and play on the Ashland team.[31]

Raymond Robinson pitched for the Price Athletic Club. He also received a call from Newark and the Philadelphia Stars of the Negro National League, and played with the Cleveland Buckeyes of the Negro American League from 1941 to 1947.[32]

All supporting evidence indicates the Boosters dominating the Richmond City County League with a winning percentage well over .800 with Tidewater on their heels. The best of league contest matched the Boosters, Tidewater and the Price A.C. Cardinals. Pitching usually decided the outcome as all three teams had some of the best pitchers in Virginia. In a June weekend encounter between the Cardinals' Ray Robinson and Giants pitcher "Lefty" Scott, the Pricemen pulled out 8–6 and 1–0 victories. Ashland played .500 baseball but remained competitive thanks in part to the addition of Lester Jackson. As the press never announced a league victor, it is merely guesswork that the Boosters also won the league championship

The arrival of the D.C.-based Hilldales in 1939 may have upset the Boosters' run as city champs when they lost a 1–0 thriller to the Hilldales at Mayo Island Park in July of '39.

The *Norfolk Journal and Guide* reported a 1940 pairing of Pearson's All-Stars and the Boosters in a best out of five series to determine a champion of northern Virginia. The Boosters were later alluded to as the victors, though how the pairings were decided or how many other teams were involved remains a mystery.[33] However, it is clear that the Boosters played every reputable semipro team east and west of Richmond city in 1940 and came away victorious. Starting in West Virginia and then traversing southwest Virginia the Boosters defeated Lexington's Cubs 18–1, Buena Vista 3–2, and the celebrated Roanoke Black Cardinals 9–0. Only the Lynchburg Red Sox spoiled the Richmonders' tour, topping them 8–7.

No mention or listings of standings for a Richmond League were published in 1940. All references to the Boosters baseball team and sports program ceased after 1940. Black baseball in Richmond continued at a recreational level until the semiprofessional Richmond Giants were formed in 1945.

In 1900 the Norfolk Red Stockings became one of the first Negro professional teams in the United States. From the beginning of the twentieth century until the end of segregated major league play in the '40s, tidewater Virginia was synonymous with black baseball.[34] New York had its Mohawk Giants and Brooklyn Royal Giants, and Massachusetts housed a fine team in the Boston ABCs but in the nineteen thirties black semipro baseball in Tidewater was unrivaled. Norfolk's Stars were the next recognized ball team out of southeast Virginia. In 1921 the semipro Stars landed journeyman Negro League catcher George "Chappie" Johnson as a player manager. Under Johnson's tutelage, the Stars' left-handed pitching ace Jesse "Nip" Winters developed into a big-league prospect.

Winters then went on to pitch for the outstanding Pennsylvania Hilldale Daises. In the Negro League World Series of 1925, the tall lefty pitched game four against the Kansas City Monarchs and earned a 7–3 win for Hilldale as they went on to win the series five games to one. Jesse Winters is touted as having been the best pitcher in the Eastern Colored League.[35]

By the thirties with the nation in the throes of the Great Depression, baseball was the best news going. Tidewater area teams received coverage in at least three black Mid-Atlantic newspapers including the region's own *Norfolk Journal and Guide*.

Prompted by the publicity and number of organized teams, black ballplayers journeyed from West Virginia, North Carolina, South Carolina, and Georgia to play on Tidewater baseball teams. The most famous visiting ballplayer of the era was Negro League Hall of Famer Walter "Buck" Leonard. Discouraged with sandlot play around his home in Rocky Mount, North Carolina, Leonard traveled north to Portsmouth to play for the Firefighters, a traveling semipro team, in 1933.

Midway through a successful stint in Portsmouth, Leonard reaped the benefits of playing in the right place at the right time when Portsmouth squared off against ex–Negro League star Ben Taylor and his Baltimore Stars. Taylor, whose entire family was involved in baseball and who had been around competitive black baseball since the teens, recognized that Buck Leonard had the makings of a professional. Despite the gamble involved in relocating with another barnstorming club, Leonard took the risk. His involvement with Taylor's Stars, and then the Royal Giants, led to his discovery and promotion in 1934 to one of the best Negro League teams ever, the Homestead Grays.[36]

More than a dozen winning ball clubs came from three different counties of the Tidewater region. Suffolk, Norfolk, Newport News, Portsmouth, and Plymouth supported black baseball though the 1950s. Suffolk's Aces played in the Richmond City County League of 1939 along with the Franklin County Elks, and in 1940 participated in the Virginia-Carolina League. Portsmouth produced five winning ball teams in the Grays of Belleville, the Senators, Dodgers, Black Revels, Firefighters, and the St. Julien Creek Tigers. Portsmouth native Leon Ruffin was one of two area players to make a mark in Negro League baseball.

Ruffin played for the Newark Dodgers in 1935 and 1936, but was released to the Pittsburgh Crawfords in 1937. The Dodgers merged with the Brooklyn Eagles and moved to Newark, New Jersey, in 1936. While with Pittsburgh in 1938 Ruffin wrote Newark Eagle owner Abe Manley asking for another opportunity with the Eagles, and Manley obliged. Leon Ruffin became a mainstay with Newark through 1946.[37] He possessed a cannonlike throwing arm, and although a weak hitter he was adept at the bunt and hit and run, coming through when the big play was needed.

The Berkley Braves of Norfolk were city champs in 1938 and 1939, and Norfolk Southern's baseball team were the railroad champs of 1940.[38]

The skills of the players, fan base, and gate attraction made Tidewater the capital of black baseball in Virginia. Negro League teams made Norfolk and Portsmouth stopovers on barnstorming tours in the thirties and forties.

Signs were posted all over the region announcing the big league matchups, "HOMESTEAD GRAYS-VS-NEW YORK CUBANS Portsmouth Stadium." Norfolk native Willie Riddick was the coordinator of athletic programs for blacks in the

Tidewater Region and it was Riddick who helped the Newark Eagles, Homestead Grays, Baltimore Elite Giants, and others secure playing dates, and oftentimes find an up-and-coming ballplayer.[39]

Overtime Josh Gibson, Mule Suttles, and Leon Day were as well known in the Tidewater area as the local standouts. Negro League owners knew that the cities and towns of Newport News, Norfolk, and Portsmouth could facilitate their players in that era of Jim Crow segregation, and in turn black residents were able to witness Negro League baseball at its peak.

When the Homestead Grays were in town or Newark toured the region, stadiums filled to capacity. The local semipros played an afternoon doubleheader and then in the evening the professionals played the featured game under the lights.

Negro League baseball was without a minor league system, and thus areas such as Tidewater with a wealth of black teams served as a feeder for the traveling professionals. For local ballplayers it presented an opportunity to showcase their skills and perhaps get picked up by a Negro League team. Like the major league system for white players, Negro League baseball was made up of the chosen few who made the cut. A candidate for the Negro Leagues had to possess talent, endurance, and a sense of adventure.

In the sandlots of Tidewater there were weekend ballplayers and traveling semipros. Semipro ballplayers divided their time between odd jobs and the road. Because they earned much less than their professional counterparts, they had to love the game.

The Giants of Newport News represented the best of Tidewater's traveling teams in the 1930s. In the press the Giants were alternately referred to as Tidewater or Newport News. By either title the Virginians dominated black semipro baseball in the Mid-Atlantic region for nearly a decade. In 1931 the Giants split a five-game series with a traveling all-star team from Florida—two wins, two losses and one tie.[40]

Defensively they seemed to never lack for left-handed pitchers, and between 1935 and 1940 carried four in Lefty Smith, Lefty Scott, Lefty Stewart, and Lefty Bowman. When called, Stewart often shored up the rotations of other teams in Norfolk and Portsmouth.

Nineteen thirty-five might have been their best season, and they rampaged through the black baseball circuit of Virginia, Washington, D.C., and the Carolinas.

An examination of the Giants' play in August 1935 reveals a string of wins over the Boston A.B.C's 7–5, 5–1; Wilson, North Carolina, Braves 4–0, 5–1; and the Williamsburg Black Sox 11–2, bringing their record to 42–9. The pace resumed in May 1936 as Tidewater whipped the Durham Black Sox in a doubleheader and then traveled to Washington to defeat the tough Hilldales decisively 6–3. After defeating the Tarboro, North Carolina, Tigers in a doubleheader and then gaining single-game victories over the Statesville, North Carolina, Giants and the Fort Eustis Black Sox in early June, the Giants had registered twenty straight victories.[41]

The Giants' schedule kept them on the road and on the ball diamond at least five days weekly. At home the Giants maintained rivalries with the Portsmouth Firefighters and Richmond's B.B Boosters that were more often than not low-scoring thrillers. The three adversaries usually played a three-game series or traded home and away games within the same week.

In 1939 the Giants scaled back their barnstorming pace and participated in league play for the first time in the Richmond City County League. Results of final league standings are incomplete, but it is not unreasonable to conclude that Newport News and their rival Richmond Boosters finished in a deadlocked tie. Of note for the '39 Giants were independent victories over the Durham Black Sox of the newly formed Eastern Colored League.[42]

Nineteen thirty-nine was one of the most exciting seasons of black baseball in Tidewater. For the first time in several seasons the Newport News Giants received all the competition they could handle from the region's old and new ball teams.

Newark Eagles to Play Grays Here June 20

The Grays referred to in this June 17, 1939, headline in the *Norfolk Journal and Guide* were not the Homestead Grays of Pittsburgh, but the Belleville Grays of Portsmouth. Businessman Bishop Howard Z. Plummer's 1939 Belleville Grays bore the closest resemblance to a big-league ball club since the turn of the century Red Stockings. Plummer was head minister of a sizable congregation in Belleville—the Church of God, Saints of Christ. He was also a Mason and local businessman with contacts and great influence in the Tidewater region and beyond. The Grays played most of their home games at the town's Sewanee Stadium. The Grays' uniforms were sharp-looking sets complete with the team emblem. Plummer's squad spring-trained in Florida and then played their way north to start their regional schedule.

Nineteen thirty-eight appears to be the first season for Plummer's Grays, and was largely played out with little fanfare. But the '39 Grays boasted an all-star lineup and were managed by Joseph "Sleepy" Lewis, who came to the team in 1939 after a two-year stint as manager of the Washington, D.C., Hilldales. Lewis was a former Negro League catcher with the 1920s Baltimore Black Sox and Homestead Grays. Baseball was in his blood and he was never far from the arena of competitive baseball. Based on his longevity as a manager inside and outside of the Old Dominion it appears Lewis' career off the field was as successful as his days on the field. He was also capable at this stage of his life of penciling himself into the lineup and using the skills that made him a professional ballplayer to help the team rally.[43]

The Belleville roster contained one of Tidewater's all-time best players. After 1939 catcher Albert "Buster" Haywood was headed to the Negro Leagues to stay. Buster Haywood played with the Birmingham Black Barons, Ethiopian Clowns, Chicago American Giants, New York Cubans, and Indianapolis Clowns. Haywood is remembered as one of the smallest catchers in the Negro Leagues at 5'8" and 161, and also one of the best behind the bat. He was a player manager for Indianapolis in the early nineteen fifties, and served as a mentor for a skinny right-handed power hitter from Mobile, Alabama, named Henry Aaron.[44] Tommy Sampson was a versatile infielder who started at second base throughout most of his career. He came to Portsmouth from Raleigh, West Virginia, and quickly made a name for himself in Tidewater with his slick fielding and clutch-hitting.

In 1940 Birmingham's Black Barons signed Sampson, Buster Haywood, shortstop James Mickey, and pitcher "Cannonball" Gentry Jessup away from Belleville. Sampson played second base for the Barons through 1944. That same year the Barons faced the Homestead Grays in the Negro World Series. While traveling between cities during the series, Sampson and four other ballplayers were injured when struck head on by a drunk driver. Sampson fared the worst, receiving a broken right leg in the collision. He remained with the Barons through 1947 as a player manager though his statistics dropped off sharply. Sampson resigned from his position as manager following the '47 season and played for the Chicago American Giants in 1948 and then the New York Cubans in 1949.[45]

Perhaps one of Sampson's greatest contributions to the game of baseball was in discovering Alabama native Willie Mays and having the Black Barons sign him in 1948.

West Virginian "Cannon Ball" Gentry Jessup carried the Belleville pitching rotation and enjoyed a solid career in the Negro Leagues after 1939 with Birmingham and the Chicago American Giants. Jessup's playing days ended with a brief minor league stint in Canada's Mandak League from 1950 to 1952. It can be surmised that Jessup's nickname alluded to the speed generated by his strong right arm that allowed him to overpower many batters on the semipro level.[46] Aside from Jessup, Tidewater pitching standouts Tony Spruill and Lefty Stewart started ballgames for the '39 Grays.

Brady Johnson owned Norfolk's 1939 Black Tars and assembled a lineup of stars of his own. Charles "Tootie" Thomas attended Boston University starring at halfback on the football team. The Newark Eagles selected Thomas in 1941 to play center field. Shortstop Vernon "Big Six" Riddick was an averaged-sized man, but on the sandlots of Virginia and North Carolina he swung a mighty bat and was known for his game-breaking hits. Newark also gave Riddick his only opportunity to play big-league ball. In the Negro Leagues Riddick's inability to hit the curveball hampered his professional career, and he taxied between semipro ball and the professional Negro Leagues from 1939 to 1941.[47]

North Carolinian Spencer "Babe" Davis played and managed for Johnson on the Black Tars. Davis was capable of playing almost anywhere on the diamond except pitcher. He played in the Negro Southern League with the 1937 Jacksonville Florida Red Caps and then the 1938 Atlanta Black Crackers. Davis began the '39 season with the Indianapolis ABCs in the Negro American League, but came to Norfolk in July after the ABCs withdrew from league play.[48]

After 1941 Davis played out his career primarily with the Winston-Salem Giants of the Negro American Association, though he occasionally played stints with the New York Black Yankees from 1940 to 1942. Tar Park was home to the New York

Yankees' minor league club, the Norfolk Tars, and a home field site for the Black Tars when the white squad played on the road.

The Norfolk Black Tars and Portsmouth's Grays seemed to materialize out of the salty Tidewater air. Both teams stormed in and snatched the region's bragging rights away from the Newport News Giants. While the Grays played their way north from Florida, Norfolk toured the Carolinas. Both teams were slated to participate in the newly formed Negro International League made up of teams from Maryland, Washington, D.C., Virginia, and North Carolina. By May '39 the league's name had been changed to the New Eastern Colored League.

Belleville and Norfolk joined the Washington, D.C., Royal Giants, Baltimore Black Sox, Durham Black Sox, Durham Lucky Strikes, and the Charlotte Black Hornets. Former Negro league star first baseman Ben Taylor managed the Washington Royal Giants. Taylor is best remembered for his play on the powerful Indianapolis ABCs of 1915. The ABCs were managed by the elder brother C.I. Taylor and featured the talents of Oscar Charleston, and Cannon Ball Dick Redding. It was Ben Taylor who gave Buck Leonard his first break towards the big leagues when he played on Taylor's 1933 Baltimore Stars.[49] Taylor probably mentored more up-and-coming black baseball players than any other manager in the history of the game.

Washington's Royal Giants opened the Eastern Colored League season on May 2, 1939, in major league baseball's Griffith Stadium.

Playing before 1000 fans in a cold drizzle the Royal Giants lost to the Norfolk Black Tars 10–6. Originally scheduled as a doubleheader the second game was canceled because of the severe spring weather. The call to "play ball" rang through Sewanee Stadium in Portsmouth the following weekend as Norfolk and Belleville clashed in a doubleheader. Belleville won the first game 7–5, and the Tars came back to squeak out the nightcap 2–1.[50]

Late May 1939 brought on allegations of misappropriation of league funds, and further questions related to the season schedule. With the credibility of the new league damaged, fewer than half a dozen ballgames were played from late May to early June, after which the *Norfolk Journal and Guide* reported the pullout of Baltimore, Portsmouth and Norfolk. No mention is made of league play beyond early June and team standings were never posted. Following the Eastern Colored League's early demise Belleville and Norfolk continued competing against Charlotte and the two Durham squads.[51]

Of the North Carolina teams Durham's Black Sox figured as the most prominent challenger to the Virginians. Prior to 1939 the Durham team was promoted as champions of North Carolina. Pitcher and second baseman Lamb Barbee was the recognized team standout. Barbee divided several seasons between the Negro Leagues and the semipros of North Carolina. As a pitcher Barbee relied on a smoking fastball and curve, and at six foot three, two hundred ten pounds, had the power to bring the heat. He was not known as a big hitter in the Negro Leagues, but in spells went on tears posting an average of .500.

He first played for the New York Black Yankees in 1937, then the Baltimore Elite Giants in 1940, and the Philadelphia Stars in 1942.

In all truth Barbee loved playing everywhere and appears on rosters of the Raleigh Grays, Raleigh Tigers, and Norfolk Black Tars. Durham was the team that he always returned to, and when not playing full time in the big leagues he returned home to manage and play.

Younger brother Quincy Barbee played for the Baltimore Elite Giants with the elder Barbee and after the collapse of the Negro Leagues played minor league baseball in Canada and the United States in the nineteen fifties.[52]

By July 1939 Belleville began to distance themselves from the regional competition. In a July 1939 matchup between Tidewater's Giants and Belleville, the Grays crushed the mighty Giants 13–2.[53] On July 22, Belleville split a doubleheader 6–5, 9–2 with Durham.

Belleville had amassed a record of 45 wins and 8 losses giving the Grays a rating of .818.[54] The Newark Eagles came to Tidewater on a tour with the New York Black Yankees during the first week of July. The Eagles and Yankees played a weekend series and on Monday Newark faced off against Belleville's Grays at Bain Field in Norfolk. It was a rarity for the professionals to play the locals during a promoted tour, but Belleville's reputation now preceded it.

Mule Suttles, Newark's legendary home-run hitter, sat out the Monday contest, but Negro league great Willie Wells played third base and future New York Giant Monte Irvin was at first. Newark prevailed 3–1 in a quiet low-scoring affair.

The loss actually highlighted the prowess of Belleville as they were able to hold a professional team to a respectable margin.[55] Next the Raleigh Grays and their right-handed knuckleballer Leniel Hooker marched north looking for the red-hot Virginians and the famed Tarheels were stopped cold in their tracks. It was Grays versus Grays, Virginia versus North Carolina, a contest between each state's best semipro club.

Only the Asheville Blues and Raleigh Tigers of the Negro Southern League could lay claim to being hands down better than the North Carolina Grays. Long tall Len Hooker was the Carolina ace who possessed an arsenal of breaking pitches and a high leg kick rivaled only by the great Satchel Paige. Tidewater pitching sensation Lefty Stewart took to the mound for Belleville and carried the matchup as Hooker debuted poorly. The Virginians swept the doubleheader 6–2, 15–3.[56]

Raleigh fared better against the Norfolk Black Tars winning two games out of a three-game series in July 1939. Hooker pitched game two and limited Norfolk to 4 hits as Raleigh routed the Virginians 9–1.

The final contest was a thriller that could have gone either way. With the North Carolina Grays up 8–7 in the eighth inning and Norfolk rallying, Hooker received the call and produced in the relief role, striking out three Tar batters in a row to preserve the victory. Len Hooker was off to New Jersey in 1940 and the Newark Eagles where he remained as a starter until 1948.[57]

Former Negro leaguer John Beckwith brought his New York Stars to Tidewater in late July, dropping two games of a three-game series. In the Stars' only win Beckwith, a power-hitting right-hander for the Chicago American Giants, played center field, and contributed a two-run home run.[58]

Belleville and Norfolk continued to barnstorm into the fall, playing independent matchups and touring together. A Tuesday night encounter might find the two Tidewater teams in Roanoke, or Richmond, and on Thursday they returned home to Tidewater for another series. It was a promotion of two of Virginia's best teams and a way of taking black baseball to the people, giving them something to see and something to talk about.

In a dozen encounters during the '39 season, Norfolk managed only four victories against the Grays. Belleville started a late August run by closing the door on the Baltimore Black Sox in a close 3–2 victory in Chester, Pennsylvania, and then dismantled the Atlanta White Sox 8–1. The Tars and the Grays hit the road together playing Wednesday and Thursday night games in Pocomoke and Salisbury, Maryland, with the Grays coming out on top 5–3, and 3–2.[59] With the exception of the Hilldales of D.C. and Richmond, Belleville had defeated every other worthy black semiprofessional team on the east coast. The Grays' view from the top was a brief one, for after the triumphant '39 season the core of the lineup moved on to the Negro Leagues. Though H.Z. Plummer kept the team intact through 1940 and Joe Lewis remained as manager, Belleville never placed another squad on the diamond to rival the 1939 team that shook up black baseball's semiprofessional ranks. The Black Tars of Norfolk all but disappeared completely. Only pitcher Herman "Lefty" Scott made the baseball headlines after the Tars disbanded.

The Newport News Giants returned in 1940 again participating in league play in the newly organized Virginia-Carolina Baseball League. Rounding out the eight team roster were the Braves of Berkley, Norfolk Cubs, Portsmouth Dodgers, Suffolk Aces and Giants, Plymouth Tigers and the lone Carolina team, the Ahoskie Black Hawks. The league schedule was to be forty games long with games on Saturdays and Sundays. The first half-season began May 4, and ended on July 3. A championship series was scheduled for the first week in September with the winner declared after a best three out of five game series. Newport News played through one half-season undefeated in league contest, while Berkley finished in second place.[60]

A meeting of league officials was scheduled on June 22 to review league business and possibly add more teams to the second-half schedule. Plans were also made for a first annual all-star game pitting the first-half league champions against a selected team of all-stars on July 7, 1940. Mysteriously, a second-half Virginia-Carolina League schedule never evolved and only independent baseball results were posted beyond July 3.

The league by all appearances was well-organized and carried enough good ball teams, but further explanations were not forthcoming in the press. The first-half league champion Giants were fan favorites in August of that year to bring home the Tidewater championship, also promoted as the state championship of Virginia.

Black teams from all over Virginia and parts of North Carolina were invited to the monthlong tourney. The tourney was oddly formatted stipulating two doubleheaders and then one single game to determine the best three out of five series.

Entry blanks were placed in the *Norfolk Journal and Guide* newspaper. After two weeks of play, three teams stood in the Giants' path to the crown—Richmond's Boosters, Belleville's Grays, and the Roanoke Black Cardinals. In a much anticipated matchup between Newport News and the Boosters a week prior to the tourney, the Boosters were pulling away 6–3 when rain halted the contest. This first meeting appeared to be a tune-up for an eventual showdown in the finals of the Classic. The Boosters had won twenty-three out of twenty seven starts by early August. Despite the addition of a few Capital City Elks standouts the Boosters were handed an early exit pass out of the Tidewater Classic by the vaunted Belleville Grays of the Interstate League 6–5, and 4–0. This was perhaps Richmond's only shot at claiming a state title.

When promotions for the 1940 Tidewater Classic began in August, the Cardinals were apparently not amongst the teams projected to snare the title. Neither the Cardinals nor their fans took the snub lightly—oversight or not. Roanoke manager Chappie Simms wrote a retort defending his ball club's record and potential to become state champs. In response, the *Norfolk Journal and Guide* extended a formal tourney invitation to Simms and his fired up Cardinals.[61] The Cardinals landed in the thick of the action first drawing the Belleville Grays and then the Tidewater Giants. It was the first recorded contest between the southwest Virginia Cardinals and the dominating southeast Virginia ball clubs. The Grays and Cardinals split a game each in their opening series, and then came the much anticipated meeting against Tidewater. Roanoke controlled Tidewater handily until the bottom half of the sixth inning when the wheels fell off the red bird's machine, and a comfortable 6–0 lead flew away. A series of unimaginable errors led to a memorable Giants rally and astounding loss for the Cardinals.[62]

After the disheartening loss on the peninsula Roanoke rebounded at home and handed Tidewater a double defeat by identical 5–3 scores. Roanoke now led the series two games to one with the next game scheduled to switch back to Tidewater. This is where the trail runs cold due to a lapse in sports news coverage. Results from the Roanoke-Belleville Labor Day matchup were not published and evidently the Tidewater Giants prevailed, winning both games over the Black Cards because ultimately the championship came down to a struggle between the Portsmouth's Belleville Grays and the Giants of Newport News.[63]

The Grays had become the new kings of Tidewater baseball a year earlier. Once again the two teams met in a doubleheader and once again the games were split. Just when the action was reaching its peak it looked as if the Grays were breaking down at the worst possible moment. A good portion of the second-half Belleville team was made up of college ballplayers and after Labor Day weekend of that year the young men returned to school. Belleville met Newport News for the finale with only nine men in uniform who may or may not have included manager Joe Lewis.

When the diamond dust cleared at the end of the monthlong tourney the Giants had been whipped decisively by Portsmouth 9–0.

For Belleville it was certainly one of their greatest victories as they were declared state champs. Newport News on the other hand narrowly missed a decade of complete dominance in both independent and league baseball. The Giants and Grays folded after the 1940 season. For the former, it was the end of an outstanding run by the team with the best win-loss record; and for the latter, it was the end of the best playing team in the pre-integration era.

III

Heart of the Order, 1940–1950

In 1940, an interstate league annexed semipro black baseball teams in Virginia and Washington, D.C.'s, metropolitan area for the first time during baseball's preintegration era. The Richmond Elks, Washington Aztecs, Georgetown Athletics, and Edgewater Maryland Giants constituted the new league teams as of April 9, 1940. Belleville's Grays of Portsmouth were the last entry in the league a month later.[1] League officials had hopes of adding at least three more teams before the league's May 26 start.

Washington *Afro American* newspaper editor Art Carter played a major role in bringing the team owners and managers together. Carter served as president of the Interstate League. League officers were chosen from amongst the five teams. John Lynch of the Georgetown Athletic Club served as vice president; Leon Calhoun of the Washington Aztecs was the secretary. Former Washington Hilldale manager Joe Lewis of the Portsmouth Grays served as the assistant secretary, Dr. Joseph Thomas of the Edgewater Giants held the position of treasurer, and Joseph Miles, booking manager for the Capital City Elks, was the acting business manager.

All teams involved in the formation of the new league either leased or owned their stadiums and potentially had the capacity to cater to crowds of two to six thousand. The short-term goal of the Interstate League was to build a consistent fan base and use revenues to enlarge the current facilities. Sunday doubleheaders were the attraction in Interstate League play, leaving the rest of the week or weekend for teams to barnstorm.

The title of the new league appears to have been related to black baseball teams located on or near the old Rt. 1 corridor which basically connected all three areas. Portsmouth's Grays were the only club outside of the plotted designation.

Given the abundance of black ball teams in Northern Virginia and Washington alone surprisingly only two District of Columbia teams participated. Pearson's All-Stars of Alexandria played in the Richmond City and County League and barnstormed the Carolinas but either passed or were passed up to play in a league essentially in their own backyard. The same can be said for Richmond's B.B. Boosters who rarely matched up poorly against any eastern semipro ball club, but chose to play in the local City-County League.

League stability was hard to come by in the Negro professional leagues and even more fleeting on the semipro level. Players and owners needed a strong showing to give them a reason to quit their barnstorming tours and the confidence in casting their lots with a new organization.

By 1940 Washington, D.C., could just as well have been the nation's capital of baseball. The tiny District of Columbia housed more baseball teams, black and white, than many states. There were at least two attempts to field Negro professional teams inside the city of Washington. Ben Taylor led the first exploratory effort towards the big leagues with the Washington Potomacs in the 1924 Eastern Colored League. The team finished a dismal seventh in the eight-team league. The Potomacs relocated to Wilmington, Delaware, and went back to the semipros. Next Taylor managed the Washington Pilots in the 1932 East-West League and then the Washington Black Senators in the 1938 Negro National League. Both forays into big-league play were doomed by the first half of the season. The pilots continued on as a semipro club through 1934 with Burnalle "Bun" Hays as the ace pitcher.[2]

The District received its first successful Negro League team when the Nashville Elites relocated to Washington in 1936, before relocating to Baltimore, Maryland, for the 1938 season. The Elites were one of the better teams in the Negro National League and certainly the top team in the Baltimore-Washington-Metropolitan area until the Homestead Grays of Pittsburgh moved into Washington in 1940.[3]

The Negro League champion Grays split their home appearances between Pittsburgh and Washington and shared Griffith Stadium with the 1924 World Series champs, the Washington Senators.

They were loaded with unforgettable stars in Hall of Famer Josh Gibson, Hall of Famer Buck Leonard, Jud Wilson, and Raymond Brown. There is no mention of organized league play amongst Washington's black semipro teams, though there were at least ten competitive ball clubs in and around the city. Before the arrival of the big-leaguers D.C.'s Hilldales, made up of college and standout sandlot ballplayers, were favorite sons around the city. The Dales were one of the stronger east coast semipro clubs and played all comers from Florida to New York. Distinguished Washington *Afro American* sportswriter-editor Sam Lacy managed and pitched for the Hilldales in the early '30s. Lacy also umpired black baseball games in the District.

The Dales wrapped up city championships in 1935 and 1936 before relocating to Richmond, Virginia, in 1939.[4] When the 1940 Interstate League season opened only the Georgetown Athletic Club and the Washington Aztecs were interested in participating. Georgetown, Anacostia A.C., and the Ledroit Tigers were tops in the city through 1935. The Georgetown A.C. won the city championship in 1933 and then defeated Ben Taylor's Washington Royal Giants for the title in 1939.[5] Green Valley, Virginia, was the Athletics home site for baseball day or night, while the Aztecs played out of Oxon Hill, Maryland. In the 1930s weekend doubleheaders in the District were a main event. The Anacostia A.C. of southeast Washington clashed with Georgetown at least six games per season leading up to the city tournament.

Neighboring Prince Georges County, Maryland, held top ball teams in the Huntsville Senators and Myrtle A.C. On a Memorial Day weekend in 1939 the Senators whipped the Myrtle A.C. 3–2, won 12–3 over the Washington Aztecs, and subdued another local team, the Vista Maryland Giants, 11–5.[6]

Several black ballplayers rose out of the D.C. sandlots displaying big-league potential and promise. Clarence "Pint" Israel of Rockville, Maryland, and Russell Awkard played semipro baseball on Ben Taylor's Washington Royal Giants. Israel held down third base while Awkard played center field. Both were called up to the professional Negro Leagues in 1940.

Israel was picked up by Abe Manley's Newark Eagles where he played four seasons at shortstop, and then played three seasons on the Negro League champion team, the Homestead Grays. "Pint" Israel, though small in stature at 5'7", was known for his hustle, and though his batting averages were at best mediocre it was his fielding that won over the Eagles and Grays. Israel's younger brother Al played with the Philadelphia Stars near the collapse of the Negro Leagues in 1950, and was one of the early black minor leaguers in the South East Atlantic League (Sally) in 1953.[7]

Russell Awkard was born in Howard County, Maryland, and grew up playing baseball in the District, becoming a versatile diamond standout on the Royal Giants. Awkard was chosen by the New York Cubans and then sold to the Newark Eagles. Manager Raleigh "Biz" Mackey moved him around the diamond and Awkard responded well, and seemingly had a bright professional career ahead. However one day into the 1941 season he was drafted into military service, which ended his professional career. After his tour of duty in 1945 he returned home to Washington, but restricted his play to the sandlots.[8]

D.C. native Norman "Jelly" Jackson started out as an infielder in the local sandlots before landing with the Cleveland Red Sox in the Negro National League in 1934. After the Red Sox demise Jackson signed on with the then Homestead Grays of Pittsburgh in 1935, staying through the team's early years in Jackson's hometown of Washington. Jackson appears on the Washington Elite Giants roster in 1937 perhaps in a move closer to home. The slight infielder never batted better than .265 but had good speed on the base path, played good defense, and was known to get a hit when the team really needed one. The Grays considered him one of their best players and Jelly Jackson was always a fan favorite at Griffith Stadium.[9]

Black baseball in Maryland was highly competitive through the mid–1930s. In 1932 there were at least twenty-four amateur ball clubs. Ten of these teams competed in the Southern League of 1933 that included two Baltimore City teams, the Giants and the Tigers. Other black ball teams hailed from Randallstown, Chase, Pimlico, and Fairfield. The Piedmont Tigers were the best of the Southern League that year winning both the first- and second-half championships.

On the eastern shore the Bi-State League matched teams from Maryland and Delaware together in an eight-team league from 1934 to 1937. Harrington was the lone Delaware team in competition against Cambridge, St. Michaels, Vienna, Georgetown, Federalsburg, Bellevue, and Denton. The Denton Tigers topped the league in the mid-thirties winning the first- and second-half titles. Twenty-five to thirty regular season games made up the Bi-State schedule.[10]

The South Atlantic League of 1937 presented the first attempt at integrated baseball south of the Mason-Dixon Line. It comprised the Harlem (N.Y.) Athletic Club, Chesapeake Terrace, Baltimore A's and Wilkens Athletic Club, and Catonsville Maryland Giants.[11]

Baltimore's Black Sox represented the state of Maryland in professional black baseball from 1916 to 1934, producing pennant winners in 1929 and 1932. By 1933 the team began fading in and out of the Negro National League and officially folded at the season's end. For a couple of seasons the Black Sox' status is vague as to whether they were a team of independent professionals or semipros. By 1936 the Black Sox were no longer playing professional baseball and played exclusively on Maryland's semipro circuit. The Elites moved from Washington to Baltimore in 1938, becoming the new professionals in town through the collapse of the Negro Leagues in 1950. After a season in the Negro American Association of 1939, the Black Sox' run on the semipro circuit ended with their merger with the Edgewater Giants in 1940.

Edgewater Giants owner Joseph Thomas operated an amusement park and bathing beach in Turners Station, Maryland, and in 1937 decided to add baseball as another summertime attraction. The new ball diamond was boasted to be second only in size to the Baltimore Orioles' facility. Thomas hired former Negro League player Joe Lewis away from the Washington Hilldales as the manager, and began to stock his team with talent. His most famous acquisition was Negro League legend and Baseball Hall of Famer Oscar Charleston whom he got to come to Maryland and play on the 1937 team, surprisingly as a pitcher. This is the only recorded time period in Charleston's illustrious career that he was known to pitch.

Certainly he had been a sensational outfielder and played a good second base, but for Edgewater the tough left-handed Charleston toed the mound rubber and pitched. Though box scores are few and far between, obtainable records show that in the rotation Charleston more than held his own.[12]

Laymon Yokely was the Giants' manager and enjoying his best outing as a team leader in the semipros. Yokely, the former Baltimore Black Sox ace, was forced out of professional ball by a worn arm in 1933. During his professional career he was credited with an astounding six no-hitters. In a 1934 encounter with white big-league all-stars Yokely pitched the Black Sox to a 2–1 victory giving up three hits and striking out five batters including the great Chicago Cubs slugger Hack Wilson. Yokely's fastball was superb and he threw it as hard as he could throw it each and every outing. The velocity with which he threw and his frequency in the rotation ultimately led to his arm problems.[13]

After a failed comeback with the disastrous 1938 Washington Black Senators Yokely concentrated his efforts on the Washington-Maryland semipro scene.

He was, outside of his athletic accomplishments, a born survivor and second only to baseball man Ben Taylor as an organizer. Laymon Yokely always landed on his feet, and more often then not on a baseball diamond with a winning team. After the collapse of the Senators Yokely finished up the season with the Washington Eagles, and to muscle up this squad he convinced Baltimore resident and former Negro League great outfielder Crush Holloway to play right field.[14]

In 1939 the Eagles folded and Yokely relocated to Baltimore, returning to the roots of his professional career, and started up another Baltimore Black Sox team. Baltimore originally planned to enter the new Eastern Colored league of 1939, but pulled out before the season started, and instead played out the year in the newly founded Negro American Association. Managing Edgewater Yokely secured part-time Elite Giants players to bulk up his roster. Maurice "Skeeter" Watkins played shortstop for the Giants in 1940. Watkins would go on to play for the Philadelphia Stars, Newark Eagles, and Indianapolis Clowns. He was known as a sure man to get on base whether by way of his bat or drawing a walk, and once on had the ability and hustle to take another bag. In the '50s the fleet infielder played three seasons in the Canadian minor leagues. Pitching for the 1940 Edgewater Giants Laymon Yokely appears to have regained the fire in his hard throwing right arm as he made headlines pitching 1-hitters for the Giants in several 1940 matchups in and out of the Interstate League. The long-armed broad-shouldered right-hander all but overpowered the best hitters in the Interstate League, and in 1943 he won 13 straight games earning one last shot at the professional leagues with the Baltimore Elite Giants in 1944. When the curtain finally came down on Yokely's big-league career, he hit the road with yet another semipro team, Yokely's All-Stars, and barnstormed until 1959.[15]

Belleville's Grays, 1939 Eastern Colored League champions, were the last team to enter the Interstate League. Gone were stars Tommy Sampson, Buster Haywood, and "Cannonball" Gentry Jessup.

To the Grays' advantage, resourceful baseball man Joe Lewis was manning the helm in the late '30s early '40s. Belleville suffered losses early on in league play struggling to a .500 winning percentage. But in the second half of the season with the additions of Tidewater's best high school and college ballplayers and a special guest appearance by Vernon "Big Six" Riddick the Grays stormed back in the second half of the season finishing three games behind the Washington Aztecs.

Virginia's other entry into the Interstate League, the Capital City Elks, known as the "Pride of Richmond," entered league play for the first time ever in 1940. Independent play in Virginia and the Carolinas comprised the Elks' schedule in the '30s, and their best season appears to have been 1934 when they were declared city champions of Richmond.[16] With the exception of Edgewater, the Elks matched up well with all other teams in the league, but played well below their potential most of the season. The Elks opened the Interstate season against the Washington Aztecs on Mayo Island, Virginia. Richmond lost the weekend doubleheader 8–5 and 6–1. A week later the two met in Oxon Hill, Maryland, and this time split a doubleheader with the Aztecs, winning game one 7–2 and the Elks taking the evening contest 5–3.[17]

The Interstate League regular season schedule was slated to be thirty-six games long. Because there were five teams, clubs dormant on a weekend filled vacancies with nonleague opponents. The Edgewater Giants met the all-white Heurich Brewers in a May doubleheader. The Brewers were champions of the Atlantic Coast and tops in the District of Columbia's Industrial League.

Laymon Yokely pitched a six-hit ballgame and the Giants took the first game 2–1. The night cap went an abbreviated seven innings and once more ended with Edgewater on top 4–0. The two teams faced off again in another doubleheader in July, this time with Edgewater taking the first game 5–1, before rain eliminated the possibility of a second contest.[18]

In June 1940 the Washington Aztecs filled in an open date on the Homestead Grays' schedule. For this Saturday night contest the two teams met under the lights at Ballston, Virginia, just outside of Washington. The contest was a one-sided affair as the Grays coasted to a 12–3 win, but it is more noteworthy because the Grays broke in a young pitcher from Manassas, Virginia, named Wilmer Fields. Fields pitched his first game that Saturday, won, and stayed with the team for ten more years becoming one of the Grays' all-time best players.[19]

The Capital City Elks lost a 4–2 ballgame to the Kinston (North Carolina) Grays, eventual independent Tarheel champs in 1940. They split a doubleheader with the Winston-Salem Giants of the Negro American Association, and were reported to have booked a game with the famed white barnstormers, the House of David.[20] Only twenty Interstate League games were reported, though it is conceivable that all of the league teams played at least twenty independent dates. Early August 1940 presented the last documented league results.

Edgewater and Washington were both fast out of the gate with Edgewater leading the first half with a record of 10 wins four losses and the Aztecs following at 8 and 4.

A month earlier Edgewater took both ends of a doubleheader away from the Aztecs, 2–1, 5–3. The final two doubleheaders between the squads would decide the Interstate League championship. The Giants arrived in Oxon Hill, Maryland, with a record of 14 wins 4 losses, and Washington's tally was 12 wins and 6 losses.[21]

The Aztecs' only hope was to force a deadlock tie with the Giants if they could win both games of the weekend encounter, almost an insurmountable feat considering the Aztecs had beaten the Giants only once during the season. Doubling the odds against Washington was the fact that Edgewater had not dropped two league games in a row all season. Pulling off the impossible, Washington stunningly took both ends of the double-header 7–2, and 8–5. This furious finish to league play saw both teams tied for first place and with a winning percentage of .700. Perhaps as a season ender, Edgewater took on the famed semipro Mohawk Giants of New York in doubleheader. Both games were titanic struggles, but the New Yorkers prevailed winning a double over the Marylanders, 4–3 and 1–0. Laymon Yokely was the loser of the first game.[22]

Belleville finished second having won and lost half of the ten Interstate League games played that season. League play was a bitter taste for Georgetown and Richmond as they lost eight of their first-half season games and never recovered, finishing well below .500.

World War II altered the playing schedules of Virginia's black teams but did not by any means halt the action. The more active barnstormers who toured the Carolinas and West Virginia reduced their travel in accordance with the wartime gas rationing, but still crossed the Virginia borders to compete. Black men were drafted into the armed services but not in vast numbers until 1942 and 1943.

Tidewater's number of black baseball teams increased. By 1941 there were the Newport News Black Swans, West Norfolk Slides, Oak Leaf Giants, Suffolk Giants, Norfolk Giants, Norfolk Battling Palms and Norfolk All-Stars.[23]

Joe Lewis stayed on in Tidewater and worked to field another powerhouse like the team he managed in Belleville. Lewis organized a new team called the Norfolk-Portsmouth Virginians. Little was reported of the team's tenure other than a couple of early season games in 1942. The Virginians received a formal challenge from the Kinston (North Carolina) Grays managed by Charlie Leonard, brother to Homestead Grays all-star Buck Leonard.[24]

World War II brought black baseball players via the military from all over the United States to Norfolk Naval Base and Camp Pickett as it was known in the forties. Commissioned black players played games in off-duty hours against each other and the best of the locals. There was more than enough talent on the military teams to make the wartime baseball competitive. Notable ballplayers serving in the military included Joe Black, who served at Camp Pickett in the mid-forties.

Pete Wilder, manager for the successful Raleigh Grays of the thirties, moved north, bringing with him his brother Joe, a power-hitting first baseman. Wilder headed up the Portsmouth Senators, a team said to be made up of locals and men from the Tidewater military installations. The Senators of '42 were the new team to beat and answered the call by routing the Berkeley Braves 21–1. They would win twenty-four games in a row before being halted by the Norfolk Naval Hospital. The Suffolk Aces were putting together win streaks of their own in 1942.[25]

Both Portsmouth and Suffolk played primarily within the Tidewater region that included military squads, and only a handful of games against North Carolina teams. Farther north competitive teams sprang up in Emporia, Farmville, and Williamsburg. Farmville pitcher James "Pee Wee" Jenkins pitched his way out of the Prince Edward County sandlots in 1944 and onto the Negro Professional League's Cincinnati-Indianapolis Clowns. From 1946 to 1950 he was a mainstay in the pitching rotation for the New York Cubans, World Series Negro League champs in 1947. At 5'8" 160, the undersized Jenkins utilized his command of assorted pitches and his steady control to carve out a career in the big leagues.

After 1950 Jenkins played on a few remaining Negro League teams—the Birmingham Black Barons in '52, and a stint back with the Clowns. Pee Wee Jenkins experienced the most success playing in the Mandak League of the Canadian minors posting a 7–5 slate for Winnipeg in 1952, and then a 5–2 mark for Brandon during his last year of organized baseball in 1953.[26]

The Williamsburg Black Sox were back in the spotlight in the 1940s. The Colonial ballplayers asserted their newfound power with victories over Suffolk, the Dixie Aces, and Maryland Alco Flashes, winning seven out of eight contests in August 1941. The team played both in Williamsburg and Richmond alternately; hence they also appeared as the Richmond Black Sox.[27] Richmond City gained a new black baseball team in the Richmond Rams.

The Rams started fast out of the gate in 1941 thanks in part to lean hard-throwing Eddie "Red" Jacobs, a star hurler for the Raleigh Grays. Jacobs debuted for Richmond in April '41 and pitched a seven-hit eight-strikeout ballgame to defeat the Berkeley Braves 8–2. The *Norfolk Journal and Guide* touted the team as semipro champs early on in the 1941 season.[28]

Semipro league play received a revival almost immediately following the end of World War II. The Negro American Association was perhaps the most successful and longest running black semipro league in the Eastern United States. The league evolved in 1939, the year that marked the failed attempts of the New Eastern Colored League. The founders of the association are unknown; however, listings in historical references about the Negro Leagues would indicate that the semipro Negro American Association was like the Negro Southern League, a minor league for black baseball teams.

League play was constructed to include black teams on a circuit of southern cities, and much as with the plans for the Interstate Baseball League, access to adequate facilities was sought to bolster the fan base. Nineteen thirty-nine is the only season of recorded play in the decade of the '30s, and six teams made up the association roster. Representing Virginia's entry in the association were the outstanding Hilldales of Washington, D.C., newly transplanted to Richmond. The Dales were enjoying a dominant five-year run, and quite possibly had the potential to branch out into a professional franchise. Through 1938 the team held their own against the Negro League's New York Black Yankees, Indianapolis Clowns, and Baltimore Elite Giants. Joining the Hilldales were the new Baltimore Black Sox, Camden (New Jersey) Giants, Greensboro Redwings, High Point Red Sox and Winston-Salem Giants.[29] F.B. Morris's Greensboro (North Carolina) Redwings played a barnstorming schedule throughout the Carolinas, Virginia, and West Virginia. The Redwings were especially well known in southwestern Virginia where they played regularly against the Bedford Athletics and developed a fierce rivalry with the Roanoke Black Cardinals.

Morris was known as "Bris." His ball team originally represented Goshen, North Carolina, until 1939 when Goshen and the Asheville Black Tourist combined to form one ball club in Greensboro. In Greensboro the Redwings played their games at Memorial Stadium, and were celebrated as the only semipro outfit in the town. When the team opened its Negro American Association schedule on May 5, 1939, a high-ranking official from Greensboro's city government was on hand to throw out the first ball, and a sizable crowd of black and white fans cheered on the Redwings.[30] On July 4, Greensboro met High Point in a titanic eleven-inning diamond duel before 3000 supporters, with Greensboro prevailing 7–6. To top off the 4th of July fireworks, the Wings defeated Chappie Simms' Roanoke Cards 13–12 in the nightcap.[31] In their decade long involvement with the league, the Redwings never earned the top spot in the association but the team always maintained winning records. Nineteen thirty-nine and 1949 were probably the Redwings' best outings in the N.A.A. as they battled for the number one spot in the first and second half of league play. C.I. Deberry managed the Redwings in 1948 while he served as vice president of the N.A.A. and Bris Morris was the acting league secretary.[32]

Otto Briggs was a former Negro League outfielder with several teams during his twenty-year career, most notably the famous Pennsylvania Hilldales. He spent the latter part of his big-league tour around the Pennsylvania and New Jersey region last playing for the Atlantic City Bacharachs. The Camden (Pennsylvania) Giants were a likely fit for Briggs who like many other ex-professionals maintained the desire to manage and play on a team of his own. Baltimore Black Sox manager Laymon Yokely was a contemporary of Otto Briggs serving in the same capacity on the Black Sox team.[33]

Complete results for the Negro American Association's first season of play were not published, but the former D.C. city champions the Hilldales continued their winning ways in Virginia's capital city. Concluding the first half of play in July Hilldale stopped the tough Baltimore Black Sox on Bugle Field in Maryland 13–6, 7–6 earning the first-half championship. Hilldale bested all of their league opponents, rarely dropping more than one contest in the scheduled league doubleheaders. In independent action the Dales won an impressive 7–6 matchup over the famed House of David bearded nine. Following their championship win over Baltimore, Hilldale met the B.B. Boosters in what might have been billed as the battle of Richmond.

Hilldale Ace Jim Stewart came away with a 1–0 thriller over pitcher Junius Matthews and the popular Boosters.[34] The Dales returned to Washington, D.C., after the '39 season, played out of Richmond again in 1941, and thereafter faded from the ranks of black semipro baseball. Greensboro and Winston-Salem continued to participate in the N.A.A. into the 1950s, though by 1949 Winston-Salem languished in the league cellar.

Negro American Association play was dormant from 1941 to 1947. Post-World War II league participants were from Virginia and the Carolinas; no black ball clubs north of the Mason-Dixon line were included in the postwar reformation. During the 1947 season black teams in Virginia and North Carolina played in a revival of the Virginia-Carolina league titled "the Carolina Semi-pro League for '47."[35]

In 1948 the association reformed and remained in existence through 1952. The reinstatement of the league led to peak seasons in 1948 and 1949 with the top semipro, and former Negro League ballplayers competing on N.A.A. teams. Five days out of seven association ball teams were on the diamond.

The majority of league games were played within the confines of city recreational facilities. Virginia ball clubs played in High Rock Park, Norfolk, and Peanut Park, Suffolk, and Richmond City Stadium. Carolina teams played in Greensboro's Memorial Stadium and Durham Athletic Park. The N.A.A. also rented Griffith Stadium in Washington, D.C., at various times between 1948 and 1950. The Raleigh Tigers played in the association in 1948 as did the famed Asheville Blues after dropping out of the Negro Southern League.

The Tigers held their ball club together through their exit from the Negro Southern League, through organized semipro play, and through the demise of the Negro National League. The Negro American League, a last-ditch effort to maintain Negro professional baseball, was the last stop for Raleigh in the early '50s. The Atlanta Black Crackers, no longer competitive in the Negro Southern League, entered the second half of association play in 1948 replacing the Danville Aces.

Atlanta enjoyed its best seasons of professional baseball during World War II, but with the integration of major league baseball and Negro National and American League teams luring players away, the team dropped down to a semipro status.[36]

Richmond, Virginia, produced the Richmond Giants, a team made up of players from various states on the east coast. The Giants began play during World War II and evidence indicates that the team had aspirations of bringing professional ball to the Old Dominion. Richmond played the second-half schedule of the 1945 Negro Southern League with the Nashville Black Vols, Atlanta Black Crackers, Asheville Blues, Knoxville, Chattanooga, Indianapolis, and the Mobile Greys. The Giants were clearly outclassed in their efforts to play at a professional level, managing one win in the first-half twenty-game schedule.[37]

The Giants played in the Carolina Semi-pro League in 1946 and 1947 and then in the N.A.A. through 1952. Pitcher Garnett Blair of the Homestead Grays was the Giants' most recognized star. Blair came to the team after the Grays disbanded in 1949, staying with the team through 1952 until he received his only call-up to the minor leagues in 1953. Led by Blair, Richmond's pitching staff moved the team up the ladder of N.A.A. competition.[38] Richmond native Whit Graves had a 16–1 record in 1949 with four shutout ballgames. Menskie Cartledge backed Graves and Blair with a 16–3 record of his own. Isaiah Hyman of Savannah, Georgia, and Walter Johnson of Baltimore, Maryland, rounded out the staff.

Tidewater waded back into competitive semipro baseball in 1947 when baseball mogul Brady Johnson acquired the farm team of the Negro American League's Cleveland Buckeyes. Johnson's new team left Ohio and came to Newport News, Virginia, where they were known as the Norfolk-Newport New Royals.

Third baseman Ed Finney, pitcher-outfielder Horace Garner, first baseman Frank Alston, and pitcher Bob Stephens all saw action with both Norfolk and the Newark Eagles in the latter part of the forties. Johnson recruited old friend and rival

Joe Lewis to manage the new squad, and in 1947 the Royals won the second half of a doubleheader against 1946 Negro World Series champion Newark 10–5. Norfolk also played matchups against the Indianapolis Clowns, Atlanta Black Crackers, and Homestead Grays.[39]

Citing a lack of fan support in Tidewater the team barnstormed throughout the northeast in 1948 playing against the semipro Hartford (Connecticut) Indians, Staten Island (New York) Giants, and Point Pleasant (New Jersey) Nine. The Royals then toured the Midwest before returning home to Tidewater. Norfolk harbored strong hopes that their barnstorming exhibitions and wins might propel them into the Negro National League the following year, but the league collapsed, dissolving Negro professional baseball in the east. Ironically, during the 1948 season the Negro American Association petitioned for an agreement preventing raids on their best players by the Negro National League.[40]

The Royals, upon close inspection, were basically a .500 ball team in the Negro American Association, their strongest season being 1949 when they pushed the Homestead Grays early on in the first half of play. Without the further additions of a few higher caliber ball players, they were not likely candidates to fare well in the professional leagues.

As with the Negro Leagues, the Negro American Association held an all-star game before the championship rounds started for the second-half schedule. Beginning in 1939 the game was known as the Upper South versus the Lower South Baseball Classic and it pitted a compiled all-star team from the association versus the best team in the Negro Southern League. The Negro Southern League included the Asheville Blues, Raleigh Tigers, Atlanta Black Crackers, Birmingham Barons, Jacksonville Eagles, and Nashville Black Vols, Memphis Tigers, and Mobile Greys.[41]

Baseball historians label the Negro Southern League as more of a minor league system compared to the Negro National and American leagues in the north. To the credit of the NSL many reputable players played their way through the lower south circuit and then excelled in the more popular Negro Professional Leagues. Among the former NSL players were Alex and Ted "Double Duty" Radcliffe, Satchel Paige, Mule Suttles, and Turkey Stearns.

Much like the selection process for the Negro League East vs. West game, fans voted and mailed in their player selections to the *Norfolk Journal and Guide* sports department before the scheduled contest. The Negro Southern League's Asheville Blues dominated the all-star contest for the better part of a decade. In their last triumph in 1946, the Blues eked out a 1–0 screamer before a reported 4000 fans, an astounding number for a semipro setting. The eighth annual classic in 1947 featured the Jacksonville Eagles, Florida, league leaders in the Negro Southern League, against a Virginia-Carolina aggregation.[42]

Before meeting the Jacksonville team the all-stars faced off against nemesis Asheville in Durham, North Carolina. Five thousand fans sat through record-setting July temperatures to witness a 4–3 dogfight that ended in favor of the all-star squad.

The tuneup against Asheville boosted the confidence of the all-stars for their August 10 encounter with the Eagles at Greensboro Memorial stadium. Playing again before 5000 fans the all-stars survived another titanic struggle to beat the visiting Jacksonville squad 7–6. Former Capital City Elk Roy Debran and Negro League journeyman Spencer Davis represented Durham as standouts in the contest.[43]

Washington's Negro National League and World Series champions the Homestead Grays were the guest professional squad in 1948. Results of the matchup are not available. In a twist of irony, one month into the 1949 season the N.A.A. welcomed the Grays again, this time as members of the semipro league. With the demise of the Negro National League the Homestead Grays were forced out of professional baseball. The Grays won their last World Series championship over the Birmingham Barons in 1948.

Rather than fold the Grays organization, S.H. Posey, son of team founder Cumberland Posey, sent the team south to play in the thriving association. By 1949 black professionals not chosen to play in the white minor and major leagues had three options: join the Negro American League, play league ball in Puerto Rico, Cuba or Mexico, or play semipro ball on the east coast semipro circuit. The 1949 N.A.A. roster pitted Washington's Grays against Greensboro, Raleigh, Richmond, Norfolk, Charlotte-Asheville, and Winston-Salem, North Carolina. The Negro National League champs continued to use Griffith Stadium as their home field.

Compared to the competition they were accustomed to in the Negro Leagues, the lower level competition in the N.A.A. was less than challenging for the D.C. Grays. Even with the loss of batting star Luke Easter to the Cleveland Indians organization, the pitching of Wilmer "Red" Fields and hitting of Buck Leonard overwhelmed Negro American Association opponents.

Washington led the league with a .812 winning percentage losing only to the Greensboro Redwings and Raleigh Tigers.[44] Results of the second-half schedule were not made available, but by all recorded accounts the second half belonged to the Richmond Giants. Managed by Richmond native and former Baltimore Elite Giant Bob Clarke, the Virginians won a record 19 straight games, setting the table for a clash with the first-half champions, the Grays, in the second-half championship. Only the opening game of the series reached newsprint, as the Homestead Grays went up one game to zero after a 6–4 victory.[45]

In late August, a promotional matchup between the Richmond Giants of the Negro American Association and the Richmond Colts, a minor league team in the southern Piedmont Association, was arranged. It was one of the first big matchups between a black baseball team and a white squad on record in the Mid-Atlantic region of the South. Precisely 3,104 baseball fans poured into Mooers Field in Richmond, an estimated 2000 of them black baseball fans supporting the Giants. The game went 13 momentous innings. Richmond Giants pitcher and former Grays star Garnett Blair matched zeros with Sal Federico until the Colts were able to capitalize on a Giants error and squeeze a run in to win it 1–0 in the 13th. The Colts gave Garnett Blair his only appearance in the organized minor leagues in 1953.[46]

The association continued a few years beyond the integration of major league baseball, but with the lack of press, and dwindling fan support, the league eventually went the way of the Negro Professional Leagues—players, teams, and games long forgotten.

While the Richmond Giants and Norfolk Royals represented Virginia on the league circuit, John "Chappie" Simms and his Roanoke Black Cardinals dominated black baseball in the southwest. Owned by W.F. "Dingit" Hughes, the Black Cards first made their mark on the black semipro circuit in the latter part of the 1930s. Chappie Simms was an outspoken manager with unwavering confidence in his ballplayers. Simms was also the team booking manager, and through promotion and referrals Roanoke played the best semipro teams in Virginia, West Virginia, and North Carolina.

The Cardinals played regular home games at Roanoke's Springwood Park and big matchups down the highway at Municipal Stadium in Salem, Virginia. The Cardinals never participated in a league, but rivaled many league teams such as the Richmond Boosters and Tidewater Giants. A typical weekend found the Cards playing a doubleheader in Gary, West Virginia, against the Gary Grays, or Slav Fork Indians, and Keystone Giants. If it happened to be a holiday weekend, Simms detoured the team through Lexington or Lynchburg before heading home to Roanoke.

The Cardinals lineup was solid at the plate, on the mound and in the field. Second baseman James Jones was a mainstay in the Roanoke lineup of the thirties and forties, batting in the heart of the order. Pitchers Ralph "Moose" Woodliff, George Skipper, and Gill held back the opposition as James Jones et al brought in the runs.

Whenever the Redwings of Greensboro, North Carolina, met the Cardinals of Roanoke it was summed up by the word "thriller." One-run, extra-innings ballgames were commonplace in the heat of their diamond battles, with each team claiming a split in most of the encounters. The Black Cardinals were a fast-paced club known for their impressive win streaks; this often aided in their press coverage. In August 1939, in the midst of a 12-game win streak, they had two wins out of a three-game series against one of North Carolina's best black squads, the Raleigh (North Carolina) Grays. Roanoke won the first contest 5–3 on August 3. Coming into the 2nd game Raleigh sported a record of 43–12, and playing at Shaw North Carolina Memorial Field made the Cardinals the 44th victim in a punishing 13–2 victory. Len Hooker allowed 6 hits and struck out 12 Cardinal batters. The two teams locked up again for the final game in Roanoke. This time the Black Cards prevailed over the Grays winning 9–4 and neutralizing Raleigh pitcher Hooker who had managed to sit on Roanoke batters in the previous encounter.[47]

In 1940 the Cardinals were out fast again, and in the second half of play in August they were 15 and 2. One loss came via a 9–0 blowout at the hands of the Richmond B.B. Boosters. Leading into the Tidewater Classic the Cardinals pushed their win total to 17, by knocking off the Danville Aces 20–6 and the South Boston A's 4–2.[48]

Their play in the Tidewater Classic was thrilling but left them a game or two short of taking the prize as champions of black baseball in Virginia. As a consolation for an outstanding season the *Norfolk Journal and Guide* declared the Black Cards independent champions for 1940 perhaps based on furnished results from numerous black independent teams around the state.

Nineteen forty-one appears to have been just as rewarding for the Star City diamond men. By July '41 the Cardinals were again on a hot streak winning six in a row, numbering amongst their conquests the West Indian Royals, South Boston Virginia Blue Sox, Danville Aces, the famous New York Mohawk Giants, and a white semipro outfit in Roanoke City. Black Cardinal losses during that season came against stellar competition. In April the Black Cards dropped a game against the Winston-Salem Tigers 16–9. Two recorded Negro League matchups spelled defeat for the Cardinals—first they lost to the crowd pleasing Ethiopian Clowns, and then to the Negro National League New York Black Yankees. The Cards also lost one-sided matchups to the popular Brooklyn Royal Giants and another semipro team from Wilmington, Delaware, the Alco Flashes. The Alco Flashes played under the charge of Negro League great Judy Johnson.[49]

The Cardinals continued play through the early years of World War II. Nineteen forty-three may have been the last season of play as they were still listed in the black baseball directory. Their last headlining win came in July 1942 when they dismantled the Capital City Elks of Richmond 3–0, and 3–1 in a Fourth of July doubleheader at Springwood Park, Roanoke. The *Norfolk Journal and Guide* listed Simms' Cardinals as 16–0 after winning the holiday doubleheader.[50]

The Cardinals suspended play through 1946 and reformed in 1947. In the reformation a few remaining players from the early '40s squads joined together with another Roanoke team known as the All-Stars. Al Holland, Sr., Richard Dawson, William Robinson, and George and Melvin Franklin banded together with Woodliff, Boyd, James Jones, and Howard Easly.

The new Roanoke team resumed an independent schedule playing in the Carolinas and Virginia. Al Holland recalls that it was an era of hard men playing hard ball. The team divided modest shares of money at the season's end, but they were basically happy to play weekend baseball, and the fact that they could buy their own uniforms was a great accomplishment during those hard times.*

---

*Reading of the Cardinals' exploits in the old *Norfolk Journal and Guide* easily captured my imagination just as the sports page did when I was 10 years old and without the advantage of advanced media tech. But more than 60 years had passed since those exploits were first in print. It was enough of a task finding players who played and still lived in the region where I grew up, let alone ball players in another region of the state 50 years prior. I made one trip to Roanoke in the summer of 2000, somehow found the city library and at the desk introduced myself and left a card. I guess the impression had been made because 24 hours later I received an email from the librarian excitedly relating that right after I left that day a popular local patron visited the branch and after learning of my inquiry declared that he himself—one Alphonso Holland, Sr.—was a former member of the Cardinals. The branch librarian connected me with Mr. Holland, and I reached him later in the week. This was a grand slam, in my celebratory expression. Mr. Holland, though an elderly man at that stage, had great recall and like his peers was an amazing storyteller. With the valuable print records of Cardinal baseball achievements and Mr. Holland's recollection, the story and that era of black baseball was complete.

Mr. Holland considered himself a very good baseball player but not great. Perhaps humble to a fault, he left out the fact that his son Alphonso Holland, Jr., was a former Major League pitcher for the Pirates, Giants, and Phillies who ended his career with the New York Yankees.

Holland recalled with amusement a night game played against the Greensboro Redwings in which the Redwings agreed to compete for the gate receipts rather than split them 60/40 as was the norm in their matchups. The traveling Roanokers prevailed and headed home with padded pockets to the embarrassment of Greensboro. Playing in a holiday matchup with the Keystone (West Virginia) Giants, Holland was approached by an opposing ballplayer with an offer not related to baseball, to work in the local mines making $7.00 a day. Easy money, Holland was assured. The next day Holland followed this fellow down into one of the shafts where they manned one of the lines to the miners farther down. One day in the dark confined shafts told Holland it was definitely not his calling and he made every excuse to get back on the ballfield and then back home to Roanoke.

Al Holland points to contests versus touring Negro League teams as the most memorable during his play with the Cardinals. Each season, teams such as the Kansas City Monarchs, Ethiopian Clowns and Baltimore Elite Giants made Roanoke and Salem a stopover on the way from spring training or before heading to the islands for winter ball.

Though the Black Cards earned rare victories over the big-leaguers, Holland says they generally held their own, and it was exciting to be on the same field with so many good ballplayers. Al Holland is still amazed recalling the mastery of Josh Gibson behind the bat, and the superior talent of pitcher Leroy "Satchel" Paige. Infielder James Jones and pitcher Frank Boyd tried out for Negro League teams, but did not make the cut. Holland remembers that the lures of Negro League ball though thrilling appeared to be a tough way to make a living, and so many talented players were satisfied to play a respectable game of baseball on their hometown teams. The Roanoke Black Cardinals lineup folded for good around 1950 with only a few surviving team members like Al Holland still around today to recall Springwood Park and matchups against the Negro Leaguers in old Municipal Stadium in Salem.

Based on a scattered record of wins and their playing schedule from season to season the Black Cardinals probably rank as the fourth-best team in the history of Virginia's black baseball teams prior to the era of integration.

The Cumberland County Sluggers were a weekend traveling squad with one of the more impressive setups on the rural sandlot circuit. The Sluggers had their own stadium complete with a fenced in perimeter, dugouts and a grandstand. Fans paid $0.50 to get into the park and young ball chasers received a nickel for every baseball returned. With the proceeds, the team bought uniforms and the best bats money could buy, Louisville Sluggers. Former Cumberland players recall the necessity of replacing the costly store-bought lumber inspired the acquisition of a few hand-crafted hickory bats.

On away playing trips the Sluggers chartered a Greyhound bus and traveled to Washington, D.C., Maryland and West Virginia. In Virginia they played independent ball against a dozen teams in the southern part of the state. The team reached its stride following service commitments by a large portion of the lineup. Left fielder

III. Heart of the Order, 1940–1950   53

The Roanoke Black Cardinals, circa 1948: Front row, from left: Tittler Palmer, Fred Rice, Jim Jones (manager), Richard Dawson, Hubert Perry, Frank Boyd; Back row, from left: George Brown, Henry Craighead, Clarence Brown and Malcolm Williams (courtesy the Virginia Room, Roanoke Main Library).

William "Rabbit" Robertson served in the U.S. Army during World War II and played baseball on a post team in California.

William "Rabbit" Robertson:

> I played ball in the service at Hickman Field. Peewee Reese was the fastest guy there. He was playing in the Navy and I was playing in the Army. I could go from first to third on a bunt. The New York Yankees taught me how to steal bases. Before a pitcher can pitch the ball he's got to stop breathing; when he'd stop breathing that's when I'd take off.

Robertson was joined on the Cumberland squad by his brother, third baseman Lawrence Robertson. Center fielder George "Pop" Reed was the best-known and most animated player in the region. The short left-hander was tabbed with the nickname "Pop" when he had barely reached his teens, leaving him plenty of time to mature into the tag. In the outfield he was fleet, and caught fly balls in his glove and bare hand.

At the plate opponents say Reed would swing at anything, all with the intent of knocking the ball out of the park. He liked to hit the ball hard, and for a man his size generated a lot of power. In the late '40s and early '50s the Cumberland batting order was distinguished by the presence of seven left-handed batters, much to the dread of any right-handed pitcher. If there was a weakness on the right side of the infield or outfield the Sluggers would find it. Cumberland secured at least two games with the Camp Pickett Warriors in Blackstone, Virginia. (Camp Pickett is now known as Fort Pickett.) The matchups occurred during the service stint fulfilled by Brooklyn Dodger pitcher Joe Black. In their only victory over Camp Pickett, a wild throw to second base propelled Cumberland to a 1–0 win. Joe Black pitched, surrendering no runs in the losing cause against the Sluggers.

Former Cumberland players remember facing many hard throwing pitchers in the region, some of them the best ever seen short of the major leagues. Victoria in Lunenburg County, and Waverly in Sussex County reportedly had pitchers throwing upwards of 100 mph. As "Rabbit" Robertson recalled vividly, "you saw the pitcher cock his leg up in the air, and before it came down the ball was there." The Sluggers had a standout pitcher of their own in Claude Lipscombe. Lipscombe tried out unsuccessfully for the Brooklyn Dodgers in the '50s. Cumberland played one season in a loosely organized league in the late '40s with teams from Petersburg, Crew, Sturgeonville, Waverly, Victoria, and Blackstone.

In their travels Cumberland struck up a friendly rivalry with a sandlot team from New Jersey made up of black and white players. The Jersey team came to Cumberland County once a year and Cumberland returned the favor.

Cumberland players housed the Jersey baseball players during their stay, and because the team owned their playing field, Jim Crow segregation laws were not a deterrent. The Sluggers played a lot of good teams home and away but their true rival awaited them in the next county west of their own, in Buckingham. The Buckingham Grays had been together since the '20s and played a regional schedule for most of their existence. Out of respect to the elders of the church, baseball was only played on Saturday not Sunday during the early years. In southern Virginia few teams whipped the Grays on a Saturday afternoon. The Chambers, Hills, Garrets, Joneses, and Agees were the kings of Dixie Hill Diamond in the community of Dilwyn. To black residents the Grays were as important as the Dodgers were to Brooklyn, and Buckingham fans were very vocal in their support. Author and Buckingham resident Charles White recalls the excitement:

> A lot of fields were located next to these black owned restaurants, and Saturday night places. During the day it was the big game, and the women brought out the chicken and cakes and pies. If the Grays were playing Shipman or Cumberland, it was like a World Series game. I'll never forget, Pop Reed came up to bat and Willie Chambers was pitching, and Willie's mother yelled out, "Pop hit a home run and I'll give you a chicken leg," and so Willie's brother said, "Mamma, whose side are you on?" But I saw some spectacular catches on Dixie Hill Diamond, guys making the kinds of catches I've seen in the major leagues.

Moses Garrett and Willie Chambers were the one-two punch for the Grays pitching staff. Moses Garrett blinded batters with his fastball and drop ball. Garrett's pitches were fast and he had great control. Willie Chambers stymied batters with his hard breaking curveballs and knuckleballs. Opponents from the era say that even if you connected on a Willie Chambers pitch it wasn't going anywhere because every pitch was pure junk. Chambers also played second base and was known to catch on occasion.

Powell Jones was the Grays catcher and one of the best in the region. Jones could block it and he could hit it out. The Buckingham Grays played locally against Arvonia, Fairview Lodge, and Rockmill. Out of the area games were booked with Appomattox, Amherst, Chase City, Shipman, and Massies Mill. In the '30s Buckingham native and educator Frank Harris was a counselor for the CCC camp at Fort Harrison below Richmond. Harris toured central Virginia with the camp baseball team playing against teams in Richmond and also bringing the talented squad of youth to Buckingham to play his hometown Grays.

Between Buckingham and Cumberland the debate has long raged as to who held the upper hand, and whether or not Pop Reed got the better of Willie Chambers and Moses Garrett. Even today the two sides refuse to cede the title of "superior" to the other. The only compromise appears to be the agreement that both teams struggled against Amherst County baseball teams.

Willie Chambers:

> I used to pitch to Pop Reed and just throw it any kind of way-anywhere, and he would try to hit at it ... whether he could reach it or not. Then I had to throw one at his body. He'd back up and it would break across the plate. He couldn't do nothing with that curveball. Buckingham was the best.

Pop Reed countered, touting the Sluggers prowess in the sandlots:

> Cumberland played everybody everywhere that had a good team and we won.

On the southern tip of Albemarle county lies the community of Covesville, long known throughout the twentieth century for its apple orchards, logging, and black baseball. Between 1944 and 1952 the Covesville Virginia Tigers reigned as independent champions in central Virginia, going undefeated for a handful of seasons. The community produced so many players, there were two teams, the Big Team and a younger squad of teenagers. Covesville was "baseball country."

On Sunday afternoons family and friends of the ballplayers filed out of the church just minutes down the road and headed for the diamond. They were still dressed in their Sunday best with the ladies in their dresses and the men wearing the popular straw summer dress hats. Everybody was going to watch Covesville play baseball. It is estimated that black baseball in the community began in the teens. There is a surety that the ball team was always filled out with the Dowell and Henderson families, and then later Mosbys, Williamses, Smiths, and Stevens made the roster.

Without the presence of a makeshift backstop, no one would have mistaken the Covesville ball diamond for a playing field at all. It was an oddly shaped cow pasture adjacent to a rich field of corn. Right-field hits carried with little might, but center field might have contained the hits of a Josh Gibson. As catcher and infielder Edward Henderson recalls, players with the least amount of seniority had to prepare the field on game day.

> We used to have to chase the cows off the field and get up the cow piles before the game, mow the grass. The boys from the city who used to come up and play against us were used to playing on good diamonds and had to get used to playing the ball off of the humps and dips on a country ball field.

Following successful seasons in the twenties, Covesville's baseball team began to show signs of aging in the nineteen thirties. The Tigers matched up poorly against the Shipman Spiders and Massies Mill Giants in neighboring Nelson County. Kelly's All-Stars of Charlottesville refused to book many games with the Tigers unless they needed to fill in a long holiday weekend with an extra game.

This all changed in the forties when a younger generation Covesville players joined the Tiger lineup alongside a few of the remaining veterans from the '20s and '30s. Albemarle County natives who saw Covesville play in the '40s and '50s compared the Tigers to a team of big-leaguers playing on a makeshift diamond. The ball field was right beside old Rt. 29 south making it easily accessible for baseball fans and teams traveling into the area. Oftentimes people out on weekend drives stopped just because there was a ballgame going on, and in this rural setting it was an added activity to the day. Cars and trucks lined the highway and surrounded the field. Drivers of state passenger buses pulled over on their breaks to watch the Tigers play ball. At one time or another it appeared everybody had their eyes on Covesville baseball, and the Tigers gave them something to see.

The Covesville lineup had character and fans came to know the players by their style of play, how they talked it up on the field, and entertained. The Tigers were lively. In the outfield James Henderson had the company of his brothers Robert and Samuel. Robert had also played on a military post team during World War II. They were a swift trio and covered the expansive outfield like they owned it. When it came to Covesville's infield play, seeing was believing.

Two left-handed infielders were playing on the wrong side of the diamond. Lefty Albert Henderson played shortstop like a moving screen, rarely missing a ball and had little problem making the out at second base. He was a big hitter in the lineup and his speed on the base path approached world class. In high school he was clocked under ten seconds in the hundred yard dash on a dirt track.[51]

Third baseman Haywood Dowell did not look like an athlete, much less a ballplayer. He was haggard in appearance and looked to be in poor shape, but when he put on the uniform, and picked up his tattered rag of a glove he was a ballplayer.

Teammates remember left-handed Haywood Dowell on the ball field as poetry in motion. He raked up ground balls with only his thumb in the tattered glove snapping it open and shut, and when he had the ball snared, threw to first base with everything he had, all the while yelling to his teammates. In his teens he was reportedly a good pitcher. Haywood was tough and he was competitive. A few teammates learned the hard way when they unsuspectingly found themselves planted in the red clay after Haywood had run over them in practice. When guarding the bag he threw his body into an opposing base runner oftentimes pinning the runner down short of third base.

According to first baseman Isaiah Mosby, one of the younger Covesville Tiger standouts in the mid-forties, it was nothing short of mesmerizing to see Haywood Dowell catch and throw a baseball.

> Haywood was left-handed, and he'd sweep up balls like you're sweeping the floor. He used to pick up a ball, turn around and throw it, and when he threw, that ball would always curve, so you had to be ready because as hard as he threw it could kill you, but it was something to see him catch and throw! He'd pick it up, and sometimes he'd skip to get his balance and throw—then again he'd go on around in a circle and throw if it was on his left side.

Other teams found the out-of-position play by Covesville peculiar, maybe even a mockery, but they could not hit the ball by Dowell or Henderson, and there was no one else in the Covesville community that came close to taking either man's position away.

Isaiah Mosby was coming of age in the forties as one of the teenaged Tiger ballplayers. He was tall with good strength and leverage in his upper body. As he looked back on his growing up in a 2000 interview, he pointed out that hard times often made hard men.

> I used to get up before sunrise and walk two miles to work doing manual labor, and sometimes on the way home I would work another job for someone else. By then it was dark, but I would cut corn by the moonlight, and then go home and do the same thing the next day. Times were hard, World War II was going on, no one had much money. People really enjoyed watching a baseball game. Compared to the way we worked back then playing ball really was easy, and it took your mind off of the hard times.

Young Mosby proved a perfect fit for the Covesville lineup making the plays in the field and at the plate the opposition soon learned he was one of the Tigers' longball threats. Former players and fans recall Mosby routinely driving balls from the field onto old Rt. 29, and on one effort depositing a shot beyond the highway.

Covesville always presented a strong pitching staff during their many seasons of play. From the 1930s Tigers pitchers Joe Martin and Luther Henderson were standouts. Former Covesville players remember tall Joe Martin resembling Satchel Paige, all arms and legs. Martin had several good pitches and often started for the Tigers. Teammates also say he would never throw a game away.

If Martin was pitching a good game but starting to lose his command he would turn it over to another teammate in the rotation regardless the inning or pitch count. Often this meant that one of the Dowells entered the game and it was truly a new ballgame.

Rufus "Junky" Dowell was not a big man but he was like a ground-level twister when he released the baseball. He had an impressive fastball, and his curveball has been described as frightening, mainly because sometimes he didn't know where it was going and did not care—it was the batter's problem once it left his hand. Decades later, younger players remarked that had they faced Junky Dowell in his prime they would have never seen the ball. The more Junky Dowell threw the ball the better he became. You could take him out of a ballgame, but you could not knock him out. As Bob Winston of the Wilmington Eagles recalls, giving up home runs never seemed to faze Junky Dowell.

> We were playing a game up at North Garden and Junky was pitching, and I came to bat twice in one inning. I said, "Lord have mercy!" And old Junky he said, "I just ain't gonna give up." We had our pitcher to hit a home run off of Junky that day, but he would not give up.

Junky was known to pitch a game for a neighboring community on Saturday and then start and win a game for Covesville the next day. Teammates remember with humor that Junky pitched nine innings warming up on the sideline, much to the dismay of his manager. Legend has it, years later in an 18-inning battle against the locally based Greenwood Hawks, Junky went all the way for the win while the Hawks used several pitchers.

Early Dowell led the Covesville team pitching rotation, and batted cleanup in the order. He worked in a sawmill all of his life and in his prime stood 6'1" and weighed upwards of 230 lbs. In the days when ball players appeared to be cloaked by the baggy wool sets, Dowell's uniform looked like a custom fit.

As a teenager he was a Covesville first baseman, but after a stint in the Army in the early forties where he played on a military squad there were few doubts that Early Dowell was a pitcher. He was schooled in the national pastime in the service playing against some of the best black players in the country, and when he returned to his Covesville, Virginia, home he put his knowledge to work in reorganizing the Tigers. Relatives and opposing players remember Early Dowell as a quiet, reserved, and very modest man off the ball field. On the field he was vocal in directing the Covesville ball team.

It is said that when Dowell returned from the military in the mid-forties no one in central Virginia had seen the kind of speed he displayed. His pitching was overpowering, with his fastball all but intimidating the best hitters and his curveball breaking sharply over the plate. Often Howard Carter, a good solid catcher, was forced to block the pitch rather than catch it. Many country ballplayers could not see Early Dowell's pitches much less adjust their swing to make contact. Dowell's teammates laughingly remember some opposing hitters swinging the bat in one direction and running in the other. Bobby Hudson who played for Nelson County's Massies Mill Cubs compares Early Dowell to major league pitcher Armando Benitez in stature and style.

He was a good fielding pitcher, due to his time playing first base, and former teammates say he could have played catcher if he desired. Early Dowell was not known for having a good pick-off move but he knew how to break up a base stealer's timing and hold him on. In a famous 1950s game of Covesville versus the Albemarle County community of Greenwood, Greenwood speedster Lewis Kelly put Early Dowell to the test.

Lenny Dowell, Covesville Tigers, Astros:

> Greenwood had a guy on the team named Kelly. I think Kelly went out for the big leagues but didn't make it, but that guy was fast! He could steal a base on you, and play around on base on you. Anytime Early would whirl back to get him he'd dive back into the base. He'd walk way off the base taking a big lead. Kelly would go on and go on just like Jackie Robinson and when Early would wind up he'd go a little further. Early threw back two or three times but he couldn't get him. Early told Albert Henderson, "When I throw you the ball back at Kelly and try to get him you won't get him this time." He said, "I'm gonna walk almost to you and then I'm gonna walk back like I'm going back to the mound." Early whirled back and got him. Got him off base and picked him off for the first time.

Though he stirred the fans every time he pitched he never let the chants and shouts break his focus while on the mound. Occasionally when he had the game under control, he offered a fleeting gold-toothed smile as he paused in his stretch.

The Covesville diamond today (Tigers-Astros) (photograph courtesy Jon Glassberg).

After his release teammates say he struck a defiant pose because he did not expect the batter to make contact. At the plate Early Dowell helped his own cause by hitting home run shots that in rural settings disappeared from sight, and in the cities and small towns crashed into facades great distances from the playing field.

Black teams outside of Albemarle County were convinced that Covesville brought Early Dowell in on loan from the Negro Leagues, but he was a local product with extraordinary skills.

Former Covesville infielder Edward Henderson sums up Early Dowell's abilities in his prime:

> Early pitched a Sunday game for Covesville and won. Lewis Tolliver came out picked him up and carried him to Charlottesville to pitch against a barnstorming black team from New York, and Early shut them down! He didn't know his own strength when he first came out of the service. He and Coach Bob Smith played together in Charlottesville. Coach Smith was a bull of a man, and he'd wear out a uniform every time he played. More than once I've seen Smith and Early Dowell bounce balls out in the street when they hit them down at Washington Park, and sometimes Early would put one up on that bank where the houses stood.

Bob Smith came to Charlottesville in the 1940s, later becoming the head football coach at Charlottesville's new black high school, Jackson P. Burley. Smith was a black college all–American at Morgan State in Baltimore; baseball was his third sport. Covesville fans who saw Bob Smith and Early Dowell team up briefly agree that Smith was the only person who could handle Dowell's high-velocity fastballs, and Dowell could really let it go when Bob Smith was behind the plate.

Perhaps because of the poor results experienced by rival teams against Tiger ace Early Dowell, many communities made a pitch for his services. Amherst County, Shipman, Massies Mill, and Charlottesville were still traveling to Washington, D.C., Maryland and West Virginia to play against black semipros. They brought along Early Dowell as an extra ace in the rotation and a deadly bat in the lineup. Early Dowell traveled with these teams because he loved to compete, and it is safe to surmise that he delivered the desired results because often he played an entire weekend of baseball for at least two teams.

Coach Bob Smith had seen many talented athletes in all sports, and as a native of New Jersey had witnessed Negro League play. He was convinced that Early Dowell could play in the big leagues.

Dowell's relatives remember Bob Smith prompting a big-league club to offer Early a contract, but though Early liked to travel and play he was not interested in leaving Covesville. Instead he kept the papers among his personal effects for the rest of his days. By the 1940s there were lots of black baseball teams in central Virginia, but attempts were never made to organize the community teams into a league. Albemarle County alone held at least eight community teams between 1940 and 1950.

A few miles down the road the community of North Garden had a ball team, and adjacent to North Garden were the communities of Chesnut Grove and Esmont. Of the three, Esmont's Giants gave Covesville the better ball game. The Giants were led by pitcher Albert "Buster" Scott. In his time the left-hander was known as one of the best around and for certain had the best pick-off move. He turned his back when he pitched, spinning around to make the delivery, and he had a wide assortment of pitches to toss to the plate. Scott was smooth. Otis Copeland was the number two Esmont starter and while Scott had the junk, Copeland had the speed. The Tigers secured games through referrals from other players and teams. Players wrote letters and made phone calls when receiving word of a good ball team. Once Covesville began its amazing run in the mid-'40s other people approached members of the team at random saying, "I know a team in Lynchburg you can play, they have a good team," or "there's a team down in Fluvanna, they play good ball." The team never charged admission to games but passed the hat to cover expenses. Covesville had a faithful contingent of white fans who turned out to see the Tigers home and away. They never ventured close to the action but watched from the perimeter of the ball field and they knew all of the players.

Later, James Henderson and Isaiah Mosby began booking games for Covesville and there were very few vacant summer weekends for the Tigers.

With Early Dowell's pitching shutting down the competition, and the batting order of Henderson, Mosby and Dowell, the Tigers were the team to beat in the region. The Tigers now handed out whippings to the teams that had put them on the receiving end in the '30s.

All of central Virginia's tried and true clubs who traveled to play the best black semipro teams fell to the Tigers. Lewis Tolliver's Charlottesville squad, powerhouse

Massies Mill, Shipman, Amherst, Orange, and the impressive Dupont Grays of Waynesboro all went down to defeat against Covesville in the '40s. It is impossible to say how many games the Tigers won or how many seasons they went undefeated. Records are long since lost and there is no evidence of press coverage from any source. Popular opinion amongst surviving team members places the number at three or four years without a loss.

One summer weekend around 1949 or 1950 the Tigers were playing a game in Louisa County, Virginia, and were playing like professionals, as if they were putting on a show for everyone in attendance, and after the game they found out that they were indeed playing for a special audience. Isaiah Mosby explains:

> A fellow saw us play a game in Louisa, and we were very good that day. He said there was a team in Richmond—the Richmond Black Sox—and he wanted us to play them. Our problem was that we preferred not to play on Saturday because some of us worked on Friday night, and would get off on Saturday morning at 8 o'clock. We had to play this Richmond team on a Saturday afternoon ... didn't get enough sleep, and for some reason we didn't have it together, and they gave us a good shellacking. That was the only time I can remember Covesville getting shut out.

Covesville traveled to Glen Allen, Virginia, just outside of Richmond, and played that Saturday afternoon without three of their starting players. Howard Carter the starting catcher was missed most of all. Without Carter blocking the plate and Black Sox batters jumping on Early Dowell, Covesville was in over its head from the first inning. Unknown to the Covesville nine, the Black Sox were seasoned semipros who had faced off against Virginia's best black teams for two decades.

This matchup was Covesville's best opportunity to climb the ladder of top black teams in Virginia. Today remaining players from that contest are divided on whether the Tigers and Black Sox crossed bats again, and whether or not Covesville got the better of the Richmonders in the old cow pasture. It has been confirmed that Covesville began to lose its air of invincibility and teams near and far began to get to the Tigers lineup, including mighty Early Dowell. Dowell's pitching exploits in the region and beyond began to present signs of wear, and by the mid-'50s he was no longer able to shut teams down as he had a decade earlier.

The Tigers were still one of the best teams in Albemarle County and by 1952 their second team showed great promise, beating every team in the area except Covesville's Big Team. Baseball continued in the community of Covesville with more standout players and teams, but each generation revered the Big Team of the '40s who set the standard for Covesville baseball.

Staunton Stands Alone 1948–1950

Ninety-year-old James Becks radiates a warmth and friendliness that is detectable not just in person but also over the phone. In certain situations, he might be mistaken for a man 20 years younger. Mr. Becks has been devoted to his community in Staunton, Virginia, since returning from World War II when he was just barely an adult, participating in different capacities but more so in the promotion of sports. As an athlete, Becks found it easy to contribute on the baseball field and the basketball court.

His contribution to black baseball in Virginia began after World War II when he joined his hometown team, the Wild Cats, in 1949. Staunton, despite its spelling, is often pronounced "Stan · tn," depending on from where you hail in Virginia.

The Wild Cats played at Montgomery Hall Park, a former mansion and farm opened in 1947 providing a recreational area for black residents of Augusta County. It had a pool, picnic areas and ballfields. The Wild Cats were debuting in style and up and running the bases from the words "Play ball!" Black baseball had been popular in Augusta County since the 1920s up through the Depression-era '30s when the Harrisonburg Red Sox, Sperryville Yellow Jackets, Kelly's All-Stars and a red-hot Front Royal 9 ruled the valley and northwestern Virginia. Staunton first had a black baseball team known as the Staunton Athletic Club or ACs. A few miles north, Bridgewater played and traveled as the ACs through relocation to Harrisonburg into the 1970s. Is it possible that at some point in time Staunton and Bridgewater faced off for not just bragging rights but also ownership of the ACs moniker?

A Staunton team was re-formed in the late 1940s but had no problem establishing contacts or lining up opponents thanks in large part to a Dr. Childs of Staunton who sponsored the new Staunton ball club in 1948. Like the Wild Cats players, returning black serviceman all over the state were soon shedding military branch colors in favor of baseball-weight woolen sets for summer play.

The Staunton Wild Cats of 1948 included George Stuart, manager, Babe Robinson, Rueben Dawson, Johnny McCutcheon, Creed Pannell, Charlie Venable, Oliver Tate, Ira Wells, Godfrey Tate, Charles Gray, George Robinson, Sidney Vaughn, Mason Miller, Allen Jackson, Raymond Huggard, Robert White, Jr., and Robert Cauls. Bat boys were Lee Epps, Samuel Tate and Archie Anderson. Visitation to Montgomery Hall Park during the summer season was estimated to have been as high as 18,000, so it stands to reason that with the popularity of baseball and visitors to the park from all over the state, the Wild Cats had packed grandstands watching them play.

Childs entered the Wild Cats into a five-team assembly called the Western Virginia League. Along with the Wild Cats were the Waynesboro Grays, Charlottesville Cubs, Bridgewater ACs, and Lynchburg Bees. Of note, James Becks had relatives in the Burgess family playing on the Bridgewater ACs club north of Staunton led by Rockingham County baseball legend Roscoe Burgess. He recalls with renewed humor playing in Charlottesville and the power hitters of the day smashing balls across Preston Avenue and off the house on the hill before park officials changed the field orientation from south to northwest. He also recalls playing basketball in the "barn" atop Washington Park used for both sports and dances.

The games were competitive and closely matched, but the Wild Cats had their eyes on the ball and found their stroke in the late '40s, dropping very few games on a schedule just shy of thirty matchups. One can surmise the few league teams played each other two to three times during the season, but Childs arranged other tilts around the region to keep the Wild Cats sharp.

Staunton traveled to Roanoke to play the Black Cardinals and the Tigers. They took on the Covington Colts in the hotbed of baseball in Allegheny County during that era. Staunton played against extraordinarily strong Amherst teams and by winning those games established regular matchups against Amherst's toughest opponent in Albemarle County, the Covesville Tigers.

Covesville versus Staunton became a regular matchup. Covesville was invincible in central Virginia during that era but there is no word on whether the Wild Cats may have bested the Tigers at Montgomery Park. From Amherst and Covesville westward Staunton played the Crozet All-Stars and the Greenwood Hawks. Occasional contests were set up via black baseball directories in the Washington, D.C., *Afro American* to play the Washington Aztecs or Arlington team from northern Virginia. Metropolitan D.C. teams loved bus trips west to play black teams in the "cornfields" often without remarkable success, but the hospitality and picnic fare were unmatched. Though ballgame accounts and scores are long lost, we know through the referenced slates of teams and by the names of opposing players of the era, Dowell, Henderson, Sims, Awkard, Burgess, and Williams, that Staunton's Wild Cats were formidable.

In the spring and summer of 1949, the Wild Cats played 25 games, winning 19 and losing six. The league championship game came down to Staunton versus Bridgewater, which was just up the train tracks, with the Wild Cats prevailing. Staunton had a much better record than the ACs, and evidenced by the outcome, was the better team in the valley at that time.

Speaking with Roscoe Burgess in 1999, Burgess fondly recalled many local and regional games home and away but did not allude to the 1949 finale against his cousin's ball team or competing for rights to the team name. Trophy or no trophy, relative or friend, it was always competitive in black baseball. The games lost were not forgotten but these players wanted scant mention of them if possible.

The Wild Cats arrived with a nearly identical record in 1950, posting a standing of 19-7, again winning the district an repeating as champions. James Becks left the team after the 1950 season to focus on his family and the mentoring of youth making their way in athletics. With lists pages long of athletes and athletic families from Staunton and Verona, it remains puzzling as to why other teams were not assembled during the peak of play in the 1960s. Perhaps players who were interested in offering their talents played in the communities of Waynesboro or Lyndhurst, Virginia.

IV

Uncrowned Champions, 1950–1960

Central Virginia

I was in the military in the fifties with a guy named Bob Buhl who later pitched for the Milwaukee Braves, and we played on the Post team together. The Braves were having tryouts in Louisville not far from where we were stationed at Fort Campbell, Kentucky. He said, "Ed you're a good ballplayer; I'm going to this tryout the Braves are having and some friends of mine are going to be there why don't you come along." So, I got a three-day pass and went down there—I just wanted to see and learn some things I had never known. They put me in the field and tried me at second base, and they saw that I had speed and could run and hit the ball pretty good.

After the tryouts were over the manager said, "Ed what are you thinking about doing after you get out of the service—would you like to come down to Bradenton, Florida, to camp? We might have a spot for you." I said, "I don't know, you guys are too good for me. I don't know." Even after I got back to the post he called my post commander before I got out to see what I was going to do. But I had my mind set on going home and that's what I did. I never gave the Braves a second thought until years later.

—Edward Henderson, Cismont Virginia Braves

Sims and Sims

Talk black baseball with anyone within a 100-mile radius of central Virginia and someone is bound to know of the Sims family. The family, and their ball team, the Greenwood Athletic Club, began play in the 1940s. At the core of the lineup were Arthur, Bernard, Elgie B and George Sims. The four brothers combined their enthusiasm for baseball and made winning a family tradition for two decades. Sims and Sims, Sims and Sims—first name changed, last name never changed, replied amused former Washington Monarch pitcher William Carter. Many players and fans around Virginia's black independent circles thought the team was one vast Sims family, when in fact they were brothers, uncles and cousins. Once the ballgame began no one on the opposition was interested in the exact nature of their family relations.

One thing was certain, these Sims men who spelled their name with one "M" could play the game of baseball.

Arthur Sims, called "Tom Cat" by his younger brothers, was the fiery leader of the Greenwood nine. He played hard, played to win and expected the same from his teammates. He was a good pitcher, outstanding catcher, and was capable of filling in at any other position on the diamond. Arthur Sims was without a doubt one of the best all-around baseball players to lace up a pair of spikes in Virginia. Brothers Elgie B. and George recall seeing him catch an entire game using a first baseman's mitt because that was all that was available. Nothing kept Arthur Sims out of a ball game, and he was the last of the brothers to hang up the glove at age fifty-two.

In the 1950s when his sons joined the Hawks' lineup many opponents began calling him "Pop" Sims. Says William Carter: "Pop Sims was the only one we recognized, he could hit and once he got going pitching he was something." Bernard Sims played first base and was a pitcher too. He had a wicked sidearm delivery that once produced a curveball that removed an opposing batter's shoe. Bernard could also knock the cover off of the baseball and hit some of Greenwood's longest home runs.

Elgie B. Sims was a quiet, skillful ballplayer, but on the pitching mound he had authoritative presence. He combined artful pitching and cunning to take over a ballgame. Elgie B. liked to make the batter work, make him guess while at the plate. He was a master of the slow breaking curve, knuckleball, overhand curve, and one of his favorites, the change of pace slow ball. When he needed to smoke a fast one across he did so with relative ease, again surprising the hitter. If he went three innings without an earned run, he might pitch a shutout or a no hitter. The longer he stayed in there pitching the more confident and formidable his performance.

Black baseball fans in central Virginia best remember the classic pairing of Arthur Sims working behind the plate and Elgie B. pitching. Arthur talked it up to Elgie B. nonstop, praising him much of the time and giving him hell at times when B. was losing his command. "Damn it B., you're not throwing the ball; you want me to pitch?" Arthur then walked halfway out to the mound and fired the ball back to Elgie B. as hard as he could.

Now that the challenge had been made, Greenwood fans knew what was coming next. Elgie B. was known to adjust his cap to the side, with Arthur still ranting "come on in here B" and the fans getting into the chant. Elgie B. would kick his leg high like Satchel Paige and pitch his way out of the jam. You could tell that Elgie B. had regained his command because he finished his pitches off with style—a little pause after he followed through on his delivery. At times when he was especially pleased with his performance he turned his head away from an opposing batter and laughed. Where brother Arthur was more vocal, B. was animated and his actions told the story.

Elgie B. Sims recalls his baseball past:

Boy let me tell you, when Greenwood was going to play ball we had cars lined up behind us. It was the same as a league game when the teams met up, no running away on either side.

Most of our scores were 4–3 6–5 and all like that, tight games. I pitched a no-hitter against a team down next to Richmond.... Red Robbins. I played short stop and pitched. I played anywhere except catcher. Arthur played catcher and anywhere else you put him. "Tom Cat," that boy was a catcher. We went everywhere and played everywhere—Barboursville, Elkton, Keswick, Orange, Harrisonburg. We played the Roanoke Black Sox over in Waynesboro under the lights at Kate Collins.

We'd be out all night on Friday and, sometimes my manager, George Collins, used to beg me to pitch on Saturday, and I'd say man I can't pitch no ball today. Then I'd go ahead and go to pitch for him boy and when you'd see me cock my leg up high in the air you knew I was right. They used to call me "Satchel Paige." My ball, it wasn't fast, but there was so much junk on it. My brother George, he'd throw sidearm, he threw hard.

Sometimes I used to throw hard but I used my head. I was going to give you something you couldn't hit. You're the one pitching but you got nine men on that field. You got seven men behind you ok, you got a catcher. As long as I keep the ball in play I didn't need to throw the ball hard. But when the bases were loaded that's the time to throw the ball, and that's when I would throw it hard. I liked to throw a fastball hard, but I liked to put the junk on it to make them swing and miss. I never get baseball out of my mind. Every time I look at a baseball game it carries me back to when I was playing.

When league play came to central Virginia's black teams in the '60s, a major league scout saw Elgie B. pitch in an all-star game and invited him to camp not knowing that B. was forty years old.

In the fifties Greenwood acquired a game-breaking crowd-pleasing player from the nearby town of Waynesboro, Virginia. His name was Lewis Kelly. Everyone referred to him simply as "Kelly," and he played baseball for the Greenwood Hawks and the Crozet All-Stars. It is not known whether Lewis Kelly was at all related to the famous Kelly ballplayers of Charlottesville, but he made his own impression amongst players in Virginia's black sandlots. Kelly was a short bowlegged utility fielder who most often relieved Arthur Sims at catcher. He was a talented receiver and a clutch hitter, but best of all he was lightning on the base path. Lewis Kelly gave a pitcher something to worry about anytime he got on base.

He chewed tobacco vigorously and ran—in the words of the old country expression—faster than you could spit. Witnesses say Kelly could bolt from third base, come within a few feet of home plate and dash back to third beating out the throw. When Early Dowell and Albert Henderson of the Covesville Tigers trapped Kelly in their famous pickoff play, Kelly swore that it was the first time anyone had ever thrown him out; no one else had ever come close.

With the added attraction of night baseball on Friday and Saturday nights in Waynesboro and Orange, Greenwood often played the entire weekend, and so it was common for the Hawks to total up 40–45 games a season. In the early '50s the team started traveling to the Valley to play Luray, Harrisonburg, Staunton, and then traveled east to play the Little Washington and Front Royal ball teams.

Greenwood played and won impressively, leading to earned invitations to holiday baseball tournaments and doubleheaders. People wanted to see these "Sims" people touted as such good ballplayers, and this "Kelly" person who ran like Jackie Robinson. When Arthur Sims' sons joined the team it changed the order entirely.

Edward "Dopey" Sims remembers baseball as a family tradition:

> Growing up, we knew daddy and our uncles worked during the week, but on the weekends they were going to play ball somewhere. In the summer, my brother Estes, Hildrie Barbour and I used to spend the early part of the morning picking black berries. We would get enough money to buy a baseball and then from eleven o'clock until five we would be on the diamond playing. Mama knew where to look if she needed to find us, Greenwood Diamond.

Edward "Dopey" Sims and Esters "Preacher" Sims also knew to bring their gloves along once they reached their teens because there was an excellent chance they might get into a ballgame. Both started playing baseball on the family team before they were halfway through high school, followed by baby brother William "Winky" Sims. They were forever addressed by their distinctive nicknames in and out of Virginia's black baseball circuit. However, for black baseball fans and players, their names followed by the last name Sims only added to the lore and legacy of the ballplaying family. "Preacher" and "Dopey" were both standouts on Charlottesville's Jackson P. Burley High's competitive baseball teams of the fifties and sixties.

Childhood friend Hildrie Barbour played shortstop with the brothers on the Hawks; some say he was the quickest ever seen to cover no man's land. He was a fair hitter and were it not for a lack of foot speed might have received more attention from major league scouts.

Dopey Sims began play in the outfield, but as he matured was moved to the infield and third base primarily because no one else wanted the hot corner. He recalls that no one knew the power of hitters in Virginia's black sandlots better than he came to know it, guarding that left field line. Preacher Sims followed in the footsteps of his father and played anywhere and everywhere on the diamond. He could have been the starting pitcher on any team around and could play catcher too. Like his father he was very competitive and loved nothing more than winning and letting an opponent hear about it when Greenwood was in control. On one end of the bench "Pop" Sims was talking loud, on the other end Preacher was talking. It was all in fun, an early precursor to trash talk so prevalent in professional sports today, but Preacher could really get under an opposing player's skin.

Dopey and Preacher followed each other in the batting order and it was promoted by their uniform numbers, #3 and #4. Given their ability to hit, one could not afford to walk either one, and they were known to hit back-to-back home runs anytime.

In the eye of the civil rights movement, Jim Crow Laws still prohibited blacks and whites from competing together within the confines of public facilities. But arrangements in the sandlots were of a special nature without funding or officers of the city or county presiding over the activities. So, here and there a few white ballplayers stood on the same diamond as black players and used the same bats and balls.

One of the first white ball players to participate and play in the all-black central Virginia sandlots was Crozet, Virginia, native Charles Shifflet. Shifflet was an excellent center fielder, good relief pitcher, and deadly hitter.

He played for both Crozet and Greenwood, and anywhere the two teams traveled and played they brought Charles Shifflet along. He performed in an environment where he was the minority, and perhaps subject to taunts. Shifflet was so good, he was chosen to compete with the Sims brothers in the all-black baseball tournaments in Lynchburg, Virginia. In those tournaments he hit the ball out just as he did in any other game. Charles Shifflet displayed a great deal of integrity and a good deal of courage in placing himself in what was a very awkward position in 1950s Virginia. Because he crossed the line of Jim Crow, a few other white ballplayers joined black teams in central Virginia in the 1950s.

George Franklin Sims was a left-handed pitcher who unlike his brother Elgie B. rarely threw anything resembling a slow ball. George liked to bring the heat, whether sidearm, overhand, curveball or fastball. By the time George Sims developed as a ballplayer he was the ace on the neighboring town team in Crozet, Virginia, called the All-Stars. On occasion another team member might pitch, or an outside guest from another team like brother Elgie B. might take the mound, but George Sims was the only regular starting pitcher for more than a decade. He was maybe 5'8" but he was strong and in excellent condition. He spent the better part of his lifetime working hard in a nearby lumber mill. George was probably the fastest of the Sims brothers and he was an aggressive base runner who came in hard every time he came into the bag.

Unlike many beleaguered aces on rural ball teams, his arm was enduring for easily a twenty year span. A few opponents called him laughing George for his good natured chuckling on the mound, but he was all business when it came to throwing strikes. Louis Carter was the Crozet shortstop and team captain. Carter kept the team's morale up and never let up himself. He was always cheering pitcher George Sims. "Come on George, show 'em what you got. He can't see it—he can't see that heat brother!" As George Sims recalled, sometimes he did not have the stuff, but with Louis Carter talking behind him, he would dig deep, bear down on that hitter, sweat pouring, and throw to the plate with what fire he could muster and often put the game away. George Sims left it all on the field when he pitched. George Sims:

> I never did play with Greenwood much. I used to play with Crozet. George Collins he was the manager and he used to schedule the games and everything. When he said, "Play ball" we were there ready to play ball. I used to love it! You'll make a pretty good player if you love to play, but if you don't care nothing about it you might as well forget it. You got to be interested if you're going to play ball, because I'd rather play ball than eat when I was hungry. We went down there to play Red Robbins next to Richmond and only had nine players, but we were ready to play.
>
> I used to go and pitch in all-star games on Saturday and then come back home on Sunday and pitch. We used to go down to Lynchburg to play in these all-star games and they had some darn good hitters in those games boy. Bobby Hudson and Fletcher Gaines came after me to play. I pitched those three innings in that game down in Lynchburg and some of those hitters were carrying me boy, I'm telling you! I used to pitch, play short stop, but I never did play second base. I liked to throw it, and I would throw it hard, overhand, underhand, sidearm or any way. I never could throw a slow ball, never threw slow.

> My catcher Herman Steppe's hand used to be swollen up. Those were some good days. I still wish I was playing. Lord of mercy it makes you think especially when you get old and you can't play anymore. I wish I was able to play because I loved it.

Aside from his pitching talents for the Crozet team, George Sims was one of the best hitters in central Virginia. In a 1950s encounter against the Orange (Virginia) Nats he hit a solo home run shot that was then disputed allegedly because of his failure to touch a base. In those times when black baseball teams were lucky to have one good umpire making the calls, disputes were often settled by replays. Unfortunately for the Nats, George Sims' replay at the plate resulted in an identical blast off the bat sending the ball out of the park in the same location. This time there was no question as to whether it was a home run.

Catcher Bobby Hudson of Massies Mill recalls George Sims' effectiveness at the plate:

> He used to stand way off the plate, and I used to try to pitch him to the outside. I said, he can't hit that outside fastball. Every time I'd try to slip that outside fastball by him he'd knock the hell out of it. He couldn't hit that ball inside. He could hit it but not as well. Arthur Sims was a good hitter too—those Sims could play ball man.

Crozet was a good hitting team, and once the ball was in play, the All-Stars had some race horses moving around the base path. There was Lewis Kelly when he was available, and John White another Hawks and All-Stars performer. George Sims was fast, and the "Crozet Flash," Lester Washington, defined the word sprint. Washington actually earned his nickname on the football field for Burley High School in the '50s. Crozet traveled and played on an identical circuit to that of Greenwood. Wherever George Collins could book a ballgame the Crozet players were ready to go. Logistically, with the two so close together, it made for a great rivalry. Nonetheless, no one can recall more than one meeting between the Hawks and the All-Stars, a close game that ended in favor of Crozet.

By the nineteen fifties with Covesville and Massies Mill regrouping, the Hawks and Crozet All-Stars were in the prime position to take over as the best teams in the area. Neither team beat the Covesville Tigers every time, but now they were at least winning games against the Tigers. Before the Hawks and All-Stars could claim the top spot, however, a new foe stepped in to intercept.

Greenwood, Virginia, lies on the north side of Rt. 250 east-west. Minutes away on the south side of Rt. 250 is the community of Avon, a rural section just inside the Nelson County boundary. Avon's All-Stars began play in the mid-fifties bringing together players from the teams of the Dupont Grays in Waynesboro, Greenfields, and Wintergreen in Nelson County, Virginia.

Pitcher Lin Awkard and first baseman G.G. Blair were two notable standouts from the Dupont Grays teams, long respected in black sandlot baseball since the '30s. The rest of the Avon team were locals from Nelson aided by some good up-and-coming ballplayers.

When Avon and Greenwood met up on a Saturday or Sunday everything stopped until a victor was decided. As "Dopey" Sims remembers the matchups were primarily about community pride.

> We didn't play for money, and for a long time didn't play for trophies, but we played for those bragging rights. The Avon fans were tough and they would get on you! You were under a lot of pressure, and it was tough playing in those games, but you wanted to have the bragging rights in the area. When we played South Garden it was the same way. It would be my grandmother yelling on one side and Mrs. Burton on the other side and they would go back and forth. Nobody wanted to lose those games.

In the fifties when Early Dowell of Covesville left the mound for good, Edward Thompson of Avon stepped up and became the new pitching sensation. Not much is known about Thompson's background in baseball, only his prowess once he earned the position of pitcher. The left-handed Thompson could throw hard and he had superb control. He had an around-the-world breaking curveball, and a diving knee-buckler that started up around the letters smoking, and broke down across the plate waist high. Thompson's letter-high fastball simply overpowered many batters—it was too high and too fast. Only the best hitters in the region caught on to hitting Thompson's heat.

Lin Awkard, a fine pitcher and ball player in his own right, enjoyed days off watching teammate Edward Thompson shut down the competition.

> We used to play Harrisonburg over in Waynesboro Park two or three times a month; we'd call them up and they'd give us a game for fun. And Eddie Thompson fanned one old boy so bad one night the boy sat down and cried. That boy couldn't hit that ball no way he tried! He sat down and cried cause he knew he could not hit the ball and he never did hit the ball! Eddie could throw it.

Through the early sixties Edward Thompson dominated hitters on the black baseball circuit, from Orange to Culpeper and Harrisonburg. Stories vary but it has been said that Edward Thompson had at least a couple of tryouts and a brief stay in the minor leagues, but was released each time. The only fact everyone who faced Thompson can confirm is that he had major league stuff and created some long afternoons for some of the best hitters in central Virginia.

Bobby and Eddie

> We were serious about that thing man. I used to bet a guy five dollars I'd get more hits than he would today. After the game was over people would invite us to their homes for dinner and cookouts. We'd talk about the game win or lose and what each player did. If we lost we talked about what went wrong—"why didn't we try this or make that play"—and we loved it, those were some good days.
>
> —Bobby Hudson, Massie Mill Cubs

Bobby and Eddie Hudson grew up in the shadow of local baseball legends around their home of Massies Mill, Virginia. The two were related to the Giles and

Ligons who'd made up the Massies Mill Giants, one of central Virginia's all-time best black baseball teams. Bobby played shortstop and catcher while Eddie pitched. Both brothers served in the military in the early '50s, making military baseball teams. Eddie pitched against Willie Mays who happened to be serving his hitch away from the New York Giants at the time. Bobby played competitive ball in the Navy, but the most memorable event was the coach of the squad telling him that he had the makings of a catcher even though he was clearly left-handed.

Upon returning home the brothers joined community friend Fletcher Gaines in revamping the ball team. By now members of the old Giants were up in age and it was time for a new generation of ballplayers. First base wizard Alex Giles remained and still amazed black ball fans with his gloveless catches and splits. He was not a great hitter, but he could bunt the ball any place he need to, making it difficult for the opposition to make a play. Team manager Fletcher Gaines was a good hitter and first baseman.

Massie Napier was an excellent all-around performer who played catcher and in the outfield, was a good hitter and had great speed even though he was one of the older players on the new team now renamed the Cubs. Eddie Hudson was in his prime in the fifties and was one of the most sought-after pitchers around. He was a tall man with good velocity on his pitches and a good variety of breaking stuff, and he was known to sit on the best of ball teams. Eddie Hudson was also one of the best hitters on the team; anything near the center of the plate was sure to be lost in the pines. Bobby continued playing shortstop as he had in the Navy, until one day, overcome with frustration at the other team stealing on Massies Mill's catcher, he took the mitt in hand and became a receiver on the spot, daring runners to dance too far away from the bag. Bobby's first thoughts were of the prophetic words of the old naval baseball coach's prediction years earlier.

The Cubs came together in what could be described as central Virginia's golden age of black baseball. Several counties had three or four ball clubs, the games were more popular than ever and overall the players were the best anyone would see during the run of black baseball in central Virginia. Home field for the Cubs was a diamond at the lower secondary school in Massies Mill, and many considered it the best around. The Rockfish River ran right by the ball field and a home run wasn't credible unless you hit it into or across the river. The Cubs played a steady local schedule against Avon, Greenwood, Covesville, Crozet and Shipman. They traveled east to play Cismont, Orange and Keswick. Massies Mill teams had a longstanding playing schedule versus Bedford Co., Appomattox, and Danville.

Amherst County, minutes down the road, was the do-or-die rival for Massies Mill. They matched up several times a year and each contest was an unpredictable thriller.

Since the two squads knew each other so well they had to do something to stir up things up. If Massies Mill brought in an outstanding pitcher, Amherst would bring in the best hitter from southeast Virginia.

Bobby Hudson:

We went to Amherst once, and they had this boy who tried out for the Cleveland Indians as a pitcher. We got up there and they told us, "Ya'll haven't got a chance today, we got a man done tried out for the Cleveland Indians." I told them, "I don't care who he tried out for, if he puts that ball across the plate I'm going to hit it!" So we messed around practicing, we weren't a good practicing team—I don't know why. We couldn't practice worth two cents, missing balls. When we got to playing it was a different story. So that guy got up on the mound, he didn't get through the first inning. We hit that scoundrel everywhere! They had to take him out—beat them 15–3. I told them they could go back to Cleveland and get some more.

Lynchburg city was only one-half hour away and when the Massies Mill ballplayers were not watching traveling Negro League squads they played against some of the city's league teams. Over time, a Lynchburg baseball promoter impressed with the Massies Mill Cubs asked managers Bobby Hudson and Fletcher Gaines to bring the team down to participate in weekend baseball tournaments. Knowing the quality of competition in tournament play, Gaines and Hudson scoured a couple of counties, lifting the best hitters and pitchers to compete with the Cubs. Arthur and George Sims, Edward Thompson, Len Awkard all filled in the lineup and the Cubs made a good showing, losing only to the best black semipro squads.

Massies Mill maintained play against a team in West Virginia that had been a competitor against the old Giants club. Playing ball in the coal mining state provided its share of memorable episodes.

Bobby Hudson:

We were playing ball in Aingine, West Virginia, and my brother Eddie was playing center field. Center field was fenced in with piles of coal kind of on a slant. Eddie couldn't get back up on that slant to get those balls. Those boys were hitting that ball way up on the slant! I told the manager, "Let me play center field, I can go up and get those balls." I ran to center field, I'd go up to get the ball—they'd knock the ball way over the pile. I couldn't get it then. Those guys could hit those balls. They beat us 13–0.

The new Massies Mill team ranked up there with the best through the fifties and early sixties. Though the Shenandoah Valley League started in 1963 the Cubs did not come in until three years later. By that time the lineup was not as strong and the team usually finished near the bottom in league play, but Bobby and Eddie were all-stars.

Mack and Barboursville

For black baseball fans, a Sunday drive east away from central Virginia led to the counties of Louisa, Orange, and Madison. To the south there were black teams in Gordonsville, Cismont and Keswick. Heading north there was Barboursville, Orange and Madison counties. There were more teams to play for and play against than time to accommodate all of the baseball action. Gordonsville in Louisa County had promoted black baseball since the '30s, first with the Bacharachs, and then the Eagles. Keswick played in an area of Albemarle known as Millers Flat at the time.

Baseball in the community of Barboursville began as a loose collection of friends from the community playing pickup games in a pasture on old Rt. 20, sixteen miles east of Charlottesville, Virginia. Aspiring ballplayers in Barboursville did not have to look far to find either a weekend ballgame or an opponent, for they were literally living inside a black baseball loop. To the north of the Albemarle County community were Orange, Greene and Madison counties, and to the South the communities of Cismont, Keswick and Gordonsville all supported ball teams.

Barboursville players took their gloves and rambled from one community to another when there were no prospects of finding a matchup at home.*

Local baseball enthusiast and Barboursville resident Southall Minor saw good potential in Brian Hughes, Charles Buddy Davis, and a young, strong-armed pitcher, Matthew "Mack" Davis, and in the early fifties united the collection of youth and became their official manager. The team found a permanent ball field in another pasture about a mile from the first Barboursville diamond on Echo Valley Road where they would play their games until disbanding in the seventies. Matthew "Mack" Davis was a competitor from start to finish. He was not the best pitcher in the region but he was one of the best. He was the anchor of the sparse Barboursville pitching staff, never using more than three pitches—his smoking fastball, curveball and the drop or sinker. Mack threw hard and all of his pitches had good movement. He was an imposing figure even in his youth. Davis stood 6'3" and as he matured he filled out with massive shoulders and arms. He could throw hard and, most of all, he always claimed his part of the plate. Batters who crowded the plate were brushed back or knocked down, and from time-to-time players who were fond of too much celebration were given a little stinger around the letters to put something on their minds.

As Covesville standout Jim Dowell remembers, "Mack was just like Junky Dowell, he was tough!" When they went out to pitch it wasn't no two or three innings. "They went out to pitch nine innings or eighteen or whatever it had to go."

Mack Davis' speed, his mound presence, and the mental toughness that allowed

---

*In the summer of 1999, I was approaching the first 50 pages of this manuscript, and early research efforts were limited to former player interviews. I decided to look up noted pitcher Mack Davis of the Barboursville Giants. Barboursville is in eastern Albemarle County and Orange County. I remembered watching Barboursville play against the Ivy Eagles as child but did not specifically recall their players. I heard about the fabled pitcher half a dozen times with either a story or a respectful compliment. I did not know if Mack Davis was still in Barboursville; he was, according to a few, alive and well, now retired. So I drove scenic Route 20 into eastern Albemarle County with not much more information than the directions to Barboursville. Whether it was fate or incidental timing, the first person I introduced myself to at a Barboursville crossroads store facilitated my meeting with Mack. It was as simple as asking "Do you know Matthew 'Mack' Davis of Barboursville?" "Yes," she said, "he's my father-in law. Who are you?" My introduction and title fell short of the legend I intended to interview but I presented my business card and a week later I was sitting in a living room being regaled by Matthew "Mack" Davis, Sr. He had played baseball all over Virginia and recalled teams near and far. Mack had plenty to say about the good days gone by and the league they played in. He was enthused about the project but made it known in no uncertain terms that he looked forward to reading a finished product. I was officially on the clock to produce *Sunday Coming*. It was a cordial first meeting and any interest in baseball was welcomed by Mack Davis, but as it turned out, my connection to his family was decades long and was through his sons. Pearlie Davis, Mack's daughter-in-law, transitioned many years ago. I never saw her again. I have called Barboursville home for several years.

him to go nine innings and win a close ballgame after giving up a home run made him one of the region's top pitchers until age forty. Barboursville players knew they only needed to score a few runs because Mack could bring it home.

Manager Southall Minor was serious about baseball and serious about organizing the Barboursville youth. His first lessons revolved around team unity and participation, from the way the team arrived to the way they hustled on and off the field. As Mack Davis recalls they learned to respect Minor, while finding humor in his disciplines.

> I used to leave here and walk all the way down to the other side of Barboursville, then ride back up here to play ball. If I didn't get down there, Southall Minor he'd raise Cain. "How come you weren't down here this morning?" And all I had to do was walk up to the top of the hill.

One Sunday morning Mack Davis received a visit from Hugo Scott and "Big Sam" Buckner. Scott and Buckner had a ball team in the community of Ruckersville ten miles from Barboursville and needed players for what was probably a tough contest on that particular day. As fate would have it Mack and Brian Hughes were available to help out Scott's Ruckersville team. Hugo Scott heard opportunity knocking and did not hesitate in making the proposal that the Ruckersville and Barboursville communities join forces. After both sides agreed, the new team remained in Barboursville and became the Barboursville Giants.

Hugo Scott was a man who loved baseball, loved working with the young people in the community, and he believed in the competitive and entertaining values of black baseball. He wanted the players to conduct themselves in a professional manner, and he wanted the team to look the part from their uniforms to their play on the diamond. Scott was one of the few managers in the central Virginia area to promote and have published the sandlot exploits of black baseball teams. Southall Minor managed through the early sixties before Hugo Scott took over the team through to its ending.

If Mack Davis gave the team its identity defensively, "Big Sam" Buckner represented the offensive side. As long as there was an out left and a run to be scored in a close game Barboursville knew they had a chance to win it with first baseman Big Sam at the plate. Buddy Davis batted third in the order and hit some thunderous shots, but Sam Buckner hit neck-craning, eye-shading bombs over the playing field.

Mack Davis remembers teammate Big Sam:

> Sam Buckner.... I believe he was one of the best long ball hitters around. Sam reminded me of big Luke Easter. [Luke Easter, Homestead Grays, Cleveland Indians.] Great big two hundred and sixty pound man no fat just big; he'd hit one of those balls—and hit it out! Get another ball because that one's gone! He hit one in Elkton and there was a cornfield behind center field. Sam hit that ball halfway across that cornfield and the ball cut corn because there was nothing left afterwards. It took three men to get that ball home and when the catcher caught the ball, Sam he hit the plate. I had been on first base and was home sitting down and he was still running. I got up and went down toward the third base line; I said, "Run Buck run!" Man he kept coming! So when he got home I said, "Great God man what were you doing?" He said

[gasping], "I had it on the floor!" He couldn't run, but when he hit 'em he didn't have to run, and you'd very seldom get him out. I've seen him go down on one knee and hit it out, and it was gone.

In 1952 the *Roanoke Tribune* published a weekly sports report covering baseball, amazingly in central Virginia. The coverage was centered around a Four-County League involving the Keswick Dodgers of Albemarle, Madison Indians, North Garden All-Stars of Albemarle, Gordonsville Eagles of Louisa, Barboursville Giants, and Louisa Eagles.[1] Since the first recorded coverage appeared five games into the season it is not known which the fourth original county might have been. Orange County makes for a good guess, as it is the only county glaringly absent from the alignment of black ball teams.

The *Roanoke Tribune* stayed with the league's exploits through the end of June 1952. Available details present the early part of the league schedule as a three-way battle between the community of Keswick, North Garden, and the Madison Indians. Keswick had at their disposal standouts Louis Johnson, Doc Barratt, Max Moore, and Bill Minor. Johnson is said to have been one of the best fielders and hitters anyone had ever seen. He played baseball in the military during World War II and in the 1950s was one of the first black ballplayers to integrate and play for an American Legion post squad. Max Moore was an excellent outfielder, covering ground as if there were two of him in uniform.

Bill Minor might have been called barnstorming Bill. Minor liked to pitch, and liked to play anywhere and often, and pitched for all of the teams in the region at one point or another. In his prime he was virtually unhittable. Minor was pitching Wiffle Ball, and the batters were swinging lead bats.

Mack Davis:

> Bill Minor would go and pitch anywhere he could find a ballgame. He didn't care as long as he played. Bill never threw his arm out, but he had the slowest curveball of any man I have ever seen. It didn't look like it would get up to the plate, but it would get up there and break. I told Bill, I said, "Bill if I had your curveball and you had my fastball, man we'd go somewhere."

The Madison Indians formed in 1950 and probably played their best baseball during that decade. The Indians' roster echoed the names Frye, Lindsay, Jackson, Ward, and Beasley. Johnny Frye was a feared long-ball hitter, and Lawrence and Willie Beasley were consistent singles and doubles hitters.

In the Indians outfield was Lewis Frye, forever remembered by his more popular nickname "Race Horse." Frye made his first start in black baseball in the '30s at the age of fifteen when the Kelly All-Stars recruited him to play center field.

In his youth he was so fast that he often overran the baseball, and later, once his timing improved, it was not unusual for Race Horse to charge a fly ball, make the catch and then circle around the infield, much to the delight of the gametime crowd. He was an entertaining player to watch even when he did not make a play. Lewis Frye made baseball his life, playing until he should not have been on the field, and only quitting when he could not make it around the field.

North Garden's community baseball team was revived by the second Covesville ball team minutes away. The younger second Covesville Tigers team needed a diamond and since the North Garden team had all but disbanded they made North Garden their home field. It was predominantly a teenaged squad but they were dynamite with a list of names that figured prominently in black baseball around central Virginia. There were the Dowells of Covesville—Lee, Jim and Lenny—and Earl Smith. From North Garden were Curtis Burton, Gene Burton, Lloyd Burton, Mack Burton, Randall Burton, Jerome Robinson, Leroy Jones, and Bernard Washington. On Saturdays the North Garden All-Stars had the additions of Esmont, Virginia, twins Donald and Willie Gray.

The North Garden All-Stars were a young team, but they had four good pitchers in Lee Dowell, Earl Smith, Lenny Dowell, and Jerome Robinson, four long-ball hitters in Bernard Washington, Randall Burton, and the Grays, and the fastest player in the region in Jim Dowell. North Garden could run you off the diamond. For the few seasons they were together they were one of the best teams in Albemarle County.

The Gordonsville Eagles were off to a good start, but fell back after half a dozen games in. Barboursville and Louisa plummeted to the cellar at 2–7 and 1–5 respectively.

As reported by the *Roanoke Tribune* it appeared the Barboursville Giants were playing good baseball, just not good enough. They lost close games and they lost games in which they were ahead, losing in the late innings. In a June doubleheader against the Keswick All-Stars, Barboursville won the first game 13–4, led on the pitching mound by a player with the last name Stewman. Shockingly in the second game Keswick came back to win 10–7, pitched to victory by Mack Davis. The losing Barboursville pitcher was listed as M. Jones in that contest and a week later in a 10–6 loss to Louisa.[2] Whether pitcher Mack Davis was lured to Keswick or went voluntarily is a mystery. However, as reported in the coverage, the Giants were a good team in trouble.

In the last recorded entry dedicated to the Four-County League the article examined the woes of the Barboursville Giants and posed the possible resignations of both Southall Minor and Hugo Scott. The Giants had dropped a doubleheader to North Garden 9–5, and 9–4. When it was alleged that Minor was unable to spark the team, he decided to call it quits and local resident John Avery took over the team. In the standings Keswick, Madison and North Garden were deadlocked at five wins and two losses with at least eleven games remaining.[3] There were no further reports in the *Tribune* as to how the season or the trials of the 1952 Giants played out, but somewhere during the stretch of seasons between '52 and '57 the Giants regrouped. Southall Minor continued to manage the team along with Hugo Scott, and Barboursville won at home and away.[4] The additions of Max Moore, Lewis Frye, Johnny Frye and Willie Beasley bolstered their level of play.

Power hitter Freddy Baker, Teddy Long, Herman Smith, and Jimmy and Walker Davis, nephews to Buddy and Mack, rounded out the lineup with good hitting and fielding. The Giants' summer schedule was always full, each year progressing beyond the previous year in competition and travel. Barboursville traveled to northern Virginia to play the Little Washington Monarchs, Sperryville Tigers, Bull Run Panthers, Manassas Black Yankees, and from Washington, D.C., a black semipro club called the Sons of Washington. On the Fredericksburg side the Giants struck up a rivalry with the Spotsylvania Tigers with Dale Douglas and Herbert Akers touted as the best pitcher and catcher combination in the eastern part of Virginia.

Over the next two decades the Barboursville Giants were one of the best black teams on the sandlot circuit, and Minor and Scott continued to raise the bar. They played and won on good hitting, pitching and great support in the field. The Giants had become a baseball powerhouse and none too soon for down the road in Orange County, manager James Washington was assembling a competitive young team to challenge Barboursville for the regional bragging rights.

Without question one of the great regional rivalries among black teams was the Barboursville versus Orange match-up. It was the county ballplayers of Albemarle against the town team in Orange County. Orange played on the town diamond with lights while the Giants played in a reworked pasture. Fans black and white supported the Orange Nats and supported the rivalry against the Barboursville Giants. The stands overflowed to standing room only around Orange's Porterfield Park.

It was Washington's Orange Nats who had the most to prove; Barboursville was already an established power. Early matchups between the town and country ball teams were one-sided in favor of the older more experienced Giants. Mack Davis simply overpowered Nats hitters, and the ones he did not overpower were intimidated. But in time the young and skilled Nats proved they could stand in and compete, making Orange versus Barboursville one of the legendary rivalries of black sandlot baseball in central Virginia. It is believed that the first Orange win over Barboursville occurred in the summer of 1959. The young Nats pulled off a stunning 6–5 upset after trailing 5–0 early in the ballgame. Mack Davis went all the way, losing the decision. Orange used pitchers Walker T. Robinson and Mettres Murrill in the win.[5]

As Mack Davis recalls his youth playing black baseball around Virginia, he remembers that more than anything it was a thrill just to get out on the diamond and compete.

> Yes sir, we had some real good old ballplayers back in those days. I believe if the major leagues had been taking black ball players at the time, it would have been a whole lot of guys from around here that would have went to the major leagues. But for a long time they didn't have many in the minors.
> Edward Thompson of Avon was a good pitcher. Edward went down to the minors and had a couple tryouts, but he couldn't hold the men on base so they say—he was a left-hander. But I don't believe that because he could hold me on; I don't know about somebody else. He always wore his cap down over his eyes, looked like he was peeping from under the cap. We had some good times back in those days boy; we played anywhere we could find a ballgame, we didn't care where, as long as we played.

Henderson's Braves

Edward Henderson came home from the Army in the '50s, but instead of returning to his native home of Covesville he and his new wife settled in Cismont, Virginia. Henderson started a job in the neighboring community of Keswick, but in his spare time he began to take notice of a group of youngsters around the area calling themselves the Cismont Braves. Henderson saw their enthusiasm, but he also saw that the young Braves did not know the game of baseball very well.

As a lifelong ballplayer, first with the awesome Covesville Tiger teams and then as a semipro player in the Army, Edward Henderson had played nearly every position and had learned the finer points of the game.

Edward Henderson met with the young Braves, talked baseball with them, and from there he led by example as a player on the team exhibiting his talents running and stealing bases. He was one of the most dangerous left-handed hitters out of central Virginia, and time after time Henderson would point and hit the ball to the left and right of the diamond at will. That was all the Cismont youngsters needed to see, and they soon elected Henderson team manager.

Edward Henderson placed a great emphasis on learning the rudiments of baseball, making plays and finishing off plays. He stressed the trademark importance in black baseball of being capable of playing more than one position, and challenged each player to become an effective hitter from his starting pitcher to his catcher.

In the mid–'50s Cismont became the surprise breakout team of the area, playing and winning against Barboursville, Crozet, Greenwood and Sperryville. The Covesville Tigers who had previously trampled the young Braves were the most surprised by the transformation achieved by their old teammate.

Lenny Dowell:

> I remember the first time Cismont started beating us, Edward was playing with them then. Edward went down there, and organized those young boys and got those boys right! They had a guy down there named Marcellus and he could smoke—struck all of us out—that guy could throw!

Montague Hawkins, a longtime area pitcher, led the pitching rotation with a fastball that rivaled any in the area. His pitches were not deceptive but they could blow an opposing player right out of the box if he was not ready. Carroll Bates was a tall brawny catcher and one of the team's best utility players. He hit the ball hard and for his size was as swift an outfielder as one could find. He practiced hard and played hard. Edward Henderson recalls Carroll Bates' work ethic in practice:

> Carroll Bates was a long-ball hitter and he hit those eye-level line drives even in his home runs. And if it was in the gap you could forget it because you weren't going to get to it. He was a good catcher but he could play center field and you couldn't hit a ball by him. I used to hit fungos to the outfielders and I used to have to call Carroll off because the other fielders wouldn't have made a catch. He could cover all fields.

There was a lot to talk about when the conversation turned to Cismont baseball, but the hot topic that had everyone talking was Cismont's new starting pitcher, a small soft spoken kid named Marcellus. Teenaged Marcellus Coleman played sparingly on the Cismont team, but he was anxious to get into the lineup at any opportunity. One day he approached Edward Henderson, and told him of his desire to pitch. Looking at the teenager, small in frame and not very tall, Edward Henderson had his reservations. But being a man small in stature himself he decided to see just what the youngster could do.

Henderson and Coleman started working together one to one and Edward Henderson discovered right away that the skinny left-hander could throw and throw hard. He had a blazing fastball and he had already learned to throw a lethal curveball. What he needed most was more control. Henderson set up a target around the farm where he worked and Coleman practiced throwing at the target until his control was fine-tuned. After viewing with satisfaction Coleman's abilities throwing the ball, Henderson stressed to the young hurler the importance of being a multidimensional player.

Coleman learned that Edward Henderson wanted his pitchers to hit as well as anyone else on the team, and so Marcellus worked rigorously on his batting, and throughout his time playing baseball became one of the best hitting pitchers around.

Coleman's pitching debut came soon after his monthlong one-on-one training sessions with his manager ended. The Braves were playing at home against a local competitor and found themselves in jeopardy of giving the game away. Edward Henderson called time, and to the amazement of the other players and everyone on the diamond, called Marcellus Coleman to the mound.

Edward Henderson was probably the only person on the diamond not surprised when he handed young Coleman the ball and the little left-hander proceeded to strike out the side and preserve the win for his team. From that day forward he became the talk of the black sandlot circuit. No one knew where such a harmless looking youth got such power but they witnessed it and often left the batter's box shaking their heads in disbelief as if they had seen or not seen the ghost of Coleman's mound heat.

If one could construct a top five pitchers category from this long ago era, Marcellus Coleman would finish near the top, if not number one. Cismont is remembered and respected as one of the better area teams of the 1950s. Edward Henderson and his Braves never made it into the Shenandoah Valley League formed in 1963, but broke up in the early '60s, with players heading to various area teams. Edward Henderson went back to Covesville for a '60s revival of Covesville baseball. Carroll Bates became a game-breaking catcher for the Barboursville Giants.

Cool Papa Winston

The only thing Robert Winston, Sr., loved more than playing baseball was recounting a good baseball story. He lived and played nearly all of his lengthy sandlot career out in Fluvanna County, Virginia, playing for the Wilmington Eagles. Along the way he played with and against some of the best black baseball players in Virginia, and remembers players and games as if it all happened yesterday.

Fluvanna County was just far enough away from the heated action of nineteen fifties central Virginia baseball to be overlooked by a few, and perhaps avoided by many. Its communities are situated between Charlottesville and Richmond. The communities of Wilmington and Fork Union had supported black baseball teams since the days of Lewis Tolliver and the Kellys in the 1930s. Many Fluvanna ballplayers such as Samuel Hearns had filled in Charles Jones' Kelly roster through the years. The Franklin Brothers—Paul, Morris, Tommy—and a few ballplayers from the Payne family filled out the Wilmington Eagles ball teams.

Fluvanna ball teams were competitive in their own local playing area but did not fare as well against stronger teams outside of the region. The nineteen fifties put Fluvanna, and Wilmington Eagles baseball, on the map to stay.

Here is "Cool Papa" Bob Winston:

> I came out of the service in '53 ... and I expect I was about twenty-eight or twenty-nine before I got hooked up with this team because I was playing elsewhere with other teams. When I came to Wilmington over a period of time we brought seven ballplayers from Cunningham—right up the road on Rt. 53, that's where I was living at the time. All seven of them were my cousins, it was a family thing. I don't want to use the term "took over" but we had seven ballplayers on that team from Cunningham.
>
> I got broke in at that time with Wilmington when they went to play Esmont. [Giants] Buster Scott was pitching. I was young and green and didn't believe nothing. I said, "If the ball comes this way I got to bring some kind of wood!" In the meantime Mr. Paul Franklin's brother was playing first base and one of the family members was playing shortstop. And he threw two balls to that guy playing first base; it was batted right to the shortstop and he threw two balls to him and he missed both of them. So, Mr. Paul he was the manager at that time, and Mr. Paul called time. I'm sitting on the sideline with a brand new glove because I had just joined the team. I walked in there that day and never left first base until I retired in '78.

Wilmington's diamond, named Honeymooners Park, located off Rt. 601 in the Kents Store area of Fluvanna County, was surrounded by dense forest and held an air of intimidation just driving in on the narrow dirt road. It was a typical rural ballfield though in time it offered an interesting obstacle—there was a utility pole placed less than thirty feet behind second base. Eagles fans lined the field during games and hit the road when the team played away. Black baseball in Fluvanna was very important to Mr. Paul as his ballplayers referred to him, and he believed in cultivating young talent to keep the tradition going. The addition of the seven ballplayers from Cunningham, Virginia, met greatly with Paul Franklin's approval.

Infielder Robert Brown, called "Big Brown" by teammates, was a holdover from the previous team and still one of the most feared hitters around. Mack Davis of Barboursville cites "Big Brown" as one of the few long-ball hitters he hated seeing come to the plate. Says Davis, "Every time he came up there the ball would go down in the pines, and he's just rounding the bases laughing." Robert Brown, much like "Big Sam" of Barboursville, was a towering man with tree-trunk arms in his prime. Any pitch thrown between the letters and midthigh was never seen again. Paul Franklin, Jr., played second base in the '50s and '60s and Paul Franklin's nephew Edward Franklin played catcher. He was cat-quick and a deadly hitter. Mr. Paul played full time, then pinch-hit until he was 59 years old, and he rarely failed to deliver.

The seven new diamond men from Cunningham were versatile players capable of playing two or three positions. Large, brawny ballplayers were an identifiable trait of Wilmington baseball teams over their two decades of domination. Batting cleanup in the Wilmington order was James Payne, a barrel-chested man who exemplified the term power hitter. James Payne often broke the will of an opposing ball team with his line drive triples and doubles. Wilmington never hesitated to employ the hit and run with Payne at bat and men on base.

Bob Winston explains:

> Any of them could tell you they'd rather jump in a can of gasoline and fire than to pitch to him! He would sit there until you'd throw his pitch and if you didn't get a strike on him forget it! A lot of pitchers didn't know James Payne that well and came in and threw a high pitch, and James Payne would knock your eyeballs out right through here [*from the letters on up*]. He loved a high ball! Men on base, you could just start them to running when he came up.

Alphonso, Buck, and Charles Payne covered the pitching duties for Wilmington. Alphonso Payne had a good fastball, complemented by an even better breaking ball. Theodore "Buck" Payne threw a good breaking ball and slider. Left-hander Charles Payne threw hardest, relying on a moving fastball. The trio hit consistently, and could carry a good fastball to the pines if the pitcher made a mistake. Arthur Martin, Clarence Payne family, played third base, had a good glove, and was known for his ability to pull a pitch. Pitchers couldn't pitch to him outside because he'd knock it into the opposite field routinely.

Bob Winston batted in the number three spot for years, leading the team in R.B.I.s and often leaving nothing for the cleanup man, James Payne, to bat in. As a hitter, Winston recalls, it was not his bat speed but his ability to find the ball that led to his prowess at the plate. He was a patient hitter, content to go to the full count at any time until the pitcher's resolve wore thin, and he then had to cross the good part of the plate with some kind of fastball.

The tall, broad-shouldered Winston chose number 42, the most recognized and talked-about number in 1940s and 1950s major league baseball. This meant he took a good deal of challenges and ribbing on the field and over time local fans started calling him Jackie Robinson. At first base he was tested aggressively and often, but his reach and fielding ability kept him in the lineup season after season. In a 1950s encounter with the Cumberland Sluggers, Bob Winston was certain that all seven of the Sluggers' left-handed batters were out to run him off of the diamond, but he snagged nearly everything hit his way.

Recalls Cool Papa Winston, "They wore my pants off, but after the game, they told me, there should be a law against the way you play first base, and that was a big time compliment you know, because those boys could hit."

The Eagles played the bulk of their games in the southern sector of Virginia, playing from Barboursville to Richmond, but they were willing to play any team from any of the counties. They might have been aptly named the Wilmington "Headhunters" because they were a hungry ball team capable of jumping on a team in an away game as easily as they did at home. Wilmington did not annihilate teams, they overpowered them, beat them without mercy, and enjoyed it. Games were booked in the counties of Buckingham, Cumberland, Amelia, and Hanover, and each booking added to the win total. As games and victories piled up, the Eagles' reputation spread beyond the counties to Richmond city mostly by way of the talk of the opposition.

Soon enough, the Fluvanna ballplayers were on their way to Richmond's south side to face off against teams in the Richmond recreation leagues. The Fulton Dodgers had been tops amongst Richmond's black recreational teams since the late '40s. Wilmington appeared to be the best outside of Richmond city in the fifties, so this set up the showdown everyone wanted to see.

Bob Winston recounts Wilmington's first big matchup:

> The people here in Wilmington used to follow the team wherever we went. We left from up here and went to Fulton on the south side of Richmond, and we had the big state bodied trucks loaded with ... everybody it could carry to follow us plus cars when we went to Richmond. They would follow that team. It was one of the best games we had played for a long time. And it was three up and three down, three up and three down, never will forget that. They threw me the wrong pitch and I batted one out of there, and we took that game from them.

After victories against Richmond teams and some of the best in the region it was apparent to everyone on the black baseball circuit that Wilmington was playing on another level—basically weekend ballplayers playing like semipros. Opponents soon realized that a team effort was required to beat the Eagles. Good pitching, hitting and tight defense in the field might help a team squeak through to victory.

Wilmington dropped some games against Covesville and Barboursville, but not many and not often. The Eagles especially enjoyed going after teams with winning records and lofty reputations. If you were considered one of the best then you had to travel to Honeymooners Park to face the Eagles of Wilmington or they would come looking for you. Season after season through the fifties and the sixties it was not a rebuilding process in Wilmington but a reloading process. Time after time the team either picked up outstanding ballplayers or the standouts came to Wilmington.

In the fifties, Barnstorming Bill Minor was one of the best pitchers in central Virginia. Friday through Sunday Minor could play any place he chose. Charlottesville's Squeeze-Ins offered Minor a steady pickup game to shore up their rotation. As Bob Winston recalls the Wilmington vs. Squeeze-Ins encounter was Minor's last game pitched for the Charlottesville team:

> We went up to play the Squeeze-Ins, and Bill Minor pitched against us. We wore the boy out and he went to third base. They put another pitcher in and he couldn't stand the pressure. Bill went back to the mound, pitched to two batters and he had to go for good. After that he came

to Wilmington and nobody could touch him! I can't ever recall Bill Minor dropping a game in Wilmington! The power shift just made him unbeatable.

Pitcher Tudie Trice came to the team from neighboring Louisa County, and by the early '60s Marcellus Coleman, the slight left-hander with a rocket arm had come to Wilmington from the Cismont Braves, but for a time it was all Bill Minor as the number-one starter. Ralph Franklin:

> I never will forget we were playing this white team from Richmond, this was back before integration and Bill Minor was pitching, loaded up the bases and walked in a run. I was in the outfield and I said, "Oh no, what are we going to do now?" When we got to the sideline after the inning, Bill Minor never sat down, he kept throwing, and when we went back out into the field, nobody reached first base on Bill Minor. He just hadn't warmed up yet.

The addition of Marcellus Coleman created more heroics and added to Wilmington's ability to shut teams down. By 1960, '61, Coleman's stuff was at its peak. He was throwing pitches seldom seen in the black sandlots. He had his blazing fastball and curveball, but when he added his own version of a big-league slider, batters were defenseless. Marcellus Coleman was not intimidating nor was he as cocky and sure as an Elgie B. Sims, but he had confidence in what he could do on the mound. When Coleman came to Wilmington he knew he had to perform. Paul Franklin and the Eagles squad took a long look at the little lefthander.

One day the occasion arrived when Coleman found himself in a jam with the game on the line. Manager Paul Franklin saw the bases loaded and called time. He approached the mound with concern and said to the little left-hander, "Marcellus you've got to do better than this. We're in a serious jam now. What can you do?"

Marcellus replied in his soft-toned voice, "Don't worry Mister Paul, I've got everything under control."

Paul Franklin went back to the bench and watched along with everyone else in attendance as Marcellus Coleman sent the other side down 1–2–3.

No one knew where Coleman's power came from or his confidence, but he thrived against the best hitters in the most threatening of situations.

Bob Winston:

> Fourth of July 9th inning, we were down in Amelia County, I think we had them 3–2. Marcellus got the bases loaded with the top of the order coming up, and he shut those boys down 1–2–3, and they were sick down there that day. That number three hitter was supposed to be dangerous, but I swear that boy missed that ball by two feet! I have never seen anybody with a ball like Marcellus had; it just dropped right down in the dirt.

Coleman was a diamond in the rough. He was never scouted by a big-league team and his early exit from high school likely limited his exposure, but everyone who saw the skinny lefty pitch and stood in against him agrees that he deserved a look from a major league organization. Coleman took ill in the '60s and passed away before the age of thirty. Wilmington was a team without trophies or championship titles, but winning and losing was something the Eagles took seriously from the first to the last game. Few teams, if any, swept the Eagles. Many of their big matchups were at the request of baseball fans around the eastern part of Virginia—a who-would-you-like-to-see pairing that usually paid off as memorable.

Bob Winston recounts two late '50s battles versus the Culpeper Dragons and major league prospect George Love:

> Seventh inning nothing nothing, eighth inning nothing nothing. Two out in the bottom of the ninth … we were in the field, and the third baseman picked up a slow roller … picked the ball up three times! And the third time he picked it up the guy had crossed the plate and they beat us 1–0 in the ninth inning! George Love beat us and shut us out on his diamond. It was one of the worst whippings we had ever taken. Games like that you never forget!

The atmosphere was perfect for a return match between the two clubs. This time the Dragons came to Fluvanna County. Bob Winston picks up the rematch:

> Man! Talk about a crowd when Culpeper came back down here. They brought a crowd with them and we had a crowd here! They brought that left-hander and honest to God—we jumped on that fella like we thought he was a ham sandwich! He tried that same stuff with that fastball—we ate him up! We beat them right down here at home! They had a good team but we were hungry! We weren't satisfied with the way that thing went down one to nothing and we'd been here, got in a little practice and talked things over and everybody that came up to bat I don't care what he threw it was gone! Men on base; that's it! And wore him out!

The 1960s Shenandoah Valley League provided more opportunities for Wilmington's search-and-destroy baseball. It has been reported by the Wilmington squad that the Eagles claimed amongst their prey the awesome Sperryville Tigers after the Tigers won their first league championship in the Shenandoah Valley League. The reported score, Eagles 7 Tigers 0 in Sperryville. There are no documents to verify the meeting but if any team stood a chance of shutting out a competitive team like Sperryville it was the Fluvanna Eagles. As Bob Winston points out, Wilmington was as good as any league or independent or semipro team in Virginia.

> We used to book teams and they said we want to play you, but we know we can't beat you, and see that attitude never struck me. I don't care who you were. You could have been the New York Yankees; with me playing first base I went out there to beat you. We were as good as any team in the league but we played for years outside of a league.

King Bee

> If anybody loved baseball more than I did they'd have to be born again; not just me but all the boys around here in Covesville loved it. Covesville used to be baseball country. I have caught doubleheaders and still didn't want to stop playing. I said, "Lord it looks like this thing is over so quick." I just enjoyed it! The boys could tell you about me if they were here. I could steal bases and I could work around catching behind that plate.
> —*Jim Dowell, Covesville Tigers*

In the fifties Covesville's Big Team fell off the pace of its performance in the nineteen forties; the Tigers now found themselves vulnerable to the other strong black clubs within the county in Greenwood and Barboursville. With Early Dowell's best days behind him someone else had to step up and inspire the Tigers.

The inspirational spark was Early Dowell's younger cousin Jim Dowell, a man of average height with a lean muscular frame who sported a mohawk hair cut that stood out amongst the processed and pompadoured styles of the 1950s. He was not just the inspirational spark for Covesville baseball, he was dynamite wherever he played baseball.

Baseball has been defined as action and then inaction, or pondering the next course of action that will punctuate an eventual swing in momentum for one side or the other. Watching Jim Dowell play was like watching a highlight reel; he put in all the action that time allowed. It was one long running series of plays and thrills that no one expected or had ever seen before. An ordinary single often resulted in a double or triple. First a half-sprint to first and then a sudden burst of speed around first to second base. Dowell came in sliding at second, but if the throw was off the mark he came out of his slide running hard for third.

Manager Early Dowell thundered up and down the sideline yelling and cursing at Jim to stay on the base, but by now the excitement around the diamond had reached a roar, and the other team was clearly frustrated and shaken. Jim Dowell was perched on third waiting for the opportunity to come home. This sort of action was actually common in the Negro Professional Leagues of years prior—fast, loose, and daring.

It was typical of the kind of pressure Jim Dowell placed on black ball teams in central Virginia all game long. When Jim Dowell came to the bat, fans put down their drinks and hot dogs. The opposing team tightened up or tensed up. Managers barked commands to players: "Watch Jim!"; "Keep your eyes on Jim!" He was often referred to as "King Bee," the one who took control and set the pace for others to follow or at best keep up with.

Jim Dowell joined the ranks of Covesville's Big Team at the age of sixteen, first playing in the outfield and second base. He was also still playing on a second team of younger ball players in the neighboring community of North Garden. Jim, along with brothers Lee and Lenny and childhood friend Earl Smith, made Covesville's second team as respected as any around. Covesville Big Teamer Junky Dowell pitched for the second team at times. On one such Saturday game away, Junky Dowell's heat began to burn a hole in the mitt of the starting catcher, Elwood Smith, who begged off with a severely swollen hand.

In a spot and not wanting to forfeit, Jim Dowell volunteered to finish the game and was given the basic rudiments of guarding the plate and signals before finishing the game as the receiver for his cousin Junky Dowell. Something about his tryout behind the plate struck a chord and until his playing days were long past Jim Dowell was a catcher anywhere he played baseball.

After Covesville Big Team catcher Howard Carter retired his mitt in the '50s, "King Bee" took over the position. Lee, and Lenny Dowell, Earl Smith, Bernard Washington and Leroy Stevens followed Jim Dowell up to the first team.

Junky Dowell, Lee Dowell and Earl Smith became the three starting pitchers for the 1950s Covesville Tigers.

Hard-throwing right-hander Lee Dowell suffered control problems at times, either sending pitches wild or right over the heart of the plate. Jim Dowell discovered that the secret to utilizing his brother's speed effectively was to make him keep his fastball down. If Lee Dowell could keep his ball down below the belt there would be a lot of strikeouts that day. Lee liked to throw it hard and favored his fastball even though he had a good curve.

He did not throw as hard as cousin Early Dowell before him, but had better than average pop on the ball. That is what brother Jim liked. You could not throw it hard enough for Jim Dowell. Former players say Jim would rather have a pitch knock him over than creep up to the plate. His hands were hardened and callused and he wore his mitt paper thin. The harder Covesville pitchers threw the more Jim Dowell whooped it up. "Woo! Did you see that thing? Lord have mercy that's heat brother!" Batters who did or did not see the pitch needed no reminder or added pressure. They could hear the explosive pop of Dowell's mitt every time they missed the ball. Jim and Lee Dowell became another of the famous brother combinations of the fifties and sixties joining Arthur and Elgie B. Sims and Bobby and Eddie Hudson. Earl Smith had heat of his own, but unlike Lee Dowell rode the wave of his curveball. He was a good hitter and rough base runner known to jump on opposing players and undress them with his steel.

Lenny Dowell remembers teammate Earl Smith:

> In my view Earl Smith had the fastest curveball of anybody around. When you got out into the field you didn't have to worry about fielding balls because Earl would strike them all out. That guy could pitch some baseball! His curveball was faster than Junky's, I swear it was. That thing would get up to the plate and dip on around the corner and it was fast! He moved away to Washington, D.C., but I heard he pitched up there and was doing the same thing he did here. Earl was one of the best in my view.

Lenny Dowell played first base but was also a pitcher. Where Junky, Lee and Earl Smith were mitt-burning hurlers, Lenny liked the breaking-ball, change-of-pace curves, and cites Elgie B. Sims of Greenwood as his greatest influence. When Lenny Dowell's stuff was working right he humiliated batters into self-damning tirades. Catching a gnat was easier than catching up with Lenny Dowell's slow curve.

Lenny Dowell:

> I didn't have the kind of power to overpower anybody. I had a three-quarter speed fastball and Earl Smith, Junky and Lee went all the way over with their fastballs. My speed was about half of their speed, but I had that good little slow thing. Power hitting teams like Greenwood and Avon, I could stop those guys because I was a slow-ball pitcher, and after they'd get used to the boys with the fastballs, I would come in with that slow stuff and strike out all those guys. I was just barely getting it up there and then it would dip down. Good drop, in curve, and out curve and then rare back and fire the fastball or best I had for a changeup. I struck out 14 Avon players one day over on Covesville Diamond.
>
> Jim liked a pitcher that threw hard all the time, but every time I did that I'd get in trouble, so Edward Henderson caught me, and he let me throw what I wanted to throw. When

you pitched to the guys around here you had to have some good stuff on the ball. It had to be curving or something, if not they would hurt you. Guys like Alfred Martin, Leroy Stevens, or Frank White. They could knock it to the moon. You couldn't throw them any kind of old fastball.

The common denominator the four shared was their love of baseball, whether talking about it or catching and throwing while growing up in Covesville. They could not wait for the weekend to roll around so they could play two or three games of baseball, and none more so than Jim.

As Jim Dowell emphasized in a 1999 interview, baseball became second nature in his life.

> I could snatch that ball so fast that the umpire didn't know what to call it. One Sunday we went to Madison and the boys told me, "Dowell, we're going to get a deacon to call the game because we know he'll call it right." I was snatching that ball so fast behind that bat and I'd throw up my hand and say, "Strike!" And the umpire said, "Strike!" Their own players said, "Damn if Dowell doesn't have the deacon cheating."
>
> When I'd get behind the bat I used to keep a hand under my chin and before the ball got up there I'd knock the mask off before the ball hit in the mitt. It was dangerous because I could have misjudged it or been hit by a foul tip and could have been killed back there. I used to steal the ball from the batter—put my hand up under there and get it—go up under the bat and get it!
>
> I used to sing behind the bat too; sometimes I'd sing a spiritual song, and sometimes I'd sing a blues song. *"Oh baby."* I used to sing that song and Covesville would try to give it everything they had. *"Oh baby, you don't have to go. I'm gonna pack up darlin, down the road I go."*
>
> The boys were right then! See, a whole lot of people thought I used to just get behind the bat hollering, and singing, but it was breaking that batter's concentration.

When Jim Dowell broke into his afternoon blues show behind the plate it was more than the Saturday or Sunday afternoon crowd could resist. Even if Covesville was the last team you wanted to see win a ball game you had to pause and listen to Dowell's gametime blues. People in the crowd laughed and cheered and yelled, especially the ladies, some of whom were into Dowell's entertainment as much as the baseball itself. A few players scoffed; most of them just enjoyed the show. Says Bob Winston of the Wilmington Eagles: "Jim Dowell was my favorite, that boy could entertain a game, and if a pitcher could pitch any, Jim Dowell would make him pitch."

After Jim Dowell's performance the crowd had the feeling and were further caught up in the excitement of the game. People left ballgames talking about Jim Dowell's singing and catching first and the score later. Arthur Sims, Bobby Hudson, and Edward Franklin were three of the best catchers in the region but none of them could make the moves Jim Dowell made behind the bat. It was his lightning-quick hands and daring moves, seldom seen or duplicated by any catcher black or white in the region, that put him at the top of the list. No one had seen a catcher do the things Dowell did behind the plate.

He moved like a crouching linebacker, shifting, jumping all the while with a batter swinging and lunging over top. Howard Carter, Covesville's Big Team catcher, and Early Dowell are credited with teaching Jim the most about catching behind the plate and working with pitchers. Carter performed some of the same moves Dowell made but they were not as quick or daring. Jim took the skills to another level. He says he did anything he could possibly do to help his pitcher whether with his singing and soulful humming or snatching a ball out of the strike zone and making it look like a strike. He received a lot of attention but it took some of the pressure off his teammates. His greatest deficiency, amazingly, was his arm, at any time probably the weakest on the diamond; but, as former central Virginia players are quick to point out, it was his speed not his arm that runners came to fear.

James "Boo" Waller, Ivy Eagles:

> You could have made it and been on second base, but you were scared. He didn't have an arm to throw it, no arm! But he was so fast getting up from behind that plate! He would be up from behind that plate and out in front of that batter and the man on first base would be too scared to run, that's how fast Jim was! And he would pull the ball off the bat on you. He could pull the ball off the bat on you man—and get out there! I have swung to hit the ball and I could feel the mitt on my bat—pulled the ball right off the bat and the guy going to second had to go back to first. I would go on him and steal second and third, but to try to steal home—I would never try to steal home against him. If you go home on him you might end up in the hospital. And once he got that ball in his mitt, you're not going to knock it out, not even out of his bare hand.

Jim Dowell's bluff paralyzed many runners who eyed the first to second base dash as impossible given that he was already standing in front of the box. Jim Dowell remembers cousin Early Dowell's words of support after a ballgame: "You might not have the arm to throw people out, but at least you can catch it and block it. You got to catch it before you can throw it, some of them can throw it; and can't catch it at all."

Jim looked up to his elder cousin Early Dowell and took his words as absolute truth for Early had seen talented baseball players near and far. Aside from being a show-stopping catcher he was one of the toughest outs in Virginia's black baseball era.

He considered himself a consistent singles hitter with a good eye for the ball, and tough to overpower. Best of all he seemed capable of adapting to any game situation and getting hits when the team needed one. If the team needed a single in the gap in left or right field or a sacrifice fly for the go ahead run, he hit them all at will. Though not known to hit home runs often, he was capable of stepping up and hitting the ball out if that was what Covesville needed to win the game.

Brother Lenny Dowell, like everyone else, marveled at Jim's ability to play at higher and higher levels.

> We were playing Crozet one Sunday evening and had played eleven or twelve innings and it was tied up. Lee pitched the last three innings and Lee was striking them out and so we had two outs before going to the 12th inning so Jim got up to bat with one man on base. If Jim could knock that man in that would win the ballgame. The guy got two strikes around Jim. "God," everybody said, "that man's gonna strike Jim out!" But when he crooked his arm and tightened up—bow! That thing looked like it was going to the moon Jim hit that thing so far down that bank. So we beat them that day! We played all those innings, but Jim knocked a home run. Jim was known to knock home runs with men on base.

The bunt was actually the favored offensive weapon in Jim Dowell's arsenal. His mastery of the bunt worked perfectly in tandem with his speed. Not only was he capable of laying the bunt down but laying it down in any direction he wanted it to go, and he was sure to beat out any attempts to throw him out. It was like a professional's touch in billiards. Players of the fifties and sixties say Jim Dowell was the only man to drop a bunt down in a full count situation. Every team knew to expect a bunt and run play from Jim Dowell; they just did not know when it was coming.

Leroy Stevens of the Covesville and South Garden Tigers witnessed Jim Dowell's base-running prowess during his best years.

> Jim played against a professional baseball player up in Nelson County; his name was Johnson and he went to the Milwaukee Braves. He really threw so hard that nobody got on base from either side until the 5th inning. And some way that guy walked Jim, and he bet Jim he would never go to another base, and Jim went to second base. Then he told Jim that he wasn't going nowhere else, and Jim went to third base. Jim had Earl Smith to put down a bunt and Jim went home on that guy, and that guy got mad and stopped pitching right then, and we beat them up there that day.

You never knew what Jim Dowell was going to do; not even his teammates knew at times. Was he going to swing away for a base hit, drop a bunt down, or could he deliver with a hit against an Edward Thompson when the rest of the order had been shut down?

All anyone knew was that it was hard to get three strikes around Jim, and the other team did not want him on base. Against the Orange (Virginia) Nats, Dowell remembers a bunt that had to be seen to be believed:

> I dropped the bunt down in that good ball park in Orange, and that thing went clear out into the outfield. It was a hard bunt! The third baseman was playing down and he didn't know it was coming, but I could drop the bunt down at any time and beat it out.

Former players say Dowell was so fast in his prime he could outrace the base runner to first, bolting out of his catcher's stance. It is probable that Jim Dowell could have clocked 9.5 in a one hundred yard dash. He was always the fastest player in any game. Dowell's coming of age coincided with Jackie Robinson's debut with the major league Brooklyn Dodgers. He points to Robinson time and time again as his favorite ballplayer; he patterned his diamond play after the Dodger great. He even wore his ball cap like Jackie Robinson with the cap creased and the bill furled over his eyes.

Jim Dowell often changed the tempo of the ballgame just by the plays that he made. Just like Jackie Robinson he learned how to make the pitcher balk with his darting and dancing off base. He made the hits that fit the situation much like Robinson who was not a great home-run hitter but could hit it out to win the game. Greatest of all, Jim Dowell created runs all by himself, and that was the signature of Jackie Robinson's play. As a tribute to his hero Jim Dowell often stole home, a major feat on any level of play.

Roscoe Burgess, commissioner of the Shen-Valley League and co-manager of the Harrisonburg ACs, recalls, "We always kept our eyes on Jim when he got on base because once he's on you know he's going to steal second—didn't matter whether it was the first pitch or second pitch and he would do anything to get on base."

Jim believed in positive mental preparation before going out to play a ballgame, so that he only needed to act and react when reaching the playing field. Says Dowell:

> I never had to think about what I was going to do at the plate, because I had done all of the thinking the night before. I don't come to the bat or get behind the bat thinking. When I come to the bat I know what I'm going to do. I don't have to stand there thinking, Can I do this or that? My thinking was that night. When I come on the ball field I know what my thinking was—to get on base! When I'd come up to bat I would throw the bat down, grab a handful of dirt and rub it on my hands, and sometimes I would rub it on my face. I'd get on any way I can, hit me or whatever, as long as I get on. We had a Henderson from North Garden that played with us.... Allen Henderson. He got on base more than anybody on my team. He'd act like he was getting out of the way of the ball [laughing] but then he'd lean into it.
>
> That's the way they used to do when I started playing baseball, they'd let the ball hit 'em. And sometimes if you tell these boys today, "If you can't hit it, let it hit you," they say, "No, I ain't gonna let it hit me." We didn't care; as long as it didn't hit us in the ankle or the head, we'd let it hit us. We didn't care how we got on as long as we got on.

His style, unorthodox, rough and shocking, was effective in a head-shaking, do-you-believe-what-you-just-saw manner. Claiming that the leather and steel spikes of the day hurt his feet, he wore canvas flats on the hard red clay fields. When he took over as the manager of the Covesville Tigers in the late fifties, he brought the same spontaneous style to leading the team, making calls much the way he made plays in the field, and as he recalls, doing things no one else would do.

> We went down to Orange one night and Lee [Dowell] pitched up until the 9th inning, got in trouble and loaded the bases up with no outs! Leroy Stevens called time. I think Lee's arm had gotten tight from the night air. So Leroy said, "What are you going to do? Put Lenny in?" I said, "No, I don't want to put Lenny in." And he said, "Well, we ain't got nobody else!" I said, "Yes there is—Jimmy Vest." He said, "Jimmy Vest! Jimmy's never pitched for us before!" I said, "He is tonight." Leroy said, "Lord! We're gonna throw the game away!" I said, "Warm him up!" And I let him throw some and I told him how to hold a man on base and so on, and he got up there and he was perfect! Jimmy had that old sidearm ball and them boys were hitting at that thing and falling down, and he struck the side out first time on the mound! Then he started pitching from then on.

Though the second Covesville Tigers team never piled up wins like the Big Team they had winning seasons and were still considered one of the better teams in central Virginia. While on the diamond Jim Dowell had the power to seemingly make things go his way through hard work and good fortune. Off the field he found his life a lot harder to manage. Jim Dowell was popular and well-liked in the community, but like the fabled bluesman Huddie Ledbetter he often found himself in the wrong place at the wrong time, having to defend himself and others for the wrong reasons. He was quick-tempered, easily offended, and never one to back down from a challenge.

In the early sixties dark clouds descended upon Covesville baseball and Jim "King Bee" Dowell. The team started to lose games to teams they had handled easily in the past. Some of the more skilled position players were getting older and losing a step. Many younger players were lured away to other communities. The biggest blow of all came after the 1961 season when Jim Dowell ended a conflict with a Scottsville, Virginia, man with a blast from his pistol. At the time of the murder, a court case was pending involving charges that the victim had fired shots at Dowell on another occasion.

In December 1961 he was sentenced to ten years in South Hampton Prison for murder.[6] No one in the region who had witnessed Jim Dowell's displays on the ball diamond thought they would see him in a baseball uniform again. At South Hampton Prison in South Hampton County, Virginia, he found that the prison officials were ardent baseball fans and that baseball was the recreation of choice amongst the prisoners. He played nearly every day and became the talk of southeast Virginia baseball.

The Covesville Tigers broke up the next season and players scattered about central Virginia. Players who found themselves on the opposite side of the diamond against Jim Dowell have for years stated that he could have been a major leaguer. He had the potential to be a great catcher at the highest level of baseball, but for the lack of a strong arm.

However, speed, power and versatility at the plate were strongly in Dowell's favor. His sprinter's speed, sharp batting eye, and game-breaking execution with the bunt and run or hit and run certainly would have made him an attractive prospect for many professional clubs.

He might have qualified as a second baseman and special situations pinch-hitter and runner. As Jackie Robinson and Willie Mays made painfully obvious during their major league careers, and in the modern times Rickey Henderson, speed rarely has an off day or suffers though a slump and you cannot teach it. Players capable of manufacturing runs on their own are invaluable.

Northern Virginia/Shenandoah Valley

Drive west away from metro Washington, D.C., and Fairfax County, Virginia, and the scenery changes over to halcyon backdrops of farms and orchards. Many of the small towns and communities have changed little in the past forty years. Here, black baseball has faded from the landscape, its diamonds melding back into the open pastures and hayfields that once accommodated the weekend pastime. From Warrenton to Green Valley, Winchester, Front Royal, and Middleburg, black baseball thrived in these small towns and rural black communities of northern Virginia from the 1930s through the 1970s. Beginning in the early thirties black ball teams such as the Winchester Little American Braves, Berryville All-Stars, Front Royal, and Sperryville Yellow Jackets were the top black teams of the region.

In Rappahannock County, Little Washington's Monarchs were the neighboring ball team to the Sperryville teams of the thirties.

It is not known what the status of the rivalry might have been in that time period but the Monarchs appear to have rivaled the Harrisonburg Red Sox of the Shenandoah Valley more than any other regional team.[7] The Sperryville Yellow Jackets lost very few games during the mid–'30s, anchored by the Williams and Aylor families; they are remembered as the best ever to take the diamond. Tom Williams, Charles Williams, Sr., Reg Aylor, Henry and George Jordan were touted as being as good as any professional ballplayers. It was rumored that the old Sperryville team was scheduled to face the Homestead Grays but details of the happening were never confirmed.

However, in 1935 the Brooklyn Cuban Giants journeyed to Winchester, Virginia, to play against a select group of all-stars from the counties of Clarke, Loudoun, and Rappahannock, and Martinsburg, West Virginia. Seven different teams were represented in the two-game series. The Virginians won the first game 10–9, and lost the second tilt, 13–6.[8] Amongst the all-stars from Rappahannock County was R.T. Walker.

Pitcher Robert T. Walker played for both Little Washington, Virginia, and Sperryville. He left Little Washington in the forties to play semipro baseball in Ohio and then after a short stint in the Army, returned east finding a spot in the pitching rotation of the Negro League Homestead Grays. Walker was a solidly built man standing six foot one and weighing one hundred and ninety-five pounds. He was a fireballer, favoring a blazing fastball and curve.

In the Negro National League he won an average number of starts and competed on the Grays' championship teams of 1944 and 1948.

Walker played alongside another Virginian, Wilmer "Red" Fields of Manassas, and stayed with the Grays until the team disbanded in 1950.[9]

The pastoral setting of Rappahannock and surrounding counties became a proving ground in the nineteen fifties and early sixties for Washington, D.C., area teams. Black ballplayers to the east knew that when the country boys were not in the fields they were either practicing baseball or playing a game and they were sure to be playing baseball all weekend.

Sam Aylor of Sperryville details growing up in Rappahannock County, Virginia, in the forties and fifties:

> Around this area we had nothing to do—nowhere to go. I'd come to your house ... let's say you lived on somebody's farm, there's a big open field out there, that's where we played ball every day! That's all we had to do after we got our chores done at home. We weren't old enough to work. You get all of your buddies together, I'd play you every day! You wear me out today, tomorrow I'll wear you out! We'd laugh, go on home and start again tomorrow. That's how we learned to play.

The post–World War II Little Washington Monarchs were more formidable than their predecessors of the twenties and thirties. They were managed by George Evans and led by team captain and pitcher Bobby Clanagan.

Bobby Clanagan was the nephew of R.T. Walker. Where his uncle was a stack of brawn, Clanagan was short and less imposing. But he had a slingshot arm, hit well and was one of the fastest players on the team. He was still in his teens when he came home from service in the military, and helped rebuild the Monarchs ball team with friends from the Little Washington community. Shortstop Arthur Bridges, pitchers Hampton Fletcher and Frederick Lawson, and first baseman George Taylor became local and regional legends. Arthur Bridges was like a vacuum cleaner at short.

Former teammates recall that it was rare for Bridges to miss anything hit his way. Bridges was also a good catcher. In the mid-fifties Bobby Clanagan recruited amongst the youth of Little Washington and Sperryville which was without a ball team at the time and came up with four standouts. New additions Charles Williams, Jr., William Carter, Jr., Arthur "Seymore" Freeman and Bill Aylor, as well as Arthur "Dolly" Glasgow, came to be some of the best in Virginia's black baseball in the '50s and '60s.

Shortstop and outfielder Charles Williams, Jr., could hit, run and throw with range seldom seen in sandlot baseball. Williams' rocket arm eventually landed him on the mound in the sixties as a pitcher for his hometown Sperryville Tigers. Junior Carter was one of the best teenaged pitching prospects in northern Virginia, starring for Culpeper's all-black Carver High School. He had good speed, great endurance and a bedeviling pick-off move to second base that came out of nowhere via the right-hander's no-look sidearm pitch backward that he had timed with his shortstop.

Junior Carter, pitcher, Washington Monarchs:

> I used to throw all during the week. I'd get three five gallon buckets and set them up against the barn and I would throw until I hit nine out of ten and then I knew I was ready.

Junior Carter was invited to a tryout in Florida with the Brooklyn Dodgers, but his mother vetoed his trip south and he never made another attempt to break away from Virginia's black sandlots.

Catcher Arthur "Seymore" Freeman's first game as a Monarch was especially memorable for he was only fourteen. It was the summer of 1950 and the Monarchs needed someone to block the plate so they called on the oversized teen with his man-sized hands. Though admittedly scared, Freeman delivered and received in a big way. It is said that the only way the ball could get by Arthur Freeman was by throwing it way over his head, because anything else he could catch, block and snatch. Monarchs players joked that "Seymore made bad pitchers look good."

Bill Aylor was the ace, an overpowering left-hander who threw balls that looked like aspirin tablets and swelled catchers' hands on every outing. Some batters never got the bat off of their shoulders against Aylor; others were just intimidated. No one dared dig in on Bill Aylor. Many say he was better at age seventeen than at any point during his sandlot career. Just like Bob Gibson, Bill Aylor was a hitting pitcher with the ability to step up and hit a baseball a fabled "country mile." According to Bobby Clanagan there were telltale signs related to the kind of mound performance Big Bill Aylor might have.

If he ever come out on Sunday morning and says, "Bobby I'm feeling good today let me go" … don't let him go. When he come out and I had to just about make him get on the mound I'm telling you he was something! That was a hard-throwing man! Culpeper had a pitcher by the name of Hackley and he came to bat one day, and he used to talk a lot of junk. Bill Aylor hit Hackley in the hip and knocked the billfold out of his pocket.

It was rare to find a black ballplayer in Rappahannock County without a strong throwing arm; they appeared to be especially blessed when it came to throwing a baseball, leaving opponents near and far to marvel at their speed and range. Pitcher Billy Shanks of the Reva Aces remembers that everyone joked about the Sperryville and Washington ballplayers developing their arms by working in the orchards and hurling fruit at one another.

It was no joking matter on the diamond and in the fifties Little Washington was the Grand Central Station of black baseball in northern Virginia. They looked like a practiced and polished ball team, and this was evident in the way they whipped the ball around on the double play. Monarchs infielders were known to hold onto the ball, loading up on the throw to first just so they could throw it a little bit harder. It was cockiness and confidence.

The Monarchs ball diamond behind the Pine Knott Inn on Rt. 211 turned into a baseball carnival. As many as seven black ball teams were known to show up on a Fourth of July looking for a ballgame. Teams were divided up for an all-day elimination style tournament the likes of which rivaled Tidewater baseball in the thirties and forties.

The Pine Knott Inn was the Saturday night spot to jitterbug and shoot pool; in the daytime the action was behind the inn on the ball diamond. Power lines ran across the outfield and anyone hitting the ball into the power lines was awarded a double that could prove to be an advantage or disadvantage for the winners and losers of the ballgame.

Local residents sold food and baked goods; the ball team had outdoor barbecues and shooting matches. Word spread that at Pine Knott ball diamond you could expect southern hospitality and good baseball. It was an exciting time in Virginia's black baseball history. A typical clipping publicizing a Monarchs ball game in 1959 read:

> The Washington Monarchs will play baseball against the Greenwood Athletic Club at Pine Knott, Sunday July 26 at 2:30 P.M. Come see two fast teams.[10]

Front Royal, Strasburg, and Marshall were tough, but former Monarchs point to the teams of Washington and Alexandria as their true measuring stick. These teams carried former Negro League players and prospective major leaguers. Greenwood's athletic club from the south gave the Monarchs fits during any match up.

Once again, manager Bobby Clanagan:

> We played all over. Culpeper was always tough and the Reva Aces were a hard team to beat. I don't think they ever had more than ten players but man they could play ball. We played a lot of games in Orange at their night stadium and Luray too because they had lights. Washington

and Alexandria were tough because they had so many good pitchers to choose from but we used to beat them and they'd beat us sometimes. The Arlington Black Sox they came here … man they looked like a major league team, came on a big bus. They went down on that field and started practicing, everybody was looking at them, and they were handling that ball like a monkey handles a peanut. When the ball game started we wore them out! [Laughs]

William Carter, pitcher, Little Washington Monarchs:

Greenwood, whew! They were something to beat and the first name changed but the last name never changed, just Sims and Sims, Sims and Sims; couldn't tell one from the other. The only one we recognized was "Pop" Sims [Arthur]. "Pop" could hit and when he got warmed up pitching he was something!

Amazingly with all of the good ball teams in the northeast, neither Little Washington nor any of the others played league baseball. There was more than enough independent action to go around. Ellis Glasgow took over as manager in the late fifties and in 1962 organized an east versus west all-star game played at Crosby Stadium in Front Royal, Virginia. Front Royal, Winchester, Strasburg, and Culpeper took on Washington, Luray, Greenwood and Orange. The west all-stars won the first game 9–4 and the east stormed back to take the second contest 5–0. The '62 all-star game was probably the event that prompted the organized Shenandoah Valley League the next season.

Before 1960 the Monarchs suffered a split, with some players remaining with the Monarchs and others going to the new Sperryville Tiger team minutes down the road at Horse Shoe. Amongst those lost were the Williams brothers, Charles Jr. and Thomas. The split itself created northern Virginia's best black ball team of the sixties, and a rivalry for the ages. Older players from the '40s and '50s, however, say that the Little Washington Monarchs were northern Virginia's best.

Culpeper County

Bordering Rappahannock County to the south is the county of Culpeper, Virginia. Culpeper County's contribution to black baseball included Reva, Mitchells, and Culpeper. Culpeper and Reva became two of the best-known ball teams of the '50s. The Culpeper ACs of the 1930s were second only to the likes of Charlottesville's Kelly All-Stars and the Sperryville Yellow Jackets twenty miles down the road. The ACs played a traveling schedule that carried them from Charlottesville, Virginia, to Green Valley, Virginia, to Rockville, Maryland, and to Washington, D.C.

As the years passed and the older ACs headed to the sidelines, the baton was picked up by Culpeper native and baseball man Charley Lane. Lane, like Kelly's All-Stars manager Charles Jones would book a game anywhere he could get one and was known to bring players into the lineup from all directions outside of Culpeper township.

The team was renamed the Dragons, an interesting moniker during the time of giants, dodgers and tigers. Lane's new team combined remnants of the old ACs and new teen stars, most of whom were Carver High School baseball standouts and well-schooled in the fundamentals of the game. The Dragons were versatile as many black teams of the day were with pitchers and hitters who were easily converted into infielders and outfielders when needed. Leading the way were standouts Jake Carter, Dee Robinson, Henry Shanks, Jr., and Leroy Hackley. The last piece in the assembly of the new Dragons was their star pitcher, George Love.

He was a brawny 6'3" left-hander with a good hard fastball and he had all of the good breaking stuff. Love possessed great strength but he had control. The deeper he went into the innings the better his control and the more dominant he became. One could either hit against George Love or not hit against him. There was no in between and after five innings the odds of getting hits against the big left-hander diminished greatly. Base runners kept their eyes on him because his pick-off move was lightning quick.

Charley Lane and other local baseball enthusiasts put their hopes on George Love and helped him secure a successful tryout with the Pittsburgh Pirates. Under the strains of early major league integration and homesickness, George Love was overwhelmed. The pressures of having to perform, the alienation and change of environment did not add up to the worth of becoming a big-leaguer and Love returned home to the sandlots of Culpeper. Back at home he was the talk of the black baseball circuit and was known as the boy who'd tried out in the "League." Teams played twice as hard against him and his Dragon teammates.

Black baseball fans still rave about encounters between George Love and Big Bill Aylor of the Washington Monarchs and Sperryville Tigers. The two often held each other's team scoreless through 7 innings. During one memorable clash both teams were scoreless after nine innings and both pitchers were courting no-hitters. George Evans, the Monarchs manager, placed himself in the game as a pinch-hitter and got a hit off of George Love that eventually led to the game's winning run.

Not only were the good hitters in the area trying to prove something standing in against Love, but other pitchers wanted to outduel the left-hander at any given opportunity. Before integration brought on early stages of social change, Culpeper like any other black team of the time played on private property, usually an open field. Culpeper's white ball teams played on the fairgrounds of Farmers Park. Blacks were not allowed into the grounds, but black ballplayers watched from the roadway for many years. But by the late fifties Farmers Park opened to blacks in the region and became homefield for the Dragons. Lane's teams played regionally and still traveled a bit but refused to play the rural teams of Reva or Mitchells because they were bush teams, woodcutting boys in overalls. The Dragons had a few rivals and played competitive heads up baseball. Culpeper battled it out on numerous occasions with Sperryville, Little Washington, and Orange. All of these teams were in close proximity to the town of Culpeper. Out of the list the Dragons probably rivaled Orange more than any other. Many of the Dragons and Nats went to high school together playing on Carver High's baseball team.

The two teams often faced off as many as six times during a summer season and all of them were hard-fought contests. Culpeper won more of the late '50s contests, but Orange stormed back with the upper hand in the early 1960s.

The Dragons played into the mid–'60s before the team started to disassemble. Reva, Virginia's baseball history began like that of many rural community teams. The players were farmers, laborers and mill workers playing Saturday and Sunday baseball in cleared pastures. Players wore overalls and work boots, but they played hard and considered themselves as good as any, especially the town team down the road who, because they had lights and uniforms, thought they were above playing their country cousins.

Billy Shanks grew up playing cow pasture ball around Reva, and when he got out of the Army in 1953 he rejoined his friends and relatives on the home team. Billy Shanks had played baseball with the 42nd Engineers while in the service and upon his return to Reva became the starting pitcher. He was a left-hander with a whipping sidearm motion, and possessed a good fastball and curveball. Opposing players respected his speed and stayed off the plate when Billy was on the mound. Reva's ball team was basically the Shanks and the Jackson families, and later the Slaughters. They were all cousins and brothers. Today there is a Shanktown Road that runs through the heart of the still rural community.

The Reva ball field was adjacent to a half-mile race track and a dancehall. There were ballgames in the morning and horse racing in the afternoon, and dances at the dancehall in the evening. The Aces had plenty of community support and fans came out weekends for the attraction of all-day and nighttime entertainment.

They played games against Brandy Station and Keswick in Albemarle County, the then Madison Indians, but the new Culpeper Dragons still refused to play Reva because they did not have uniforms. Charley Lane and Billy Shanks were schoolmates. Billy Shanks remembers Lane's explanation of why there would be no Reva-Culpeper matchup.

> We were just an old bush team around here; we didn't have uniforms. Charley Lane was the manager of the town team, the Culpeper Dragons—a good manager with a good team. We kept after them, told them we would play them in sweat jackets and overalls and they said no. There was a man from Culpeper named Mortimer Marshall; he was the undertaker. He said, "Why don't ya'll go ahead and play those boys; you must be afraid they'll whip you!" Charley said, "We ain't afraid of no old bush team," so we went to Charlottesville and bought uniforms. That's how the Reva Aces first come up with uniforms. We bought our uniforms and put our name on them, "Reva Aces"; before, the team was just Reva.

With new uniforms the Reva Aces now had the Culpeper Dragons cornered. There were no further excuses the Dragons could use for not playing against Reva's bush team. Not long before the first Reva versus Culpeper encounter the Aces received a new addition in the form of teenaged Richard Slaughter.

Billy Shanks:

General Jackson, Richard's uncle, told me one day, "You know we ought to put Richard on first base." General said, "I'm practicing him every day, and I'm almost knocking the glove off of him." But when Richard came out there General had been giving him batting practice and Richard could scoop a ball up. Richard was good and he was no more than fourteen or fifteen.

Richard Slaughter was exposed to baseball growing up in Reva watching his relatives play ball and by his early teens all he was interested in was being on the diamond. He was growing and his skills were becoming sharp, far exceeding those of many youngsters his age and showing up some adults. He appeared in the Reva-Culpeper showdown at first base and played like a natural.

Everyone, including Charley Lane, who gruffly berated Richard's youthful enthusiasm on the diamond, knew the youngster was a star ballplayer in the making. No one could hit a ball by the young left-hander on first base and he even managed a couple of hits against grown men pitching.

Billy Shanks recalls with a smile, "Sure enough the first game played against Culpeper the Aces beat the Dragons." The last out was made by Richard Slaughter who was jumping up and down on first base before the ball reached his glove. Afterwards Charley Lane replied, "That old boy on first base would be all right if he didn't jump up and down like a monkey." For Culpeper it was an unbearable lesson and humbling defeat, losing to their country cousins. It is said that some Culpeper players turned their bats into kindling wood after Reva's first victory. The first Reva victory came in Culpeper. When the Dragons came to Reva in a return game they left the field 0–2 against the newly uniformed Aces.

Soon Charley Lane would also recruit Richard Slaughter for his Culpeper lineup along with Billy Shanks. In the '60s John Henry Price Powhatan Nelson and Warren Nelson made their presence felt in the Dragons lineup. After two losses along with some impressive play by Reva's players, Culpeper manager Charley Lane needed no further convincing and employed an "if you can't beat them join them" pitch to the Reva ballclub. But the Aces had purchased brand new uniforms, so they were not contemplating folding their team to join the Dragons. The result was Reva talent playing back and forth on the Dragons roster on many occasions. Against Culpeper rival Orange, Billy Shanks was employed in every night engagement against the Nats and always came away with the victory.

The amazing thing about the Reva ball club was that at any time there were not more than ten players on the team roster. Billy Shanks was the number one pitcher 95 percent of the time. But the Aces were a fantastic ball team and just tough to beat.

They stood up to everyone in the region—Sperryville, Washington, Culpeper, Front Royal—and more than held their own. Richard Slaughter began pitching later in his teens and was renowned early on for his breaking curves. Slaughter recalls that his pitching career might have taken off were it not for an outing against a Maryland all-star team. The teenaged Slaughter pitched the first game, earning a grueling 10 inning win. Billy Shanks started the second game of the doubleheader but got in trouble around inning 4, and Richard Slaughter was called upon again. After that weekend doubleheader Richard Slaughter was out of commission for over a month and his arm never responded quite the same though he was an effective pitcher in the sandlots through the mid-'60s.

The Aces received additional supporting play from another member of the community and the Shanks family in the form of Billy Shanks' cousin Robert Shanks. Robert Shanks had played with the old Culpeper ACs. On many summer afternoons when it was time for the Reva ballgames, cousin Rob, as he was known, would appear wearing an old uniform and expecting to play with the team. Invariably he put his younger cousin Billy on the spot as to if and when he would play that day.

Billy Shanks remembers his elder cousin's infield plays as part of a past era:

> That bat cracked—I didn't hardly see the ball, but I heard his hand crack when he caught it and he'd say, "Come on, come on" and you knew he was going to first base; that was cousin Robert Shanks. He had a little small glove looked like a kid's glove, but he'd catch that ball barehanded and he'd throw it as hard as he could throw it—didn't matter where he caught it he'd fire down on you. He wore this old uniform made of pure wool and you'd see him coming with his glove strapped to his side.
>
> He was up in age but he still wanted to play, and would get mad if you didn't let him in the game, so I would always play him here and there and he would make those catches with his naked hand.
>
> We had a one-armed man that played for Reva; he was from Gordonsville. He was supposed to have made the pros but he fell out of a tree picking cherries and broke his arm and they had to amputate. He come and asked me one day, "Billy can I play ball with y'all?" I said, "Yes Gladys you can play." But I said to myself, how's Gladys going to hit? Don't you know when he come to batting practice he showed me what he could do. He choked up on the bat about four inches and he could hit good. He'd play the field and when he'd catch that ball he'd throw it up in the air, put his glove under his other arm, and catch it again, and he'd shoot it on into the infield pretty good. He played good ball! Played just as good as some of them that had two hands.

The Reva Aces were playing thirty or more games a summer and winning more than their share against the top teams in northern Virginia and central Virginia. They had rising stars like Richard Slaughter and Roy Jackson playing with the team and then tragedy struck. In September 1959 the team's third baseman, shortstop, and second baseman, General Jackson, perished in an automobile accident on Rt. 522 in Woodville, Virginia. The accident sent shock waves through the community and decimated an already sparse lineup.

The Aces were listed for matchups during the 1960 season but never played again beyond that season. Many players like Billy Shanks, surveying the loss and examining their own lives with families, figured they had played enough good baseball, and thus the Reva Aces disbanded after a storied stint on the black baseball circuit. Reva players wanting to continue their baseball found welcomed spots on the now dominant Sperryville Tigers baseball roster.

"Stove Pipe" and the Harrisonburg ACs

Black baseball in Virginia's Shenandoah Valley has a time line as long as that of any other region in the Old Dominion. The counties of Augusta and Rockingham fielded ball teams in the '30s. Between 1930 and 1980 black baseball existed in Luray, Harrisonburg, Staunton, and Waynesboro. The Harrisonburg Red Sox and the Waynesboro Dupont Grays were the first documented black teams from the valley in the 1930s. The Red Sox played a large portion of their schedule against teams in north central Virginia such as the Washington Monarchs, Sperryville Yellow Jackets, Front Royal, and Winchester, and as far north as Martinsburg, West Virginia. Dupont's Industrial Grays traveled as far as Washington, D.C., and Maryland. Staunton, Virginia, is listed in matchups versus the Kelly All-Stars of Charlottesville.

Rockingham County supported two black teams in the late nineteen forties: one team representing the city of Harrisonburg and the other representing the neighboring town of Bridgewater, Virginia. First baseman Junious Whitelow managed the Harrisonburg team, and the rival Bridgewater team was led by Roscoe Burgess. Little did they know that they would be linked for life by baseball and family.

Roscoe Burgess of the Harrisonburg ACs:

> We had a team in Bridgewater, and we wouldn't use any Harrisonburg ballplayers, and so you had a rivalry with Harrisonburg and Bridgewater. But a couple of the guys from Sperryville would come over and play with us and a few of us would go over there and play with them. When Harrisonburg's older guys quit playing my future brother-in-law Junious Whitelow and I got together and formed the Harrisonburg Monarchs and then switched to the ACs.

Junious Whitelow and Roscoe Burgess co-managed the ACs, now a strong team by way of the union of town and city ballplayers. By the late 1950s the Harrisonburg ACs were a well-traveled, and well-known baseball team on the black sandlot circuit. They played everywhere they were able to schedule a ballgame. To the young players it was a great weekend adventure in a time before there were televisions in every living room, because blacks had very few outlets for entertainment around small towns and communities. Harrisonburg players loaded up their cars with bats and balls and brought their wives and girlfriends along, sometimes driving two hundred miles round trip on a weekend, but it was enjoyable.

The ACs played throughout three regions of Virginia in the fifties and early sixties. Driving south down highway 81 the ACs booked and played matchups with the Greenwood Hawks, Avon All-Stars, and Amherst, and went farther south still to play against Roanoke and Salem, Virginia. In the east, Sperryville, Washington, Orange, Barboursville and Charlottesville were regular opponents.

Before the initial move towards integration in the '50s Harrisonburg played against two white ball teams, Clover Hill and Briery Branch, of the all-white Rockingham County Baseball League. Staunton and Elkton became rival valley teams to the ACs, and night games were played at a lighted stadium in Grottoes. First baseman Junious Whitelow was one of the team's best hitters. Roscoe Burgess caught and was a consistent singles hitter who inspired the play of his teammates by creating bets on who would strike out first during a ballgame. The competitive Burgess remembers dropping down his best bunt to avoid paying all of his teammates on the bench.

A strong pitching staff and timely hitting made the ACs one of Virginia's top sandlot teams. Coincidentally, much of the long ball power came by way of the team's pitchers. Leif Washington, the team's starting pitcher, was said to have lost fewer than a dozen games in his six years of play with the ACs, and hit the ball out of the park as well as any slugger. The ace of the original ACs squad was Melvin "Jack" Allen, a next door neighbor to Roscoe Burgess in Bridgewater.

Left-hander Jack Allen was clearly a cut above the competition; at times not even the competitive ball teams of Roanoke could touch him. He possessed a full arsenal of pitches, and his pick-off move came out of nowhere. Allen played with the young team briefly and then moved on to semipro black baseball in Boston and Negro League ball in New York. South Carolina became a summer destination when a fan of the ACs talked up the team to his relatives down south.

Roscoe Burgess:

> I'll never forget that one game we played down there in South Carolina. We had 'em 3–2. And in the last inning we had two outs with the bases loaded and they stopped the game when some guy come up in a car. And a guy took his uniform and gave it to him. Boy! And when he came there everybody started hollering. "Here he comes; the games over now!" "Big guy!" So, my first cousin was pitching—Don Burgess, people called him "Turkey Neck" or "Stovepipe." He was tall and skinny and he'd throw his leg up high and when he'd come down you couldn't see the ball until his long arm came forward. Don could throw hard. He had a good fastball, knuckleball and every now and again he'd throw one underhand or sidearm. No one knew which way he was coming.
>
> I went up to the mound; I was the catcher, and I said, "Look this guy must be good with all this carrying on!" Guys in the stands started betting, saying, "OK I'll bet you on the game now!" And I said, "I don't know about this guy ... what do you think cousin?" And he said, "You call it and I'll throw it." Guy came to bat looked at me and said, "Goodnight turkey!" I said, "We're waitin on a guy like you anyway; we want you up here!" Don did his windup and I gave him the signal to just fire it hard down there. It didn't have to be a strike—just fire down there. Ah! "That's what I want!" he said, and he jumped back, and patted his shoes. And he [Don] fired down there again and he swung and he missed. And it was a ball and a strike. And he threw again and he swung and he missed.
>
> I said, "This guy can't hit! I don't know why all these people are up there hollering. This turkey's already out of here!" I used to talk a lot back there trying to get your concentration off the game. I said, "What do you want? You can't hit a fastball. What do you want? You want him to throw you a curve?" Can you hit a curve? He said, "Anything you throw down here I can hit!" I thought to myself, he saw two fastballs so I'm sure he's looking for another fastball. My cousin could throw a knuckle pretty good. I didn't want to throw it because he was liable to kill it, but I went ahead and called it, and this guy's still swinging, didn't touch nothing! Guys were up in the stands chasing each other through the stands trying to get their money! Afterwards I was told that was the first time they had known him to strike out in a long time because that guy could hit a ball. And later he told me, he said, "I would have never believed that I wouldn't have touched the ball! I didn't even touch the ball!"

Don "Stovepipe" Burgess is probably one of the more fabled players from the Shenandoah Valley area and perhaps one of the best remembered black pitchers

Harrisonburg ACs, 1965 (author's collection).

from Virginia's sandlots in the '50s and '60s. Almost every player of the era has their own story to tell of Don Burgess' high-velocity pitches and ever-changing delivery. Burgess stood 6'5", his lean frame draped by his uniform, and on the mound he appeared to be seven feet tall. His high leg kick did not make it any easier to keep track of the baseball.

The only consistency in Don Burgess' pitching was the whooshing sound of the baseball moving through the strike zone. Former Shenandoah Valley league players recall hearing but not seeing Stovepipe's pitches, and his underhand submarine ball all but chased some batters from the box altogether.

Sam Aylor on the perils, and humor, of facing Stovepipe:

> We were playing Harrisonburg over in Luray one night. Louis Butler was batting against Stovepipe and the ball came by Louis Butler and hit the board of the backstop. When Lewis Butler heard the ball hit, he started falling because he thought it was coming back just as hard. I can still see Louis Butler falling.

It was quite a spectacle to see Stovepipe and his cousin Roscoe Burgess work a game together. They were opposites, one as short as the other was tall. Roscoe Burgess knew that many batters were flat out intimidated by his cousin's pitching and played on their fears to the hilt. Because the average batter expected to be blown away by the lanky pitcher, it afforded the pair opportunities to sneak in the knuckleball. At catcher Burgess was always a good-natured competitive player who liked to talk it up to opposing players, rib them about their performance, and at times make a target of his mitt just close enough to a batter's ear to get the full effect of Stovepipe's rockets.

Stovepipe is said to have made a number of appearances on Rockingham and Rappahannock County teams tagged with varying nicknames. Kenny Diggs, Avon (Virginia) A's remembers:

> When I was a little boy, my dad took me to a ballgame. I'll never forget it, they called him "rooster." This guy when he threw the ball he looked like he was staring you in the face. I stood behind the backstop with my hands gripping the screen and watched—I did not see the ball! You could hardly see the ball. That's how hard he threw. My God, if somebody had put a radar gun on him, he must have been throwing 100 mph. And he was long, and when he turned the ball loose it looked like he was staring you in the face. He amazed me as a child. Burgess could throw. I had a buddy that went with us to the game, and I remember telling my buddy, I'm going to throw hard like that one day.

West Virginians Bobby Lee and Roy Taylor found spots in the Harrisonburg lineup in the early '60s. Taylor was an ace pitcher, and another deadly hitter in the ACs' order. Roscoe Burgess:

> When Roy Taylor walked out on the field Orange was through. It was always a close game, but they just couldn't do anything with Roy Taylor. One guy told me, "All he's got is a curve, a drop and a fastball—that's all he's got." I said, "And you can't hit either one of the three can you?"
>
> Roy Taylor, Bobby Lee, and another guy lived in Romney, West Virginia, and started coming to Harrisonburg, and dating some girls over here, and they'd come all the way over here just to play baseball with us. They would get over here Saturday night, and stay at my house, all three of them, and go home Sunday night after we played a ballgame.

Elkton, Virginia, to the east, was Harrisonburg's closest local rival, and some players from the ACs left the team to play in Elkton, adding fuel to the competition. Harrisonburg dominated most of the matchups but Elkton was known to steal a game here and there. By the late '60s Elkton was one of the top regional teams.

V

Bases Loaded, 1960–1970

Black baseball in Virginia reached its peak in the 1960s combining the best of the older tried-and-true stars, and the best of the new sandlot hopefuls. The decade showcased athletes groomed by two of Virginia's most competitive black high schools, Jackson P. Burley in Charlottesville and George Washington Carver in Culpeper. The last recorded black baseball league in Virginia history gave teams from central Virginia, the Shenandoah Valley and northern Virginia the opportunity for the first time to play for a championship.

As baseball's following declined nationally, that of black baseball in Virginia soared with more teams and players and larger throngs of devoted fans. Decades after regular play by black teams began in the Old Dominion, the sixties became a decade of promise for the youthful black ballplayers of the era who seemingly stood the best chance of advancing to the next level of competitive baseball.

Charlottesville Squeeze-Ins

Thirty years after the storied reign of the Kelly All-Stars, Charlottesville's black baseball scene completed a changing of the guard as the last of the original town stars retired their gloves. The Cellar Dodgers, sponsored by an eatery on the University of Virginia Corner, were rostered by remaining players from the Kelly team and ball players returning from World War II and then Korea in the fifties. Jackson P. Burley, Charlottesville city's new black high school, opened in 1951 and it was the standouts and stars of the school's athletic program who recaptured the recognition for Charlottesville in the sandlots of black baseball.

Burley High School's football team, the Bears, carried the praise as the state's best in the mid-fifties, but the same coach, Bob Smith, who'd built up the football program was now doing the same thing with the baseball team. Smith and assistant coach Greene practiced and drilled their charges like major leaguers with most of the emphasis on fielding, running, and more running. Each season the Bears base-ball team finished higher until only the powerful George Washington Carver squad of Culpeper stood in their way. John Spears was a member of the Cellar Dodgers and after witnessing the high school play of his teenaged son Jackie, and his friend Alfred Martin, he decided the two were old enough and good enough to help the aging Dodgers team out.

Covesville Yankees, 1964–65. Beloved umpire, coach and manager Gene Burton is at the far left in the back row (author's collection).

Alfred Martin and Jackie Spears received their first exposure to the local sandlots with the Cellar Dodgers before either of them could drive. However, the pair exhibited a maturity and a physical presence that easily allowed them to fit in with the team. Charlottesville Squeeze-Ins center fielder, Jackie Spears:

> The Cellar Dodgers had a game on a Friday night and they came and got Alfred Martin and I out of high school to play a game in Farmville, and we were excused from school to play baseball. We thought that was one of the greatest things in the world.

After filling in on the Charlottesville Dodgers roster for a season, Spears and Martin, along with several teammates from Burley High, decided to form their own team called the Squeeze-Ins, given their new entry into the black sandlots. The Squeeze-Ins were a young persons' social and athletic club focused on community events and fundraisers. The baseball games were the highlight of the summer and in the winter there were Squeeze-Ins basketball games.

Chuck Chisholm and Little Willie Lewis were veterans of the new team. Chisholm's days on the diamond reached back to the Kelly All-Stars of the thirties. Lewis was an uncle to Jackie Spears and held down the hot corner on third base and was still a clutch-hitter in the batting order. Lewis came to the team after the breakup of the Cellar Dodgers in 1959. Lewis' father, Willie, Sr., had played on the

Kelly team. Jackie Spears recalls that it was the display of natural baseball talent and amazing displays of athleticism by Willie Lewis, Sr., and Charles Yancey of the old Kelly team that inspired him and many other youngsters in the community to play baseball.

The Squeeze-Ins made fundamentally sound plays and were already good ballplayers. Manager Flip Murray and assistant managers Theodore "Creeper" Gilbert and James "Rat" Brown kept the young Charlottesville squad ready to play and perform.

The Squeeze-Ins were a well-organized club; they dressed out in two different sets of uniforms looking the part of ballplayers. Murray and left fielder Pat Shelton coordinated the season's schedule prior to the start in late spring.

It was a spirited squad, and every manager and player had a nickname or tag name. There was Asher "Gingus" Conn, William "Locust" Douglas, James "Jimmy" Mills, Charles "Dinky" Woodfolk, Percell "Rabbit" Jones, William "Colesy" Coles, Percell "Red" Berkley, and Charles "Doll Baby" Douglas. Outfielder Jackie "Moon" Spears was a powerfully built youngster with broad shoulders and massive arms. He hit the ball with power, and was known to hit it far at times. Spears had a strong arm and once made an outstanding outfield play on a well-hit ball that almost ended in disaster.

> We were playing a game against Avon at Washington Park. I played center field and I had a pretty strong arm and this guy hit the ball and really hit it out there. I recall that it was one of the longest balls that had ever been hit. He was circling third base and somehow I got that ball back to the infield—I fired it in and he thought he had a home run ... the ball hit him in his head and knocked him out! Eventually he got up and he wasn't hurt but the ball just knocked him out, and I thought I had killed the man.

The Shelton brothers—Nathaniel "Pat" and George, called "Chico"—contributed good hitting and fielding. Team captain Chico Shelton was a starting infielder and led the team in R.B.I.'s. Chico was the hitter counted on most in important scoring situations. Only Alfred "Pepper" Martin hit the ball harder than left fielder Pat Shelton.

As one of the area's top contenders, pitching was the only category in which the Squeeze-Ins lacked depth. Sterling "Boo" Dudley was Charlottesville's ace, starting almost every Sunday afternoon game for the team. Right-hander Boo Dudley rarely failed his teammates often striking out as many as ten batters on game day.

Alfred Martin was the team's best all-around performer. At Jackson P. Burley High he was a member of the state championship team of 1956, and was a standout in basketball. He earned all-state honors in the years 1959 and 1960.

The Squeeze-Ins put him anywhere they needed him except at catcher. Martin started at first base, but played shortstop as well as any player in the region. By the age of sixteen grown men feared facing the hulking youngster; word spread in a hurry that Martin was the terror of the Squeeze-Ins batting order. The best advice on handling his at bats was summed up in two words—back up.

Martin and Jackie Spears both worked out under the eyes of a Cincinnati Reds scout in Charlottesville while still on the Burley Bears baseball team. Drafted into the United States Air Force in 1961, Martin landed the enviable duty of traveling and playing fast pitch softball for the 4600th Air Base Wg. ENT. Colorado. He now stood six feet four inches, weighed well over two hundred pounds and his tag name "Pepper" Martin followed him to Colorado where his home run displays were chronicled in the base newspaper. The 4600th went on to become champions of the military league winning the ADC softball crown in 1961. Playing fast pitch no doubt increased his bat speed and sharpened his fielding ability to a fine edge.

Upon his return from the military in 1964 Alfred Martin's sandlot exploits made him a lasting legend in the history of central Virginia's black baseball teams and stars.

While with the Squeeze-Ins, Martin further displayed his versatility, starting at pitcher in place of Boo Dudley when the team engaged in weekend doubleheaders, and also making appearances in a relief role. Lloyd "Booty" Brown started at catcher, pitched at times and was a consistent hitter in the heart of the order.

Percell "Red" Berkley and Percell "Rabbit" Jones were the speediest on the roster, usually compiling many of the team's game-breaking steals between the two of them. When faced with a particularly formidable opponent manager Flip Murray called on barnstorming area pitcher Bill Minor of Keswick, Virginia. If Minor could hold a team down with his off-speed junk-ball pitches, Murray knew his Squeeze-Ins could generate enough offense for the win.

The community-oriented fundraisers sponsored by the Squeeze-Ins Social Club created a following in support of the team's diamond pursuits. Jackie Spears volunteered his time to the Jackie Robinson Little League, the only organized play for black youth ten to fourteen. Reflecting back today, Spears is as proud of his work and association with the little league youth squad as he is of his participation with the Squeeze-Ins adult team. Spears points out that there was a sense in the black community in those times that baseball was of great importance socially, and playing the sport aided in building character.

The Squeeze-Ins played on the same Washington Park diamond that had served as a springboard for the traveling Kelly All-Stars in the '30s. Compared to the rock-strewn and uneven fields still utilized as weekend diamonds in outlying areas, Washington Park was almost big league.

The old diamond was actually bookend to the Burley Bears baseball field, and was located walking distance from black residents of Rose Hill, Tenth Street, and the Vinegar Hill neighborhoods. The new Charlottesville team had the summer crowds supporting them and they had a team to see and talk about.

Former opponents of the sixties Squeeze-Ins team still marvel at the immediate impact of the young Charlottesville club that never carried more than a dozen players. The players were well-coached and strategically placed around the diamond according to their strengths. Stellar performances in key positions and good execution when presented with scoring opportunities made the Squeeze-Ins as good as Greenwood, Orange, or Barboursville from the words "play ball."

As Jackie Spears remembers, the Squeeze-Ins were competitive and confident:

> When the umpire said play ball we were excited and inspired because that was what we came out to do on Sunday afternoons; to play ball and winning was what it was all about for us. I can remember playing down in Wilmington and there was an old sign behind third base, and either Alfred Martin or Pat Shelton hit a line drive over third base, and the ball was hit with such power that it knocked a hole in the sign. And it was a landmark for years because the sign was never fixed. Alfred Martin was an excellent athlete. He played baseball, basketball, football; talk about power, he could hit a ball a country mile as people used to say.

During their tour of Virginia's black sandlots the Squeeze-Ins played everyone, and were one of the few teams in the region to play regularly against the vaunted Wilmington Eagles, one of the best black ball clubs in the Old Dominion. Charlottesville won very few matchups against the Wilmington Nine but they loved the high level of competition and former Eagles still talk about games against the Shelton brothers and Alfred Martin. Alfred Martin would later star at shortstop for Wilmington in the late sixties.

Charlottesville played a local schedule but also spent much of the summer traveling out of the area to play black teams in Buckingham, Lynchburg and Farmville, Virginia. An examination of the team's play in August 1960 finds the Squeeze-Ins taking a night game away from the Orange Nats, 5–2, and then returning home the following day and rolling over the Covesville Tigers 11–2.[1]

In the contest versus Covesville, Alfred Martin's pitching limited Covesville to three hits and he helped his own cause at the plate by driving in four of the eleven Charlottesville runs.

The following week the Cismont Braves visited Washington Park sporting a 10–3 record and in search of a win that could put them ahead of the Charlottesville team. The Cismont Nine was similar in makeup, essentially another new team on the black sandlot scene of Central Virginia that mirrored the Squeeze-Ins at almost every position.

The encounter was an offensive thriller as both teams put nineteen runs total on the scoreboard. By the time the game was called in the midst of a downpour in the bottom of the ninth, starting Squeeze-Ins pitcher Sterling Dudley had gone all the way and held on long enough to get the win.[2] The next Squeeze-Ins triumph came in a one-sided victory of 14–3 over the Ivy Virginia Eagles.[3] The victory over Ivy was the eighth consecutive win for the team. If anyone wondered about the credibility of the new Charlottesville team they now had more than enough supporting evidence of the youngsters' prowess.

The remainder of August and September were spent battling against Orange, Wilmington, and Greenwood. Greenwood versus Charlottesville was a thriller that packed Washington Park to capacity. It was a hard-fought ballgame that featured two top teams. Preacher and Dopey Sims of the Greenwood Hawks were teammates of

Top: Charlottesville Squeeze-Ins (1960s). Back row (l-r): William "Locust" Douglas; Theodore "Creeper" Gilbert, assistant manager; Freddie "Flip" Murray, manager; James "Rat" Brown, assistant manager; James "Jimmy" Mills. Middle row (l-r): Asher "Gingus" Conn; Charles "Dinky" Woodfolk; Percell "Rabbit" Jones; Jackie "Moon" Spears; Lloyd "Booty" Brown; Linwood "Chuck" Chisholm; Percell "Red" Berkley; Sterling "Boo" Dudley. Front row (l-r): Nathaniel "Pat" Shelton; George "Chico" Shelton; Charles "Doll Baby" Woodfolk. *Above:* Charlottesville Squeeze-Ins at Booker T. Washington Park, August 6, 1961. Front row (l-r): Sterling Dudley, Jackie Spears, George Shelton, Lloyd Brown, Charles Douglas, and Nathaniel Shelton. Back row (l-r): Charles Woodfolk, "Little" Willie Lewis, and Percell "Red" Berkley.

many of the Squeeze-Ins players at Burley High, so they knew each other's strengths and weaknesses. Games between Charlottesville and Greenwood often came down to the last at bat to decide a winner.

All of the games were an exciting display of hustle and athleticism by young players of the decade. Charlottesville-Orange was an instant feud in the sixties. The series of games played each summer placed Burley High baseball players against Carver High diamond champions.

During the school year Carver always came out on top, either defeating Burley in the regional or state finals. Carver baseball teams were the product of three counties—Rappahannock, Culpeper, and Orange. Burley teams consisted of Charlottesville city and Albemarle County athletes. Burley's only championship occurred in 1962 when the team finally hurdled their nemesis in Culpeper County to bring the title home to Charlottesville. Each time the Squeeze-Ins and Orange Nats met up the two teams knew that one successful inning could determine the outcome of the ballgame, so it was a challenge to see who could make the first strong rally.

The 1961 season was one of the best ever for the Squeeze-Ins, with an early run of consecutive victories that included a 12–6 win over the Harrisonburg ACs.[4] It almost appeared the team might have an undefeated season but in August diamond play got hot and rivals Orange and Wilmington caught up with the Charlottesvilleans. After a Saturday night loss at Orange the Squeeze-Ins boasted a record of 21 wins and 6 losses.[5] It was just the beginning of the month of August and, though without further proof, it is feasible that the Squeeze-Ins won thirty to thirty-two games in 1961.

For reasons unknown the Squeeze-Ins were not part of the Shenandoah Valley League in the early sixties. Undoubtedly they would have been an excellent addition to the new league; but perhaps like many sandlot clubs they felt that they were able to get in enough ballgames playing independently each year. The Squeeze-Ins began to break up in the mid-sixties as players from the original lineup began to fulfill military and college commitments outside the area.

A couple of attempts were made to revive baseball in Charlottesville through the remainder of the decade. Gene Burton of Albemarle County started a teenaged squad in the mid-sixties that had a two-year run, and then at the end of the decade Burley High teammates Dopey Sims and Johnny Nowell headed up another decent Charlottesville team for another brief run. Neither team compared to the Squeeze-Ins.

Nats Are Mighty

The Orange Nats were a team of young men representing black baseball in Virginia and during their tenure they came to represent the town of Orange, Virginia. In the fifties the Orange Black Sox, the first successful black ball team in the town,

Top: Greenwood Hawks, August 6, 1961, Charlottesville's Booker T. Washington Park. Kneeling (l-r): Roger Howard, William "Winky" Sims, James Blair, Hildrie Barbour, Estes "Preacher" Sims, and Edward "Dopey" Sims. Back row (l-r): Unknown, Arthur "Pop" Sims, Charles Shiflett, Harry Brooks, George Collins, manager; Homer Brown, Robert Watts, and Sidney Diggs. *Above:* The Charlottesville Elks pictured sometime in the 1930s outside Rivanna Post 195, 2nd Street, Charlottesville. Team members are unidentified.

disbanded. James Washington, a well-known pitcher and sandlot performer in the region, took it upon himself to form and shape a new team from the black youth coming of age in the town. Washington took a special interest in the team, from their appearance to where they played and the avenues through which the team garnered publicity. He was proud of the young men under his guidance, then and now referring to them as "his boys." The Nats traveled as much as any black team in Virginia, and they played on one of the best ball diamonds in central Virginia at Porterfield Park. Though the Nats played baseball from the late '50s to the late '60s, 1961 and 1962 were seasons that made a case for the Orange ballplayers being as good as any black team in central or northeast Virginia. The name Nats was derived from the Washington Senators who were often referred to in the press as the "Nats."

By 1961 all the pieces were in place for James Washington's Nats. The team had been together for three years, and the players were maturing and had learned a lot about playing ball in the sandlots. Almost all of the starters on the Orange team were current or former George Washington Carver baseball players. At Carver, Orange County ballplayers learned to play like champions and they won their share of state titles.

Bootney Alexander and Isaiah "Zeke" Walker captained the Nats. Some say Walker was one of the best shortstops ever to put on a glove in the sandlots; a few say he was simply the best they had ever seen anywhere. Walker was of average height but had tremendous strength in his shoulders and arms. At shortstop he played with his pants high and his cap pulled low, and one wondered if he could see anything at all; but no one could get a ball by Zeke Walker. Pitchers facing Walker were satisfied when he hit doubles and singles because it was no secret that any fastball or curve belt-high could be seen leaving Porterfield on the rise when Zeke brought the bat around.

He was powerful and he was consistent. Orange players rallied around Walker because he performed week in and week out and that made him an obvious choice as one of Washington's team captains. The Nats carried no fewer than twenty-four players in the early sixties. Many players sitting on the bench in Orange could have started from week to week elsewhere. It was a competitive atmosphere and only the best players started for James Washington.

There were a few players from outside of Orange township shoring up the roster. Robert "Butter" Ware, Chin Ware, and Walter Ware were from Culpeper County but gave their allegiance to Orange. Clarence Snead, Jr., was the son of fabled slow ball pitcher Ned Snead. Snead pitched and played shortstop.

He bore a similar sleepy appearance to his father and had learned a few of the same creeper pitches that his father had used to vex the best batters years earlier. Edward Scott, Vernon Junior Watkins, Mettres Murrill, Robert "Red" Terrell and Randolph Howard completed the regular starting Orange lineup. Mettres Murrill was one of the more versatile Nats and one of the team's best athletes, holding down infield and outfield positions. Murrill was also called on to pitch as a starter and take the mound in a relief role in the early '60s.

In a 1961 win over the Culpeper Dragons, Murrill struck out 18 Dragons batters.[6] Robert "Red" Terrell was the youngest of the Nats starters but his accomplishments belied both his age and his size. Red Terrell was short and thin in 1961 and 1962, certainly the least imposing of all the Orange players, but he was possibly the best athlete in Orange County. At Carver High School he was an all-state halfback leading Carver to their own championship season in the '60s. On the gridiron and the diamond he was fleet and powerful. For a time opposing players in the region and beyond underestimated the power the skinny left-hander possessed, though Terrell soon earned their respect.

Bobby Slaughter, Sperryville Tigers:

> The first time I played against Red Terrell I was playing right field for Sperryville. Red come up to bat and he wasn't a big guy no way, but Charles Williams was playing center field and he told me to back up. I took two little steps back. "This little man isn't going to hit it over my head." Ray Jackson was pitching and Charley was saying "Back up!" I still just backed up a couple steps. Ray cocked his arm—Red put one off that brick concession stand behind center field.

No one knew whether the long drives came by way of Red Terrell's swing or strong wrist and powerful lower body. It mattered little because during a decade of play for the Nats Terrell hit the ball with power all over the field. Zeke Walker placed Terrell in the outfield but did not hesitate to bring him into the infield at first base.

Later on as he matured Red Terrell pitched for the Nats. In game-breaking situations with Red Terrell on second, James Washington and his captains knew a good single into the outfield was all that was needed to bring Red Terrell home for a score because he had sprinter's speed.

The Nats used their fully staffed squad to their advantage. Whenever Zeke Walker played catcher, or Junior Watkins and Clarence Snead pitched, another capable player filled the infield position. Bobby Robinson, Charles Robinson, Clarence Robinson, Gilbert Robinson, Ronnie Robinson, Clarence and Moses Humes all contributed the Nats winning seasons of '61 and '62. These Nats were platoon players, some still in their teens getting a taste of baseball with the adults. They came off the bench to hit or start a position in the field when another player went down, and they distinguished themselves with clutch plays throughout the Nats' early sixties run.

Essentially, the seven gave Orange another team of ballplayers to rotate in and out, keeping the competition wondering and making adjustments.

Junior Watkins and Clarence Snead were good pitchers, but Nat ace Randolph Howard was the sensation of the region. A left-hander, Howard wasted no time impressing his teammates and opponents with his mound dominance. By the time he reached the age of seventeen he was one of the best pitchers in the region, striking out many veteran hitters in the black sandlots. Howard had size and good speed. The better the opposing pitcher the better Randolph Howard became.

In duels with Mack Davis of Barboursville, George Sims of Crozet, and George Love of Culpeper, Howard went the distance and usually recorded high double-digit strikeouts. Teams unable to get over Randolph Howard pitching after three innings, often found no success at all. Porterfield Park in the sixties was the premier spot for black baseball in Virginia. The atmosphere and enthusiasm was similar to that experienced by the Washington Monarchs on their diamond behind Pine Knott. Black ball teams first gained access to the park in the mid-fifties when civil rights efforts toward desegregation were just getting in motion. It was the excitement created by the all-black teams and their thrilling play, and it was the following by loyal black fans and then white fans that made Porterfield a great place to play baseball and watch great baseball games. Unlike any black team within a hundred miles of central Virginia, the Orange Nats had a home field outfitted with lights for night baseball.

The accommodations afforded the young Orange team the luxury of playing day and night double headers or Saturday night contests followed by Sunday afternoon matchups. The diamond was well-kept, there was an actual home-run barrier in comparison to other black ball diamonds where home run balls were hit onto the highway or trees and the field was level and regulation. Other teams in and out of the region loved coming to Porterfield for night games because it gave them an extra game for the weekend. Most of all, former players agree that they played well on scores of rural diamonds but on diamonds like the Nats' at Porterfield Park, they played like major leaguers.

Manager James Washington still reflects back with pride on the time when "his boys" were the highlighted entertainment in the town of Orange.

> The Washington Senators' attendance was going down in the '50s—they were playing in an empty stadium. When my boys played I had 1400 fans at Porterfield Park, black and white, before integration. A big roll of tickets would sell out every weekend easy.

The atmosphere was a sports fan's dream, especially in the setting of a small town. The games were overall unforgettable, and a few of the matchups added to the lore of black baseball in Orange. Porterfield Park had a twelve midnight curfew, which ordinarily would suffice for most weekend events, but not an Orange Nats ballgame. In the early sixties the Washington Monarchs came to Porterfield and played a thriller still talked about on both sides. William "Junior" Carter picks up the story.

> I'll never forget a night game we played down in Orange that went 16 innings. I sprained my ankle in the 7th inning and was just hopping around and pitching on one leg. We played 9 innings before anybody reached first base. About the 12th inning they shut the lights off on us because that was the deadline. Somebody called the man in charge of the stadium and he said we could keep playing but it would cost us twenty-five more dollars. So both teams scraped up $25.00 and they turned the lights back on and we played until 2:30 in the morning before we won 1–0.

In July 1961 Orange hosted Spotsylvania's Tigers on Porterfield in a battle that featured a pitching duel between Spotsylvania speedballer John Akers of the Tigers and Junior Watkins for the Nats. Up until the sixth inning the game went scoreless.

Then Spotsylvania posted a run and added two more in the eighth. But the Nats rallied in the ninth when Clarence Robinson, Edward Scott and Roger Jackson all singled and then scored on singles and doubles by Gilbert and Bobby Robinson. This was all either team earned because at the stroke of twelve the game was halted at 3–3 without a reprieve this time to prolong the contest.[7]

As exciting as the out-of-town battles made Nats baseball, nothing compared to Barboursville versus Orange. As the teams were situated twelve miles apart, this was the game for the bragging rights to the area. Seasoned old-school players against the new generation, they knew each other's strengths and weaknesses, but it was always a titanic struggle between the two. Mack Davis took the mound for Barboursville; Orange used Randolph Howard and Junior Watkins alternately to try and solve the riddle of stopping Barboursville's dangerous heavy hitters in Johnny Frye, Buddy Davis, Sam Buckner and Carrol Bates. Fans witnessed a lot of strikeouts and many key plays made to swing the momentum from one side to the other. No one left a Nats-Giants game early.

Players on both teams knew that they had to step up the level of play and assert themselves and became decisive factors in the outcome. In the late fifties Nats batters were plainly intimidated by hard-throwing Mack Davis, but the more the teams met, the better Orange sluggers such as Zeke Walker learned to hit Davis' heat. It was emphasized to the young Nats by James Washington to go out and battle, keep the game within reach, because if Mack Davis gained a comfortable lead no one in Virginia could overtake him. Mack was known to close the door on good hitting teams in close games routinely, and he certainly sat on teams in one-sided contests. Years later Howard Ware mused that Mack Davis, also an umpire when he was not on the mound, used to *umpire* the Nats' Saturday night games and then pitch against them on Sunday's knowing what they could or could not hit.

The community and the city met up several times a season with the last of the battles taking place in early October. The Nats were tough to beat at Porterfield Park as were the Giants on Echo Valley Road, but the outcome was usually an even split between the rivals. Scores were always close, 6–5, 5–3, 2–1. Occasionally one side pulled away decisively from the other early in the game.[8]

There was an attempt in 1961 to maintain a six-team league amongst the teams of Barboursville, Gordonsville, Cismont, Lahore, Orange, and Culpeper. This attempt at league play was a precursor to the Shenandoah Valley League formed in 1963. Details and games chronicled to support play in the '61 league were not published. The interleague standings posted in the *Charlottesville Albemarle Tribune* at the season's end illustrate that the league was a competition between the Cismont Braves, Culpeper Dragons, and Orange Nats. Gordonsville and Lahore finished poorly with records of 7–12 and 4–7. Barboursville only completed ten games, leading to the assumption that in 1961 the Giants were still traveling around the region and northern Virginia to fill out their schedule.[9]

Culpeper was heralded as the second rival for the Nats in the fifties and sixties.

Orange and Culpeper ballplayers attended George Washington Carver high school together, played sports together, so it was basically a divided Carver baseball squad facing off in the summer months. Of the four recorded encounters between the Nats and Dragons in 1961, Orange won three of the four ballgames. After a barn burning 12–10 Orange win at the start of the season, Culpeper, paced by pitcher George Love, earned a 4–2 July win at Culpeper. Love limited the Nats to five hits total.[10] The next clash occurred on the last day of August at Porterfield Park.

Zeke Walker sent Mettres Murrill to the mound and Murrill worked Culpeper over for nine innings, striking out 18 Dragons with only 2 walks as Orange cruised to a comfortable 6–2 victory.

A week prior Murrill had gone to the mound against the Esmont Giants of Albemarle County and fanned 12 Esmont batters before self-destruction set in the 7th inning and Orange lost an 8–7 heartbreaker.[11] Labor Day weekend set the stage for the final game of the season and series at Farmers Stadium in Culpeper. Randolph Howard started his last game before moving on to the collegiate level with a stunning performance as he held the Dragons and their best hitters scoreless until the bottom of the ninth. Culpeper pushed over two scores when Howard walked two batters who were then brought around after a hard hit single to the deep part of the field. Orange jumped on Culpeper early in the game with Ware, Zeke Walker, Robinson and Murrill each posting marks of 2 for 4. The win gave Orange their 16th victory against 6 losses and a near seventeenth when a final showdown with Barboursville was called early due to rain.[12]

Prompted by strong wins over the experienced ball teams in central Virginia that included Barboursville, Culpeper and a Richmond semipro club, manager James Washington placed the Nats on a road schedule in 1962 against the best black teams in northern Virginia and Washington, D.C. Only rivals Barboursville, Cismont, Gordonsville, and a Culpeper County team, Lignum, were within an hour of Orange. All other competitors scheduled were far north and east. Surprisingly the Culpeper Dragons were dropped from the summer schedule, replaced by the Sperryville Tigers of Rappahannock County. The Tigers were a multi-talented team that would set the baseball standard for the young Nats and many other black ball teams in 1962.

Orange stumbled, leaving the gate in a hotly contested 6–5 loss in Lignum, then hosting the Tigers of Sperryville the following week, lost by an identical 6–5 tally. The Nats regrouped and posted a satisfying 14–9 win over longtime foe Gordonsville, before traveling north to Rappahannock County to play on the Tigers diamond at Horseshoe. It was as if the Tigers were in charge of the Nats' trial by fire introduction to black baseball. Sperryville handed Orange an 18–6 walloping, letting the young Nats know that they were competing on a different level of baseball. James Washington held council with his team leaders, Bootney Alexander and Zeke Walker, and plotted a plan to snap the team back into the reality that they were ready and capable of playing and winning against Virginia's best. Orange marshaled its forces together after the humbling Sperryville defeat, and then forged ahead into a winning streak eleven games long.

Playing two needed games at home, Orange stepped back onto the diamond and battled, first triumphing over Gordonsville the second time 6–5, and then winning a 6–5 confidence booster against the Alexandria Braves. At that point and time the Braves were considered to be the best team in northeast Virginia with the best position players available. With two momentous wins behind them the Nats began their streak giving the entire town something to talk about. Orange rolled over Centerville 15–7, crushed Falls Church 11–1, and then posted three straight wins over Washington, D.C., the last victory a 9–1 trouncing. The next victories came over Inlet, Cismont, and another return win over Falls Church 3–1. Holding down the Fairfax County team once again, Randolph Howard whiffed 17 the Falls Church order. In a Saturday contest, Orange cruised to a severely one-sided win over a white Staunton, Virginia, team, Pine Grove, 19–5. Clarence Snead struck out 18 Pine Grove batters in six innings of work.[13]

Orange was hot; it appeared that the young Nats might only lose two games all season long. Mid–August presented an open weekend on the Orange schedule prompting James Washington to enter his team in an all-star game promoted by Ellis Glasgow of Little Washington, billed as "East versus West." The Nats were allied in the East with rivals Luray, Little Washington, Sperryville, and Greenwood, versus Culpeper, Strasburg, Winchester and Front Royal. The West All-Stars won the first game of the doubleheader 9–4, but the East stars charged back in the nightcap and shut the door 5–0. Fans in attendance best remember Dopey and Preacher Sims hitting back-to-back home runs.

The highway awaited the Nats—their destination, Alexandria. The Braves had not forgotten the 6–5 squeaker they had lost down in Orange. Winning was serious to the Alexandria squad; losing was all the more serious. Led by the best pitcher in northeast Virginia, known only by his last name, Stanley, the Braves shut down the Nats 12–0 ending their impressive winning streak. The Nats could not cave in after the loss and there was no time left for a breather. With two weeks left in their season Sperryville and then Barboursville awaited.

In those two remaining games in early October, the Nats played like champions. Sperryville arrived at Porterfield Park riding its own winning streak, having beaten the best in northern Virginia and West Virginia all summer long. Randolph Howard put the Nats' season on his shoulders and pitched a three hitter against one of the best hitting teams in northern Virginia.

Going into the fourth inning the game was scoreless before Sperryville secured a man on and then worked their precision like squeeze play to score the runner. The run would be the only tally for the Tigers. The Nats' Red Terrell shook up the Sperryville defense, later racing home on an errant wild pitch to the plate. Terrell seized the momentum again in the 7th, drawing a walk, stealing second and third, and then bringing home the winning score on a clutch Clarence Robinson single.[14]

Barboursville came to Porterfield for the first time during the '62 season. Normally the Barboursville-Orange diamond duels were a best two out of three during the season, but it would be only a single October game for the neighbor-against-neighbor bragging rights.

Junior Watkins received the call for the Nats, entirely reasonable since Watkins had been rested with an arm injury most of the season. Randolph Howard was weary after going the distance in close ballgames the previous month. Mack Davis took the mound in Porterfield as always. Watching Mack Davis warm up, hearing the pop of his fastball, his pause to spew out some tobacco, one gained the sense that he claimed Porterfield as his house as much as any Orange pitcher. It was always a personal challenge Mack Davis issued—he was going nine, could you?

Five innings into the Saturday night ballgame it was zero to zero. Mack Davis was sending Orange batters back to the dugout, and Junior Watkins was cutting the Giants batting order down to size. Both teams rallied for scores but the Nats came up with four to Barboursville's one. Chinn Ware crashed a double against the Porterfield barrier and scored on a single by team captain Zeke Walker. Orange now sat on a 5–1 lead that dwindled at the top of the ninth when the Giants earned two quick scores.

Pandemonium ringed Porterfield as Junior Watkins faced the heart of the Barboursville batting order with one out, and the Giants' winning runs on base. Johnny Frye, the Giants batter known to smash home-run balls out of sight, went down swinging for the second out. Still Orange was in jeopardy of losing their last game. Charles "Buddy" Davis was at the plate and he was a game breaker.

Davis could either tie or win the game with one swing of the bat, and if the Giants went ahead it was going to be three tough at bats against Mack Davis, not known to throw a game away. Watkins went into his windup and Buddy Davis hit it hard, but Watkins had accomplished what he needed with the final pitch—he had kept the ball down and though Davis had hit it with all of his power, Chinn Ware controlled the hot grounder down the third base line and make the final put out.

It was time to celebrate for more than one reason. The Nats first congratulated each other on a 14–4 season record, they could now appreciate the eleven-game winning streak that pushed them to the season mark, and they had preserved the record by defeating their all-time toughest opponent, Barboursville. Robert Red Terrell, still in high school, was the team's most valuable player for 1962. Terrell saved many games with his defensive play in the outfield, produced run-scoring rallies with his timely base stealing and ended the season with a batting average of .312. Four other Nats batters were right behind Red Terrell. Edward Scott batted .309, Roger Jackson posted a .305 average, Zeke Walker finished at .303, and Chinn Ware splintered the lumber dead on .300.[15]

All Orange pitchers with the exception of Randolph Howard posted undefeated marks. Clarence Snead had four wins without a loss; John Akers on loan from

Orange Nats, 1962. Front row (l-r): Butter Ware, Chinn Ware, Edward Scott, Clarence Snead and Randolph Howard. Back row (l-r): Roy Long, Red Terrill, Zeke Walker, Junior Watkins, Clarence Robinson and Ronnie Robinson.

Spotsylvania went 3–0 for the Nats. Due to injury Junior Watkins made only one appearance and perhaps his most gratifying, the 5–3 win over Barboursville. Nats ace Randolph was the workhorse called upon nearly every weekend against all comers. Howard won six ballgames and lost just one—the crushing defeat at the hands of Alexandria. Randolph Howard was now a matured ballplayer, having persevered against some of the best hitting teams in the north and northeast of Virginia.

The '62 season was the Nats' best during their days at Porterfield. This was pre-Vietnam; players were not yet conscripted for service, and some were college bound but returned to play in the summer. Nats players were 17 to 21 at the time, not quite settled with families. Only the Tigers of Sperryville, to whom Orange lost two games during the season, finished with a better record. Despite playing only 18 games, it was the quality of competition and road victories that makes a strong argument for the '62 Nats being one of the best teams of the decade.

ORANGE NATS 1962 SCHEDULE

Lignum	6	Nats	5
Sperryville	6	Nats	5
Gordonsville	9	Nats	14
Alexandria	5	Nats	6
Centerville	7	Nats	15
Falls Church	1	Nats	11
Wash DC	4	Nats	8
Wash DC	1	Nats	9
Inlet VA	0	Nats	10
Cismont	3	Nats	6
Falls Church	1	Nats	3
Pine Grove	5	Nats	19
West Allstars Vs East Allstars Winchester VA*			
West	9	East	4
West	0	East	5
Alexandria	12	Nats	0
Sperryville	1	Nats	2
Barboursville	3	Nats	5

*All-Star Game coordinated, promoted by Ellis Glasgow of Washington, Virginia. The 1962 East vs West Allstar game was held at Porterfield Park in Orange not Winchester, matching the Orange Nats, Gordonsville Eagles, Buckingham Grays and Wilmington Eagles vs. Cismont Braves, Sperryville Tigers, Esmont Giants and Greenwood Hawks.

NOVA

NOVA, Northern Virginia. The National Pastime in twentieth-century America was no less popular around the nation's capital with several presidents onsite at the old Washington Nats' opening days to throw out the first pitch. D.C. was also home to the Negro League champion Homestead Grays for several seasons. Thus, not surprisingly, black baseball became popular from south D.C. to Manassas in Prince William County, Virginia. Loudon County hosted a Leesburg town team and also had the Purcellville Athletics who rivaled the Arlington Athletics. Middleburg had its Braves in seasons gone by; counties outside of the District of Columbia maintained a residential, business and rural landscape, undeveloped areas making perfect sites for baseball fields and games.

Because they were in reach of the nation's capital and around more paved streets and sidewalks NOVA ballplayers were still city boys traveling out of town on Saturdays and Sundays to play against the country boys—and loving every visit. NOVA teams loved the change of scenery and more, the hospitality, win or lose, and even if they did not notch a win, they traveled east again well fed with the best in Mid-Atlantic Virginia country cooking.

Today, driving in any direction withing 30 miles of the nation's capital takes one past subdivisions, youth league fields, shopping centers, new business parks in Fairfax, Springfield and Manassas; it is no longer your grandfather's Northern Virginia scenery.

The Falls Church baseball team played at James Lee Community Center, the aligned playing field facing Virginia Route 50 north and south to and from Arlington and D.C. Today it is impossible to fathom Richard Slaughter or Robert "Red" Terrell hitting home run blasts into Route 50 without causing a traffic pile-up and incurring the wrath of destination-bound motorists. With the development of shopping malls throughout Fairfax County, a mid–1960s capital beltway and more residents in and around D.C., the changing landscape changed the prospects for available playing space. The 1960s were the final inning in the golden era for black baseball in Northern Virginia.

Barnstorming Boo Waller and the Ivy 9

Every level of athletics has a noncompetitive team or two. These teams are the hapless but often loveable underdogs always seemingly playing against the odds and more often against themselves. The 1960s Ivy Eagles were much like the early 1960s Mets. The Eagles made outstanding plays which were nullified by disastrous blunders. There were a few dedicated players and scores of unreliable ones. The team was often short of equipment, short of players, but they never stopped playing baseball. The community support never declined; fans came out with the incentive to root the Eagles on to a win on that given Sunday. And when they won it was cause for a celebration.

The Ivy Eagles had been around since the thirties, but never seemed to generate baseball talent in the numbers that other Albemarle County, Virginia, communities such as Esmont, Greenwood or Crozet put on the playing field. In days gone by Henry Ivory, Sr., and Clarence Abell had been the standout performers and were sought-after to play on other teams outside of the Ivy community.

Wee Willie Armstead, William Maupin, Sr., Frank and Raymond Jones were mainstays through the nineteen fifties.

Even though the teams were not very competitive, they had fun and passed the enthusiasm and spirit along to the next generation of players. There are always good players on poor teams, and Ivy had its share during its tenure in the sandlots of black baseball. In the '30s and '40s it was Henry Ivory, and in the '50s and '60s James "Boo" Waller stepped up and carried the team with his strong left arm.

Waller was the classic throwback to the days of Negro League baseball when players moved freely from team to team by way of their much sought-after skills. Amongst his many talents in baseball, Waller was a talented infielder, outfielder and a formidable switch hitter. But the highlight of his performance was watching him pick the runner off first base. Anytime an opposing player danced off the bag even a few feet the chant went up from the crowd, "Pick him off Boo!" Win or lose, Boo Waller competed in black baseball leagues and independent contests using his explosive fastball and deadly curves until there was nothing left in reserve.

By the fifties a tight band of neighborhood friends began to make their way into the Ivy lineup. John Armstead, James Perkins, Sr., George Mayo and James "Boo" Waller grew up watching Ivy baseball games and spent every spare moment practicing on the diamond while the adults worked. It never mattered how hot it was outside or whether they had real equipment as long as they were out on the field going through the motions of playing baseball. John Armstead remembers substituting a mattock handle for a bat and having a contest with his friends to see who could drive a tennis ball the farthest.

The progress of the teens did not go unnoticed by the older ballplayers. For them, it was easy to see that the youngsters, as they approached their mid-teens, were ready to take positions in the Ivy lineup.

Manager Willie Wee Armstead, Sr., and assistant Henry Waller, Sr., made two important placements among the young additions to the Eagles' lineup. John Armstead, who loved to play shortstop, was convinced by his uncle to catch temporarily because he had good hands. For nearly two decades after putting on the catcher's equipment John Armstead was Ivy's number-one catcher. The other position change was a surprise for Boo Waller—when the adults approached him about his strong left arm and going to the pitching mound. Learning to pitch was the furthest endeavor from Waller's mind.

James "Boo" Waller:

> Uncle Henry and Mr. Willie Wee Armstead started me pitching. One day we were on the ball diamond practicing and they said we need a left-handed pitcher. They said, "You're the only one up here that's left-handed; a left-handed pitcher is good, and that's what most people can't hit." I said, "No Uncle Henry and Mr. Armstead. I don't like that; I don't like to pitch. I like playing that infield and that outfield." And Uncle Henry told me, and I'll never forget, he said, "Pitch now or never!" That meant not to play ball and that's how I started pitching.
>
> I could throw hard already and I just got in with my brother-in-law James Perkins and George Mayo. They were pitching and they showed me how to grip the ball for different pitches, and I just started practicing how you hold your fingers and seeing what the ball would do and just practice, practice, practice. My best pitch was my curve and drop [slider] and my fastball was untouchable at the time.

Managers Willie Armstead and Henry Waller had made an unimpeachable call in sending teenaged Boo Waller to the pitching mound. He had a strong young arm, and a knack for mastering various pitches in a short period of time. With Boo Waller pitching sight unseen by a large contingent of area teams, Ivy started to win ballgames riding on Waller's sheer dominance.

The downside to Boo Waller's almost overnight talent—every other community team wanted to borrow his services for their pitching rotations. Helping the dilemma along was Waller's eagerness to go almost at a moment's notice and display his mastery for other ball teams before his own home game on Sunday. At the height of his barnstorming circuit he pitched for four different teams throughout the summer months.

This sort of rambling sandlot exploit had played out before with other notable pitchers such as Keswick sensation Bill Minor. Unlike Minor, though, Boo Waller threw hard in every game. It was an accepted fact in black sandlots that hard-throwing pitchers were not only effective but drew big game-time crowds. Securing a pitcher like Boo Waller was a win-win situation, and no one loved it more than Boo Waller. Before a matchup against the Crozet All-Stars, Crozet manager Collins remarked that if his All-Stars lost to Ivy the team would quit playing. Boo Waller pitched Ivy to victory and Crozet lost by three runs. Collins did not call it quits, but he took a personal interest in securing Boo Waller for the Crozet pitching rotation.

James "Boo" Waller:

> I was pitching for four different teams at one time: Greenwood, Ivy, Crozet and Chesnut Grove. I used to rub my arm always but on Monday morning when it was time to go to work I could hardly lift it. Then about two days later when it was time for practice that arm was ready again.
>
> Then on Thursday night it might hurt a little bit, but on Friday the hurt was gone. On Friday and Saturday I would rub it up real good. On Sunday I would rub my arm up good and I would keep my jacket on to keep the heat in and man I could fire a ball.
>
> Greenwood was my favorite team because I was already playing with Dopey and Preacher Sims at Burley High when I started playing there in 1959. On Saturday nights I played on a second younger team George Collins had started. I went over to Stuarts Draft when Stuarts Draft had a team, and Wesley Dean Durrette was pitching for Crozet and they got eight runs off of him in the first inning. They put me in there and Stuarts Draft didn't get another run, didn't even reach first base. Arthur Sims from Greenwood caught me that night, and I swelled his hand up. George Collins who managed Crozet got me from Ivy to pitch against Stuarts Draft in case they needed me and he brought Arthur Sims from Greenwood, and we ended up beating Stuarts Draft 19–8.
>
> I should have went to the major leagues but I started fooling around in high school and cutting classes. I was scouted by the Pittsburgh Pirates at Burley. I started getting bad grades and knew my dad was going to get on me and I just quit school. And I tell everybody that was the worst mistake I ever could have made in life.
>
> If I had the chance again I would have been in the major leagues. That was my best shot.

Childhood friend and teammate John Armstead and many others around the community recognized the value of Boo Waller's skills. Armstead also tried to counsel his teammate to save some of his talent for the big leagues where he was sure Boo Waller was destined to perform. Remembers Armstead:

> A scout came and discovered Boo before he came out of Burley High School. We didn't let him pitch that much for Ivy, but then he started pitching for Greenwood and Crozet. I tried to talk to him and his uncle talked to him, and after a while his arm was shot. He had the talent for the major leagues. There wasn't a left-handed pitcher around that could pick you off base better than he could pick you.

In the nineteen fifties and sixties, major league requirements and expectations were rigid; for black ballplayers the rules were absolute. High school dropouts were not a part of the chosen few to put on a professional ballplayer's uniform. When Boo Waller dropped out of Burley High, none of the major league teams cared how often or how well he pitched because he had failed one of the requirements for selection.

It never dawned on Boo Waller at age 17 that his big-league dreams were done. It was evident, however, that he loved to play baseball, and for the next decade he planned to enjoy the best black baseball had to offer, in Virginia's hardscrabble sandlots. It was not surprising that Boo Waller received invitations to pitch for other ball teams, but it was surprising that he managed to play so well for every one of the teams he played for. He made adjustments as he went from team to team, dealing with the pitching mound, the unpredictable slope of any and all rural diamonds in central Virginia, and most importantly working with an unfamiliar catcher.

Emphasizing the fact that he was indeed on loan when paired with another catcher, Waller was unbending in calling the pitches he wanted to throw. After working his way around the sandlot circuit for a few seasons he was sure he knew the hitters better than anyone. Many disagreements arose between Waller and his catcher of the day because Waller continued to shake off a selected pitch. Boo Waller says, reflecting back, that he preferred being removed from a ballgame rather than serving up a sure home run pitch.

> Sometimes you would have hard feelings between you and your catcher. You are feeling one thing and he feels another, but if I didn't want to throw it I'd just keep shaking him off. He'd call time and come out and I'd say no I'm not throwing it because the batter's gonna send it, and I wouldn't throw it. I'd call the manager out there and say take me out, and I would not throw that pitch. I'm not going to throw a pitch to that guy if I know he's going to knock it out the park. I'm going to keep you down on the infield or in the air, but I'm not going to give you something good to hit.

From game to game and several playing locales, it didn't matter if the catcher was Arthur Sims or John Armstead, they all knew Boo Waller's pick-off move was money in the bank. Adding the cobralike pick-off move to first doubled Waller's defensive value. Here Boo Waller dissects his famed pick-off move:

> It took me three years to get that pick off move and I worked on it and worked on it and finally I became good. I picked off the most men when the sun was shining really bright. Their shadow was on the ground and I wouldn't even have to look at them. I'd just look down at the ground and my eyes would see their shadow and see which way they were going, toward second base or back to first. When I started the motion my arm was on an angle being left-handed and the guy on first thinks you're going home and next thing you know the first baseman has the ball and he's out.
> When the sun wasn't shining the catcher would give me the signal when the guy took too much of a lead and I was so fast going to first base you thought I was going home and I had you out! Jim Dowell was one of the worst guys I was afraid of on third base. Jim Dowell would get on third base and he was a threat. That dude would steal home on me all the time. I'd go into my windup and stop and the umpire would call me for a balk and automatically give Jim home.
> Finally I realized what I was doing wrong, and when Jim would get that big lead I would just back off the rubber then I'd go towards him and get him trapped in a run down with no

way in the world for him to go back to third, and between the catcher, third baseman and myself we had him.

Jim was quick! If he bunted a ball you didn't get him out because he was moving down that line. He never tried me off first base, but on second and third base he gave me a fit until I learned what to do for him.

Over time as Waller exhibited exceptional talent and picked apart the best hitting teams in the region and was basically given free rein by managers to make his own pitch selections. They would win it or lose it on Boo Waller's call. His calls must have been on target because he was called back time after time. Here he details some of the strategy that led to his success.

On a full count I'd send a straight fastball on the inside corner, keep it close to him down around the knees. If I don't get the call and there are no men on base I'm going to work on you on first base until I pick you off. I have held the game up for five minutes just to pick you off of first base. If I walk you I'm going to get you out one way or the other. When the bases were loaded I never liked to get into a lot of curve balls and drops when the bases got loaded because I had a good arm and I had good speed behind my fastball. If I got ahead of you and got two strikes I would throw you that knuckleball or that curve and drop at the same time.

I had a real good knuckleball. If I got two strikes on you when I threw that knuckleball you weren't going anywhere because I was going to get you out one way or the other. And sometimes when I got two strikes on a batter I'd throw two or three knuckleballs in a row and you could count the seams when it was coming up to the plate.

And if my ball wasn't working right my brother Alexander would burn my hand up when he threw that ball back. Alexander could sit down and throw you out going to second. Now when I got a real good hitter up there I had to stick with that curveball and that drop on him. You couldn't feed that good hitter no fastball. I don't care where you put it he was going to send you. The guys that played for Sperryville [Tigers], they were good hitters! You had to keep nothing but curves and drops on them and keep that ball down and sometimes they would send you then. Sperryville had the best team in the league, they were something to beat man! They didn't have nothing but those old pulpwood cutters and they would ride you and send you. They were the top team. Then we found out that Sperryville couldn't hit against a man throwing that slow junk and we started using James Perkins. They couldn't do nothing with a man throwing that slow ball; they can't catch up with it. They were a stone fastball hitting team.

There were some guys that would throw at you and hit you intentionally, but I wasn't like that. Now I might throw a ball close to you intentionally to get you afraid of me especially if you were a real good hitter. I could throw two balls close to your head, and the only way it would hit you is if you run the opposite way and run into it. But if you fall back from that ball, and I come back with it again and you fall back; then you belong to me because I'm going to get you out! I'm not gonna hit you with it but I got you scared now and you're out of there 1–2–3.

On game days when Boo Waller played for Greenwood he was pretty well resigned to concentrate on pitching a good ballgame. Teams like the Greenwood Hawks generated plenty of offensive power to keep a good pitcher in the ballgame. At home in Ivy it was a different story. Every good bat on the ball was needed, and Waller knew he had to get out there and hit, and prided himself on helping his own cause by batting in the heart of the Ivy Eagles order.

During the course of becoming an accomplished hitter he discovered, like many who faced him in the batter's box, that left-handed pitching was especially vexing to left-handed hitters. So without a great deal of deliberation Waller decided it was time to make an adjustment.

> When I was hitting, the left-handed pitchers were hard for me to hit so I started switch-hitting. I said one day, I'm going to get on my right side because I just cannot hit this left-handed pitcher. I'll never forget it was on Armstead Hill and the first time that I got my right side to hit against a left-handed pitcher I got a single. And from that day on I stayed on that right side and the more I stayed on that right side against a left-hander I became real good, and then a lot of times I batted from the right side against right-handed pitchers. I parked the ball down in Orange twice in one night. I knocked that ball out of the park and clean across the road twice in one night on my right side and my left side. John Armstead and I and Frank Frye, we were famous for knocking the ball out of the park. We used to have a little bet at the end of the year we'd put up money for the person who hit the most home runs. One year I beat Frank Frye, the next year John won, then Frank Frye won two years in a row.

While Boo Waller burned up the circuit for other teams Fridays and Saturdays, Ivy made calls of their own to recruit players for their struggling lineup. Herman Howard, just out of the Army, played a few seasons. There was always something to contend with on the Ivy team other than the opposition—either a shortage of ballplayers, a shortage of baseballs on game day, or for a time a quandary over where the team might play its baseball. Besides the old diamond on Armstead Hill the team worked on another tract of land practically throwing distance from Armstead on Rt. 708, now the site of a subdivision.

It was a temporary experiment, much to the relief of visiting ball teams and Ivy ballplayers. The pitcher threw downhill to the batter, and the batter batted uphill. A throw from first base to third base traveled uphill and the third baseman had to lower his aim to prevent sailing his throw over the glove of the first baseman.

It was an improbable setup for regulation baseball, but it was a part of black baseball that nearly every team had to contend with. As long as you could play the ballgame out, complaints were few. In the late sixties Armstead Hill was the permanent site for Ivy ballgames.

Its only drawbacks were in its rising infield that could give a hard hit ball an interesting bounce, and center field sloped off toward the surrounding forest. Any catcher squatting down behind the plate was not likely to see much of the center fielder from the neck down.

The Shenandoah Valley League was in its fourth season when Ivy made its entry. Not being a part of the league, the Eagles played independent ball and had to play many games on Saturdays because league teams were certain to be booked on Sundays. Joining the league afforded the Eagles an opportunity to play more games consistently, but the league presented criteria that made playing and winning that much more difficult for the beleaguered nine. Boo Waller:

> We played independent for years and years until Mr. Scott and Roscoe Burgess formed that league in '63 [the Shenandoah Valley leagues]; then everybody started to join. The way the league worked you had to be fully uniformed, and Ivy didn't have all of their players in

uniform because sometimes we didn't have enough guys to even play. Teams like Ivy were beating the top teams but the teams protested, and the game was forfeited to the other team because we didn't have the full uniform, but we actually beat that team.

The teams made it understood before the game started that they were protesting because we were not fully uniformed, but went ahead just to play the game out on that Sunday. Some of the smaller teams had not raised enough money to buy all the players uniforms. We used to beat Harrisonburg, but the game was forfeited to Harrisonburg because we were not fully dressed. I remember one time over in Harrisonburg they took a spectator, you know—some guys that would like to play ball—just to give us nine players because some of our players didn't show up. It was a long time before Ivy had full uniforms, not until John Armstead took over in the '70s, and then Ivy started moving up with the better teams.

Organized league play did not slow Boo Waller's trips around central Virginia; rather, he became more in demand. Pitching around the league also gave Waller a good overview of the running of the new league and the rabid aspects of competition now that teams were finally competing for titles and trophies.

If you could have been more than one person on a Sunday and followed those games, then you would have seen it all and know it all. There was so much conflict early on in the league that Mr. Scott and Roscoe started appointing umpires to each game, no more home team umpires. When it came down to the play-offs, teams were pulling good hitters and pitchers to play with them so they could go to the championship, and then we started turning in rosters. If I pitched a game for a team and we won but I wasn't on their roster then that team had to forfeit. If you had a good team—oh man! You had to fuss and argue to win a game because nobody wanted to lose back then.

It was a lot that guys didn't know about the league back then because they were not keeping up with the meetings going on and so forth, so a lot of times they missed out on some important league business. But we had plenty of good times. You could fuss and argue with a guy and twenty minutes later he was still your friend.

Certainly, Boo Waller experienced the best and worst of the Shenandoah Valley League in the sixties. He was an all-star, but in spite of his diamond travels he never pitched on a championship team. Near the end of the decade the good times for Waller almost came to an abrupt end when his enduring left arm finally started showing signs of wear and tear. These were signs he laments that he should have heeded years prior. At first he received cortisone shots like the ones that prolonged major leaguer Sandy Koufax's career. But in time the weakest link gave way.

After I pitched so much—pitching for teams on Friday night and then I was right back out there on Sunday and I'd win them both, but that's what messed my arm up. I pitched from 1959 to '67 before I started having problems with my arm and I had an operation on my collarbone on the day after Christmas in '67. I pitched for more than two teams for eight years before I started having problems with my arm. Whoever called me I would go, and that's when Uncle Henry got mad because I was pitching for other teams and finally put me off of Ivy diamond. Uncle Henry kept telling me and talking to me to slow down. Next thing I knew they wouldn't even let me back on the ball diamond.

I could understand why he got mad at me, but I won for Ivy too. If they lost it wasn't because of my arm, it was because the guys behind me weren't playing. I'd keep the ball down on the infield but then there were guys bobbling balls and missing balls. So I went and played with Greenwood and then I went to Keene [Colts] in the seventies.

At Keene I was going to the games and never did get in any of the games so I just gave up baseball period. But I should be retired from the major leagues right now, and I blame myself—I could have been there. My arm doesn't bother me anymore. I'm fifty-six years old and I know I can still throw a baseball given the chance.

Sperryville

As the 1960s unfolded, Sperryville, Virginia's, recognition in black baseball returned after a thirty-year hiatus. Located in a pastoral setting of farms and country stores bookended to Little Washington, Virginia, Sperryville's Sunday sounds of silence gave way to cheering fans and echoing bats around a new ball diamond at Horseshoe on Rt. 211. The formation of the new Sperryville team a few years earlier was not without controversy; half of the lineup came from the Washington Monarchs' 1950s squad. No one recalls why or how the division occurred, only that it created an intense rivalry and made black baseball in the north central section of Virginia twice as popular as it had been before. Once again, Sam Aylor recalls growing up around his lifelong home of Sperryville:

> Around this area we had nothing to do—nowhere to go. I'd come to your house … lets say you lived on somebody's farm, there's a big open field out there, that's where we played ball everyday! That's all we had to do after we got our chores done at home. We weren't old enough to work. You get all of your buddies together, I'd play you every day! You wear me out today tomorrow I'll wear you out! We'd laugh, go on home and start again tomorrow. That's how we learned to play.

The Tigers were a new ball club with a competitive spirit and competitive goals. They played well and presented themselves well, somehow raising enough money to not only cover the cost of equipment, but also uniforms.

For a time Sperryville shared the Washington Monarchs' diamond behind the Pine Knott Inn on Rt. 211. With the developing rivalry between the two ball clubs it was only a matter of time before the Tigers looked for their own playing space. Sperryville residents supported the new team, happy to have baseball back in the community. Local resident Harry Starks donated his hayfield for the team diamond, and Howard Butler laid off the field's dimensions. Butler contributed much of his time and support to help the team make a positive impression in the community. The players built a grandstand with a roof out of scrap parts from old buildings from area farms, and there were dugouts for the home and visiting teams. These were amenities largely unheard of in Virginia's black sandlot baseball, but the Tigers were goal-oriented young men who wanted to project a progressive attitude.

There was a one dollar admission fee to home games gladly contributed by black and white fans from the Sperryville community.

The Sperryville Tigers lineup in the late '50s featured half a squad of seasoned performers in black sandlot ball, and new up-and-coming ballplayers like Sam Aylor still in the learning and developing stage. Sam Aylor's father was a standout catcher on the highly competitive Sperryville teams of the '30s and '40s. The Aylor children were raised under the disciplinary ethics of church, work, and school. Any other digressions except baseball were forbidden. The black youth of the community poured themselves into baseball on the local team; it was what they looked forward to from week to week. Consequently, since the adult team was the only source of team-oriented baseball, youngsters had to become ready to play with the adults at an early age or not play at all.

Sam Aylor explains:

> Louis Butler was the manager and I started playing when I was twelve. I started out as a left fielder because I could run and if a ball was hit in the gap I'd run it down and catch it; but I couldn't hit! Two outs and my turn at bat everybody would just start gathering up the gloves. The reason I struck out so much [was that] I was afraid of the ball. Everyone was bigger than I was, faster and stronger and I was afraid of the pitchers. As the time went on I quit being afraid, and I could knock the cover off a ball. On the Sperryville Tiger team we went out with one thing in mind—winning fair and square. But we went out there to win. We didn't go out there just to play a game and have fun, we went out there to win. They were hard games, I was catching a lot back then, and I was kind of small. Those bigger guys would bowl me over, I'd get up, brush myself off and keep on catching. It hurt me but I didn't let them know it hurt me. Those guys played hard.

Younger players skilled enough were placed in the outfield for their speed, and at the bottom of the batting order until their hitting came around. The Aylors, Williamses, Fryes and Jacksons formed the roster of the 1950s and 1960s Tiger teams. William "Moody" Aylor played third base and started at catcher. He was a solid hitter and also served as team manager in the '60s. Sam Aylor played the outfield into the '60s holding down right or center field. Center fielder Jesse Frye, the fastest player on the team, moved Sam Aylor to right field; he could run any ball down, and he had a good arm. Young Sam Aylor, though one of the smallest players on the diamond, eventually ended up at catcher because his hands were a bit faster than those of older brother Moody.

In the late fifties, Charles Williams, Jr., was recognized as one of the best shortstops in Northern Virginia. He was tall, had great speed, and had a cannon for an arm that made him become a Tigers pitcher. He would have remained at shortstop were it not for the development of his younger brother Thomas, known to all as "Dootley."

Dootley Williams compared to the modern day shortstops; he had size and possessed great range. The younger Williams had the ability to go into the hole behind second and third base, backhand the ball and fire a rocket to first base for the out. The one asset both Williams brothers shared was their ability to hit monster home-run blasts. As Mack Davis recalls, "If you made a mistake against the Williams brothers you had to get another ball." Charles and Thomas Williams were reportedly scouted in the 1960s for the major leagues. The St. Louis Cardinals in particular had an interest in Thomas "Dootley" Williams. Opponents to Sperryville in the sixties remember all of the Tiger infielders having strong arms that whipped the ball around the diamond almost faster than the eye could keep up with.

Outfielder James Johnson, Jr., was the most consistent hitter in the Tigers order, routinely going 4 for 5. Johnson had the ability to shift his feet and smash hits through holes in the other team's defense. Many believe his ability came from his strong wrists and lightning-fast hands. He was not known to hit many home runs, but because he could hit them anywhere he wanted, Johnson batted cleanup.

In the pitching rotation for the Tigers, Charles Williams pitched, and had a good fastball and overhand curve. Ray "Shotgun" Jackson had it all. Jackson could throw heat, but he had more breaking pitches than the average country ballplayer. Jackson was Sperryville's ace due to his versatility. Says Sam Aylor, "Some hitters would have been better off staying on the bench than to go up and face Ray." Jackson had speed and great control, and the catcher barely moved his mitt when Shotgun Jackson pitched a ballgame. Junior Carter of the Little Washington Monarchs filled a spot in the Sperryville rotation at various times during the sixties.

Big Bill Aylor, the former Monarch standout, sided with his kin when the Little Washington squad split in the '50s. Bill Aylor played first base and pitched for Sperryville. Bill Aylor's arm may have been at its strongest in his teen years, but he was still one of the hardest-throwing pitchers in Virginia, almost knocking his cousin Sam over when he released his fastball. A little wild at times and known to hit batters, Aylor was both intimidating and effective. Bill Aylor batted in the heart of the order where he was still one of the biggest long-ball threats around.

On the Sperryville squad of the early sixties, Big Bill Aylor is most famous for an unforgettably poor performance against the short-lived Cismont Braves in Albemarle County. "Big" Bill Aylor lived and worked around Gordonsville, Virginia, for a time, but befriended a few of the ballplayers from the Cismont community. Being a baseball man and living nearby, Bill was prompted to attend the Cismont team practices and even volunteered to pitch batting practice. As fate would have it Sperryville came to town to play, and the Tigers' starting pitcher was shelled from the words "play ball."

Every time Sperryville players looked up, the ball was sailing into the trees surrounding the short Cismont ballfield.

A fuming Bill Aylor surveying the scene said, "You won't smell no more," and promptly took to the pitching mound for Sperryville! Big Bill's first pitch boomed off the bat of a Cismont batter and disappeared into the pines for a home run, and "Big" Bill Aylor was through before he started.

Adding insult to injury, Cismont's winning pitcher, a skinny left-hander without the power to break a window pane, had the Sperryville batters breaking their backs trying to hit a slow breaking curveball. The final tally, Cismont 21, Sperryville 7.

It was the worst whipping the team had ever endured, but it left the door open for a rematch of special significance in Sperryville. Sam Aylor picks up the story:

> They had a little left-hander—he didn't weigh a hundred and ten pounds soaking wet with an

overcoat on—just barely getting the ball up to the plate, and we couldn't hit him to save our lives. So, that's how we got to know Richard Slaughter. We'd heard about him, but he was living in New York at the time. So somehow we got a hold of him, wrote him a letter and told him when we were going to play and would he come down and pitch for us if we paid his bus fare. I guess he said yes because he was here.

There was a left-hander here wasn't a pitcher or a ball player just threw the ball, and we took batting practice off of this guy every day for a solid week! This little left hander come back up here to pitch against us at Horseshoe [and] we wore him out! We actually wore him out! And Richard pitched for us against them and they had never seen him, didn't know where he was coming from and we wore them out. Down there Cismont beat us bad, and that little left-hander was just barely getting the ball up to the plate and we couldn't hit it. We beat them by four or five runs but it was no such score as what they beat us by down there. Cismont never did beat us after that.

The Tigers were so humiliated and humbled by the lopsided Cismont loss that they had begged the services of Richard Slaughter who was by then playing semipro ball in New York State. Slaughter, originally from Reva in Culpeper County, was glad to return home to play baseball. In the redemption contest versus the Braves Richard Slaughter struck out 18 Cismont batters, walking only 2 in Sperryville's 8–2 win.

When he became a member of the Sperryville Tigers, he brought a few of his cousins from Reva along. Roy Jackson, Henry Shanks, Jr., and Bobby Slaughter all played for Reva and Culpeper. The Reva team was gone after the fatal Woodville car crash in 1959, so the remaining players were welcomed in Sperryville.

A very good team became great when Richard Slaughter joined the Tigers roster. He was experienced, having played ball with adults since age fourteen, and at any time Richard Slaughter was one of the best players on the diamond. In his time it was said that if you wanted him to play the third out he could play it better than anyone.

Slaughter was a stellar first baseman, a left-handed pitcher, and a left-handed hitter, excelling at both. He had an excellent curveball, and he was the Tigers' best hitter.

Watching Slaughter's effortless swing it was hard to believe the ball went anywhere, but he could hit a shot four hundred and thirty feet easily. In one memorable at bat, a blast from Slaughter's Louisville Slugger knocked the window pane and sash out of a local resident's window, the ball coming to rest on the bed of the distraught lady of the house.

Despite being left-handed, Slaughter could play catcher if the team needed an emergency backup catcher. With the addition of Richard Slaughter, the Sperryville batting order was terrifying. In the words of Sam Aylor, "If any pitcher went through the Tigers lineup twice he was good." While it seemed Richard Slaughter could hit almost any pitch, 6'5" outfielder Lawrence Hutcherson could hit them even farther. Sperryville played a game against an Arlington team in Northern Virginia. Hutcherson came to bat, and on the second pitch got the cut in on the ball he wanted, and it was gone. Fans and teammates were tracking the baseball, waiting for it to disappear, but it was a windy afternoon in Northern Virginia that day and unbelievably they saw the ball get trapped in a gust and move back toward the field! The ball was blowing in the wind, and when it finally dropped, it was still over the outfield fence—that was Hutcherson at bat.

Bobby Slaughter on batting in the Sperryville order:

> They had some good baseball players around here back in them days. I was playing in Pittsburgh when I left to come down here. They had some good ballgames and good ballplayers in Virginia. I thought I could play pretty good—that first year I played for Sperryville I was hitting .352 and there were five guys beating me. Richard Slaughter was hitting about .500.

Former players from Virginia's 1960s era of black baseball endorse the Tigers as one of the best hitting teams anyone had to face. Without a doubt their batting order personified power, but the Tigers also prided themselves on the strategic run-scoring maneuvers.

The hit-and-run and squeeze play were constants in the Tiger offense. They thrived on winning low-scoring ballgames, because there was good speed in the lineup and several players were proficient in the bunt technique. The Tigers won a close 1–0 ballgame over their rivals the Monarchs on a walk, stolen base, bunt to advance the runner to third and then a sacrifice fly to score the runner.

The Sperryville Tigers reached their stride of dominance during the 1961 and 1962 seasons. The Tigers played every good team from the Shenandoah Valley to West Virginia to Fairfax County, and won. Compiling a playing schedule was fairly simple for the Tigers since many of the players such as Moody Aylor had been

Slaughter stretching out at 1st base where he most often played, 1968 (author's collection).

playing in the sandlots since the early fifties and knew of teams and players to contact in several locales. To the south Sperryville matched up against Cismont, Barboursville, Madison, Orange, Reva, Culpeper, and Louisa.

In the west games were booked with Elkton, Luray and the Harrisonburg ACs who'd enjoyed an alliance with the old Sperryville teams of the forties. In the region of Rappahannock County, Millwood, Marshall, Winchester, and Front Royal highlighted the Tigers' summer schedule.

Traveling east towards Washington, D.C., Sperryville played home-to-home games with several Fairfax County teams including Alexandria, Falls Church, Vienna, and Merrifield. The Tigers' greatest diamond battles occurred against the Arlington and Alexandria teams where low-scoring contests were the norm. The most talked-about games of the summer were always the Sperryville versus Little Washington pairings.

Richard Slaughter turns on a high fastball, 1967 (author's collection).

Created out of a natural rivalry after the split of the 1950s Monarchs, the Sperryville–Little Washington match-ups were something to talk about from the first game in the fifties to the last game in the early seventies. Unfortunately, other than announcements in the local Rappahannock news promoting the contests, there are no documents listing the outcome of a single Sperryville-Washington ballgame. This is where popular opinion and player recollections come forth. Players outside of Rappahannock County give the edge to the Sperryville Tigers in the '60s, while others proclaim the Little Washington 1950s team as being far superior.

Certainly the intense rivalry that players on both sides speak passionately of even today did much for the popularity of the two teams and further boosted the reputation and excellence of black baseball in Rappahannock County.

By mid–July 1961 Sperryville sported a winning record of 17 wins, 1 loss and 1 tie. The tied ballgame came in a June matchup against the Luray Eagles. The

Tigers captured win number seventeen over a Martinsburg, West Virginia, nine in Martinsburg.

Sperryville got off to an ominous start as Martinsburg bombarded pitcher Charles Williams for six runs in the first inning. Moody Aylor pulled Richard Slaughter off of first base, and sent him to the mound. Martinsburg never earned another run and the Tigers pulled ahead to win 7–6.[16]

The Tigers high-stepped into early August with an eleven-game winning streak including victories over Harrisonburg (7–4), Martinsburg, West Virginia, and a Falls Church ball team. Pitcher Ray "Shotgun" Jackson had an 8 wins 0 loss pitching record and Sperryville's team record stood at 21 wins, 2 losses and 1 tie. They would add four more victories to their record before the season's end.

Former players on the 1962 squad point to that summer season as the best during the team's existence. The '62 Tigers won 30 ball games, lost 2 and tied 1, bettering their mark from the previous summer. The last game lost was a 2–1 nail-biter against a fired up Orange Nats squad finishing up their own winning season down in Porterfield Park.[17]

Sperryville never again equaled their mark of '62 but they continued to win and dominate into the late sixties. The Tigers received their greatest recognition participating in the 1960s Shenandoah Valley League where many central Virginians labeled their northern counterparts the best black ball team of the era. Summing up the playing history of the Tigers, Sam Aylor asserts: "A lot of teams whipped us too. If you beat us today, we'll shake hands, smile and go on, but next time we're going to beat you. We weren't the best of the best but we were right there with them."

The Shenandoah Valley League

Between 1939 and 1979 there were five recorded black baseball leagues in the Commonwealth of Virginia. Over the span of five decades 75 percent of Virginia's black sandlot baseball teams played independent ball. The highest concentration of league teams played out of the southeastern part of the state through the fifties.

In central Virginia the 1952 Four-County League was the only attempt at league play. Black baseball in central Virginia was more popular than ever in the 1960s with more teams and a larger following. Roscoe Burgess, co-manager of the Harrisonburg ACs, and Hugo Scott, manager of the Barboursville (Virginia) Giants, both headed ball clubs who had traveled and played black teams all over Virginia and beyond. They had encountered good teams, great players and the best and worst of playing facilities. One thing stood out when Burgess and Scott compared notes—the ills of playing independent baseball. In some seasons the best teams in a geographic area matched up, sometimes not.

Playing schedules constantly varied because of weather and cancellations.

Often after a much-hyped and -promoted matchup, the weekend rolled around and the ballgame had been called off. After conferring over the course of a year Burgess and Scott agreed that it would be more efficient to know with confidence from week to week who your team would play, and the start time. They were especially convinced that the tradition of black baseball had thrived long enough in Virginia to make organized league play entirely possible.

The first order of business was in convincing area managers and players to participate in the formation of a league, and after years of independent play it was not an easy task. But Burgess and Scott went after the region's well-known managers and players from teams with longstanding traditions and reputations in black baseball. Hugo Scott recruited his nemesis James Washington and his Orange Nats, and Roscoe Burgess convinced Harrisonburg rival Elkton to throw their hat in the ring.

The Greenwood Hawks by the early sixties were one of the best-known independent teams in Virginia. George Collins, former manager of the Crozet Virginia All-Stars, took over as manager in Greenwood and entered the Hawks into league play. The last of the entries was a new Albemarle County team, the South Garden Tigers. South Garden was the product of Covesville's Tigers disbanding after the '61 season, and a few players from the Charlottesville Squeeze-Ins. It was a new team but a powerful collection of skilled players.

Burgess and Scott developed a mixed schedule of league games between the six ball clubs and continued independent games on open weekends. The league operated as the Shenandoah Valley League with ball teams located on both sides of the National Parkway. Players later shortened the title to Shen-Valley.

A structured playing schedule was made up months in advance with a noncancellation policy. A fifteen-minute grace period preceded the start of a game, and a penalty of forfeiture was installed for severely late starts. In the developing stages of league play Burgess and Scott worked on criteria for participation in the league. Standing out amongst all other issues were promptness and presentation.

Former Shen-Valley Commissioner Roscoe Burgess:

> Independent you played on Sunday. The game was supposed to be at 3 p.m., but you might get started at 4 p.m. or 4:30 and it was many times that you were playing when you couldn't see and the game is still not over. When we got the league, it was 3 p.m. You started on time or you forfeited the game. Mr. Scott and I decided that if you're going out there—look like a ball team. You got guys out there with cowboy boots on, straw hats and overalls, and then some guys in baseball suits. That doesn't look like a team to me. If you're going to have a league, then let's look like a league. I gave each manager a few months to come up with uniforms. I was proud to go around to each team. I'd go to your home game, then I'd go to somebody else's and they had uniforms on and I liked that.
>
> [Laughing] Sometimes if there was a really good visiting player at a game and he was willing to play, the manager would take somebody out and give that guy his uniform but at least he was in uniform. Later on we started turning in rosters.

Teams were allowed to carry twenty-five man rosters submitted before the start of the season. Allowances were made for additional players in a team lineup after the all-star break. September signaled the start of the best-of-three play-off series and then an October best-of-five series followed for the championship of the league. For the first time in thirty years Central Virginia's black community teams had a championship series to secure the bragging rights amongst the counties.

For the more dominant teams of Harrisonburg, Barboursville, Greenwood and Orange, clothing was not such an issue; they had played in uniform for years. Other teams struggled either because of lack of team funding or personal finance, but they were all moving in the direction of outfitting their club, and that is what Roscoe Burgess was looking for.

Twenty-four games made up the season length, one game per week from May to October. Teams were permitted to play as many ballgames as they could fit into a weekend but all league games had to be played out, no cancellations.

In 1964 the Avon Wrecking Crew and Lyndhurst from Augusta County joined the league. The following year, Sperryville and Luray joined the league lineup, bringing the total to ten teams. Nineteen sixty-five may have been the first year the Shen-Valley League held an all-star game. Orange's Porterfield Park was one of the chosen sites. The '65 all-star game pitted Barboursville, Orange, Luray, South Garden, and Lyndhurst, versus Harrisonburg, Elkton, Sperryville, Greenwood, and Avon.

These teams carried a lot of respect in black baseball and started the ball rolling for a full-fledged league. Teams playing independent ball outside the league found it increasingly more difficult to book ballgames, because all of the better teams were playing league ball. This encouraged more sandlot teams to consider joining the Shen-Valley League.

In 1966 league champions were awarded team trophies, and individual trophies were awarded to the best players. Soon there were twelve teams as the league grew in popularity. Burgess and Scott worked well together consulting with each other on various discrepancies around the league. They were proud of the all-black league and wanted to project that pride throughout the communities and beyond.

Roscoe Burgess recalls his duties as commissioner:

> Sometimes after games were over I'd come in the house and there would be two to three calls protesting the other team's appearance or arrival time. But then it got down pretty good, and the league ran real well. Mr. Scott was a good man. He wanted the league to do well. He wanted teams to be proud of. "It was an all Black league, but look at them, they look good and they're playing well, and we had some good players in that league."

Competition on the sandlot circuit was at its peak, as rewards and recognition previously unavailable playing independent ball were now possible to garner through effort and unparalleled play. After a few seasons of organized play, major league scouts finally started to make their way around to watch central Virginia's black ballplayers. For many it was flattery arriving a little too late. Major league scouts found a source of untapped talent located on the back roads winding through black communities.

By 1966 the league had grown to twelve teams with the Madison Orioles, and a young team in North Garden. Madison's ball team, formerly known as the Indians, had been together since the early '50s. The Fryes, Beasleys, and Lindsays all played together on the Madison team, and subbed in and out of the Barboursville Giants lineup. Madison played in an area known as Wolftown. North Garden had a ball team for many years, but lacked consistency in its lineup. The Burtons played for a time on the North Garden team. The Smiths and Dowells along with the Gray brothers of Esmont gave the community a good ball team in the early '50s, but the teams were always fleeting as players either quit playing altogether or moved on to other teams.

In the mid–'60s the team again went through a rebuilding process with a few young players from Charlottesville, and a large segment of young players from the Shipman area of Nelson County who traveled north seeking a place to play after losing their ballfield.

The 1960s Shen-Valley League was dominated by four teams. In the east Harrisonburg and Sperryville totaled up the most wins per season, and in the west Avon and South Garden blocked the path to the championship round. Greenwood and Barboursville were top contenders and play-off teams but were always thwarted by the four top teams. Avon constantly blocked Greenwood from advancing and Sperryville or Harrisonburg stood in the way of Barboursville. Orange, Elkton and later Charlottesville were on the fringe of contending for a championship run but usually ran out of gas late in the season.

Covesville became a contender again in the '60s when Jim "King Bee" Dowell returned from prison in 1964 and started up a new team in Covesville that reunited the Dowells and the Hendersons, and added some young talented teenaged ballplayers from the Covesville community. Jim Dowell brought back his singing and talking behind the bat that complemented his playmaking. Though he was in his thirties, everyone could see that he was still every bit the ballplayer he had been in the '50s. After a couple of seasons the Covesville Astros had one of the best records in the league but had to get by neighboring rival South Garden to reach the play-offs. Covesville versus South Garden was a championship series alone.

Late '60s entries of the Ivy Eagles, Massies Mill Cubs, and Madison Orioles fought to avoid the cellar of the Shen-Valley League. Good hitting and fielding were important, but it was usually the team with a deep pitching rotation that contended in the play-off and championship rounds.

Take Your Ball and Go Home

Equipment and uniform issues and playing field conditions during the heyday of black baseball in Virginia are as storied as the games and players. Their version of the pastime was both inventive and unconventional. A former player related with humor buying a box of new baseballs for a game one weekend, only to have another teammate return the box of new balls for twice the number of a blemished lot. You never knew. No one ever saw any of the ball chasers who bolted into the forest after foul balls jumping over trees and tearing shirts on briars for dimes and quarters retrieve a baseball and put it in their pocket. Those baseballs either went into the equipment bag or were put back into play soon after. Thus, it is fitting to revisit the following recollection of which there are several versions.

One Sunday, the Greenwood Hawks traveled across the county to play the Barboursville Giants, two communities as far away from one another as any destination in the league. Both bordered county lines east and west. The two teams had faced off since the early 1950s. Arthur Sims of Greenwood and Mack Davis of Barboursville, both past their primes, were old rivals and old friends too. Age was just a number to the two managers. Arthur was Mack's senior but the force driving the Hawks team at catcher, in clutch hits and always on the bench talking it up to his team and the opposing team. Mack was the last Barboursville manager, super vocal and still one of the toughest pitchers for hitters to face in the league, keeping the Giants in contention late into the summer.

As usual, it was a tight game, tilting back and forth, Barboursville's fans willing their team to win, and Greenwood, who traveled well everywhere, had their faithful fans. Esters "Preacher" Sims pitched that day while his father Arthur, still capable at catcher, coached and managed from the bench.

Esters was pitching well but his curveball was not breaking, and he and his father knew there was something wrong. For Preacher, throwing a sharp curve was like turning a doorknob; his ball should have been falling off the table, but instead it was rolling and tumbling. Giants hitters Johnny Frye and Carrol Bates put slow breaking curves over a row of cow pasture fences.

From the bench Arthur Sims had seen enough and decided it was not Preacher's mechanics that hot Sunday but the baseball, by now a little too brown and a little green in spots too. Edward "Dopey" Sims playing centerfield had a clear view of the unfolding events:

> "Daddy called time and stopped the game. He told Mack Davis, 'Mack, this baseball is no good. We need a new baseball. It's worn out.'" Mack, up from the bench, said "No Arthur. There isn't nothing wrong with that ball. We're not using no new baseball, keep playing!"

Was the worn-out baseball working for Mack and the stuff he was throwing that Sunday; we will never know. Esters "Preacher" Sims did volunteer decades later that the ball slipped just enough upon release to check the rotation he ordinarily expected throwing the curve.

The Shen-Valley League had assigned umpires but no witnesses at that event corroborating whether the umpire asserted any sort of authority or if he chose self-preservation over game managing protocol. Arthur Sims never consulted the umpire; he went straight to the person he knew best in Barboursville, holding his old rival accountable to right a wrong situation—for the Greenwood Hawks' interest.

Years later, Dopey Sims still couldn't believe what occurred next.

> Daddy didn't throw the ball back to my brother. He turned and threw that ball way down into the woods somewhere! My brother Esters said, "Daddy what are you doing? We ain't gonna make it out of here, that was crazy!" It was a long time ago, but I still can't believe Daddy threw that ball away. I'll never forget it.

By the mid–1960s Arthur Sims' role as a player was scaled back to catching alternate games and managing. However, he still had a strong arm, strong enough to toss a beat-up baseball cleanly out of sight.

The Sims brothers had traveled to Barboursville for games since receiving their first gloves and mitts. Nothing had changed with either the atmosphere or layout. It was still one way in, one way out, and the way out was a quarter of a mile away with nothing but Barboursville and Davis kin enroute and they were making a lot of noise. Silence, "Ooh, ahh," then a crescendo of shouts that rivaled the choir and congregation on Sunday.

No matter. Arthur was deaf to the noise; for him the controversy was over the condition of the baseball, not his sense of justice in bringing the game to a halt: he wanted a new baseball.

The Hawks were in from the field and the Giants left the bench ringed around home plate where the Arthur and Mack standoff was in full swing. Maybe a few tried to defuse the situation, but the disagreement was between two strong-willed men and had to play out until the fire was put out. It never got out of hand; it is supposed that Arthur and Mack had their say and decided to play some more baseball. Barboursville was not going to forfeit. The umpire threw in a new-newer baseball. No one remembers the score or who won the game. Did Ester's curve start working? The only thing anyone remembers is Arthur Sims' strong toss. The game-stopping display was bigger, more memorable, and more talked about than any in-game heroics or exciting final score.

Arthur and Mack repaired the hard feelings after the home plate dust up just like that ... with Arthur probably stopping at Mack's house on the way out; Mack always had a chair and a cold one waiting for him. When I was a kid, we often played with one ball and an odd number of players. The only thing agreed upon or satisfactory to both sides was, if the ball was lost, the game was over and everyone went home. In this Greenwood versus Barboursville contest, the ball was not lost; it was tossed. Despite the disagreement Barboursville and Greenwood were going to play on because Mack and Arthur loved competing against one another, *unconditionally*. It was another storied matchup that made black baseball in Virginia.

A.W.C. Inc.

Nelson County had at least four black ball teams in the '60s, but when black fans talked about baseball in Nelson they talked about the community of Avon. A few former players remember the team name being the All-Stars, but former '60s and '70s manager Doswell Diggs remembers that they were the Wrecking Crew. On the back of their new uniforms were the letters *A.W.C.* Diggs unleashed his wrecking crew at least twice a week. Hard-throwing lefty Edward Thompson was trying to work his way into the minor leagues, and Lin Awkard was on the sidelines coaching his younger sons. Doswell Diggs, Jr., called "Junior" by family and friends, was just returning home after a stint in the Army that had taken him as far as Germany; he'd been pulled out just before the completion of the Berlin Wall. Avon manager Junior Diggs reflects on the secret to his team's success:

> The team in Avon was already in place and playing. I got involved the second year after Mr. Scott and Roscoe Burgess formed the league. Robert Jackson was the manager, and then I was voted in as the manager the next year. Avon was well-balanced because we had guys we could pull off of the bench. If one guy wasn't hitting or somebody was having an off day we could substitute another player. We always had a pretty balanced attack with players who could play more than one position.

The ball diamond was a rural used-car lot owned by player Robert Jackson's father. Doswell Diggs convinced the elder Jackson to let the team use the land for their ballfield.

Avon players built bleachers for the fans, and a large concession stand that practically paid for everything the ballplayers needed down to gloves and cleats. Hot dogs, candy, and sodas were fine, but the real attraction was the home cooking served during the game by a relative of the Diggs family. Junior Diggs:

> We had a lady named Elenora Diggs that did all of our cooking for us, and we had people come just for the food. She would cook chicken, ham, cake, pies. People were hollering for her food before the game was started good. People loved her cooking!

Avon's Wrecking Crew made their presence felt immediately going all the way to the championship series against newly formed South Garden in 1964. They lost the '64 championship to South Garden who received a late season boost with the addition of Jim Dowell. Jim Dowell, on his return:

> When I'd first come home from prison in the '60s Covesville didn't have a team—they were all down in South Garden. What happened was I finished that year up with South Garden. So South Garden went to play Avon and I played with them. I got a base hit and I stole to second and stole to third. Leroy Stevens was managing for South Garden so Leroy asked me, "Do you think you can make it home?" I said, "Sure I can, all I want you to do is tell me." He said, "All right, I want you to go!" So I run up the line a little ways and come back studying the pitcher.
>
> The next time I guess he thought I was going to do the same thing. I run up the line and stole home. You couldn't see nothing but dust. I didn't know whether I was out or safe so I just laid there and the umpire called me safe.
>
> So I come back to the bat again and jumped and did the same thing again! I stole second, and stole to third and Leroy Stevens asked me, "You think you can make it?" I said, "All I want you to do is say it." And I run up the line again and went back and then ran up and stole home again. I stole home twice in the same inning.

Avon's Wrecking Crew stormed back the following year to win the west division and face Sperryville for the championship. Diggs' ball teams never lacked offensively or defensively. Avon had good hitters, and several good pitchers. Good players often sat on the bench waiting for a chance to get into the ballgame. It was a key to Avon's success; they produced talent in waves. Doswell Diggs had to beg Roscoe Burgess to permit him to bulk up his roster each season. The standout players were almost too many to mention.

There was the Jackson family, all brothers and cousins. John "Skeebo" Jackson and Robert Jackson were brothers, and Alex, Alvin and Donald were brothers. Alvin Jackson was Avon's best bunter and speediest base runner; once he laid it down he could beat it out. Skeebo Jackson played the outfield and pitched. He was known as the man of a thousand and one slides which he took great pride in displaying during his playing days. Skeebo Jackson demonstrated techniques in sliding that were not seen on televised major league play until the '70s. He had the headfirst slide, the straight on slide into the bag coming up on his feet, and the hook slide around home plate reaching back with the left hand. Jackson's show-stopper was a hook slide around second base and back into the bag completely tying up the opposing infielder's tag. Jackson was a good-humored crowd pleaser and he kept the morale high amongst his teammates.

Most of his sliding displays are commonplace today, but in his era they were rare and magical and masterful.

All Avon ball teams were said to have had several hitters in a row capable of breaking a ballgame open.

Sidney Diggs, a former standout on the Greenwood team, was a deadly hitter and a valuable Avon player performing in the pitching rotation and second base. Shortstop Stanley Harper was considered one of the best hitters and the team's toughest out. Alex Jackson was a consistent hitter, but teammates laughed at his batting technique that appeared to place his head directly into the path of the ball. John Wallace was a power-hitting center fielder. Third baseman Harry "Buck" Flippen was known for his glove and his bat. Flippen, who batted left-handed, once crushed a drive beyond the limits of Avon's diamond, the ball coming to rest an estimated 600 ft. away.

Phillip Clark, Marshton Awkard, Clyde Lynch, and Frankie Fisher staffed Avon's pitching rotation. Robert Jackson pitched and played first base. The five had good stuff on the baseball, but Howard Alexander was the big-game pitcher and big-game player. Alexander's style was a combination of those of Juan Marichal, the famed 1960s Giants pitcher, and Luis Tiant, the Boston Red Sox star of the '70s. He was six feet tall, two hundred plus pounds, and he began his windup by turning his back away from the batter, not as far as Tiant but halfway. Once he completed his turn, then came the Marichal-like high leg kick straight up into the air, and then he turned loose a smoking pitch.

Nineteen sixties Shen-Valley League players agree that Alexander was the hardest-throwing pitcher of all. He was left-handed and threw a curveball that broke two feet down into the strike zone every time. His control was excellent, and he was a very knowledgeable pitcher.

Overview of the Greenwood Hawks ball field as it looked in 2001 (photograph courtesy Jon Glassberg).

Former players point to his windup, though, as the most confounding aspect of facing Howard Alexander, something akin to balling up in a knot. When Alexander came out of that knot the leg was pointed up and the ball was gone. His pitching excited the fans, and they always knew that when sweat began to pour from Alexander's brow he was getting into the ballgame and about to take control.

At his best, 9-inning ballgames pitched by Howard Alexander lasted 90 minutes. That was all he needed to cut a path through the other team's order. Many batters could not see his ball much less swing through it.

In a 1960s thriller against the Barboursville Giants, Alexander pitched thirteen innings versus Junior Strother and won.

He was also one of the big hitters in the lineup and could knock the run in or hit it out. In another encounter with the Giants Howard matched Mack Davis in a 12-inning pitching duel decided when Howard came to the plate and hit a grand slam home run to secure a personal and team win.

The Wrecking Crew developed a reputation as a hard-playing ball club doing whatever was required to win. They were loud, tough, and everyone in the league wanted to beat them. Avon rivaled the entire Shen-Valley League. When a team defeated Avon on any given Sunday it was an accomplishment regardless of the team's winning record. Sam Aylor, Sperryville Tigers:

> I'd say in the league Avon compared more to us than any other team. They had hitters and pitchers, you didn't beat Avon every day—they could play. Avon they played hard. They would

Backstop of the Greenwood Hawks diamond (photograph courtesy Jon Glassberg).

break up a double play and they would come in with the spikes up, and I did too. That's how we played ball back then—we went out to win!

Avon and Greenwood were both in the west, and one had to outplay the other to get to the championship. Greenwood was a play-off contender capable of beating Avon's Wrecking Crew at any time, but luck was usually on the side of Avon, as another team out of the division would often trip Greenwood up, ending the Hawks' play-off and championship run.

Junior Diggs recalls the Avon-Greenwood rivalry:

Every time Greenwood and Avon played we'd draw a crowd. When we played in Avon it was always a big crowd, and when we played in Greenwood it was a big crowd. The first time we beat Greenwood was in Greenwood. The games were always pretty close, no runaway scores. Both teams were shuffling players, and switching positions because most of the players could play more than one position. One team would try to outmaneuver the other, trying to get the upper hand.

Avon came away with one championship in the sixties, but they were always in the hunt, and usually at the top of their division. The longer the season went the tougher Avon played, and they welcomed strong competition.

Outside of league play the Wrecking Crew took on the semipro Waynesboro Generals though without success in any of the matchups.

Many Friday nights the team traveled to Lynchburg to take on teams in the City Stadium in Lynchburg. Saturdays Avon matched up against teams from

Appomattox, Virginia. As good as Avon was in the '60s it was merely a tune-up for their diamond prowess in the early 1970s.

Tigers in the Hunt

After the 1961 season, "King Bee" was gone, and then the team lost their home diamond when the property it was located on changed hands. Half of Covesville's younger ballplayers, led by Leroy Stevens, traveled minutes down the road to join a team in the community of South Garden. They took with them the Covesville team name "Tigers."

Leroy Stevens' brother Wayne Stevens was already a player-manager on the South Garden team, which was made up of older players in the area. Neil Martin from Covesville pitched and Leroy Stevens moved to shortstop. A year later Leroy Stevens took over as manager and brought in a new generation of ballplayers to the South Garden team with ballplaying experience. Leroy Stevens:

> South Garden was good because we had a lot of boys coming out of high school who played under Coach Smith at Burley High, and all of those boys knew how to play before they started playing around the communities. All you needed to do was make up a team because the players knew what was going on.

Albert Singleton played at Burley and then South Garden filling in the pitching rotation. James Vest was a tall overpowering pitcher with a scary fastball that vexed batters as it moved around the plate.

Harold Burton, Meredith "Butch" Whindleton and William Johnson completed the pitching staff. William Johnson's rising sidearm heat may have been the most confounding of all. His sidearm delivery naturally added more movement to his pitches, but he was known to throw a quick pitch as well. Johnson's pitches were all over the plate, so batters never knew where he was coming from.

Donald Byers, another Burley High product, is considered one of the best first basemen of his time. Not only was his gloving ability superb, but he made seemingly impossible stretches for put-outs time after time as if he were made of rubber. Byers was a consistent threat to drive-in runs at the plate. He was joined by his two brothers Clinton and Curtis. Donald Byers shared time at first base with Alfred Martin. By the mid–'60s Alfred Martin looked like the quintessential first baseman—tall, strong arm, broad frame. When Martin stepped up to the plate the crowd hushed.

If you were rooting against South Garden you hated to see "Pepper" Martin come to the plate, because any pitcher's mistake would never be seen again. Backwoods diamonds with outfields that ran forever were not long enough to contain Alfred Martin's blasts. Barboursville pitcher Mack Davis on pitching to Alfred Martin:

Alfred Martin ... when he hit it man it was gone! We were playing against South Garden at Red Hill School and he hit one off me and I don't know where it went, but it went out of sight somewhere. When he first come out of the service, Alfred was a dangerous hitter! Don't throw him nothing around the letters.

Slugger Randall Burton first played for South Garden, and then joined the Nellysford team, but found his way back to the Tigers lineup for Saturday ballgames, and no one complained because he could hit a baseball out of sight.

Donald and Willie Gray from Esmont played Saturday games with South Garden. Johnny Nowell, an experienced area player, could play any outfield position and though Leroy Stevens often had to drag him out to the pitcher's mound, Nowell was outstanding pitching in relief.

Former Covesville ballplayer Rodney Kirby, a left-handed catcher and hitter with long-ball power, led the team in home runs. Teenaged Michael Smith was tall, muscular, and did not know his own strength. His strong arm earned him a try at pitcher, but a lack of control limited his starts. Smith could throw it hard but you never knew where it was going. Abraham Watkins and Raymond Turner were both good ballplayers but often sat on the bench because better players filled positions ahead of them. Harold Burton was not a starting pitcher but against the power-hitting teams of Avon and Sperryville, Burton's slow ball crippled batters swinging at stuff barely making it to the plate.

Left-handed pitcher Mitchell Carter led the South Garden attack. Carter threw heat, whipping a blazing high-riding fastball most of the time. A few compared him to local legend Edward Thompson, but opponents also remember Carter's sharp breaking curveball that made your knees buckle. He complemented his pitching with a professional pick-off move. He was not one of the better hitting pitchers in the league, but he was a proficient bunter and the fastest runner on the team, guaranteed to steal two bases per game. Stevens placed Carter in the lead-off position, and once he was on base, South Garden only needed a single by the next batter to bring Carter in for the score.

Mitchell Carter appeared to be a candidate for big-league ball, but arm problems and then a broken arm pitching in an early '70s game ended his hopes for the major leagues.

By 1962 Leroy Stevens was well known on the black sandlot baseball circuit for his play on the Covesville team. He excelled at a few different infield positions, but became South Garden's number-one catcher.

Stevens was short and stout, and he swung the bat with power, his wrist and forearms flexed, demolishing the baseball. In a 1960s matchup with the Greenwood Hawks Stevens hit three homeruns and on a Sunday afternoon against the Ivy Eagles, hit two homeruns in a row off of former Burley High teammate Boo Waller.

Aside from his duties as player-manager Stevens participated in the organization of the Shenandoah Valley League schedule. South Garden versus Covesville was the hyped community event in southern Albemarle County. By 1965 Jim Dowell had reassembled a Covesville ballclub, and the next year entered the Covesville Astros into the Shenandoah Valley League placing them in the western division with now bitter rival South Garden.

Smiling, Leroy Stevens reflected on Covesville versus South Garden as the most hyped event he has ever witnessed.

> When Jim came back and started the Covesville team, they were in the league and we were in the league. I think they had won a couple, and we hadn't lost a game. They pitched Lee Dowell down there in South Garden against us. Lee probably would have done all right if he had thrown some curve balls but Jim was calling for plain fast balls, and I hit a home run off of Lee that day. Lee got the bases loaded in the first inning, and I hit a home run off of him, and that's what broke those boys' hearts in that first inning when we jumped on Covesville down in South Garden. And we had more people at those games, people with cowbells man, they wanted to see that game; it was like the Yankees playing Boston whenever we played Covesville.

Lenny Dowell remembers the Covesville–South Garden rivalry and Covesville's first redemptive win:

> South Garden was good but I can't give them one hundred percent credit because our guys left us and went down to South Garden, that's why they were good. They had half of Covesville and half of Charlottesville. So we didn't have nothing much because all of our top guys were gone. South Garden had an all-star team and we just had a plain old team. So they had been beating us for two years in a row because they had all of our players down there. They beat us down there. So they came up here and Jim said we're going to try something different to beat South Garden up here today. So what we figured we'd do is put Junky in there. Junky was getting older then and slowing down, but if Junky could make at least four or five innings Lee could do the rest.
>
> So Junky pitched four or four and a half innings and kept them down maybe 5–2. So we put Lee in and he struck the side out. Then Lee got up there with one man on and knocked it clean down into that cornfield! I mean he wooded that thing!

South Garden via their championship wins ruled the organized play of the 1960s, making five championship appearances and winning three. They were able to turn away strong contenders Greenwood, Barboursville and Orange in the play-offs and withstood challenges from rival champions Avon. Only the other Shen-Valley League Tigers of Sperryville interrupted South Garden's onslaught of the mid–'60s. Leroy Stevens:

> I would say South Garden won the most championships, but Sperryville had the best team in the league. We were in it five times, and won it three times. We beat Sperryville twice, once in the play-offs and once in the championships.

League play was competitive, exciting and at times controversial. Commissioner Roscoe Burgess tried to remain neutral, preferring to let the team managers work out differences during scheduled league meetings. If by chance the two parties in dispute were not able to reach an accord then Burgess became the judge or, in some cases, umpire for ballgames mired in controversy. Burgess and Scott implemented assigned umpires a few years after the league's start-up to eliminate unfair advantages and rulings made by any team's "home" umpire. Still there were protests, accusations and unbelievably poor sportsmanship. Says Roscoe Burgess, "There were guys who would protest and almost cry over a ball game, and some of these guys were on the better teams."

There were protests over the other team's arrival time, uniforms and dress, and occasionally the playing field itself. None of the protests were more infamous than that surrounding the 1966 Avon-Sperryville championship game in Avon. The '66 Shen-Valley play-offs came down to Harrisonburg versus Sperryville with Avon awaiting the winner.

Sperryville handled Harrisonburg easily and surged into the league championship against 1965 champs Avon. The two teams notched two games apiece in the best of five series with the home-field advantage finally swinging in Avon's favor for the decisive series winner. Sam Aylor recalls the shocking finish to game five:

> Avon had us beat! They had us beat!
> The pitching mound was supposed to be 60 ft. 6 in. and they had it 66 ft. The reason we caught it was we had a guy who could pitch—he could throw a curveball through your car window and have it come out of your trunk, and it would never get to the plate and we wondered why. So me, "Mr. Smarty," I brought out a tape measure and measured from the mound to the plate.
> Their pitching mound was 66 ft. instead of being 60 ft. 6 in. that's how we won. If we hadn't protested Avon would have beaten us but we protested the game and had their measurements by them, and had their umpire sign the book to the facts. Avon actually beat us but we protested the game and on the protest I won because their diamond wasn't official. The next Sunday we played at Harrisonburg High School and Roscoe Burgess umpired the game. He said, "I don't have anything to do with either team." It was so cold! Lord it was cold! We played in jackets, that's how cold it was, and we wore Avon out. I don't think it went the full nine innings and that was the last time we beat Avon.

There was little argument or controversy in selecting players for the all-star game each season that matched the eastern division against the western division. Porterfield Park in Orange, Luray, Virginia, and Burley Field in Charlottesville all hold memories for former participants in the all-star contest. Leroy Stevens, South Garden Tigers, recalls the late summer contest:

> We went to Luray to play an all-star game and we were playing with the Barboursville Giants and I'll never forget Mack Davis was pitching and Carroll Bates was catching. Bates was a good catcher and used to catching Mack, but that night over there under the lights it was kind of shady and Mack Davis was throwing that ball so hard that it would hit the wood of the backstop and come back out to Mack Davis. So the other team was getting on base and oh boy Avon was riding us, saying they were going to clear us out tonight! They got two scores off of Mack Davis. I went out to talk to Bates because I was managing that night, and Bates said, "Leroy I just can't see!" I said, "What?" He said, "When I see that ball it's going by my head!" I said, "Well you'll get hurt back here!" I didn't hesitate at all. I asked Bates, "Do you want me to catch?" He said, "Yeah!" and went on away from there. But we needed Bates because he was a good hitter, but Bates took himself out of the game. I go back there and I told Mack to throw me two or three balls to get my eye on it.
> You were only supposed to pitch three innings, but Mack Davis pitched four innings and it was scoreless. Nobody touched Mack Davis after that. The only way that they got scores off of

Mack Davis was walking around the bases when the ball was thrown and the catcher couldn't catch it because Mack Davis could throw that ball!

There were so many good players and standouts in the '60s that it is impossible to expound on the qualities of them all, but a few names surface time and time again. Alfred Martin was a favorite player and friend, one of the nicest guys to ruin your team's chance at winning a ballgame. Leroy Stevens remembers that few expansive country ballfields were long enough to contain Martin's prodigious home-run clouts. He was most dangerous in a full count situation. Jim Dowell:

> We went down to Wilmington, and my brother Lee struck Alfred out every time he'd come to the bat. The last time he come to the bat Lee had three balls and two strikes on him and he threw it too perfect; we had them whipped, and he hit that thing deep in the mountain! And won the ballgame off of it.

A scout for the Pittsburgh Pirates approached him in the mid–'60s and invited him to camp, but ironically a groin pull from his days as an athlete in the Air Force hindered his ability to perform at 100 percent. Locally Alfred played for the Charlottesville Squeeze-Ins, South Garden Tigers, Wilmington Eagles and Ivy Eagles.

Wilson Blakey was a smaller-sized strikeout leader for the Harrisonburg ACs in the '60s. Blakey relied chiefly on his fastball, overpowering and intimidating would-be batters. He had starred on another Rockingham County team, the Harrisonburg Nationals, before joining the ACs in the Shen-Valley League. Sam Aylor:

> Wilson Blakey, his nickname was "ski king"—that's the name we gave him. He could throw almost as hard as Bill Aylor. I couldn't hit him because I was scared of him. He threw too hard for me! The rest of the team could eat him up, but I always had the thought that this man was going to hit me! If he hits you in the leg he's going to break your leg! No, I'm not afraid to say it, I was scared of Wilson Blakey! Match for match I don't know who could throw harder, he or Bill Aylor. I still believe Bill threw harder, but Wilson could throw a ball!

The Barboursville lineup of the '60s featured the addition of soft-spoken, sure-handed shortstop Vance Brock. Vance broke in with the team in his early teens, becoming an infield prodigy with big-league potential. He was a deadly hitter, but his fielding skills amazed teammates and opponents. Mac Davis:

> Vance Brock—that boy played three years and never made an error, and when he made the error I'll never forget, we were playing in Gordonsville. The guy hit the ball down through short and he missed it … he was crying and apologizing. I said, "Boy, go back there and catch the rest of these balls." That boy could catch anything!
>
> Vance played with us for six or seven years and then went into the service and Vance got messed up in the service. Vance when he was playing ball with us he didn't drink smoke or nothing. But when he got into the service…. I don't know what happened. He got messed up in the service, got hit by shrapnel and when he came back he was just gone down to nothing. He was just a quiet and funny young man always joking, but you'd never hear him raise his voice. You'd never know he was on the diamond if you didn't see him. He'd kid along with you … but he never raised his voice. He was one good guy.

Esters "Preacher" Sims could play anywhere on the field, including catcher. He was a starting pitcher, and one of the deadliest hitters in the league. Sims played semipro ball with the Waynesboro Generals for several seasons while keeping up his schedule with his home community, Greenwood, in the Shen-Valley League. He, along with brother Edward "Dopey" Sims, received encouraging words from major league scouts, but neither Sims made it beyond the tryout stage. The late Alfred Martin named Preacher Sims as the best player in the Shenandoah Valley League. Sam Aylor, Sperryville Tigers:

> Preacher! Lord—you didn't throw Preacher anything good no time! No time! Preacher was a good ballplayer. One Sunday up at Greenwood he hit one off of Charles Williams or Ray Jackson and I don't believe anybody ever went to find it.

Later in the sixties Richard Slaughter pitched more often in selected matchups, right handed power hitters, teams unfamiliar to the Tigers. He did pitch enough against the Sims Brothers to summate their abilities at the plate:

> I used to try everything I could throw against them—it never worked, and you had to pitch to them being three and four in the line-up. You couldn't pitch around them putting men on base. Greenwood was too dangerous. I remember the last time I pitched against them I had decided I was going to try a new pitch. We were way ahead, killing Greenwood that day, so I said OK, let me try this pitch out. They were down nine runs and wound up beating us by three or four. Man, I never heard the end of that.

Howard Alexander was a starting pitcher and a closing pitcher. He had heart and made many of the formidable Avon squads of the '60s and early '70s go. His pitching style was both interesting and vexing. Players who struggled against Alexander compared his delivery to balling up in a knot and then releasing the ball. He joined Preacher Sims on the Waynesboro Generals roster in the late '60s. Alexander was also a barnstormer locally and would pitch right through an entire weekend if he could get in the games. Ultimately it led to arm problems that sidelined him for good in the early '70s.

From the beginning of the 1960s to the end, Robert "Red" Terrell of the Orange Nats was an all-star. He played the infield, outfield, became a reliable starting pitcher and hit for average at the plate. Teammates and coaches depended on his solid performances to fuel the Nats machine. In 1967 Red Terrell sported a batting average of .413.[18] By the decade's end several major league organizations were giving Terrell a look.

James Bannister played catcher and pitched on the late '60s Orange teams. Bannister was a towering six footer instantly respected for his arm. He was known to stand up out of his catcher's stance and throw perfect strikes to second base, the ball not more than three feet off the diamond dust. It was this ability that earned Bannister a tryout with the Atlanta Braves.[19]

Preacher Sims lived in the western part of Virginia and Richard Slaughter lived in the east, but their abilities were all in the same areas on the ball diamond—pitching, hitting and fielding. Richard Slaughter was a left-handed pitcher and hitter who belted out tape measure home runs that pain former opponents to think about even today.

When Slaughter pitched, if you didn't get by him in the first couple of innings you were through. He had excellent control and his pitching was described as sneaky fast. Richard Slaughter appeared to be a lock for the majors from his first foray into A league ball at the start of the '60s. In a one-sided 1967 Sperryville loss to the amateur baseball team the Madison Blue Jays, Slaughter was offered a position. Recalls cousin Bobby Slaughter, "Major league scouts saw Richard and went crazy until they found out he was thirty years old." Slaughter, Sims, and Alexander were some of the first black players to break the color barriers of Virginia's amateur baseball in the '60s.

Mack Davis was an enduring strong-armed pitcher who loved playing baseball and loved to compete. Though the independent and league play statistics were rarely noted, Mack may have been one of the all-time strike-out leaders on the black baseball sandlot circuit. He fanned batters with numbers reaching double figures as a teenager, and he was still doing the same at forty. Davis and Barboursville catcher Carrol Bates were one of the best pitcher-catcher setups of the Shen-Valley League. Towards the end of the decade Strother Jackson, Jr., of Madison sided with Mack Davis, shoring up the Barboursville pitching staff.

Mel Perrow, Shipman Angels, Massies Mill Cubs:

> Mack was older by that stage, but Mack could still pitch that ball. Then they had a dude named Strother—called him "Big Red." Man, Red had a fastball, and curveball out of this world, and Mack's boys could just flat out play ball.

For those who faced Jim Dowell and his Covesville team in games in and out of the Shen-Valley League King Bee is hands down the favorite and most talked about catcher around. Whether it was talking it up behind the bat, stealing the ball from the batter, or beating the runner down to first, Jim Dowell mastered the position.

Of course his base stealing and being one of the toughest outs at the plate may have given him all-star status alone. By the time league play was at its peak King Bee was in his mid-thirties, and players and fans just coming along probably missed seeing Jim Dowell at his superlative best.

Donald Byers is one of the more talked about ballplayers from the 1960s. Former opponents have high praise for Byers' all-star fielding skills and his consistency to hit well at the plate. Outside of championship runs with the South Garden Tigers, Byers was sought-after by several teams, among them the Wilmington Eagles, Charlottesville, and a local white ball club, the Charlottesville Royals. Donald Byers left the sandlots in the early '70s to devote himself full time to a career in law enforcement.

Byers' teammate and manager Leroy Stevens played more than a decade in Virginia's black sandlots, excelling in the field and at the plate. Stevens had loftier goals coming out of Burley High School, and in his prime made an attempt at the major leagues, participating in a tryout camp with Leroy Powell and Estes Sims. Leroy Stevens:

They'd give you a shirt, a cap and something to eat. You had to have your own glove and spikes. Nine o'clock in the morning man—you're throwing all day long, and then the next day the same thing. Three days of nothing but throwing the ball. Neither one of us made it; Leroy [Powell] had the best chance of making it because he was an outfielder. Estes came back and he had his arm in a sling!

They really worked on him up there because he went up there for pitching. I went for shortstop or either second base. But your range up there was from shortstop to third base and then from shortstop to the back of the hole of second base. So, that's the range they had you running ... steady running and throwing!

Despite the lack of sponsorship, adequate playing facilities, and the obstacle-course fields, the Shenandoah Valley League was largely successful. League records are long since lost and most of what remains are player recollections and a few old newspaper clippings for documentation. The Avon Wrecking Crew won the 1965 championship, and were dominant throughout the '60s. The Sperryville's Tigers capped off the '60s with two championships in a row and are touted by many former players to have been the best playing team in the league. South Garden made four 1960s appearances in the league championship and claimed two trophies while maintaining one of the best playing records in the league.

The Harrisonburg ACs won the first and last '60s championships in the Shen-Valley League. The 1969 win over South Garden was their last before the team became the first all-black entrants into the Rockingham County Baseball League in 1970.

By the late sixties the more competitive ball teams in the Shen-Valley League began to play against college all-star teams in the Valley League. Accounts of such contests were on the minus side for the all-black teams. However, it can be surmised that had they faced off against these amateur players with an all-star lineup of their own, the contest would have been evenly matched or overmatched in favor of the black sandlotters.

Avon lost to the Waynesboro Generals on more than one occasion. Orange and Sperryville both lost one-sided contests to the Madison Blue Jays.

The end of the sixties and early seventies brought on the demise of Orange and Madison with the remaining ballplayers from both squads joining ranks with Barboursville. The 1960s formation of the Shenandoah Valley League could be referenced as the peak of black baseball in the sandlots, and on record was the longest running black league.*

---

*1965 Championship: In this book's original edition the Avon Wrecking Crew is documented as the 1965 Shenandoah Valley League Champions. Updated research utilizing previously unavailable resources and materials reveals that Avon played Sperryville in 1965 with Sperryville prevailing as champions in 1965 and 1966; *The News-Virginian* 1966–68.

VI

Bottom of the Order, 1970–1980

The '70s marked the last decade in which black baseball received active support from its fan base and full participation by black youth. Ballplayers of the new generation pulled ball caps over high-standing tufts of hair called afros. There were more young players who were now getting their chance after watching their grandfathers, fathers, and uncles perform. They brought with them the new attitudes and expressions of the decade. In the vernacular of the times, "this was their thing." A few established stars played their way into retirement with their sons on the same roster. Mack Davis of the Barboursville Giants played with all four of his sons before stepping down from the pitching mound for good in the mid–'70s.

Mack Davis, pitcher, Barboursville Giants:

> Greg played but he was more interested in track; Ricky and Keith played regularly. Towards the end we got Stanley in and he played a little outfield. Vance Brock, Lonnie Trice, Zeke Walker and Ricky Davis are about the best infielders I've ever seen. You couldn't hit a ball by them and if they got to the ball and you weren't on that bag forget about it because you weren't going to make it! You weren't going to make it! And Keith [Davis] was just as good an outfielder that you could find, and if you got off that bag—brother you're gonna be out!
>
> We were in Avon one Sunday playing and this boy hit a double. Hit a double and it rolled under the fence, but you could go back and get it. Keith jumped over the fence got the ball and ran back on the diamond. And the boy rounded second and faked like he was going to third and Keith acted like he was going to throw to third, and just whirled and threw to second and threw the boy out from the outfield! When the boy was walking back through the infield he passed by me and he said, "I don't believe it." I said, "What?" He said, "I don't believe he threw me out," just shaking his head. He couldn't get over it. Ricky and Keith both had terrible arms.

Through the final stages of integration in the South, white players appeared in black baseball lineups on a regular basis for the first time in forty years of play. It was 1970 but black baseball leagues in Virginia were still 99 percent black.

Mel Perrow, Shipman Angels, Massies Mill Cubs, on his generation carrying on the tradition of black baseball:

> We were having fun, we thought we were good athletes, and there was not much for us to do in terms of recreation. People didn't have anywhere to go. So, a lot of it had to do with just plain recreation. It was good fun up until twenty years ago [1981], and you could see the change. Softball was beginning to make a statement, so it was more lucrative for the guys to

play softball and we started losing players to softball. And we also lost players to the white amateur teams, Madison Blue Jays, Charlottesville Hornets.

The Harrisonburg ACs were now members of the Rockingham County Baseball League, but co-manager Roscoe Burgess still served as commissioner of the Shen-Valley League with Hugo Scott as secretary. Nineteen seventy would be Burgess' last year as commissioner. Players began to doubt his leadership, labeling Burgess' enforcement of league rules and policies as too harsh. Teams quit the league, teams joined. Stories vary on naming the league officials of the early '70s.

Several teams dropped out but organized play continued under the title Inter-County League. Most accounts name Hugo Scott of Quinqe the successor to Roscoe Burgess as league commissioner. Despite the leadership quandary, teams held to organized play and players of the era say that black baseball only got better in the '70s.

Here Comes Ivanhoe

> Whether we were winning or losing I always hustled.
> —Ivanhoe Nelson

Through three decades and twenty-five years of play Ivanhoe Nelson played baseball with dedication and a passion. He never considered himself one of the best players of his time, but he prided himself on his performance every time he stepped on a diamond. He was always willing to play anywhere and everywhere to help the team. In his time in the black sandlots, Nelson would play baseball for five or six central Virginia teams, starting in Charlottesville in his early teens on a junior league team created by local baseball promoter Gene Burton.

Burton moved the team to North Garden, Virginia, and into the Shen-Valley League. The team struggled; no one remembers the team name, but much of the time it gave Nelson and others the kind of exposure to playing against the big guys that they needed. Ivanhoe had his own struggles. First, there was his name *Ivanhoe*: fine for literary circles, but clearly out of place in the setting of the rural sandlots of black baseball. Secondly, he was a poor hitter which made him feel he was letting the team down. Nelson's bright spot was his play in the outfield. He had sprinter's speed that allowed him to chase and run down would-be home run shots in country ballfields that seemed to go on forever. Remembers Nelson, "I could run and cover some ground, and back up the right and left fielders."

After playing in North Garden, Nelson, at the urging of former classmates at Albemarle High School, joined an already loaded South Garden Tiger squad that Nelson touts as one of the best teams ever in the black baseball leagues. South Garden manager Leroy Stevens placed Nelson in center field where he beat out starter Mitchell Carter. That was really not a problem as Carter was South Garden's pitching ace. South Garden's field was a country mile long and its outfield sloped uphill, so Ivanhoe had all the running and climbing he was fit for on a Saturday or Sunday.

Nelson recalls the competition peaked with hotly contested division games against Greenwood, Barboursville, Covesville and vaunted Avon. Capping South Garden's divisional wins were the championship matchups with the other Tigers of Sperryville. Looking back, Nelson says, "You had to come to play ball."

> At South Garden if you missed practice you lost your starting position so guys didn't miss practice. That team was seven deep in the lineup with five guys who could hit home runs in a row. You had Curtis Byers, Rodney Kirby, Leroy Stevens, Curtis Dowell, Donald Byers right down the line. Sperryville had the best team. Oh, Mitchell and Johnny could hold them back for awhile, but about that 4th or 5th inning you better be backing up. Those Slaughter boys, whoo! I could get back 400 feet. and they'd still knock balls over my head. But I could get back and judge them pretty well most of the time. People in Sperryville would be hollering, "Don't y'all hit it to the center fielder."

Ivanhoe was tops in the outfield, but still struggled at the plate. He knew his fielding and ability to run were the only things keeping him in the lineup because he was not hitting. Compounding his woes was the number of times he was hit by pitches while crowding the plate. Once on base he soon learned that it was there that the challenge really began. Players of the era would get you out one way or the other.

> They used to throw at me and I got hit a lot because I used to stand on top of the plate, so I learned to switch-hit and I became a better hitter. I got spiked plenty of times. I dove back into third base and the guy could have missed my hand, but he came right down on it with both spikes! They would try to hurt you.

Aside from improvements at the plate Ivanhoe became an all-around utility player. The fans on all sides began to reward him for his hustle and his improving play. Ivanhoe was a standout. He had a sizable afro that almost made his ballcap look like a beanie, and then more people were picking up on his name which made him truly unique wherever he played baseball. People liked the name. Nelson was amazed. The team might play a game against Elkton in Rockingham County, and before South Garden took the field fans were calling out, "Here comes Ivanhoe." When starting catcher Cornell Carey left South Garden to reform the ball team in his home community of Esmont, Ivanhoe accepted the move to part time catcher, a move that might have prompted some to quit the team, but Nelson learned to catch and catch well.

Small in stature, he played aggressively and mastered the old catchers' trick of submarining the bigger, stronger players seeking to plant him at the plate. Many hulking base runners were embarrassed to the point of wanting to brawl after being tossed into the screen by the smaller Nelson. His strong arm had been an asset in the outfield and added value to his catching.

Leroy Stevens decided Nelson's arm was strong enough to bring to the pitching mound so Ivanhoe started pitching and did so until the end of his playing days. Little by little the overachieving Nelson was gaining the recognition of an all-star performer.

Players inside and outside of the league took note. Teams like the amateur Charlottesville Hornets saw potential in Nelson's play in games played on their homesite at Burley Field. Ivanhoe was offered a spot on the team and accepted it as an opportunity to move up and gain the exposure to major league scouts. But after spending a month on the bench he quit the team and went back to the all-black Inter-County League. South Garden's dynasty began to crumble at that time, and the early '70s were dominated by the new Avon Twins.

By the mid-'70s the team broke apart for good, and many players went back to the community of Covesville from whence many of them came. Ivanhoe also headed home and restarted the team in his community of Keene, and was joined by a few teammates from South Garden. Organizing the team was a project, and the playing field was located literally in the mountains. The handful of devotees adopted the name Colts, and with a dedicated core of players they pulled together to build a team. There were the Agee brothers, Jack, Richard, and Parkey; youngsters Bobby and Wayne Gardner, and Archie Jackson; and Ren and Early Anderson from Buckingham, Virginia, played in and out of the lineup.

The Colts could not beat the Avon or Covesville squads, but they fought every other team for nine innings and beyond to pull out a victory. In the mid-'70s the competition was at its best.

Covesville reloaded, seemingly with players from everywhere. Avon was in its stride already and getting stronger, and topping it off, the Wilmington Eagles of Fluvanna, considered amateurs by many, had entered the Inter-County League in 1973.

If your team was average or subpar, a .500 winning percentage was all you could hope for at best. Ivy, Nellysford, Madison, and Shipman were all in good company with Keene as they all struggled to keep lineups together and please the home crowd by winning one on Sunday. Keene and Ivy were both rebuilding teams, playing from week to week to avoid the league cellar. From a fan's perspective many of the best games were between the struggling league teams like Keene and Ivy, or Shipman and Keene.

The Colts whipped Madison and Elkton, but Keene versus Ivy matchups were usually decided in the late innings, sometimes extra innings. In a 1977 encounter on the Ivy diamond the two teams were tied 7–7 going into the eleventh inning. With two outs in the bottom of the inning, manager John Armstead came into the game as a pinch-hitter and hit a solo home run to push Ivy ahead to the win 8–7.[1] Keene began experiencing the same problem other community teams were faced with in the late '70s. Who was going to show up to play on a Saturday or Sunday and would there be enough to field 9? Esmont and Keene were two communities close together and were bitter rivals, but as they both struggled to field 9 players and struggled to win games they realized that they might be able to put their rivalry aside and help each other.

So, on Saturdays the special Esmont-Keene connection was formed. Not only did they have enough players, but they steamrollered some of the better teams in the area. Players of the era recall with humor that one never knew who was going to play for Keene or Esmont. In the late '70s when the mighty Wilmington Eagles broke apart, Keene picked up Michael Carey and all-star shortstop Lonnie Trice. Ivanhoe Nelson recalls that it was only after these additions that they were able to defeat Avon, and the team appeared to be rolling into the '80s.

However, Keene suffered from the same lack of on field support that plagued many other black community baseball teams. The interest of young black teens in playing baseball diminished, and the overwhelming popularity of softball around central Virginia that took away skilled players and ballfields. Here, Keene and Esmont put aside their rivalry and merged, lasting a couple of seasons before Esmont was no more. Black teams in Virginia were running raggedly along, but dedicated players like Ivanhoe Nelson and others were still interested in playing ball. So even though it was almost the mid-eighties and Nelson was beyond his window at the big leagues, he went outside of his home community one more time, this time to play with a young Nellysford team whose players were coming of age and showing promise as ballplayers.

Nelson continued to pitch as the team matched up against Elkton in the north, Grottoes in the west, and Madison Heights to the south. Massies Mill was on the rise again after merging with Shipman.

Ivanhoe played seven summers with Nellysford, and the team won at least two championships in a row. He cites his greatest reward as playing with his older and younger sons near the end of his playing days. Once that enjoyment had passed he put away his cleats and gloves, but remained active coaching Little League baseball and supporting his sons in their endeavors on the diamond. Ivanhoe's best memories of his days playing are of the great response from the communities that supported black baseball, and the respect of teammates and rivals during his days on the diamond.

New Eagles Land

In the '70s, the Bad News Bears, a trilogy of movies about hapless Little League team underdogs who overachieved and won the hearts of their fans, ruled the box office. During the same time period the Ivy (Virginia) Eagles baseball team rallied in the same fashion. There was always a ball team in the community but never a very good one. As Mel Perrow of Shipman remembers, there was always something missing.

> Poor Ivy, they never really had enough of anything. Boo Waller was a good pitcher, but if you had pitching you didn't have a good infield, so your pitcher's pitching all he wants but the guys are making errors. The next year we formed our team back in Shipman because we said, "We can beat these guys," and sure enough, we formed the team back and we went over to Ivy and beat them.

VI. Bottom of the Order, 1970–1980

When it seemed that the Ivy ball team might finally collapse in the '70s, fate intervened. Greenwood broke up after more than three decades of play. Players still in their prime from the last Greenwood squad, and younger up-and-coming ballplayers from that community came to Ivy to continue playing baseball. Some say the new players came to Ivy because they did not want to join rival Avon; others point out that teenaged Johnny Ivory already playing on the Ivy team maintained a friendship with many of the Greenwood ballplayers, thereby influencing their decision to play for Ivy.

Overnight John Armstead had at his disposal some very good ballplayers who had played together since childhood, and the young squad carried much of the area's black baseball history when they stepped on the diamond. Johnny Ivory was one of the first of the younger generation to step up and express an interest in playing ball for his community. He played second base and also filled a spot in the pitching rotation. Larry Ivory, younger sibling to Johnny, was simply a great athlete capable of playing almost any sport and playing any position on a team. He was a good gloveman in the outfield and his speed was second to none. The Ivory brothers were the grandsons of Henry Ivory who had played on the early Ivy teams and had played for the Crozet All-Stars in the late '40s and '50s.

Chris and Frankie Barbour were walking, breathing, playing representatives of area baseball in the seventies. They were both versatile players holding down several infield positions, and they were both good pitchers and hitters. They were the sons of George Sims, an area baseball legend, from a legendary baseball family. Chris and Frankie Barbour inherited their competitive spirit honestly. The brothers starred on a local CB Baker league team for high school all-stars. They literally played baseball four out of seven days a week in the summer months. Their cousin Harvey Sims was small in stature but he was quick, and had great hands. Sims played in the closing years of the Greenwood Hawks club, playing ball from his early teens. Typical of the time, he wore an Afro, but when playing ball had his hair in braids that hung down from his ball cap. From a crouching stance Sims took a couple of warm-up swings and waited on his pitch.

He preferred the high-rising fastball. Any pitcher not knowing better made a mistake throwing a high pitch Harvey Sims' way because he could hit it into the pines. It was amazing that a man the size of Harvey Sims could hit the ball with such power. Joseph "Peewee" Washington came from the disbanded Greenwood Hawks landing in Ivy with his cousins. He was probably one of the best outfielders in the league and had great speed for the position. His lean frame belied the power he possessed to both hit and throw.

James Perkins, Jr., called "Man" by family and friends, played off and on holding down first base. When serious about showing up for a Sunday game he performed well because he was actually a good athlete, though distracted most of the time. He could run and hit and may have had one of the quickest glove hands around. A backhand grab on a hot line drive past first base was Man's moment of glory and one of the memorable plays of the '70s on the Ivy diamond.

George Mayo, Jr., called Took from the time he was able to walk, was a quiet, sleepy looking youngster, but that was just one dimension of his character because once on the field he was one of the best athletes anyone had ever seen throughout the counties. Took was big-league material. He could hit, run, throw, pitch and play anywhere else one needed him including as catcher. He learned the rudiments of pitching from father George, Sr., and was working out with the team by age fourteen. Two years later Took was moving around the field in the starting lineup.

He played a good outfield, learned first base and caught for hard-throwing Boo Waller. He had a good eye at the plate and ran the bases with sprinter's speed. In high school he was a standout in baseball and football, and once loaned his speed out to the track team to set a school record on the mile relay team with childhood friend Larry Ivory.

With John Armstead's guidance and the support of the Ivy community the young Eagles built a competitive team by their second year together. They were beating the teams in the middle of the pack and on any given Sunday gave one of the top teams all they could handle. Ivy won games against Covesville and Elkton, almost unheard of in years prior to the mid-seventies. They were good, and not only the people in the community of Ivy started to take notice, but people following sandlot ball in other communities started showing up to see Frankie Barbour pitch and to see Took Mayo make some spectacular infield plays. It gave the community and the league what sports fans enjoy most—watching young athletic people perform.

In the close games where Ivy needed to make a ninth inning run to win it the stage was set for the team elder and manager, John Armstead. The team knew and the opposition knew that if they let the young Ivy players keep the game close or get into position to win then John Armstead could bring it home. The pitchers on other teams were scared because they knew that if Armstead got that last at bat with men on, they could "say goodbye to the baseball," that John Armstead, now in his late thirties, could send it not only into the pines but over the pines.

In the late seventies Ivy made it to the play-offs for the first time and fared well before being eliminated in a controversial game against the Massies Mill Cubs.

Wilmington's Big Red Machine

Bob Winston, first base, Wilmington Eagles:

We went to Madison and for an old man I had one of the most electrifying days there were. The lineup came up and everybody struck out 1-2-3. I think I was batting five that day and I didn't strike out cause I led off with a triple and that blew that crowd's mind, blew that crowd's mind! See this old boy he done pitched in the league; yeah, he done pitched in the league and he had some real stuff! But see he messed around and threw me that high ball and I'm telling you right now—if you throw me that high ball you can kiss it goodbye!

Bob Winston, "Cool Papa" to the younger generation, was in his forties, still playing for the Wilmington Eagles, still loving baseball. At the close of the '60s

Winston and cousin James Payne remained, but the rest of the brothers and cousins who had stocked the overpowering Eagles lineups of the '50s and '60s were now on the sidelines.

Attracting players to the Fluvanna community had ever been a task. Wilmington had probably hosted more top regional ballplayers than any other black community team since the '50s. Marcellus Coleman from Albemarle County, touted as one of the best in black baseball, pitched for the Eagles in the mid–'60s. Alfred Martin, whose reputation for hitting and fielding preceded him, played shortstop in the late '60s. Major-league prospect Phillip Turpin of Richmond played shortstop a couple of seasons in the Wilmington infield.

Fluvanna County produced its own talented ballplayers. Local ballplayer Cyril Carey ran down fly balls from his center field position that no one else could possibly get to. Paul Franklin's younger son, Ralph, played all over the outfield, playing center field as well as he played in right. Robert Brown, Jr., who had grown up around the team watching his father hit tape-measure home runs took over his dad's old position at third base. Claude Winston and Robert Winston, Jr., both catchers, joined the lineup with their father Bob Winston, Sr., in the early '70s.

In the spring of 1968 Wilmington managers Paul Franklin and Robert Brown attended a Fluvanna High School baseball game. They were especially impressed with the pitching of teenaged Roger Bowles, already an imposing youngster with good baseball skills. Paul Franklin, an acquaintance of Bowles' father, asked if Roger might be interested in playing baseball with the Wilmington team that summer. Roger Bowles accepted and stepped into a new era in Wilmington Eagles baseball.

Roger Bowles was the only white player on the roster and although 1970 is just back around the corner, he was very much a minority in games against all of the community baseball teams.

However, he was drawn into the camaraderie and spirit of the Wilmington team as much as the baseball itself, and came to revere Paul Franklin and Robert Brown. Through the team leaders, Bob Winston and James Payne, Bowles learned the importance of the Eagles' winning tradition and the pride taken in their displays of excellence on the playing field. Roger Bowles' play as a pitcher and infielder immediately earned him respect from opponents. In the fall he left Fluvanna for the University of Richmond where he played Division II baseball, but returned home in the summer to play for Wilmington.

By 1970 with additions to the lineup the Eagles started their run toward dominance in the new decade. They continued to play their regional opponents in Buckingham County, Cartersville, and Amelia with some wins, maybe a loss or a close game here and there. But many games did not go nine full innings because Wilmington easily overpowered a lot of teams. Steve Sheridan, a Louisa native playing baseball at Bridgewater College, joined the lineup in the early seventies and brought to the team good fielding and good base running. Sheridan was a competitive, powerfully built player who hit the ball with the kind of consistency that would eventually place him in the lead-off spot. Lonnie Trice, also from Louisa, and Tim Shelton from Goochland had both been Wilmington opponents, but in 1972 both joined the Eagles lineup.

Cat quick and built like a tank, Lonnie was probably the only two hundred and forty pound shortstop around. He was not very tall and at the plate offered a limited strike zone to opposing pitchers. However, Big Lonnie hit the ball with enough power to topple a brick wall and he could hit it almost anyplace.

Tim Shelton was a good hitter, played the infield and was a hard-throwing right-handed pitcher in the Wilmington rotation. Between 1970 and 1972 Wilmington retooled and tuned up the ball team, rolling over every team in their path. Through contacts in Richmond, Roger Bowles arranged ballgames against Richmond's semi-pro teams.

The Eagles performance was the same against the Richmond teams. Semipro ballplayers who were playing at least three times weekly could not stay on the diamond with the Wilmington order. In 1972 Wilmington met up with the unbeaten Spotsylvania team. They too had a tradition of strong black baseball teams. Each side had heard of the other through mutual opponents but had never matched up. The game was arranged by a Wilmington relative living in Spotsylvania County and it was worth every bit of hype and promotion. Bob Winston recalls the thriller:

> Spotsylvania had beaten everything over on that Fredericksburg side, and they came down here undefeated. I'll never forget the score. We're going into the fifth inning, and I'll never forget they were hanging around 1-1, sixth inning, still 1-1. Seventh inning we started chipping on the ice, beat the old boys 3-1. That was a game I'm telling you right now! They come hungry! I'll never forget those games!

Once again the Eagles were the uncrowned champions of independent baseball, but in the season of '73 the team finally made a move towards league play, joining the Inter-County League, known as Shen-Valley in the '60s. Roger Bowles:

> Back in those days Wilmington was going to play different community teams but no leagues. They knew about this league [Paul Franklin, Robert Brown], so we got in that league, got brand new uniforms with white pants and red shirts. Steve Sheridan and I went to Richmond and ordered the uniforms. Solid red jerseys with a "W" on the front, two toned letters on the back. At that juncture they were really nice uniforms in comparison to what the other teams had.
>
> Most of the other teams didn't have all the same type of uniform. Some people played in blue jeans or they would have mixed up stuff, gray pants, white shirt, but that's all we had. It was Avon and South Garden when we came into the league and they fought it out every year. We heard this that those two teams fought it out every year for the championship. In those days it was very important in these communities to win. Everybody took it seriously. If you knew where there was a real good pitcher that could stop a team, you went and got him. I'm sure some of the players that we played against were paid by the fans.
>
> I invited this guy up from Richmond, I said, "What are you doing? We've got a big game coming up in this league I'm playing in up here, but don't expect anything because we're going to be playing on a rock pile." I think we were playing Barboursville. He came once, and then he came back week after week, because of the spirit and the competition, and the way that we were all accepted in the predominantly black league. Once we got into the league and

started to win some games against the established powerhouses then everybody was after Wilmington, everybody.

Wilmington's newest roster addition, Dave Brooks, was short for a collegiate pitcher at five feet eight but was stout, weighing in at one hundred and ninety pounds. He easily clocked 92–93 mph on any given pitch. More than once players and fans saw Brooks load the bases and then strike the side out. Good hitters around the league got their bats around on Brooks' heat, but they went down swinging more often.

The 1973 team's entry into league play astounded players and fans. Onlookers had never before witnessed the power and skill displayed by the Eagles lineup. They were big guys, strong afield, and their batting order 1–6 was devastating, riding pitchers right off of the mound. The Fluvanna Eagles were all about the business of winning.

Wilmington flexed its muscles against a lot of ball teams in the '70s, but the best illustration of their power took place in a ballgame against the Ivy Eagles. Roger Bowles:

> I never will forget we played Ivy on their field. Ivy had Chris and Frankie Barbour, they were great athletes and ballplayers, and I believe Chris was pitching. Steve Sheridan led off, and singled. Michael Carey hit a home run—second man up. I hit a home run as the third guy up, and Lonnie Trice the 240 pound shortstop hit a line drive back at Chris Barbour, and he fell right on the mound and the ball went right over top of his nose. I thought it had killed him ... he didn't hit him. Chris Barbour came over—just walked right off the field. He said, "Not for me." So we had hit two home runs, and Lonnie Trice took a line drive that almost took his head off in the first four guys that were up, and he just laid it down. I think we beat them that day over 10 runs in five innings and just quit. Where our team was so dominant was that you could take any guy in the lineup and any guy in the lineup was a good hitter and could play in different places.

Paul Franklin's Big Red Machine breezed through the regular season and the play-offs without dropping a single game. But waiting in the finals were the Avon A's. The A's players were no strangers to tough competitive play and in '73 Avon was defending titles from the past two seasons. The A's lineup was a roll call of standout players: Estes "Preacher" Sims, Howard Alexander, John "Skeebo" Jackson, Brad Awkard, Kenneth Awkard, and Kenny Diggs. Wilmington prevailed in the series winning three games to Avon's two. It was a battle between two evenly matched teams whose lineups mirrored each other in experience, size, power and speed. Wilmington had "Big Bowles"; they in turn referred to Kenny Diggs as "Big Kenny." The pairing set the tone for what black baseball fans could expect over the next seven seasons. Roger Bowles:

> Preacher Sims hit a home run off of us in a series game down here in Wilmington, and at the time there was a real competitive finger-pointing type deal between Avon and Wilmington. Never trouble, but just get in your face stuff. And the next inning I hit a grand slam home run off of him that Mr. Paul Franklin called "the shot heard round the world." We had some wars, and the thing would go way into October.

At the end of the 1960s when black baseball teams pulled out of the league, disbanded or regrouped, Avon surged to the top. In 1971 after the Greenwood team disbanded, Preacher Sims and Roger Howard came to Avon joining Sidney Diggs, John Skeebo Jackson, Robert Jackson and Howard Alexander. The Avon Twins claimed the 1971 and 1972 league championships. At the beginning of the decade Avon had enough players for two teams. Waiting on the sidelines were a younger generation of ballplayers: all of them were from ballplaying families in either Avon or Greenwood; most were related.

The second Avon team of the '70s had their own identity and renamed themselves the A's, likely in comparison to the new-attitude West Coast major league franchise in Oakland, California. Elgie Sims, Jr., played shortstop, Brad Awkard second, Stuart "Turkey" Sims third, Kenneth Awkard first, Skeebo Jackson remained in left field, Teddy Berkley played center, Roger Clark in right field, and Kenny Diggs was the catcher. The youngsters also started a new trend in Virginia's black sandlots—the use of batting helmets.

Kenny Diggs was a high school baseball player who lived to play baseball. At age seventeen he was a hulking youngster 6 ft. tall, 220 pounds. He followed baseball watching his uncles play for the 1960s Avon teams, and he tagged along with his high school coaches taking in amateur baseball games in Waynesboro, Virginia, where he attended school. By his late teens Kenny Diggs knew his baseball. Size, quickness and a strong arm made him an obvious choice for catcher.

He played to win, and played tough. Once on a close play at the plate, Diggs barreled into an opposing catcher taking him through the makeshift wire backstop screen. When his stunned opponent threatened a violent retort, Kenny Diggs replied, "nothing personal, it's just baseball."

Kenny Diggs caught Howard Alexander the last two seasons before Alexander's arm began to fail. Catching for Howard Alexander was something of a dream come true for the teen, and he was looked upon as an impact player immediately; but he did not know the degree to which he would have to help carry the team. Kenny Diggs:

> When Howard's arm started acting up that's when they said, you're going to have to pitch some. I said I ain't no pitcher, I'm a catcher. I had two pitches—curveball, fastball. I threw the curveball every twenty pitches. I let them know what I was throwing. I'd look over at Peewee Henderson and I'd say, it's a fastball coming, see if you can hit it. But I was accurate and I knew I had to keep the ball down. Once I got a couple of games under me I was mowing people down—with a fastball. Wilmington had a telephone pole right behind second base. I hit a shot that I know was on the rise. It was on the way out and it hit the top of the pole and went into left field. A pole in the middle of the diamond—that's dedication, that's wanting to play the game of baseball.

Back at the University of Richmond word of Dave Brooks' summer league baseball adventures in Fluvanna County got around to U.R. teammate Mike Walton, a pitcher and second baseman. Mike Walton came to Wilmington the next season and later convinced brother Reno, a left-handed pitcher at Manatee Junior College in

Florida, to pitch in and out of the Wilmington lineup. Four out of the five starters for Wilmington lived outside of Fluvanna. Dave, Mike, Lonnie, and Tim Shelton could have played baseball anywhere in the state, but quit other leagues and teams to play summer baseball for the Wilmington Eagles.

The makeup of Wilmington's ball team was an interesting parallel to the progressive steps toward integration in 1970s Virginia. Black ballplayers were just beginning to break into the lineups of the college or amateur baseball leagues.

Dave Brooks, Mike and Reno Walton, Roger Bowles and Steve Sheridan had integrated the traditionally all-black leagues, and in a sense paid tribute to the history of the event of black baseball, its value to the black community, and the quality of the competition. When they put on their uniforms they were representing the community of Wilmington and black baseball, and in return the fans showed their appreciation. This all took place under the guidance and unifying spirit of Paul Franklin and Robert Brown.

The influx of new talent meant limited or no playing time for some who had been starters years prior, but they still remained with the team and gave their support home and away. Everybody wanted to be a part of Wilmington's "Big Red Machine."

Teams that rarely practiced consistently before Wilmington's entry into the league now practiced often and began to look around for extra talent of their own. The Eagles did not drop a single regular season game in '73, and '74. When a team faced the Eagles they were in against an onslaught of talent. Wilmington used the availability of talent to their advantage. They platooned players, often using as many as three pitchers in a game to wear a tough team down. Against a power-hitting right-handed batter, left-handed Reno Walton went into the game and Dave Brooks went to the infield. James Payne, one of the elder statesmen of the team, caught fewer ballgames in the latter part of the decade, but Paul Franklin could still send him in as a devastating pinch-hitter for Dave Brooks who batted at the bottom of the order.

Wilmington took over the league the first few seasons. Thereafter they lost a close game occasionally to Covesville or Waynesboro, but otherwise it was a paved road to the play-offs. Every year waiting at the end of the championship road were the Avon A's.

Avon was defending its championship run and forced Wilmington to five games every single meeting. It was a seesaw battle each season between two competitive and skilled ball teams. Fans from several black communities loaded up their cars and traveled back and forth following the matchup. It was one of the most exciting events in the history of the all-black leagues because it was a championship series and it was guaranteed to go more than three games. It was not uncommon for a series game to go scoreless after several innings.

Roger Bowles hit home-run bombs, matched by Brad Awkard's own blast into the thicket. Brooks who had pitched against division I and division II ballplayers considered left-handed hitter Brad Awkard the best hitter and toughest out in the league. Kenny Diggs recalls that teammate Brad Awkard offered little or no zone for pitchers, so that he was looking directly at the baseball. He was short, muscular and had power, much like Wilmington cleanup batter Lonnie Trice. Diggs returned from the service in the late '70s, finding his way back into the lineup, and along the way the A's had picked up a stellar pitcher of their own in Phil Doyle of Waynesboro.

Doyle had command and threw all of the pitches a manager dreamed of: slider, curveball, knuckleball and a fastball. He was very adept at picking up on hitters' tendencies and taking the time to talk things over with his catcher. Doyle's speed was in the upper 80s, sometimes 90 with men on base—not as fast as Dave Brooks but just as effective. The opposing aces often dueled late into the ballgame waiting for the other to blink.

Phil Doyle's brother Curt was also a pitcher and a good first baseman for a season or two. The Doyle brothers were minorities on the Avon squad, but by no means the first to play ball for the Nelson County community. With the addition of the Doyle brothers and Kenny Diggs back behind the plate, Avon claimed the '77 and '79 championships.

Tip of the Cap and the Upper Hand

In the fall of 1977 Avon was leading the five-game championship series and on the verge of putting away another trophy. The series was tied 2–2 and playing out on the Eagles diamond, nine innings back and forth. Avon was ahead but in the ninth Wilmington put men on base in scoring position with two outs.

If Doyle could put away one more Wilmington batter, they could take the party back to Nelson County. This was where Wilmington was always dangerous, not known to have weak hitters in the line-up. Phil was focused on the hitter at the plate but was also aware of what was going on around him. By the 1977 season he had played with his teammates a couple of seasons, knew what they could do and what Avon could do as a team. The Eagles had a man on third coached by Mr. Paul Franklin, Sr. The runner, pumped up by the home crowd, was primed to go home on contact and to shorten that distance was a stride off third base. Phil threw the next pitch that might have been a ball, might have been a strike, but when he received the ball back on the mound, turning toward third base, Stuart "Turkey" Sims, his third baseman, caught his attention.

Turkey was tracking the Eagles baserunner but not overplaying the runner's actions to score. He didn't stick his glove out, didn't make the runner feel cut-off from the bag, but when Phil glanced over Turkey tipped his ballcap, tapping the brim, and Phil did the same in return. Doyle kicked the dust just behind the rubber, stepped up again, paused, eyes cast down on the mound and went into his motion. But instead of stepping into a pitch home, he threw a strike to the hot corner. Sims, who was expecting the throw, blocked the bag and tagged the Wilmington runner down in the red clay dust too late, too far to tag back up—game over. Avon lineups had power, speed and a depth chart of talent but also generated wins with well-executed defensive strategies.

Bob Winston was forty-six years old when the team entered the league and by 1978 he had decided it would be his last season in a Wilmington Eagles uniform. Winston had already been a part of four championship wins but for Cool Papa the '78 championship against rival Avon was probably the sweetest. Here is "Cool Papa" Bob Winston:

> Talk about a crowd of people and talk about an electrifying game, we went past five and nobody scored! We went past six and nobody scored ... we're going into the seventh and Avon is leading us 1–0. In the eighth inning we got a man on base and the old man kissed one! We took that championship down here from them 2–1 and I batted one out of the park with one man on! That was a good way to go out because I hung up the uniform that year.

After the '78 league title and finishing as runners-up in '79 the Eagles' display of dominance began to slip, though they never dropped beyond 2nd place in the final two seasons. Dave Brooks and Mike and Reno Walton of Richmond became less motivated to travel weekly, and moved on to other pursuits. The disbandment of the Wilmington dynasty actually mirrored the changing tide, as many of the old community teams began to fold area by area.

Dave Brooks was selected by the Houston Astros coming out of the University of Richmond, and though his stay was a short one it is nonetheless noteworthy and says a lot for the level of competition in the community baseball league.

Managers Paul Franklin and Robert Brown both passed away within a couple of years of each other in the nineties, leaving behind beloved memories of their dedication to the youth of the community and baseball.

Steve Sheridan is a longtime coach at Fluvanna County High School and has also served as the school's athletic director. Roger Bowles played baseball into the early '80s before settling down to concentrate on starting a family. He coaches off and on and still lives in Fluvanna County, as do Bob Winston and James Payne; they never see each other without recollecting Wilmington baseball.

Avon picked up the pace again and rolled into the early '80s winning two out of three Tri-County League championships. The Avon A's remained intact through most of the '80s, playing ball all over as the black leagues began to crumble. Center fielder Teddy Berkley discovered another black league in southern Virginia supported by the teams of Blackstone, Lawrenceville, and Victoria. Once part of the Avon team began to travel and play in the league they became known as "the boys from the Shenandoah Valley," and black baseball fans were glad to have their company. During their stay for play-off games and league championships, a house was set up in the community for Kenny Diggs, Teddy Berkley, and Brad and Kenneth Awkard. Kenny Diggs:

> I'll always remember that championship game we played against Blackstone. We were playing for the championship in that league in Lawrenceville. Kenneth Awkard pitched the first game—struck out 13 or 14 batters. I said, "You get the first one and I'll bring the next one home." We beat Blackstone 2–1, and I struck out 17 that night, and Brad Awkard caught the whole game. He was the only catcher that could catch me. We won the game when Brad Awkard hit one out around 400 feet and it was still going.

Wilmington Eagles, 1974 Inter-County League Champs. Front row (l-r): Jerry Kidd, Ralph Franklin, Freddie James, Lonnie Trice, William Johnson, Bobby Brown. Back row (l-r): Mr. Paul Franklin, manager; James Payne, Michael Carey, Robert Winston, Sr., Tim Shelton, Paul Martin, Claude Winston, Robert Winston, Jr., Steve Sheridan, Roger Bowles, Robert Brown, Sr., manager.

Big Kenny continued to play baseball into the late '80s before retiring his mitt and mask. He was in the midst of starting a family of his own. Diggs' greatest joy outside of his family and baseball has been working with other children, whether coaching them or counseling them on life.

Pee Wee and David

Jim Dowell:

In '65 I got all of my boys together who wanted to come back to Covesville and then I started adding younger ones on. I put David Johnson on the team first, and he played with us that year. We went to Dilwyn [Buckingham Co., Va.] that was the first team we played after we got the team up. Then the next year I put Pee Wee Henderson on and just kept putting the young ones on until we got them all in.

Covesville, Virginia, was still one of the more recognized locales for black baseball in the '70s. For decades it had been the Dowell and Henderson families filling out the ballteam. In the '70s it was the Hendersons and Johnsons who stood out on the community team that had changed its name to Astros in the mid–'60s. Jim Dowell managed and played into the early '70s. His brothers Lenny and Lee pitched and played during the early part of the decade, but it was essentially a new younger lineup. Andrew Wells came to Covesville from neighboring Nelson County in the 60s and became one of the team's most valuable performers. Jim Dowell worked him into the lineup, continually moving him around the field. Initially Wells had a good arm and pitched for Covesville, but a little over-confidence and some barnstorming quickly dissipated the strength of his throwing arm. At the bat Wells was a tough out and a reliable hitter in clutch situations.

If you talk about Covesville baseball in the '70s, opponents and team members will tell you, don't leave out Alec Smith. Alexander Smith, Jr., started playing for Covesville at age eighteen after playing on the Junior Covesville Yankees team managed by Gene Burton of North Garden, Virginia. Alec Smith on his start in Covesville's lineup:

> They put me in left field and I was terrible. I couldn't play the outfield at all. Then one game the guy playing second base got hurt on a play and they put me on second base and that is where I stayed.

Alec was competitive and showed a lot of hustle early on while his ballplaying skills developed. He was not afraid of putting his body in front of the ball or getting plowed over by bigger, stronger opponents, breaking up the double play. On the field Smith was as lively as they come and one of the all-time jesters of the black sandlot leagues.

He held a lot in common with Skeebo Jackson of the Avon team; neither hesitated to break up a game and the crowd with their antics. Many times Smith feigned injury after just missing a hot grounder. The sight of Smith lying prone on the diamond brought teammates and opponents running only to find Smith with a grin on his face. With a collective "Damn!" and a good laugh play resumed.

Smith developed into a consistent singles hitter, and was one of the fastest players on the team. Jim Dowell counted on him in many contests to get into scoring position by stealing around the basepath. No one unwilling to bunt the baseball played for Jim Dowell.

As Alec Smith recalls it was often win it or lose it with the Covesville squeeze play:

> Jim believed in the squeeze play rather than hitting the ball out to score the run. I'll never forget the all-star game we played in at Burley Field [Charlottesville, Va.] We were down by two runs and Jim had three of us bunt in a row. My bunt tied the ballgame or won the ball game, but the scores all came on bunts, and it just shook the other team apart. I used to hate to bunt the ball, but I laid down a perfect bunt that night and we won the all-star game—never will forget it.

Gilbert "Rabbit" Johnson grew up watching friends and relatives play ball for Covesville and sometimes traveled with the team. When Johnson was a youngster, manager Jim Dowell allowed him to sit on the bench with the admonishment, "You sit there, don't say anything, watch and learn." He was the baby in a family of Covesville baseball players behind brothers David and Lawrence Johnson.

By the time Rabbit was of age he was not only ready to join the team but had learned the ins and outs of playing for Jim Dowell. Rabbit Johnson possessed three things Jim valued in a ballplayer—commitment, courage, and speed. Rabbit Johnson was the fastest player on the Covesville team and for a time, in the entire league. He held down center field and excited the crowd as he ran Covesville's odd-sided outfield all afternoon. Rabbit Johnson:

> Harold Henderson was in right field and James Smith was in left and I would play center field because I could back up right field and left field. Some balls were home-run balls but I ran 'em down to the road [29 south] and I ran 'em down to the cornfield. They were supposed to be home runs but I went and got 'em. When I hear the crack of the bat I take off running but I keep my eye on the ball—chase it right down. We didn't know where we were going to play—never did. Before the game we'd sit there on the bench and Jim would walk that aisle back and forth in front of us making his mind up—don't say nothing to nobody. Then he'd disappear with his scorekeeper, and that whole lineup would be different. When it was time to play ball and he was calling off positions you'd say, "What? I'm thinking I'm going to be in center field today and now I'm out in right field," but you had to be ready to go and that's the way we practiced too.

Rabbit wore number #1 and led off at the top of the order because he was a consistent threat to get on base. Like his manager in style of play in the preceding decades, Johnson would do anything to get on base. Rabbit Johnson:

> I was just a base-hit man, but once I was on I could steal so I would get on anyway I could. I'd make the pitcher hit me or walk me because the next man up is a power hitter. Once I'm on base I'll worry the hell out of the pitcher. Jim would give me the signal from third base. He'd turn his back like somebody called him from the crowd. When I see his number, next pitch I was gone. My brother David could take a pitch and put it over 29 and my brother Puggy could do the same thing so I said my God where's my power but I just got the base hits. We always worked that squeeze play but nobody ever knew when it was coming.
>
> There would be a man on third and you're standing there at the bat and Jim would call time like something's wrong, "Time, time! Mr. ump." We'd walk out of the box and meet him—okay what am I doing wrong? We had to make it look good too. I want to tell you something; when that man said play ball we're coming up through there. So the batter better know to drop the bunt down because if you swing you're going to hurt your man coming in. Drop that bunt down whether it's foul or not foul, and it doesn't matter if you're a power hitter or a base hit man, when Jim called for the bunt you drop that bunt down, and that's another score! Then Jim would jump up and say, "I told you I could beat 'em like that!"

In a late '70s all-star game Rabbit Johnson won four trophies. He was named the best hitter, made the most outstanding play of the day, was the fastest on the diamond, and was selected for the overall MVP.

Players came and went on the Astros roster but none made their appearance, then disappearance, more interesting than a pitcher known to many simply as Boswell.

There is little known about this fireballer who appeared in the early '70s. His racial makeup and nationality were also undeclared—he was a mystery. But there was no secret to anyone during the mid-'70s that this new Covesville pitcher, Vincent Boswell, had above-average skills and abilities. Was he a major league prospect on the way up or down? No one will really ever know for certain. Only the pitching display that Vincent Boswell put on during his brief stay in the Inter-County League truly says anything about him. Jim Dowell remembers his chance meeting with Boswell:

> I got two players, Boswell and Logan. He and Logan came to me at the same time. I was working at the Downtown Motor Inn at this service station, and a fella signaled for me to come over. They wanted to play for that Valley League but this guy didn't want them so he sent them over to me. I was at the right place at the right time, and I brought them to Covesville. Boswell—phew! That scoundrel could throw! Three up and three down, that's what it was, and Logan was a good outfielder.

Lenny Dowell was scheduled to pitch in an early '70s all-star game, but he did not know who brother Jim Dowell had scheduled as a guest in the rotation.

> We were going to play in the all-star game down at Washington Park [Charlottesville, Va.] under the lights and where Jim found this boy I don't know. South Garden didn't know Jim had found this guy. I was shocked because we didn't know, and Jim told me, said, that white guy's going to pitch tonight. South Garden didn't want that, said it wasn't fair. We had a hard time getting the game started, they didn't want that boy up there. But they didn't know how good he could throw, but Jim knew because he had already tested him out. Went down to Washington Park, and that boy shut everything down—shut them South Garden boys down to nothing! He had a fastball, but he had that big-league fastball. That thing would get to you and go down, all of his balls would go down! No matter how high it was thrown when it'd get to the batter it would go down fast. Jim's hand was all swollen up the next day.

Vincent Boswell stayed around and pitched for Covesville for another season, shutting down Avon, Massies Mill, and Waynesboro.

Still, the Astros failed to win a championship even with Boswell's major league heat. Boswell disappeared as quickly as he appeared with rumors and mystery surrounding his whereabouts or condition.

William Dowell was a pitcher who could throw hard, plain and simple—he could blow you away. A lack of control was the only thing standing in Dowell's way to becoming a top area pitcher. Playing for the South Garden Tigers he was used as a starter, but often he whiffed a batter or two and then loaded the bases with runners. Soon Dowell lost confidence and the team and the manager lost confidence and so he was pulled to the bench. In the mid-seventies he spent more time on South Garden's bench than in the field, so when approached by Covesville team captains Henderson and Johnson, Dowell was willing to give playing in Covesville a try.

Jim Dowell agreed to bring him onto the squad and caught him, and had William practice with the team before deciding he was ready to start. Jim Dowell:

> We put him on the mound and he did the same thing, loaded the bases up, but one thing was different, I didn't pull him out. Peewee and David called time, said, "What are you going to do?" I said, "He pitched himself in it, let him pitch himself out." I went up on the mound and

talked to him, patted him on the back. I said, "You got yourself in this jam, now get yourself out." I said, "Just rare back and let it go," and he pitched himself out. He could throw hard cause he was left-handed anyway and he pitched good ever since.

After pitching his way beyond his old sticking point William Dowell was one of the touted pitchers on the sandlot scene, and attracted the attention of the amateur Charlottesville Hornets made up of college players in line for the big leagues. William Dowell tried out and made the squad, but opted not to play on the team. He did, however, end up playing for Elkton's baseball team when he met a sweetheart from that community and moved to Rockingham County.

Whether you were a fan or a player, baseball games on Covesville diamond were memorable. Hot rods growled back and forth moving in and out of the parking area, James Brown and Parliament Funkadelic blaring from their speakers.

The new Astros were something else. The young team made plays and whipped the baseball around with flair. They swaggered around the diamond with a gait they named the "Covesville Strut." Not only were they a good ball team but they were entertaining in an unforgettable way.

Two names are forever linked to the Covesville teams of the '70s: James "Pee Wee" Henderson and David Johnson. Henderson and Johnson took the baton and carried the tradition of Covesville baseball into the '70s. By '71 they were both veterans of the Shenandoah and then Inter-County black baseball leagues.

In the mid–'60s, Henderson and Johnson played on the Junior League community team the Covesville Yankees under Gene Burton, but by the time they reached their teens it was apparent to everyone, especially Jim Dowell, that they were advanced well beyond the Junior League level. The two teens were already burly, well-muscled young men who threw and hit as well as the average ballplaying adult in the league.

All they needed was the exposure, and further maturation. The older of the two childhood friends, David Johnson, came up first and took over a position in the outfield. Jim Dowell recalls the youngster dropping maybe one ball all season long.

Pee Wee Henderson followed the next year and joined Johnson in the outfield and the two proceeded to run and defend the outfield green like they owned it. Cyril Dowell, Covesville native:

> Pee Wee could run that field all day long. He could cover from center field to right field and from center field to left field. Guys used to get mad because he would catch balls out of his territory, but he could run it down and catch it, so you couldn't really be mad at him.

After a couple of seasons, Henderson and Johnson became as renowned for their hitting as they were for their outfield play. The Covesville teenagers were known game breakers around the league and teammates rallied around them.

The long-ball power of Henderson and Johnson was what the fans came out to see from week to week and the pair rarely disappointed them. They batted number three and four in the order and both could drive the baseball across the north and south bound highway lanes. In the Inter-County League of the mid–'70s Henderson and Johnson were in the top five best long-ball hitters in the region, the other sluggers being Kenny Diggs and Brad Awkard of Avon and Roger Bowles of Wilmington. When comparing the two Covesville power hitters, David Johnson's home-run shots traveled a little farther more often.

Johnson grew up swinging axes and sledgehammers; swinging a baseball bat was child's play. He had powerful legs and batted out of a wide stance.

When he connected fans could tell by the sound of the wooden bat on the ball whether or not it was playable, and David Johnson knew it too. He was a good-natured fellow who displayed a mile-wide grin. At the times that he connected with a monster blast that sent the baseball over the two-lane highway or into the forest he was already grinning with the ball on the rise. He would then glance over at the Covesville bench and then Pee Wee Henderson as if to say "your turn." Sometimes, if the pitcher was shaken, Pee Wee Henderson followed with a home-run smash of his own.

Opponents knew he and Henderson loved hitting against pitchers who threw heat and they loved the long ball. For Henderson and Johnson the toughest part of playing for Jim Dowell was executing the squeeze play, bunting the runner around, because they wanted to hit the ball out of sight. Johnson was once benched because he received the sign to lay down a bunt and he hit a line drive.

Each new season Jim Dowell grew to rely on them more and more, over time moving them around to play different positions in the infield and outfield. By 1972 both Henderson and Johnson were learning the rudiments of catching from Dowell.

Johnson had a strong arm, and besides his ability at catcher, he developed into a fine pitcher and closed many ballgames for Covesville. Pee Wee Henderson caught and played everyplace else except pitcher. He was fiery and emotional to Johnson's laid-back demeanor.

While Henderson was known for his hitting and fielding, it was his base running that made the difference in many close ballgames for the Astros. Countless times Henderson stood on third knowing that he was the winning run in the famous Covesville squeeze play, and he charged home without hesitation for the winning run. Covesville baseball was on the rise in the '70s.

Hotly contested games between Covesville, Avon, and South Garden were the highlight of the summer season. It was always Avon or the South Garden standing in the new Astros' way to the final rounds of play.

Farewell Jim

> We played South Garden on Covesville diamond. I didn't play that day, I just sat on the bench and coached. The score was tied 5–5, and here comes Pee Wee. He said, "Jim, it's Arthur's [Henderson] time to bat," but he said, "I want you to pinch bat for Arthur." I said, "Okay." I think Arthur could hit the ball too, but the boys didn't have confidence in him. So me being an old ballplayer I didn't go for no home run, I didn't try to go for no triple, all I wanted was

connection and I got a base hit. A base hit was a double for me anyway so I stole to second. I didn't try to go no farther, I just wanted to get out of the double play. So the boys had been hitting the ball all that day but Andrew Wells. He come up behind me and hit a little looper right in the infield. It was an easy out, but instead of the guys getting the ball they were watching me running! And I scored from second to home on a little soft hit on the infield and won the game 6–5. [laughing] They had that ball all the way but they were so busy watching me running they had their eyes on me and let the ball get through.

Led by Jim "King Bee" Dowell, Covesville was at last liberated from the dominance of nemesis South Garden. The team had been playing its best baseball and a strong championship run appeared guaranteed. Then despair set upon the Astros. Jim Dowell was arrested and again charged with murder. Once again the ball diamond was the arena for the last of his positive deeds as a free man. After he received a sentence of twenty-five years no one in the community of Covesville expected to see Jim ever again. He served fourteen years in all, memories of his days on the ball diamond in Covesville preserved in a warp of bad time.

Puggy

Lawrence William Johnson was a Covesville ballplayer, but in the stronghold of black baseball in central Virginia, he meant something to all that played. He stood six feet tall and it is estimated that he weighed one hundred and sixty pounds. His features were vaguely Native American and reminiscent of those of Negro League great Smokey Joe Williams. Unlike the hulking frame of Joe Williams, Lawrence Johnson's body belied the power he possessed in his right arm; it was an arm like a rocket launcher. On his best days he was untouchable with his 90 mph fastball and his high seventies change up. No one hit against him, not Avon's batting order, Wilmington's order—no one could touch his heat. But on his worst days he appeared to have little interest in playing at all.

Around his Covesville home everyone knew him as Puggy not Lawrence. To Covesville and other communities, he is something of a tragic hero.

The middle son of the Johnson family was a distant individual, making it difficult to really know him on a personal level. Teammates rarely dared ask him of his thoughts. Everyone, friends and rivals included, marveled at how a man his size could throw a baseball 90 mph, and what an exceptional talent this was in the middle-of-nowhere sandlots. He grew up in a house overlooking Covesville diamond, and was taught the ins and outs of pitching by his uncle Rufus "Junky" Dowell. By his teens he was playing several positions on the Junior Covesville Yankees team, before going up to the big-team Astros in the early '70s. In comparing his size and ability to generate his own power to those of another pitcher, major leaguer Pedro Martinez comes to mind. Martinez was another average-sized man who generated the power of a man forty pounds heavier.

Puggy sat on the bench behind starters Lee Dowell, Lenny Dowell, William

Dowell and Vincent Boswell. He played shortstop and pitched in relief, and for his size he was a dangerous hitter. As Covesville's rotation dwindled and Jim Dowell's arrest jolted the team, Puggy finally made his debut as a starter in 1976. Players and fans around the league and in various communities who did not know what kind of skills Johnson possessed received an immediate and overwhelming performance. Black baseball fans in return delivered a frenzied response. His form was excellent, his delivery effortless; some say the baseball whistled through the air upon the release of his fastball. When he or Kenny Diggs came on the mound to pitch, new baseballs were thrown out into the game to sharpen a hitter's batting eye.

There was an air of excitement surrounding Puggy Johnson's success. Many fans came out, not to cheer for Covesville or another team but to see Johnson pitch.

Other ball teams around the league wanted him to pitch for them and initially he did, but he more or less shrugged off the adoration as if wondering what all the fuss was about, even though he was the talk of the league and beyond. Mel Perrow, Shipman A's:

> I always said I could hit against any pitcher. The first time I faced Puggy he threw that ball on by me. The next time up I was prepared and knew the kind of stuff he had. Same thing—strike out! The third time up I dropped a bunt down with two strikes against me! Now that's not good baseball but that was all I could do against him!

Kenny Diggs:

> I never will forget Puggy and I hooked up in a pitching duel at Covesville that went almost 11 full innings scoreless. Covesville got their first score when Pee Wee homered to deep left field and that made it 1 to nothing. We came up at the bottom of the inning and Elgie Sims, Jr. doubled, I singled, and Brad Awkard hit a triple and we won it 2–1. But we had a pitching duel that lasted 11 innings, nobody hitting. That was Pee Wee, David, Brad, all of them going down. I could throw.... I could throw. He's the only man in my era that I know of that could ever come close to my arm—if it wasn't better.

At times it appeared that he played baseball because others wanted him to play and not because of the nature of his abilities or sheer desire. Older brother David Johnson along with team members tried to convince Puggy to attend major league tryouts, but he always came up with an excuse not to go. League officers who knew baseball and the special nature of his talents offered their support and urged him to go to an A League rookie camp, but each time he balked at the offer. Puggy never seemed to realize the nature of his talent. He grew tired of everyone's advice and prodding, and became more moody and introverted.

This was more evident on the ball field when he would simply excuse himself from the game by walking off the mound in the midst of a ten strikeout performance without an explanation, only offering, "Damn it I'm tired. Let somebody else pitch."

Rumors of substance abuse circulated and he began to show the strains from personal problems that no one else could comprehend. Opposing players began to take note that he was not the same, and physically he appeared not to have the same power that had made him one of the area's most unhittable pitchers.

The summer of 1978 would be the last season of baseball for Puggy. On a suffocatingly hot humid Virginia day, when no baseball games were scheduled, his life came to a violent end.[2]

He was killed by a single shotgun blast in an armed confrontation minutes from where he played his best baseball. Throughout the region those who simply appreciated his talent lamented what could have been. At age 22 Puggy was gone, taking with him the last bit of excitement in black baseball. Though his death did not mark the end of the league or black baseball it seemed to present itself as a marker beckoning the end of the tradition. Athletics and the sports we love are made up of heroes, whether they choose to be or not, and black baseball in Virginia was not any different. It was the players with their personalities and abilities that made the games special.

Lawrence Johnson never played pro ball or claimed the status of a major leaguer, but he is remembered as one of the best of the best by all who witnessed his performance.

M & M's Are the Best

Through the '70s in central Virginia black baseball thrived; there were good players and devoted fans. Conversely, it became more difficult for community ball clubs to field enough ballplayers in their own local area to remain competitive. Managers of area teams began to actively pursue talented players outside of the community. As black baseball in Virginia came to a close within the next decade nearly every team experienced the dilemma of finding enough interested ballplayers.

The Shipman Angels baseball team were well-acquainted with the struggle to field a team. Players like Mel Perrow, Charles Miles, and Herman Bell had traveled to other communities to play ball as far back as the '60s. Mel Perrow:

> I played for Gene Burton in North Garden [1960s] and we were basically a pickup team of what was left over from different teams, because in Shipman we didn't have enough players and that's how we ended up in North Garden.

From North Garden the Nelson County ballplayers traveled to Ivy, Virginia, for a season, before finally going back to their home community at the start of the new decade. They named their team after the new major league expansion California Angels team around Los Angeles.

A majority of their seasons were spent putting nine good players on the field, and playing their way out of the league cellar. Of course, defeating neighboring Massies Mill or Nelson County champs Avon was always a coup at any time. Curtis Perrow was the Shipman Angels' manager. He was a strong advocate of organized league play amongst black ball clubs and particularly the enforcement of regulated rules and stipulations. However, he also illustrated the importance of gamesmanship, a lesson younger brother Mel never forgot.

> My brother Curtis was the manager at Shipman. We were playing a game and there was something that we did that wasn't quite right. So the other manager challenged it. My brother Curtis looks at him and says, "No, no, have you got your rulebook?" The other manager looked at him funny. Curtis said, because on page so and so, paragraph so and so, it states thus, thus and thus and he beat the other manager down with that. I'm standing there trying to keep from turning green. I knew the rule book backward and forward. It was not there, and even if it had been there it would not have been in that order. But Curtis looked at the other manager without a rule book and got one over on him, and the guy had to deal with it. Whatever it was that we had done, he had to let it go because he didn't know the rules at the moment and he didn't have any way to prove it otherwise, and he had to take it.
>
> On the way home I said, "Curtis, whoever heard of a rule book being laid out like that." I said, "Man that book's not laid out like that!" He said, "I know it, but he didn't." So I learned that from my big brother—beat them with smarts.
>
> I never went to a game without my rule book, because there was always something in there that would kind of catch you off guard, and you might have to sit there on the side while the game is going on and take a look.

Aside from the stratagem applied by Curtis Perrow at appropriate times Shipman became a fair team in the league. They held their own against teams playing .500 baseball and at times played over their heads to prevail against the dominant Inter-County League teams. Herman Bell was probably the best player on the team. A manager could put him anywhere on the diamond—he had a good arm and he played catcher. Bell was fast, and he was a good hitter. Shipman left two extra spaces open on their roster for two out-of-town ballplayers native to the community.

Eugene and James Scott both lived in New York, but during the summer they came home for visits, and when they came home they played baseball for Shipman. The Scott brothers were power-hitters. Their addition throughout the season often meant the difference between Shipman finishing near the middle of the pack or the bottom. By the late 70s it was the same story. After six or seven seasons Shipman once again had problems fielding a team. Keene, Esmont and Ivy were beginning to bring their young ballclubs around, getting better and rising in the league standings. The only place for Shipman to go was down. Looking around Nelson County, Massies Mill and Nellysford were in the same situation.

A meeting of team managers from the three Nelson County teams was held and the managers sat down and discussed how they might help each other continue baseball in the heart of Nelson. Mel Perrow:

> In my time Shipman was never strong. Nellysford had lost a few players, we had lost a few, Massies Mill was beginning to lose their strength. We got together and started talking, and decided "Well we got a good team, if we join together," and we had a strong team that year, so it was the Massies Mill Cubs.

The newly aligned Cubs brought together the talents of Mel Perrow, Bobby Cabell, Herman Bell, T.B. Baker, Charles Miles, Fletcher "Buddy" Gaines, Jr., and Elmo Gaines. The Gaines brothers were sons of Fletcher Gaines, Sr., long time manager and black baseball promoter of the second Massies Mill squad in the '50s and

'60s. The Cubs were good; they played hard and they played tough. Backed by managers Bobby Cabell and Mel Perrow, the team made no mistake about going out there to win. At times they were accused of being overly aggressive, but they were hungry. Their last ballfield, "Ebony and Ivory Field," still stands today on Rt. 151.

Best of all they were moving up in the rankings, and after the month of August, the Cubs stood on the doorstep to the play-offs, a first since the merger to form the new Massie Mill Cubs. Mel Perrow actually preferred spending more time on the bench coaching and surveying the happenings on the playing field. Though he was still a good player, he was very candid about his abilities as a player. Mel Perrow:

> I knew my limitations. I played because there was nobody that was playing any better, so when this kid showed up that was the end of me. He said, "I want to play." I said, "What position do you play?" He said, "Center field." And this kid was young, fast, he could run the ball down and catch it, and he could throw. I could still run it down, but then there was so much pain after, in getting ready for the next one. I could outhit him, but hey, I could sit on the bench and pinch-hit and do that every now and then and that's basically how I finished up. I managed a couple more years, but I didn't do much playing.

In the '80s Massies Mill became contenders; they were battling Covesville and Avon for the go-ahead nod to the championship rounds. The play-offs contained the usual excitement, and also had their share of twists and controversies. Mel Perrow was no stranger to disputes or controversial calls. He was now acting secretary to Hugo Scott, the commissioner of the league, and very detail-oriented.

> We were moving into a time of real strict rules. The uniform rules had to be enforced or you looked like a bunch of clowns—one guy out there in khaki pants and so forth. Anything out of uniform was a big enough reason to protest, or get a guy kicked out of a game. Bobby Cabell and I were co-managers at Massies Mill, and we beat Avon in a play-off game. Avon was always loaded with players and they could always get somebody that could flat out play.
> One of Avon's better players ... for some reason or another he got there late and he was on the bench. The game is going on—and the game is tight, but they are ahead and they are beginning to pull away from us. And I saw the manager when he pointed to that guy. By him getting there late, he's not fully dressed and he's forgotten all about it. The minute he pointed to him I touched Bobby, I said, "No don't say a word."
> I waited until the manager called his name and he stepped to the bat; everything had gone down, then I sent Bobby out, I said, "Go protest." Bobby lodged an official protest. Man they were so mad at Bobby—they were mad at Bobby for almost a year. And I laughed. I said, "Bobby, I sent you because you were bigger than me—they thought you were the bad guy." And we beat them.
> I beat you with my wits. I never was a power-hitter. I played until I was 35 years of age and I think I knocked one home run during the whole time, but I never really tried. I would get a single, double, or triple, and I was fast so I would bunt you to death.

Massies Mill went on to claim an early '80s championship before the team split, with the Nellysford community reforming a ball team. Mel Perrow stayed with the team into the '80s while serving as the commissioner of the Tri-County League. The Cubs were the last of central Virginia's black baseball teams. When the Tri-County League folded in the '80s, manager Bobby Cabell entered the Cubs in an integrated baseball league in Lynchburg, Virginia. After four years of play Massies Mill claimed

Snapshots. Clockwise from top center: Avon Twins; Avon Twins; Culpeper Dragons; Henry "Bubba" Waller, Jr.; John Armstead; and Henry Waller, Sr., at left, Henry "Bubba" Waller, Jr. The Sperryville Tigers are at center.

an early '90s championship. On that note the Cubs folded for good, with many players, including Bobby Cabell, turning to softball.

Snapshots

Rapid-fire digital photo takes, selfies, and GoPro action footage have become commonplace in the 21st century, but if you were born between 1950 and 1970, you remember the Kodak and Polaroid instant cameras that produced sticky three-by-three snapshots. Soldiers sent them home in letters from Vietnam showing the enlisted troops posed near bunkers and artillery with buddies. Snapshots were pinned to boards in college dorms and high schoolers snapped them leaving football practice and at favorite after-school hangouts. Like the images that today's camera phone capture, these photos were taken spontaneously. Unlike today's digital mastery, the quality was low and there were no back-ups.

Snapshots were stuffed into notebook binders for safekeeping only to be discarded accidentally when school was out. Albums were filled with them; they were easy to place and hard to remove; they were tossed and scattered about in desk drawers and in dresser drawers stuck in between drawers. They were voluminous in number but hard to keep up with, and finding a classic snap was almost like finding your favorite currency in between the cushions. If you could identify or remember the person and place it brought an instant smile.

The following features are snapshots of players from the 1970s who stood out on the baseball team, in their families and in their communities.

David Wyant, Home and Away

David Wyant from White Hall, Virginia, grew up working on his family farm and playing sports. Outside of church on Sunday and school during the week, it was all he knew. His grandfather did run a country grocery store—Wyant's—which meant a little more work. Wyant's upbringing and disposition turned him into an affable student athlete.

David was a three-sport standout at Albemarle High School in Charlottesville. Baseball was his favorite sport and upon his acceptance to the University of Virginia he continued his athletic career under then-coach Jim West. UVA was not as competitive in the ACC when David Wyant walked on the grounds in the mid-sixties but building toward some very good teams in the late sixties and early seventies. David was a very good ballplayer, a good pitcher, but he quickly realized that he was on a higher tier of baseball and still had a lot to learn to distinguish himself as a player on the Division I level.

David Wyant crossed eras with Charlottesville boy wonder and future Major League third baseman Mike Cubbage. Cubbage, inducted into the Virginia Sports Hall of Fame in 2017, was a few years behind Dave Wyant but also a talented three-sport athlete who came of age knocking out windows across from Lane High School Field.

Not long after graduation Wyant returned to his high school alma mater to coach baseball, soon meeting young Ricky and Keith Davis from Barboursville. First impressions were mutually positive and the teenaged Davis brothers recruited their coach to play for the Barboursville Giants. Coach Wyant accepted and added another sports commitment to his arm's length list of endeavors, coaching high school, apprenticing as an official in little league sports through high school sports, then suiting up for his own games in the evening.

Barboursville rehabbed and formed up with a new lineup of players in the 1970s. Mack Davis was now the unquestioned team leader buoyed by his sons, nephews, and close friends in the community. He was also still amazingly good as a pitcher—sometimes still intimidating to younger hitters. But Mack needed relief in the rotation to save his arm and keep opposing teams also retooling off balance.

Wyant brought with him the enthusiasm and revitalizing spirit to lift the Giants back to the heights of contention where they were decades prior. David might have enjoyed playing ball more than Mack Davis. David had a closet of uniforms. He was already playing on another independent baseball team, the Charlottesville Royals.

According to his Cavaliers and Royals teammate Coach Tommy Bibb, the Royals were invented out of necessity.

As Bibb explained, like all other student athletes when the semester and regular sports season ended, you were looking for a team to join for summer ball in June. For Central Virginia collegiate baseball players this meant latching on to a team in the Valley Baseball League. However, at the time an ambiguous ruling as to eligibility of collegiate players left Dave Wyant and Tommy Bibb odd men out.

So Tommy and David, with input from a few former high school teammates and rivals, found a sponsor, got new uniforms and started playing regularly on the former Burley High School Field under the lights. The Royals played all comers during the week including a few of the best area black baseball teams, winning all except a couple of matchups with the South Garden Tigers, Covesville Astros and Wilmington Eagles. The cost was 50 cents to walk through the gate, and full stands kept the field lights on and the Royals in bats, baseballs and beer.

Incidentally, through the Royals' matchups versus South Garden, Donald Byers was invited to play for the Royals weeknights then returned to the home team on Sunday. Byers was the only black player on the Royals roster but this was also an early move in desegregating local sports in the Charlottesville-Albemarle community.

On those Sunday afternoons, David was a smash hit in the new Barboursville lineup, winning over the loyal fan base. Recalling the community years later, he chuckles at the Barboursville matrons over-feeding him between innings to the point he was worried about his continued play as he waddled, belly full, back out to the mound. Playing in a black baseball league David learned a side of life he was isolated from growing up in his own part of Albemarle County. Listening to his new Barboursville teammates he quickly caught on to the differences in how he grew up playing sports and the schools he had attended. Teammates regaled him with stories of athletes who had attended George Washington Carver and Burley, two schools whose alumni exploits were becoming distant memories but still vivid for those of a different generation in the 1970s.

David won his share of games on the mound for the Giants, standing out in a small percentage of white ballplayers in the early '70s, sometimes standing out too much. Infrequently, but here and there, he received the same taunts and racist vitriol black players maneuvering through the minor leagues and early major leagues endured decades prior. He was in the wrong community and in the wrong culture and he was too good, incurring the ire of a few fans.

The racism was evidence of minor discontent but not representative of the majority as Wyant remembers his teammates and keen competition that he always lived for during his time in athletics. With the passage of time and ballplaying seasons, neither David Wyant nor his teammate remember clearly how many games and seasons he played Barboursville Giants baseball, but it seems he made himself available somehow through the mid-'70s before devoting himself to the more popular game of softball that swept the 1970s.

Outside of his family two undertakings tied down reference points throughout life, going to work as an engineer for the then-Highway Department of Virginia and moving up the ranks of football officiating. As an official he started from the ground up, in his words, learning from the best game to game, and as he got better people in the right place and right time began to take notice. Key correct calls in some important college football games led to interest and interviews toward professional sports officiating. David became an official in the NFL, making an appearance in America's most popular event, the Super Bowl, working Super Bowl XLVIII as a side judge.

Brother Leewood

Elkton, Virginia, and its hollows were a storied stop along the historic path of black baseball in Virginia. Former players junior and senior never forgot the trip up Route 33 near Skyline Drive, with vivid recollections of leaving the main highway to a rural gravel road and then to a cattle path, one way in, one way out—Bryant Hollow. But on the way into the hollow there was a ball diamond somewhere in the trees and there were houses, houses of relatives and supporters of the Elkton Bucks baseball teams, letting you know you were in Bucks country.

Black baseball in Elkton was just as popular in the 1930s as the 1960s, according to Roscoe Burgess, Sr., who counted the East Rockingham team among a steady slate of rivals in his early years of playing ball in the 1940s. The community was among a select list of prospective teams in the early 1960s when Burgess and Hugo Scott formed the Shenandoah Valley League. We cannot speak in totality to the makeup of the early Elkton teams, but by the early '60s the lineup was largely composed of the Davis family, eight Davis brothers and cousins including Leewood, rivaling the Sims family of Greenwood for kin in the lineup. Bryant Hollow became "Davis Hollow" on Sundays in the Shenandoah Valley League. Leewood joined the team in his late teens when he was already a good baseball player recognized by black and white players in the Shenandoah Valley. He played on his home Elkton team and preceding integration played on all-white Rockingham County baseball teams.

Playing in either league there were conflicts, but Leewood was purely a baseball player who showed up to play winning baseball, playing hard but fair. Admittedly, he avoided winning via conflict at all costs. Leewood left it to the other fellows to sort out their hyped feelings one way or the other, and when the umpire finally uttered, "Play ball!" Leewood was back in action.

The only piece missing from the story is how good his Bucks teams were. Player recollections, fond as they may be, are sometimes lacking in regard to the success of a rival or competitor. All former players confirm that there were regularly scheduled playoff games played in Bryant Hollow.

The South Garden Tigers, nearing their peak in the late sixties, battled Sperryville in Rappahannock County and Harrisonburg and Elkton in Rockingham County late into the season so it is quite possible that Elkton made at least one championship appearance between 1968 and 1970. A mid-season *Charlottesville-Albemarle Tribune* article highlighting the Shen-Valley standings before the all-star break showed the Bucks with a strong 5–1 start, placing them a game behind their rival, the Harrisonburg ACs.

Leewood continued playing for his family team but by the mid-'70s relegated his play to the Rockingham County Baseball League. Stunningly, Rockingham County Baseball League statistics credit him with 22 years of play, a 15-time all-star playing first base per his 2017 induction into the league hall of fame. It stands to reason that in his heyday Leewood was rarely out of uniform. It is certain he played for the Bucks on Saturdays and Sundays and probably played two games a week in the Rockingham County League. He played most of his seasons in the county league first with the Harrisonburg ACs, then Linville and he also aided Shenandoah in reaching the 1982 championship, bowing out in a 4–1 final to Clover Hill. Leewood is still on the go, still active throughout the week—not on the diamond but volunteering time in his home community of Elkton.

Michael Carey

Michael Carey made his way onto the famed Wilmington Eagles Baseball team much like many others over the decades: by invitation. A standout athlete since his teen years in Fluvanna County, Michael was not at all unfamiliar with the Wilmington team or their winning history. He was not from Wilmington but from Fork Union and so played ball with friends in lower Fluvanna and Richmond County.

However, a mid-'70s chance meeting with a Wilmington player watching Michael's team play charted his diamond career with an exchange along the lines of "You are one of the best outfielders I've seen" and in turn Michael volunteering, "I would really like to play for Wilmington"—done. There was always room in the Eagles lineup for a good arm, deadly bat and glove men tracking baseballs like hawks.

Besides his skills Michael Carey fit into the Wilmington lineup right away because he "loved" playing the game of baseball. No wonder in the 1975 team photo he is standing shoulder to shoulder with James Payne, his manager, Mr. Paul Franklin, and Cool Papa Robert Winston, immediate good company. Carey was also part of a younger generation of players that continued Wilmington's winning tradition and continued its lore that carried on long after the team's end. His favorite Major League player was hard-charging, Venezuela-born Dave Concepcion, #13 of the Cincinnati Reds, and so Carey first played shortstop and then moved to the outfield playing beside Steve Sheridan. The two complemented each other with their fielding skills and both smashed singles and doubles ahead of the long ball threats in the lineup.

Then there were Roger Bowles, who was either behind the plate or at third base; Big Lonnie Trice, who guarded everything between second and third; Tim Shelton out of Goochland, Virginia, who pitched and played the infield; and Roger's friends making semi-permanent appearances, David Brooks, Reno Walton and brother Mike. How much love did Tim have for the game? Well, with a matchup with the retooled Barboursville Giants and a commitment to his wife's graduation in competition, Michael did the right thing and put family first. Wilmington lost a close one, 5–4, away, and years later Carey still laments his absence from the lineup that weekend as a factor in the Eagles dropping a game to one of the better teams in the then–Tri-County League.

Michael Carey wanted to play, he wanted to win and he always played like a winner, sometimes stretching singles into triples and going home for a score every time Wilmington put men on base in scoring position. In his own words, "you needed to make a perfect throw and catch to put me out." He was determined to score and make those runs count. Before games Wilmington players made bets on who would get the most hits that day and the most home runs; the winner got the pot after nine innings. With the drive and enthusiasm Tim brought to the diamond, it is no wonder that when jersey number #13 was presented to him he never batted an eye; he liked the number, creating his own luck, and fans at home and away easily identifying him in the lineup. Like Virginia's old-time players before him, for Tim it was not enough to just be on a good team or in the starting lineup; he had to stand out, from the crisp elastic stirrup socks that aligned #13 to his ballcap. And then there was his personal selection of bats. Even teams of the most humble means kept a bag of bats but most often players went out and purchased their own, whether a matter of weight or new design.

Michael, newly married and starting a family, was on a budget but still needed good equipment. The average player in those times played with gloves until they were rag soft but bats were another story. Once again an acquaintance carrying on conversation about baseball helped Carey solve an equipment issue. This acquaintance worked at Fork Union Military Academy as equipment manager for the Athletic Department.

The college preparatory school had sports programs that propelled and prolonged the careers of athletes far and wide. Athletic gear was in great supply and replaced when worn out. When Michael Carey heard that broken bats were tossed into the trash, he experienced a moment of inspiration.

Rather than picking a bat out of the bag at random or taping together a broken bat, he put in a running order for discarded bats courtesy FUMA's baseball team. Once he received the discarded bat, he simply nailed the bat back together using the best weight nails to tack up the fractured shards, taped it up, and put it in play. If the bat broke again—not too often—he selected the next repaired slugger in his own equipment bag of bats. Perhaps this innovative move typifies the spirit and creativity of black baseball in Virginia as much as the scrabbled diamond cutouts.

Wilmington won before entering league play and were winners during, maybe winning three to four out of five years entered. The Eagles' greatest worry was lack of competition in the league because competition on hot summer Sundays outside of the league had run dry. Michael Carey was an all-star the years he played on a team of all-stars. Then and now he feels his Wilmington Eagles team was special, records and championship wins standing on their own. Perhaps most astonishing is his confession that the team never practiced during their run of dominance; too many players were spread out over longer distances. "Wilmington players showed up and won." By the '70s, with a few remaining starters still in the community and everyone else spread out in the region, practices according to Carey were not logistically possible, so the Eagles just showed up, played, and won. The Wilmington Eagles still had rivals in lethal line-ups, including outfielder Keith Davis of Bar-

Looks like he could still play. Michael Carey (right) with the author, 2019 (author's collection).

boursville, Ivanhoe Nelson of Keene and a slew of rivals on Nelson's vaunted Avon teams. He remembers Avon as the measuring stick no matter what level of experience you had under your cleats. But he always looked forward to standing in against Phil Doyle and Kenny Diggs or tracking home run balls hit by the Awkard brothers. He played for the Eagles transitioning from the old Wilmington obstacle course diamond to Fluvanna High School's Field until the team folded and then he finished his diamond career with the Keene Colts in Albemarle County.

Awkards, Avon and All-Comers

During the heyday of black baseball in Virginia the name Awkard was synonymous with baseball—often mispronounced and not as well known or remembered as Sims or Davis but present and in place when the competition reached that higher level. Avon is a village below the magnificent Blue Ridge Mountains in Nelson County. Players walked to church and the ball diamond. Linwood Awkard had already distinguished himself as a baseball player when he started the Avon Allstars in the late 1950s. "Lin," as he was known, was still a very good player but became more focused on mentoring the younger talented teenaged Allstars, Durrette, Jackson, Diggs, Alexander, and his oldest son Marshton. Sometime between the Allstars and the Avon Wrecking Crew, sons Kenneth and Herman Brad, "H.B.," began substituting in and out of Avon lineups at age 13 much like Aaron and Mays in their formative years of Negro League ballplaying. At 17 H.B. was credited along with other Avon players with bringing trophies home to the base of the Blue Ridge. By 21 H.B. and cousin Kenny Diggs were leading Avon into the last bow of black baseball play and new incarnation as the Twins.

Players from within and outside of the community came, conquered and went, but members of the Awkard family remained through the decades as players, managers, and scouts finding talent. Father Lin loved watching his sons play, but at times, with their games secured in the early innings, he was known to show up in other communities, recollecting, visiting and scouting other teams on Avon's schedule. In the last decade there remained younger son H.B. and a few relatives but Avon also remained dominant in baseball. Different decades, different uniforms but always, Avon, Awkards versus all-comers, amateurs, integrated teams, travel squads. Every third hitter in the lineup was dangerous. Avon may have recorded more grand slams than any team in league play. Batters 3, 6, 9, four to six runs scored, game over. Watching Avon round the bases resembled a track relay team as much as a baseball lineup at times.

H.B. Awkard, Jr., 1989 MLB draft, Boston Red Sox (photograph courtesy H.B. Awkard, Sr.)

Into the 1980s, playing in the mode of a select few versatile all-star Central Virginia players, H.B. pitched with the best, roamed the outfield, and played catcher, receiving from some of the best on the Avon A's teams. Among his high points in a long-running baseball career were playing with the stars of the heyday including his father and members of the old Wrecking Crew, pitching a three-hitter and a 1–0 no-hitter, playing for the Grottoes Cardinals where he batted .400, and lastly going behind the plate as receiver for his son H.B. Jr., a 1989 Major League Baseball draftee.

H.B. still lives in central Virginia, heading up a successful family enterprise in limousine transportation.

A haul of Avon baseball trophies, late 1970s to 1991 (photograph courtesy H.B. Awkard, Sr.).

Robert Anthony

The 1965–66 Barboursville Giants were still a force to be reckoned with. Mack Davis and Carrol Bates were the mainstays with the addition of the Brock kin from neighboring Greene County. During the decade more representatives of the Davis family began entering the lineup, including Mack's nephews, Marshall, Jimmy and Walker Davis. Watching from the bench from the time he was old enough to tag along was Robert Anthony, Mack's sister Charlotte's son. Charlotte was one of Barboursville's greatest boosters, always vocal home and away and one of the Sunday cooks enticing fans with home cooking. Robert grew up cheering for the Giants and his uncle often traveling to away games anywhere the Giants played in the region. Uncle Mack was also a father figure for Robert Anthony throughout his lifetime. He could always count on his uncle and "Uncle Mack" could always count on him.

Responsibility came at an early age with Robert taking on jobs before his teen years, chopping wood, working on a farm and then working for a well-known local brick manufacturer, Webster Brick, in his last years of high school.

He was on the Barboursville Giants team by his teens along with a couple of relatives and friends in uniform—but still watching from the bench. In his words, he, Freddy Baker and Burrill Brock were the "water boys" and equipment managers—they rarely made it on the ballfield. To sharpen their skills, for a time they played in a few of their own teen pickup baseball games with a junior Barboursville lineup against the communities of Esmont, Covesville, Chestnut Grove and Elkton. Assisted by Ms. Dorothy Churchman and Will White, the younger team could usually get in half a dozen games during the summer.

Robert, Freddy and Burrill really wanted to play on the big team, but securing a position in the Barboursville Giants lineup, relatives or not, was not easy with many players a generation ahead unwilling to hang up the glove voluntarily. Outside of injury, you had to best them, actually displaying what you could do at the plate and in the field during late winter and early spring practices. Recalls Robert Anthony in the present day, "Once we got the chance to prove ourselves and play in those games, Freddy and I—those older guys never did make it back into the lineup."

Robert, Freddy, and friends entered the Giants lineup in the last decade of Barboursville baseball, 1970. Robert was a dependable singles hitter and Freddy hit the ballpark blasts that made the fans holler and leave the generous concessions area. Freddy Baker established his own Barboursville Giants home run lore at the expense of the Madison Orioles. Madison, seeking to dress up their ballfield, installed "temporary" fencing clearly demarcating home run territory. Freddy had a field day hitting so many home runs that game that the *temporary* fencing was never seen again.

Robert contributed in any way he could as a team player and with pride remembers playing with his brother Michael and younger cousins Ricky, Greg, and Keith. Keith Davis was an all-star in centerfield with Robert next to him in left. Reminiscing with humor he recalled that cousin Keith actually covered so much field so fast that he sometimes had to stop himself short so that Robert could make a couple of catches during a game. They both chased down balls on a few of the better outfields, Porter Field and Burley Field, but also the lopsided gorge areas where infielders had to alert the outfield that balls were headed their direction.

Outfield play on the black baseball diamonds of Virginia was not just about running fleet of foot with an eye on the ball but also about maintaining a bead on the ball, striding over dropping and rising terrain. The cousins also had the chance to play in the summer all-star game representing the family and the team.

Like a true competitor, Robert's lasting single memory of the all-star classic is not making a game-saving play but misjudging a ball under the lights of Porterfield that he was sure that he would not have misplayed under normal daylight conditions.

Robert also recalls early '70s growing pains with the transition to a new lineup. The Giants were not winning. After hearing the displeasure vocalized by loyal Barboursville fans, and then Uncle Mack reading the young line-up the riot act, Barboursville started winning again, and with additions to the roster the Giants were again among the top area team contenders in the newly-formed Inter-County League. The late Kansas City Chiefs receiver Walter White, a tremendous all-around athlete then of Cismont, Virginia, played summers on the team along with friend Raymond Bates. Barboursville finished runner-up to the Avon Twins a couple of seasons and then, making things even more challenging, Wilmington entered the league. The Giants were still winners, stealing their very first encounter with the big league–appearing Fluvanna team. Anthony years after the fact has a healthy perspective on the team and his time playing, maybe not outright champions or very best but a team and community respected and remembered.

When Barboursville folded in 1978, often struggling to field nine players, Robert remained active with family playing in the more popular softball games that took over Central Virginia and sometimes pickup and league basketball with his younger cousins the Davis brothers. Teenaged Robert was a brick maker and held down this demanding physical task after class and continued the craft after graduation from newly-integrated Orange County High School. Aside from a military commitment in the Air Force and a brief stay in the city, Robert has lived his life out in Barboursville.

He became a devoted father and grandfather, and just as significant, Robert Anthony became the Reverend Anthony and is pastor of his home church, Blue Run in Barboursville. Alas, he has performed the eulogies for cousins Greg and Keith Davis and his beloved uncle Matthew "Mack" Davis in 2020. He is a few years older than his uncle when I first interviewed him back in 1999 but remains busy six days out of seven and is an integral part of the annual black baseball reunion held in Orange County.

VII

*Race Against Time**

In the spring of 2019 I attended a baseball game at the University of Virginia. The Cavaliers were playing Norfolk State University in a nonconference matchup. The Division III Spartans were not an equal match for the Cavaliers judging from the pitching, hitting, and fielding that day.

More revealing was the fact that half the Spartans roster was comprised of white ballplayers. Following the mostly one-sided matchup, I mused over why a significant percentage of non-black student athletes would attend an HBCU. Are they recruited like black athletes at the school for a sports team? Are there not enough amateur level African American players to fill the roster? Baseball was the national pastime into the 1970s and had a strong presence in black communities in urban and rural areas. Baseball gloves were guaranteed presents for birthdays and at Christmas. With the glove next came hours and hours of playing catch with friends and relatives, learning to catch a baseball, handle grounders and fly balls, and pitch.

Invitation Only

In 2017 Major League Baseball commemorated the 70th anniversary of Jackie Robinson's integration of professional baseball. Annually there is Jackie Robinson

---

*"Race Against Time" was a chapter omitted from the first edition of *Sunday Coming* due to time constraints for the original submission in 2001. From the inception of the project in 1999, the deeper I got into the research, interviews, recollections, and celebrations, the stronger and more persistent the question became—what happened to black baseball players in Virginia? Several old-timers offered their perspectives but we are still without one definitive answer to what precipitated the decline or if there exists the possibility for a revival. The Native Americans invented lacrosse but in large part are not participants anymore. Black jockeys were winners of the Kentucky Derby in the 19th century but not seen in the modern era. Even these examples fall short. What if African Americans eschewed anything to do with today's game of basketball on any level? Black baseball in a bygone era was a family game, a neighborhood and community game. It started with a glove and a baseball, learning to play catch with your father, catch with a friend, your relatives, watching them play and then, in your time, progressively learning the game of baseball.

Fifty-plus years on it is still nearly impossible for me to watch a baseball game on TV or in person without remembering my first exposure to black baseball in the very neighborhood where I grew up, the energy, excitement, intensity. From the Gen X vantage point, it was a sport your father played, your uncles, older brothers and cousins, receiving the new ball glove at Christmas and or for your birthday, outfitting you for that rite of passage beginning with playing catch, resulting in midweek ballgames, mastering a position and, hardest of all, hitting a baseball.

Of course, it was also routine to watch and follow several black professional baseball stars of the 1970s: Aaron, Blue, Jackson, Morgan, Stargell, Baker. Conversely, today there are few African American players to follow; the sport is almost foreign to African American youth who often view it as uninteresting, too slow and too expensive.

Day, when every Major League player dons #42. This is special because Jackie Robinson was an impact player in his time and he became a Hall of Famer. It is more significant because the figurative color line disappeared and a Black American, a descendant of enslaved ancestors, was on the field, not in the stands as a paying customer or looking through an open part of the outfield fence. With the richly documented history of Black Americans throughout baseball, questions have arisen as to what has become of African American baseball players in the twenty-first century. Robinson and Larry Doby desegregated the Major Leagues in 1947 with Brooklyn and Cleveland, respectively. Between 1947 and 1959 more than 100 documented black Minor League players followed Robinson and Doby but only a few received promotions to Major League teams and an even smaller percentage starred playing big-city baseball.

Raymond Dandridge, third base Negro League and Latin League star, delighted fans in Minnesota, increasing the gate for the Minor League Millers club, but he never received the honor of a cup of coffee in a Major League stadium.

No one outside of Brooks Robinson could field like Dandridge, but he was deemed too old with the thought that a promotion for an aging vet took an opportunity away from a white Major League prospect predicted to have a long career ahead. Negro League players comprised the first wave of black players desegregating professional baseball.

Negro League baseball did not have a Minor League system. Players were selected from amateur and sandlot teams, either sticking to a professional lineup or being released, but if capable they played and displayed their talents immediately.

Players played their way into shape, played their way into the lineup without extra Spring Training instruction and thus played their way into the league where they stayed for as long as their skills and interest carried them through.

Former Negro League stars and drafted players remained on Major League rosters as long as they performed to expectations, but underperformance meant a trip back down to the minors. This was also the case for younger white ballplayers, but black Major Leaguers knew if they expected to make it back to the league they had to persevere and put up the numbers to earn another call up. This was the case with Newark Eagles baseball legend Monte Irvin, drafted by the New York Giants and outfield teammate of Willie Mays. Drafted in 1949 with Hank Thompson, Irvin played here and there in the lineup batting .224 with a handful of runs batted in but no demonstration of the power that he was known for in the Negro National League with the Eagles. Starting in 1950 out of spring training on a Minor League club, Irvin's bat came to life. He hit 10 home runs in 18 games, inflating his average to .510, waking up in the Majors and becoming an integral part of the Giants' championship teams.

The Negro Professional League continued with shuffled lineups and new league formations. The Negro Southern League was revived and included teams from Richmond, Virginia, and Chattanooga, Tennessee, and new teams in the Midwest.

Baltimore's Black Sox, a Negro League team that probably went through more incarnations than any other club from amateur to professional, supported a new team through the 1950s. A couple of things were different post–1947: the fan following and coverage in newsprint. Black baseball fans were following the exploits of the Dodgers and Indians, not the Grays and Monarchs. The leading black newspapers, *Pittsburgh Courier* and *Baltimore Afro American*, were dedicating their coverage to Jackie Robinson and Larry Doby as well as other black athletes making strides and making their presence felt in other areas of desegregated American sports. Negro League baseball results were relegated to the back page and edge of the page results in brief, no longer sports page features.

It was not until 1960 that every Major League team had at least one black position player. In the preceding decade a number of black players debuted as Major League prospects, but only future Hall of Famers were granted promotion. Age and personal and social conduct were under scrutiny for black players. Many of these players were the same age as white prospects but were called up nearly a decade later after playing their prime years in the minors. The catcher, often considered the team leader, was sparsely represented by black position players in the Majors despite having legendary catchers during the decades of the professional Negro Leagues: Biz Mackie, Josh Gibson, Roy Campanella.

Only Elston Howard and John "Junior" Roseboro were able to carve out notable careers behind the plate in the Major Leagues, playing for the Yankees and Dodgers, respectively.

The last Major League team to draft a black player was the Boston Red Sox when second baseman Elijah "Pumpsie" Green received a call-up from the Minneapolis Millers to pinch hit and run in a Sox game in July 1959.

Best of the Best

In the 1950s, black baseball thrived with teams and in some cases leagues in every corner of the Commonwealth of Virginia. With the passage of civil rights acts in the 1950s and 1960s, signs of progress were evident with the integration of public schools and parks. *Brown v. Board of Education* in 1954 and other rulings forecast changes in public education in the South. Extracurricular activities reflected desegregation in greater numbers on football teams, basketball teams and track teams than on baseball teams; those few who did participate represented 1 percent on teams with all white classmates.

Teenaged black players who had played all the way through junior league baseball as starters and all-stars or played summers in their communities on still-existing black baseball teams against adults failed to either make the school lineup or try out at all. There was something regressive about the integration of the national pastime.

Outside of the confines of public education, black players appeared in integrated lineups on the sandlot level and in amateur organizations like the Rockingham County Baseball League and the Apple Valley League in the Shenandoah Valley. In 1967 Richard Slaughter and the Williams Brothers of the well-traveled Sperryville Tigers played in an integrated lineup with the Culpeper Cubs, an independent team. Slaughter later played for a Cubs opponent, the Madison Bluejays of the Valley League. Previously, Virginia Jim Crow laws prevented integrated sporting events in publicly maintained parks. The Orange Nationals (Nats) of Orange, Virginia, were permitted to play before capacity crowds at the town's Porterfield Park but were prohibited from holding practices on the field.

The 1950 Danville Allstars participated in the Negro American Association, a high amateur league of the best black baseball teams from North Carolina and teams from the southern part of Virginia. Danville played through a season and a half and were replaced by the former Atlanta Black Crackers of the Negro Southern League. Baseball continued in Danville, but the news surrounded a young man not yet out of his teens: Percy Miller, Jr.

Percy Miller, Jr., son of former Negro League pitcher Percy Miller, Sr., was playing sandlot ball and part of a summer stint with a traveling Jacksonville Eagles team. From the age of 15 he played on his father's Danville team, knocking in runs as he gained confidence and a following, enough of a following to earn an invitation to test the waters during the early days of integration. A local businessman with connections to the Carolina League secured a try-out for young Miller with the hometown Minor League Danville Leafs. The team's logo was symbolic of southern Virginia tobacco production over the centuries. The Leafs were a farm club of the San Francisco Giants.

Percy Miller came in hitting from game one, a sold-out 1951 event that drew the bulk of the Leafs' white fanbase and an overflowing section of elated African American supporters from the town and surrounding areas. Though off to a promising start, Miller struggled with the still-existing Southern segregationist practices and all but complete alienation from teammates who had rarely been in any close proximity to a black man. Danville made efforts to work with him through a playing slump, but in their assessment Miller's development in the minors was not where they envisioned, so he was cut from the team in the spring of 1952.

Joe Vann Durham, originally from Newport News, Virginia, signed with the Baltimore Orioles in 1954. He played eight games before being let go and was out of the Majors for two seasons before being picked up by the Cincinnati Reds in 1956.

Outfielder Charles "Charley" Peete was drafted by the St. Louis Cardinals in 1955. Peete, signed by Portsmouth in the Piedmont Association in 1953, played his way steadily upward smashing hits, hitting .311 with 17 home runs and 79 RBIs.

The Cardinals planned to send him to Caracas, Venezuela, for winter ball with the plan to ultimately bring their rising prospect up to the big team during the 1956 season. Sadly, this was not to be. Charles Peete, his wife and three children, among twenty-five passengers making their way to Valencia, perished when their plane struck the side of a mountain.

Black ball stars enjoyed the most exposure during the late 1950s and 1960s. Frank Robinson won Major League Baseball's Triple Crown, Hank Aaron consistently hit 40 home runs each season, pitcher Bob Gibson became an all-time great pitcher setting an ERA stat not likely to be equaled and Willie Mays seemed to make everything exciting at the plate and in the field. Maurice Maury Wills, a Washington, D.C., Cardoza High School grad drafted by the Brooklyn Dodgers in 1950, debuted in the newly minted Los Angeles Dodgers in 1959. He became the Major League all-time base stealing leader in 1962 tallying 104 stolen bases.

The 1970s Black stars appeared in all of the best lineups: Vida Blue pitched for the A's, Reggie Jackson was in the outfield for the A's and Yankees, and Willie Stargell and Henry "Hank" Aaron blasted home runs.

Between 1961 and 1967, Lou Brock, Tommie Agee, Blue Moon Odum, Cleon Jones, and Vida Blue were drafted into the Major Leagues. All were World Series winners. Brock and Blue are Hall of Famers,

Diversity in Major League Baseball has been charted above 40 percent with more players of color hailing from the islands, especially Puerto Rico and the Dominican Republic, continuing a long history of great baseball by Black players designated as Hispanic–Latino.

African American players make up 6 percent of professional baseball rosters, down 12 percent from the early 1990s. In the history of the Negro Leagues black American players were celebrated from the South to the North and West to the islands as the best of the best, but at home 78 years after Jackie and Larry Doby, they are scant at the highest level or hard to distinguish from island-born players. Reflecting back on his professional baseball career in Bruce Adelson's 1999 book *Brushing Back Jim Crow*, Joe Durham succinctly assessed the turbulent decades he endured along with his ballplaying peers, their goals and ultimate impact of crossing the color line in Major League Baseball.

> Once the teams became integrated in the different leagues, there was the possibility of [widespread] integration someday. But it was hard to make changes. Some people didn't want to make changes. People said, well we've got the black players in. "There are enough black, motels, hotels to house these people and restaurants to feed them." Most teams traveled by their own bus, so you didn't have to worry about segregation on your own bus. But sooner or later they would have to get around to integrating the restaurants and hotels because times had changed. We were pioneers for sure. There are a lot of things you would like to [change] and hope the guys who come behind you follow instead of coming in with a hot head, because if you do, you're in trouble. Just go out and do your job. Forget about everything else except, just remember one thing. The people up in the stands have paid their way in. If they want to be ignorant to call you all kinds of names, let them do so. You can't let that sort of thing get close to you. If it does, you can just wipe out the season, because every town you go into will be practically the same thing. You have to do your job.

Only three African American players appeared in the 2023 Major League Star game compared to nearly a dozen fifty years prior. Of the trio, Los Angeles Dodgers outfielder-infielder Marcus "Mookie" Betts is already on an all-time list of greatest all around Major League players.

Historically Black Baseball

Historically Black Colleges and Universities (HBCUs) are institutions of higher learning founded for the educational advancement of the African American populace, beginning during the mid–19th century in the Northeast. They then flourished in Southern states during Reconstruction. The HBCU experience includes academics, fraternal orders, arts, and sports. Baseball was played at tiny Storer College in Harpers Ferry, West Virginia, and at famed Grambling University in Louisiana. With the folding of the Negro Leagues in the 1950s HBCU play was the last bastion of organized black baseball but sanctioned as amateur athletics. The NAIA (National Association of Intercollegiate Athletics) was the first sanctioning body to accept the membership of HBCUs in 1953, and today the majority of HBCUs are under NCAA (National Collegiate Athletic Association) sanctioning.

The Mid-Atlantic MEAC conference consists of eight schools: Coppin State, Delaware State, Howard University, Maryland Eastern Shore, Morgan State, Norfolk State, North Carolina Central and South Carolina State. As reiterated by Bob Kendrick, president of the Negro League Baseball Museum, in the prime years of the Negro Leagues a great number of the players were student athletes at HBCUs recruited to play summers on Negro professional league rosters. Limited documentation exists pointing to HBCUs producing major league talent during the desegregation of professional baseball, but black ballplayers were more often drafted out of high school and selected from the sandlots like their white counterparts.

Baserunning and base stealing legend Lou Brock of the champion St. Louis Cardinals played collegiate baseball for Southern University before a 1961 draft date. Tommie Agee, drafted in 1962, of the New York Miracle Mets played at Grambling State. Agee's 1969 teammate, left fielder Cleon Jones, played football and baseball at Alabama A&M and then baseball at Grambling before his 1962 draft date.

Cecil Cooper played baseball at Prairie View A&M in the late '60s before being selected by the Boston Red Sox in 1972. He moved on to the Milwaukee Brewers, where he made his Gold Glove career and once batted .352, finishing only behind George Brett in the American League.

After baseball Cooper became an agent, notably guiding the careers of Hall of Famers Randy Johnson, Wade Boggs and Yankees player and later manager Joe Girardi. In 2007 he became the interim manager and then manager of the Houston Astros, the first black manager in Astros history.

Evident in HBCU athletics today are desegregated lineups with white ballplayers attending colleges like Norfolk State University on scholarship. The irony is that what once was an area that had no fewer than four of the best black baseball teams in a fifty-mile radius now generates a small percentage of skilled baseball players.

In the first edition of *Sunday Coming* I chronicled the rich history of black baseball in the Mid-Atlantic beginning with the powerful teams from the Tidewater and the peninsula, the North versus South season-ending championship versus North Carolina's best all-star teams and also the long play of popular teams along the eastern shore.

The state of Maryland had its only professional team for part of the twentieth century with the Baltimore Black Sox, before the Major League Orioles transitioned from Minor League to Major League contenders.

Out of the eight MEAC Schools only four have baseball teams, Coppin, Delaware, Maryland Eastern Shore and Norfolk State. Team rosters are integrated with black and white scholarship athletes, Delaware and Norfolk State have white head coaches.

North Carolina A&T in the Coastal Athletic Association is the only HBCU in the state with a baseball team made up of predominantly white players with a white head coach. Norfolk, Newport News, Portsmouth and Suffolk, Virginia, had some of the best black baseball players and athletes in the early twentieth century.

Richmond has a long history of black baseball from Church Hill, downtown home to Raymond Dandridge, to Glen Allen in once rural, now suburban Henrico County, and neighboring Hanover, with only Virginia State still offering baseball among its athletics. Al Bumbry of the 1970s championship Orioles teams played ball at Virginia State.

Further examination of HBCUs around the nation reveals a similar pattern. Famed Florida A&M, champions of the SWAC Conference in 2023, where Andre Hawk Dawson, Vince Coleman and Marquis Grissom played, has a white head coach and predominantly white roster. Grambling State, Alabama A&M, Jackson State and Prairie View A&M have black coaching staffs with integrated lineups.

Southern University and A&M College in Louisiana sent 15 players to the Major Leagues beginning in 1958 with their most famous player being outfielder Louis "Lou" Brock of St. Louis Cardinals fame. Southern's modern-day integrated roster is predominantly black with an all-black coaching staff. The Southern University Jaguars had five position players selected for the HBCU Swingman's Classic in the summer of 2023.

These scenarios are not revealed to disparage the presence of white players and coaches but to illustrate the absence of black baseball players and coaches at Historically Black Colleges and Universities, some of which now lack baseball programs entirely. Baseball scholarships are harder to earn, and prospective players, be they white or Hispanic, are applying to and playing ball for the schools wherever they are accepted. Participation among black American athletes on collegiate ball diamonds is still charting at a very low average as an overwhelming number of scholarship NCAA black athletes make weekend headlines in the sports of basketball and football.

The HBCU Swingman Classic, sponsored by T-Mobile and backed by the MLB-MLBPA and Youth Development Foundation (YDF), is an annual all-star showcase for baseball student-athletes from Division I programs at HBCUs.

The inaugural event was held during the 2023 MLB All-Star Week on July 7 at T-Mobile Park, home of the Seattle Mariners. Three players who participated in the inaugural 2023 event were selected in the 2023 MLB Draft, and two players signed with MLB clubs as undrafted free agents. The 2024 HBCU Swingman Classic took place during 2024 MLB All-Star Week at Globe Life Field, home of the Texas Rangers.

Selections for the HBCU Swingman Classic are made by a committee representing Major League Baseball. Topping the list is Hall of Famer Ken Griffey, Jr. MLB scouts and player association representatives also play supporting roles in player selection.

2023 HBCU Swingman Coaches

- Vince Coleman
- James Cooper
- Andre Dawson
- Marvin Freeman
- Ralph Garr
- Cito Gaston
- Ken Griffey, Sr.
- Marquis Grissom
- Trenidad Hubbard
- Jerry Manuel
- Troy Marrow
- Bo Porter
- Lester Strode
- Lenny Webster
- Rickie Weeks

Vince Coleman, Andre "Hawk" Dawson and Marquis Grissom all played college baseball at Florida A&M University. A footnote to this well-meaning event: white HBCU baseball players are being selected to participate on their merit, also attracting the attention of Major League organizations. It is an HBCU classic and showcase for HBCU players. While the promotion and attention are valuable, lack of participation and overall promotion of black American baseball players remains at the same low percentage. Arenas and promotion geared toward the revival of black baseball and the participation is still at a stage of stunted growth without the participation of the best black athletes.

Athletically Inclined

Talented prep and collegiate black athletes are apt to choose the sport with the highest potential for a full scholarship offer, basketball and football leading the list. Name, image and likeness (NIL) licensing in a new century offers compensation for participating college student athletes, pay being based on their athletic achievements and draft potential. Basketball posts the most NIL funding, followed by football and then limited but growing numbers of baseball players. The College Baseball World Series offers some of the most exciting baseball during the year.

The percentage of black players in World Series lineups is low but the players are for the most part of college all-star quality though few of these players are seen again in post-college play. On June 26, 2021, Vanderbilt captured the College World Series championship, their second within a five-year period.

Vandy pitcher Kumar Rocker of Alabama, the MVP of the Series, is of African American and Indian descent. The 6'5" 250-pound right-hander Rocker won his starts with dominating mound performances, tossing cut fastballs that veered and disappeared at the plate and rising fastballs that added extra digits to the radar gun. He shared rotation duties with Jack Leiter, the second overall pick in the 2021 Major League Baseball draft, son of former New York Mets pitcher Al Leiter.

Baseball fans of a different era might see Rocker as a throwback to the Houston Astros' J.R. Richard, a lookalike minus a few inches with the same fire on the fast ball.

Kumar Rocker recorded a no-hitter in the regional championships with 19 strikeouts and in his last start recorded 11 strikeouts for the win, extending the series versus Michigan for a game three and ultimately the championship.

Not only was he one of the few dominating black players in SEC baseball but undoubtedly one of the few black pitchers to dominate in the College World Series in recent years and claim the players award. Rocker was drafted in July 2021 by the New York Mets but did not sign. Pitching for the high A-League Hickory, North Carolina, Crawdads he incurred a torn ligament injury to the elbow necessitating Tommy John surgery during the spring of 2023, ending his season. In September 2024, however, Rocker made his Major League debut with the Texas Rangers.

A few other black collegiate baseball players made their presence felt during the playoffs and series: Michigan Wolverines game-breaking infielder Ako Thomas, outfielders Jordan Brewer and Cristian Bullock and on the winning Vandy team DH and All-American first teamer Austin Martin. All received honors during the 2019 season.

2024

Twenty-five years ago, I began assembling the stories that made *Sunday Coming*. This spring in my hometown of Charlottesville, two-sport standout African American pitcher Jay Woolfolk from Richmond, Virginia, just started spring training. Woolfolk is a right-handed pitcher with a mid–90s fastball coming out of the bullpen for the University of Virginia. Already an MLB prospect, he is a business major entering his junior year in Charlottesville. He won a high school state championship at quarterback in football and pitched for St. Benedictine in Richmond.

Woolfolk is not the first two-sport African American athlete from the commonwealth. Dell Curry, who grew up in Grottoes, Virginia, was a three-sport athlete at Ft. Defiance High School and drafted as a baseball player in the 1982 draft. At Virginia Tech Curry played basketball and baseball. He was drafted by the Baltimore Orioles in the 1985 draft as a pitcher, but by the mid-eighties Dell Curry's basketball talent was more than an obvious strength, and he went on to achieve all-star status during an esteemed career with the Charlotte Hornets.

Following his 2023 sophomore season Woolfolk announced his decision to focus on baseball and his role as a closer. Woolfolk played two seasons on the football team at backup quarterback. The Cavaliers were 2015 College World Series champions. He was named to the USA Today Collegiate post-season roster playing in twin five-game series matchups versus Chinese Taipei and Japan.

More than three quarters of a century after Jackie Robinson and Larry Doby, African Americans are no longer breaking the color line in baseball but moving the line toward diversity. Jackie Robinson Day, held annually by Major League Baseball, pays tribute to one of the most important events in civil rights history, and all Major League players wear #42. Ironically not every Major League team has an African American player on the roster. Robinson and Doby represented less than 1 percent participation in the initial efforts toward desegregating professional baseball. In 2024 African American baseball players are at the plate and in the field numbering fewer than 10 percent. Race against time.*

---

*Adelson, Bruce. *Brushing Back Jim Crow*. Charlottesville: University Press of Virginia, 1999; MLB.com. http://www.mlb.com>hbcu-swingman-classic.

VIII

Game Over: Vacant Sandlots

> Baseball's dying down on account of the country just don't play baseball no more. I remember when I was coming up, every community had a baseball team and Covesville had two.
> —Jim Dowell

With the close of the '70s, black baseball in Virginia began to fade into the cultural past of the black community. At the time few realized the significance of black teams folding region by region, or the loss of a tradition recognized as far back as the Depression era. More people began playing softball on Saturdays and Sundays, and in the '80s young black males were no longer gravitating towards baseball— it was pickup and summer league basketball that held their interest. Older players tried from time to time to revive interest in black baseball leagues, but received little if any support. There was a revival of a team in Greenwood, Virginia, that lasted a couple of seasons, but without a solid lineup of supporting players it was difficult to remain competitive.

A few longstanding black baseball teams continued play by joining integrated baseball leagues. The Sperryville Tigers played in the integrated Apple Valley league before merging with their rival Little Washington in the '80s. The Harrisonburg ACs had been in the Rockingham County Baseball League since 1970; Massies Mill joined an integrated league in Lynchburg, Virginia.

Sam Aylor, Sperryville Tigers:

> We played a year or two in a league down in Fairfax—and we came in second or third a time or two, but that was too much traveling for us, so we got out of that league, and that's when we went to Apple Valley, much closer.
>
> Rappahannock, Winchester, Strasberg, Edinburg, Luray, Hay Market and New Market were in the league. Anyone from teenaged on up could play in the Apple Valley League, the oldest league in Virginia. The first year we got in the Apple Valley League we won two games … we knew we needed a whole lot of good ballplayers.
>
> We were in it for five years, and we won three trophies out of the five years. I was the oldest guy to hit a home run in the Apple Valley League—I was fifty or fifty-one. Then the team folded.

David Clanagan, elder son of Rappahannock Monarchs manager Bobby Clanagan, started playing for the team at age 15. David Clanagan loved baseball and was one of the most dedicated ballplayers of his generation. He became the manager in the '80s and did his best to promote and carry on baseball in the area.

VIII. Game Over: Vacant Sandlots

The Massies Mill Cubs ball field today (photograph courtesy Jon Glassberg).

David Clanagan, manager, Rappahannock Monarchs:

At the end of the all-black teams, it just came down to getting teams to show up. We would have Marshall on the schedule for Sunday, Sunday comes around and Marshall doesn't show, so that's when we decided to join the Apple Valley League. I coached and managed the team for nine years and we won two championships. Things were going good, then everybody just got tired of baseball and it was hard to find some guys who would commit to a whole season. We missed going to the championship round the last year we played because half of the starters didn't show. I tried renting Crosby stadium in Front Royal and the guys were excited about playing again but then the same thing would happen—guys wouldn't show for games or it was too hot for them to play baseball. And so finally that was it—the Monarchs folded. It almost makes you tear up sometime when you sit down by the old ball field and think about the good times and all the players and games.

Covesville, Avon, and Elkton kept playing baseball as long as they could field nine. Covesville, Avon, and Massies Mill promoted outdoor events such as discos and car shows in conjunction with their '80s ballgames to renew interest in black baseball.

Central Virginia's DJ Sam "The Beast from the East" Clark was the most popular and best known DJ in the Mid-Atlantic area in the '80s. Unfortunately, depending on the perspective, his shows outshined the baseball game, so that the crowds were showing up after the ballgame, and the promotions were lost on the after parties.

The old ballfields are silent now, some barely recognizable. Many were converted into privately owned property for housing, or returned to their original role as farmland. Few if any of the first-generation founders and promoters of black baseball in Virginia are around to illustrate the auspicious beginnings of the cultural pastime. Second-generation ballplayers are scattered about, and have a decent recall of games and people, but a lack of documentation makes it difficult to detail all but the most memorable games and people. Sadly, the ranks of the younger ballplayers have thinned over the past thirty-five years, with many standouts and teammates leaving the game too soon. Gone are Robert "Red" Terrell, Isaiah "Zeke" Walker, Alfred Martin, David Johnson, Marcellus Coleman, Jr., "Big Red" Strother Jackson, Jr., Herman Bell and Vance Brock.

Signs of black baseball, and the men who played it, are long since removed. But the memories and stories remain, increasing in value as the years roll by.

Roger Bowles, Wilmington Eagles:

Kids today, they don't have any idea of what we played on. Wilmington was completely surrounded right in the middle of the woods, and had a light pole twenty feet behind second base. Avon; you played on a hillside with power lines running across left field. At Elkton there was a hog lot with a barbed wire fence behind left field; if you hit it over that it was a home run. But it was a barbed wire fence, so when the outfielders go back they go into a barbed wire fence. But I probably had more fun playing in this league for the years that I did than four years of college ball at the University of Richmond and some semi-pro stuff in Front Royal. I had more fun playing in this league on a Sunday afternoon. It was important to the guys and it was a big part of a Sunday afternoon after church and the guys took it serious. It was a very competitive type of situation and winning was very important.

We never see each other now that we don't revert back. James Payne and myself, when we see a high school ballgame, ask, "Would you like to go back and play one more in the bushes?" It was that important to everybody.

Kenny Diggs, Avon A's:

I played for semipro teams when I was in the Army in Oklahoma, and none of them could compare to this league [Inter-Co, Tri-Co]. In our era, there was so much talent through that league. If we took four people off of Avon's team, three or four off of Wilmington, three or four off of Covesville, I wouldn't be scared to say we could have competed with any pro team in that era.

The author with Matthew "Mack" Davis (right), Barboursville Giants, at a reunion in 2019 (photograph by Alan G. Johnson).

Esters (left) and Edward Sims, the #3 and #4 hitters for the Greenwood Hawks, the heart of the order. Donald Byers is in the background at left, with an unidentified player (photograph by Alan G. Johnson).

A Good Man for the People: Commissioner Roscoe Burgess

I met Roscoe Burgess a few months after beginning the writing of *Sunday Coming* through my old neighbor and friend Ivy Eagle John Armstead. What I realized quickly in our first phone conversation was that Mr. Burgess was on a tighter time schedule than I even though he was 70 years old, a grandfather, and a retiree. Unlike other retirees and former players Roscoe was still on a schedule, still in demand Sunday to Sunday. The Saturday afternoon we met up at his Bridgewater home, he was returning from doing a tiling job he had taken on that weekend. In his prime Roscoe was just as apt to take on countless commitments but at the same time a dyed-in-the-wool baseball player-manager.

Roscoe was very accommodating and welcoming during the first and only in person interview. Afterward we spoke a couple of times by phone and he gladly fielded questions about the league. He assisted in getting his former players from the Shenandoah Valley out for the early reunion events held before the publication of *Sunday Coming* in 2002.

What impressed me the most besides the fun and fact-filled baseball recollections was that it was easy to tell that he had taken a personal interest in associates, friends, and teammates, even opposing players and managers. It was very easy for Roscoe to relate something about these men whether talking about how they

Group reunion, 2019. Front row, from left: Lawrence Frye, Alex Jackson, unknown, author Darrell Howard, Leewood Davis, Matthew "Mack" David, Keith Davis, Thomas Waller. Back row, from left: Charles Ellis, Otis Kilby, Justin Kilby, David Williams, unknown, unknown, George Ellis, Walter "Chinn" Ware, Howard Ware, Herman Smith, unknown, Robert Anthony, Stanley Davis (photograph by Alan G. Johnson).

played on Sunday or how they earned their livings off the diamond, what church they attended and what they were now up to.

He was quick to give credit where credit was due when it came to the competition. Even though he played on some very good Bridgewater and Harrisonburg teams he had no problem acknowledging players and teams from around the region like Sperryville, Greenwood, South Garden. He confessed to being a little louder and demonstrative and cagey during his heyday behind the plate, a little different than his affable public persona.

Never let anyone trick you into making a bad play as he did to other unwitting players on more than one occasion. Always keep your head in the game.

As witnessed by a former playoff and championship round foe, the late Leroy Stevens of the South Garden Tigers, Roscoe often had more up his uniform sleeves than the signs used by the ACs.

> We were playing Harrisonburg on our field, Mitchell Carter was pitching, bases weren't loaded but men on the corners. Roscoe was coaching third and before Mitchell could throw the next pitch he called out, "hold on, let me see that ball, there's something wrong with that baseball!" Mitchell was confused but he stopped and threw the ball to Roscoe, but Roscoe stepped back and let the ball pass on by. Oh Lord, the man Harrisonburg had on third went on home and the man on first ended up on third; needless to say, we lost that game.

Leewood Davis, Elkton Bucks, 2019 (photograph by Alan G. Johnson).

Roscoe Burgess did not call time, Leroy Stevens did not call time, the umpire did not call time.

And lastly, sadly, Mitchell Carter did not call time and South Garden's chances sailed away. I suppose the then-young Mitchell saw Roscoe as an authority figure—commissioner Burgess—and hesitated with the risky request, but that day he was also a competitor who wanted to win that game. When I quizzed Roscoe about the episode a year or two after publication he confirmed the event after a good long laugh. "Keep your eye on the ball and your head in the game, because if I could get your mind on something else, I could turn it into an advantage, and I used to tell our players the same thing."

Hidden baseball trickery aside, Roscoe Burgess also mentored young men playing baseball in that era along with his brother-in-law Junious Whitelow. Together they created a winning team and a positive culture that ballplayers in the region, even other states, wanted to be a part of.

Mr. Burgess was a humble, gifted storyteller but he was also a great presence in his community and beyond, a mentor and mitigator. Founding a sports league over

Orange Nats Walter "Chinn" Ware (center, with arm extended) and brother Howard Ware (left) reminisce with Matthew "Mack" Davis (wearing a Washington cap and holding a cane), Barboursville Giants center. Stanley Davis (far right) listens in on the Nats version of games gone by (photograph by Alan G. Johnson).

an area of a hundred miles is an ambitious undertaking requiring good planning and excellent management skills at nearly every turn. The fact that Burgess umpired almost as long as he played baseball made him no stranger to conflict or controversy when it came to baseball. Umpiring in the Rockingham County League gave him a blueprint and helped him envision how he would structure the Shenandoah County League. More impactful now than twenty-five years ago was when he stressed sticking to the schedule on those Sundays long ago. "Get all of your games in. If something is not right or outside of the rules, we'll look at it later and fix it, but get your games in. I stressed that to all the managers and it still happened that teams didn't play their games but not too often."

Commissioner Burgess took into consideration not just the playing of a scheduled game but the promotion of the league. There were plans and preparations made by the home team, plans made by the traveling team, friends and visitors attending the games and supporting the league, all very important. Roscoe knew that letting a single thing spoil the event would hinder the stability and longevity of the league. He had a vision for how he wanted to play the game of baseball; what he did not count on was having two separate, diverse visions come to fruition at almost the same time.

The ACs and Elkton team played weekend games on backwoods diamonds off the record against Rockingham County Baseball League teams like the former Briery Branch Braves, the 1968 league champs. Roscoe grew up watching Briery Branch play baseball games and knew many of the players and managers. Roscoe Burgess was the first black player to play on an interim basis in the league in the 1950s playing for Briery Branch. With complete school desegregation in 1967, the stage was set for more players and perhaps a team to desegregate the Rockingham County league. Burgess' two sons, Ron and Roscoe Jr., were part of the first wave to desegregate Rockingham County public schools and participate on the sports teams.

Co-managers Burgess and Junious Whitelow petitioned the Rockingham County Baseball League for entry as early as 1965 and were added in 1969, playing their first official season in 1970. Even in 1970 Virginia the ACs were an all-black team set to play on the record on city-county funded diamonds for the first time in forty-six years. The settings were familiar because the players were from the Shenandoah Valley, but the makeup of the attending fans

Robert Anthony, Barboursville Giants, 2019 (photograph by Alan G. Johnson).

was not familiar to how they were received playing in predominantly black enclaves around Virginia. While the ACs were not an integrated team in the all-black Shen-Valley League they did have white ballplayers on the roster in the Rockingham County Baseball League.

The ACs were one of the best teams in the Shen-Valley League but the Rockingham County League was another notch higher still. Players in the league were former high school and college players and some Major League prospects. The ACs were game but struggled mightily during their initial seasons. Hits and wins were especially tough to get early on because they were facing a greater variety of pitches from a slew of talented pitchers.

Roscoe, then on the verge of 40, led the ACs in hits, especially clutch hits that made the difference between winning and losing.

Despite the departure of the ACs from Shen-Valley contention he was still co-commissioner of the league in 1970, presiding over affairs of teams in the Valley while working closely with Hugo Scott. As commissioner, Roscoe was always firm but fair, but by 1972 some of the players felt he was a little too unyielding in his rulings over certain matters and wanted to move away from the original league model. Burgess and Scott were the founders of the league, no one had been elected or appointed, and the entity remained the property of the co-commissioners; thus the name change in the early '70s.

Roscoe realized legality but rather than rally supporters in his favor he above all wanted to avoid conflict over a league that had flourished and continued to flourish a decade after its inception. So he decided to step down while Hugo Scott in Greene County, Virginia, remained as sole commissioner of the new Inter-County League.

Roscoe Burgess passed away in May of 2013 after a lengthy illness. In recent months he had been elected to his town council for the sixth time and in this same year was elected to the Rockingham County Baseball Hall of Fame. Again, two events transpired at the same time beyond what he had envisioned.

Still, the city council of Bridgewater felt there was something missing in the way of a final tribute to the Virginia gentleman of Bridgewater, so the Roscoe Burgess Riverwalk was created as a lasting tribute to a favorite citizen whose greatest accomplishment outside of baseball was in giving of himself, helping his family and community. In the words of the town manager Jay Litten, "the idea to dedicate Riverwalk to Roscoe [was made] on the basis that Riverwalk establishes a new connection to Bridgewater. He was always connecting people, forming bridges."*

---

*HMdb.org; THE ROSCOE BURGESS RIVERWALK.

Appendix 1: Norfolk Journal and Guide Baseball Directory

1939

Richmond Royal Giants, Richmond VA, Benjamin Puller, manager
Rocky Mount Monarchs, Rocky Mount NC, William A. Bryant, booking agent
Kinston Grays, Kinston NC, William Foye, booking agent
High Point Red Sox, High Point NC, Dr. H.C. Eccles, booking agent
Philadelphia Stars, Darby PA, Edward Bolden, owner
Homestead Grays, Homestead PA
Ethiopian Clowns, N. Tarrytown NY, Syd Pollock, booking agent
Pearson's Allstars, Alexandria VA
Berkley Braves, Norfolk VA, Allen Wilson, booking agent
Washington Senators, Portsmouth VA, Joseph Faulk, manager
Belleville Grays, Portsmouth VA, Benjamin H. Young, booking agent
M. & W. Giants, Norfolk VA, Carl Surrat, booking agent
Tidewater Giants, Newport News VA, Harry Mills, manager
Newark Eagles, Newark NJ, Abe Manley, owner
Bladenboro Tigers, Bladenboro NC, Ted Reynolds, manager
New Bern Cubs, New Bern NC, William Jones, booking agent
Rocky Mount Black Swans, Rocky Mount NC, Chas. D. Leonard, booking agent

1940

Ahoskie Black Hawks, Ahoskie NC, Allen B. Wilson, booking agent
Berkley Braves, Norfolk VA, B. Wilson, manager
Tidewater Giants, Newport News VA, Willie White, manager
Norfolk Cubs, Norfolk VA, James Booth, manager
Portsmouth Dodgers, Portsmouth VA, James Staten, business manager
Plymouth Tigers, Plymouth NC, A. Jeannette, manager
Suffolk Aces, Suffolk VA, Thomas James, booking agent
Suffolk Giants, Suffolk VA, Charles Brown, booking agent
Oxford Braves, Oxford NC, James Holden, booking agent
Gary Grays, Gary WV, John Barksdale, booking agent
Gilmerton Black Sox, Gilmerton VA, Bryant Sleight, business manager
Fighting Rebels, Norfolk VA, Junius Roberts, booking agent
Roanoke Cardinals, Roanoke VA, John "Chappie" Simms, manager
Kinston Grays, Kinston NC, D. Leonard, manager
Long Ridge Sox, Hickory VA, Jesse Jones, booking agent
Eagles Baseball Club, Winston-Salem NC, W.B. Bitting, booking agent
Colored House of David, Greensboro NC, Archie Robinson, booking agent

1943

Campostella Braves A.A, Norfolk VA, Robert Wilson, manager
Camp Pickett Warriors, Blackstone VA, Lt. Basil Oliver, booking agent
Capital City Elks, Richmond VA, Joe Miles, manager
West Norfolk Slides, West Norfolk VA, Larry Drumgold, manager
Oak Leaf Giants, Norfolk VA, William King, manager
Charlotte Red Sox, Charlotte NC, Sam Douglas, manager
Norfolk Allstars, Norfolk VA, William Manley, manager
Portsmouth Senators, Portsmouth VA, Pete Wilder, manager
Uptown Clowns, Portsmouth VA, Jesse Braxton, booking agent
Churchland White Sox, Churchland VA, Willie Johnson, manager
Franklin Allstars, Franklin VA, Henry G. Chambliss, manager
Raleigh Tigers, Raleigh NC, William Bridgers, manager
Fire Fighters Ball Club, Elizabeth City NC, E.V.C. Alexander, booking agent
MT. Hermon Boosters, Portsmouth VA, Eddie Joyce, manager
Portsmouth Hoboes, Portsmouth VA, Edward Joyner, manager
Twin Pine Tigers, Churchland VA, Odell Loney, manager
Elizabeth City Woodpeckers, Elizabeth City NC, James Davenport, booking agent
Norfolk Tigers, Norfolk VA, Carl Dudley, booking agent
Durham Redcaps, Durham NC, Dock Jenkins, booking agent
Suffolk Aces, Suffolk VA, Thomas E. James, manager
Gilmerton Esquires, Portsmouth VA, Leroy Winston, manager
Carolina Black Hawks, Ahoskie NC, Roscoe Moore, manager

1950

Carolina Bees, Asheboro NC, L.C. Everett, manager
Bristol Blue Sox, Bristol VA, Jimmie Spann, manager
Liberty Park Aces, Norfolk VA, E.L. Ratliff, manager
Sportsman Athletics, Portsmouth VA, C. Swann, manager
Sportsman Tigers, Norfolk VA, J. Harris, manager
Richmond Eagles, Richmond VA, L. Robinson, manager
Winston-Salem Indians, Winston-Salem NC, Z. Wilson, manager
Raleigh Grays, Raleigh NC, W.A. Wilder, manager
Winston-Salem Stars, Winston-Salem NC, A. Alexander, manager
Battling Palms, Norfolk VA, L. Gray, manager
Norfolk-Western Giants, Norfolk VA, J. Thornton, manager
Norfolk County Aces, Norfolk VA, J. Fogg, manager
Norfolk Orioles, Norfolk VA, R. Owens, manager
Esquire Club, Millers Tavern VA, S.R. Wilson, manager
Bladenboro Blue Caps, Bladenboro NC, L. Davis, manager
Danville Athletes, Danville VA, P. Ross, manager
Roanoke Tigers, Roanoke VA, A. Hodnett, manager
Norfolk Badgers, Norfolk VA, W. Wyatt, manager
Covington Colts, Covington VA, W. Burke, manager
Silver Moon Tigers, Asheboro NC, W.A. Gailes, manager
Philadelphia Giants, Philadelphia PA, G.M. Victory, manager
Dupont Grays, Waynesboro VA, W.B. Woodson, manager
Edenton Sluggers, Edenton NC
Washington Aztecs, Washington, D.C., T. Brown, manager
Norfolk Eagles, Norfolk VA, P. Tanner, manager

Appendix 2: Leagues and Teams

1939

RICHMOND CITY-COUNTY LEAGUE

A Class
Granite-Manakin
Boosters Jrs.
Page's Semipro
Centralia Allstars

AA Class
Richmond B.B. Boosters
Newport News Tidewater Giants
Price A.C. Richmond Cardinals
Ashland Tigers
Richmond Royal Giants
Franklin Elks
Pearson's Allstars

NEGRO AMERICAN ASSOCIATION

Richmond (VA) Hilldales
Baltimore (MD) Black Sox
Camden (PA) Giants

Greensboro (NC) Red Wings
Winston-Salem (NC) Pond Giants
High Point (NC) Red Sox

NEGRO INTERNATIONAL LEAGUE

Baltimore Black Sox
Washington Royal Giants
Portsmouth Belleville Grays
Charlotte Black Hornets

Durham Lucky Strikes
Durham Black Sox
Norfolk Black Tars

1940

INTERSTATE LEAGUE

Washington Aztecs
Edgewater (Maryland) Giants
Richmond Capital City Elks

Georgetown A.C.
Portsmouth Belleville Grays

VIRGINIA-CAROLINA LEAGUE

Newport News Tidewater Giants
Ahoskie (NC) Black Hawks
Plymouth (VA) Tigers
Berkley (VA) Braves

Suffolk Giants
Portsmouth Dodgers
Norfolk Cubs
Suffolk Aces

Appendix 2: Leagues and Teams

1947

Carolina Semipro League

Norfolk-Newport News Royals
Raleigh (NC) Grays
Danville Aces
Greensboro Red Wings
Richmond Giants
Durham Eagles
Columbia
Winston-Salem Giants

1948

Negro American Association

Asheville Blues
Raleigh Tigers
Jacksonville Allstars
Orangeburg
Greensboro Red Wings
Norfolk Newport News Royals
Richmond Giants
Winston-Salem Giants
Danville Allstars
Atlanta Black Crackers*

*Atlanta replaced Danville in the second half of play.

1949

Negro American Association

Washington Homestead Grays
Greensboro Red Wings
Raleigh Tigers
Richmond Giants
Norfolk-Newport News Royals
Charlotte-Asheville Blues
Durham Eagles
Winston-Salem Giants

1952

Four-County League

Keswick Allstars
Madison Indians
Gordonsville Eagles
North Garden Allstars
Barboursville Giants
Louisa Eagles

1959

Amelia, Ashland, Hanover and Spotsylvania, Virginia

Ellerson Tigers: Mgr. H. Chambliss
Georgetown Giants
Jack's Grill
Amelia County Cubs
Spotsylvania Tigers
Spotsylvania Yellow Jackets

1960–1970

Northern Virginia

Alexandria Braves
Arlington Athletics
Arlington White Sox
Bailey's Crossroads
Falls Church
Manassas
Merrifield Giants
Vienna

1972

Virginia Commonwealth League

East
Prince George Blue Sox
Tidewater Tigers
Petersburg Lions
Wakefield Nationals
Chuckatuck Trotters (Smithfield)

West
Dinwiddie Co. Giants
Dinwiddie Orioles
Carson Cardinals
Lunenberg Tigers
Chase City Dodgers
Petersburg Royals

1964*

Shenandoah Valley League

Harrisonburg ACs
Barboursville Giants
Orange Nats

Greenwood Hawks
South Garden Tigers
Elkton Bucks

*Inconclusive evidence as to first year of organized league play. Listed as 1963 in edition I, organized in 1964, formalized play with 10 teams in 1965.

1965

Shenandoah Valley League

Harrisonburg ACs
Barboursville Giants
Orange Nats
Greenwood Hawks
Avon Wrecking Crew

Sperryville Tigers
Lyndhurst Wildcats
Elkton Bucks
Luray Allstars
South Garden Tigers

1966

Shenandoah Valley League

Harrisonburg ACs
Barboursville Giants
Orange Nats
Greenwood Hawks
Avon Wrecking Crew
Elkton Bucks

Sperryville Tigers
South Garden Tigers
North Garden
Covesville Astros
Lyndhurst Wildcats
Massies Mill Cubs

1967

Shenandoah Valley League

Harrisonburg ACs
Barboursville Giants
Orange Nats
Greenwood Twins
Avon Wrecking Crew
South Garden Tigers

North Garden
Covesville Astros
Lyndhurst Wildcats
Ivy Eagles
Madison Orioles
Massies Mill Cubs

Appendix 2: Leagues and Teams

1969

SHENANDOAH VALLEY LEAGUE*

Harrisonburg ACs	Waynesboro
Barboursville Giants	Ivy Eagles
Greenwood Twins	Madison Orioles
South Garden Tigers	Massies Mill Cubs
Elkton Bucks	Charlottesville
Covesville Astros	Sperryville Tigers

*No record of an Avon team participating in league play during 1969.

1970

SHENANDOAH VALLEY LEAGUE

Avon Twins	Massies Mill Cubs
Greenwood Hawks	Charlottesville
South Garden Tigers	Elkton Bucks
Barboursville Giants	Waynesboro
Madison Orioles	Shipman Angels
Ivy Eagles	Nellysford
Covesville Astros	Orange Nats

1977

INTER-COUNTY LEAGUE

Covesville Astros	Massies Mill Cubs
Avon A's	Ivy Eagles
Waynesboro	Wilmington Eagles
Elkton Bucks	Esmont Rattlers
Keene Colts	Nellysford

1980

TRI-COUNTY LEAGUE

Massies Mill Cubs	Keene Colts
Avon A's	Wilmington Eagles
Covesville Astros	Elkton
Ivy Eagles	Grassland Sluggers*
Esmont Rattlers	

*Grassland Sluggers, Louisa-Orange County players combined, replace Wilmington Eagles, 1980 season.

1986

TRI-COUNTY LEAGUE

Tri-County League	Madison Heights
Massies Mill Cubs	Red House
Avon A's	Grottoes
Covesville Astros	Remington
Nellysford	Greenwood

Virginia's Negro League Players

Norman Earl Banks, Richmond, Virginia; 2b, 3b, Capital City Elks; 1945 Newark Eagles

Jesse "Jess" Barbour, Charlottesville, Virginia; 1910–1926, of,1b, 3b, Philadelphia Giants, Chicago American Giants, Bacharach Giants, Detroit Stars, Pittsburgh Keystones, Harrisburg Giants

Harry Butts, Suffolk, Virginia; p, Suffolk Aces, 1949 Indianapolis Clowns; Minor Leagues 1952, 1953 Vancouver, Portsmouth, Richmond, Piedmont League

Robert "Eggie" Clarke, Richmond, Virginia; c,1b,ss, mgr., Richmond Giants 1922–23; 1923–32 Baltimore Black Sox, New York Black Yankees 1933–40; Baltimore Elite Giants 1941–46, Philadelphia Stars

James Crump, Norfolk, Virginia; 2b, Norfolk Giants, Washington Braves; 1921–24 Hilldale Daisies, Philadelphia Giants; 1925–38 Negro National League umpire

Raymond Dandridge, Richmond, Virginia; 3b, Richmond Allstars; 1933–49 Newark Eagles, New York Cubans

John Davis, Ashland, Virginia; of, p, Mohawk Giants (NY), Newport News Royals; Newark Eagles 1941–48

Macajah Marchand "Mack" Eggleston, Roanoke, Virginia; c, of, 3b, 1919–1934 Dayton Giants, Hilldale Daisies, Harrisburg Giants; Homestead Grays, Nashville Elites, Baltimore Elites, Philadelphia Stars

Jim Elam, Richmond, Virginia; p, if, Better Business Boosters; 1943 Newark Eagles

Wilmer "Red" Fields, Manassas, Virginia; Virginia State College; 1941–49 p, 3b, of Homestead Grays

Albert "Buster" Haywood, Portsmouth, Virginia; c, Belleville Grays; 1940–50 Chicago American Giants, Cincinnati-Indianapolis Clowns

Chauncey "Rats" Henderson, Richmond, Virginia; p, Richmond Giants 1922, 1923, Atlantic City Bacharach Giants 1923–29; Detroit Stars 1931

John Preston "Pete" Hill, Culpeper County, Virginia; cf, lf, rf, 1b, 2b Mgr, Philadelphia Giants, Leland Giants, Chicago American Giants, Detroit Stars, Buffalo Red Caps

Lester Jackson, Richmond, Virginia; mgr, p, Ashland Tigers; of, Newark Eagles 1938, New York Black Yankees, 1940, 1941

James "Peewee" Jenkins, Farmville, Virginia; p, Farmville Giants, 1946–50 New York Cubans

William Percy Miller, Jr., Danville, Virginia; of, Danville Aces, Danville Allstars, Jacksonville Eagles NSL; Carolina Minor Leagues, Danville Leafs 1951

William Percy Miller, Sr., Danville, Virginia; p, Danville Allstars, Chicago Giants 1921, St. Louis Giants 1921, St. Louis Stars, 1922–26, Kansas City Monarchs 1922, 1934, Nashville Elite Giants 1930–34

Charles "Mule" Peete, Franklin, Virginia; of, Indianapolis Clowns 1950, minor leagues 1950, 1951; St. Louis Cardinals 1956

Vernon "Big Six" Riddick, Norfolk, Virginia; ss, Norfolk Tars; 1941 Newark Eagles

Ray Robinson, Richmond, Virginia; p, Richmond Cardinals Price Athletic Club; 1938, 1941 Newark Eagles, Philadelphia Stars 1947

Leon "Lassies" Ruffin, Portsmouth, Virginia; c, Belleville Grays; 1936–50 Newark Eagles, Pittsburgh Crawfords, Philly Stars

Robert T. Walker, Little Washington, Virginia; p, Washington Monarchs; 1945–49 Homestead Grays

Charles Henry "Lefty" Williams, Madison County, Virginia; p, 1915–1934 Homestead Grays

Ernest Judson ("Jud" Boojum) Wilson, Remington, Virginia; 3b, Baltimore Black Sox, Homestead Grays, Philadelphia Stars

*Compiled from listings in Robert Peterson's *Only the Ball Was White* and James Riley's biographical *Encyclopedia of the Negro Baseball Leagues.*

Appendix 3: Virginia Player Register

Abell, Clarence, c, Crozet Allstars, Ivy Eagles
Agee, Charles, 2b, Buckingham Grays
Agee, Floyd, Buckingham Grays
Agee, Joseph, (p), Keene Colts
Agee, Randolph, Buckingham Grays
Akers, Herbert, c, Spotsylvania Tigers
Akers, John, (p), Spotsylvania Tigers, Orange Nats
Alexander, Forrest "Duke," of, Avon Twins
Alexander, Howard, (p), Avon Wrecking Crew, Avon Twins, Avon A's
Allen, Jimbo, Avon Allstars
Anthony, Michael, lf, Barboursville Giants
Anthony, Robert, of, Barboursville Giants
Armstead, John, ss, c, mgr., Ivy Eagles
Armstead, Sterling, Ivy Eagles
Armstead, William (Willie Wee), Ivy Eagles
Arrington, Jimmy, 2b, Madison Orioles
Arrington, Paul, 3b, Madison Orioles
Avery, Pete, c, rf, 1b, Gordonsville Eagles, Kelly's Allstars
Awkard, Herman Brad (H.B.) Sr., 2b, Avon Wrecking Crew, Avon Twins, Avon A's
Awkard, Ernest, Avon Twins
Awkard, Kenneth, 1b, (p), Avon Wrecking Crew, Avon Twins, Avon A's
Awkard, Linwood "Lin" (p), Dupont Grays, Greenfields, Avon Allstars
Awkard, Marshton, (p), Avon Wrecking Crew
Aylor, Bill, (p) 1b, Little Washington Monarchs, Sperryville Tigers
Aylor, Reg, Sperryville Yellow Jackets
Aylor, Sam, lf, c, 1b, mgr., Sperryville Tigers
Aylor, William (Moody), 3b, mgr., Sperryville Tigers
Baker, Freddie, ss, 2b, Barboursville Giants
Baker, T. B., Nellysford, Massies Mill Cubs
Banks, Arthur, Kelly's Allstars
Banks, John, c, Madison Orioles
Banks, Marshall, Culpeper Dragons
Bannister, James, (p), Orange Nats
Barbour, Chris, (p), 3b, Ivy Eagles
Barbour, Frank, (p), ss, Ivy Eagles
Barbour, Hildrie, ss, of, Greenwood Hawks
Barbour, Kenneth, (K.B), 2b, Ivy Eagles
Barbour, Payton, ss, Madison Orioles
Barbour, Stanley (Greasy), Ivy Eagles
Barratt, "Doc," Keswick Dodgers
Bates, Carroll, c, Cismont Braves, Barboursville Giants
Bates, Johnny, Gordonsville Eagles
Baugher, Garland, Elkton Bucks
Beals, Kern, Elkton Bucks
Beasley, Lawrence, 2b, Madison
Beasley, Robert, (p), Madison
Beasley, Willie, (p), Madison
Beasley, Willie, Barboursville Giants
Becks, James (p) Staunton ACs, Staunton Wild Cats
Bell, Herman, Shipman Angels, Massies Mill Cubs
Berkley, Percell (Red), of, Charlottesville Squeeze-Ins
Berkley, Teddy, Avon Twins, Avon A's
Blair, David, c, Waynesboro
Blair, G. G., 1b, Dupont Grays, Avon Wrecking Crew
Blair, James, Greenwood Hawks, Lyndhurst
Blakey, Hiram, lf, Madison Orioles
Blakey, Charley, Kelly's Allstars
Blakey, Wilson, (p), Harrisonburg Nationals, Harrisonburg ACs
Boswell, Vincent, (p), Covesville Astros
Bowles, Roger, 3b, (p), Wilmington Eagles, University of Richmond
Boyd, Frank, (p), Roanoke Black Cardinals
Brackett, Tyrone, South Garden Tigers
Bridges, Arthur, ss, Washington Monarchs
Briscoe, Henry (Red), Richmond Cardinals, Virginia State University
Brock, Burrell, 3b, Barboursville Giants
Brock, Robert, if, Barboursville Giants

Appendix 3: Virginia Player Register

Brock, Vance, ss, Barboursville Giants
Brooks, David, (p), if, Wilmington Eagles, University of Richmond
Brooks, Harry, Greenwood Hawks
Brown, Arnold, "Arnie" 1b, (p) Greenwood
Brown, Emanuel, Keene Colts
Brown, Clarence, ss, Roanoke Black Cardinals
Brown, George, cf, Roanoke Black Cardinals
Brown, Henry, Wintergreen
Brown, Homer, 1b, (p), Greenwood Hawks
Brown, James (Rat), asst. mgr., Charlottesville Squeeze-Ins
Brown, Joe, Orange Nats
Brown, Lloyd (Booty), (p), Charlottesville Squeeze-Ins
Brown, Robert, Jr., 3b, Wilmington Eagles
Brown, Robert, Sr., mgr., 3b, Wilmington Eagles
Buckner, "Big Sam," 1b, mgr., Barboursville Giants
Bumbry, Al, Fredericksburg, Baltimore Orioles
Burgess, Don (Stove Pipe, Rooster), (p), Harrisonburg ACs, Elkton
Burgess, Ron, (p), Harrisonburg ACs
Burgess, Roscoe, Harrisonburg ACs, commissioner of Shen-Valley League
Burton, Addie, mgr., Avon Allstars
Burton, Curtis, Covesville Tigers
Burton, Edward, c, mgr., Avon Wrecking Crew
Burton, Gene, North Garden, Chesnut Grove
Burton, Harold, South Garden Tigers
Burton, Lloyd, South Garden Tigers
Burton, Randall, c, North Garden Allstars, South Garden Tigers
Byers, Clinton, c, South Garden Tigers
Byers, Curtis, South Garden Tigers
Byers, Donald, 1b, South Garden Tigers, Wilmington Eagles, Charlottesville Royals
Cabell, Bobby, Massies Mill
Cabell, Bud, Kelly's Allstars
Carey, Bernard, Kelly's Allstars
Carey, Cyril, of, Wilmington Eagles
Carey, Mike, lf, Wilmington Eagles
Carpenter, John, 3b, Madison Indians, Madison Orioles, Barboursville Giants
Carter, Howard, c, Covesville Tigers
Carter, Jake, Culpeper Dragons
Carter, Lewis, ss, Crozet Allstars
Carter, Mitchell, (p), South Garden Tigers
Carter, Richard, Crozet Allstars
Carter, William, (p), Little Washington Monarchs, Sperryville Tigers
Cauls, Robert, Staunton Wild Cats
Chambers, Willie, (p), Buckingham Grays
Chisholm, Linwood (Chuck), if, Kelly's Allstars, Charlottesville Squeeze-Ins
Clanagan, Bobby, (p), Little Washington Monarchs
Clanagan, David, of, ss, Little Washington Monarchs
Clark, E. Chester Sr., Wintergreen
Clark, Phillip, Avon Wrecking Crew
Clark, Roger, Avon Twins, Avon A's
Clark, Walter, Avon Wrecking Crew
Clark, Willie, Avon Wrecking Crew
Coleman, Leroy, Grassland Sluggers
Coleman, Marcellus, (p), Cismont Braves, Wilmington Eagles
Coles, William (Colesy), of, Charlottesville Squeeze-Ins
Collins, George, mgr., Crozet Allstars, Greenwood Hawks
Collins, Johnny, Barboursville Giants
Conn, Asher (Gingus), (p), Charlottesville Squeeze-Ins
Cotrell, Frank, Shipman Spiders
Coward, Bud, c, 2b, Kelly's Allstars
Crawford, "Doc," Wintergreen
Crawford, "Monk," Wintergreen
Crosson, James "Boo," 3b, Roanoke Black Cardinals
Dabney, Joe, Wilmington Eagles
Davis, Charles (Buddy), 2b, Barboursville Giants
Davis, Donald, Buckingham Grays
Davis, Greg, Barboursville Giants
Davis, Jimmy, Barboursville Giants
Davis, Keith, cf, Barboursville Giants
Davis, Leewood, 1b, of, Elkton Bucks, Harrisonburg ACs, Linville Patriots, Shenandoah
Davis, Leroy, Elkton Bucks
Davis, Lewis, Elkton Bucks
Davis, Matthew (Mack), (p), 2b, cf, Barboursville Giants
Davis, Paul, Elkton Bucks
Davis, Randall, Elkton Bucks
Davis, Randolph, Grassland Sluggers
Davis, Ricky, ss, Barboursville Giants, Shenandoah University, Bridgewater College
Davis, Roger, Elkton Bucks
Davis, Stanley, of, Barboursville Giants
Davis, Walker, 3b, Barboursville Giants
Davis, Walter, Elkton Bucks
Dawson, Reuben, Staunton Wild Cats

Dawson, Richard, of, Roanoke Black Cardinals
Dickerson, Frank ("Brownie"), (p), Gordonsville Eagles, Barboursville Giants
Dickerson, Tom (Butch), Gordonsville Eagles
Diggs, Doswell (Junior), mgr., Avon Wrecking Crew, Avon Twins
Diggs, Kenny, c, Avon A's, Staunton Braves
Diggs, Sidney, (p), 2b, Greenwood Hawks, Lyndhurst, Avon Wrecking Crew, Avon Twins
Doffelmeyer, Larry, ss, c, Barboursville Giants, Shenandoah
Douglas, Charles (Doll Baby), if, Charlottesville Squeeze-Ins
Douglas, William, Charlottesville Squeeze-Ins
Douglas, William (Locust), c, Charlottesville Squeeze-Ins
Douglass, Dale, (p), Spotsylvania Tigers
Dowell, Curtis, Covesville Tigers, South Garden Tigers
Dowell, Early, (p), 1b, mgr., Covesville Tigers
Dowell, Haywood, 3b, (p), Covesville Tigers
Dowell, Jim, (King Bee), c, of, 1b, mgr., North Garden, Covesville Tigers, Covesville Astros
Dowell, Joe, Covesville Astros
Dowell, Lee, (p), North Garden, Covesville Tigers, Covesville Astros
Dowell, Lenny, (p), 1b, North Garden, Covesville Tigers, Covesville Astros
Dowell, Rufus (Junky), (p), Covesville Tigers, Covesville Astros
Dowell, William, (p), South Garden Tigers, Covesville Astros, Elkton
Doyle, Curt, 1b, (p), Avon A's
Doyle, Phil, (p), Avon A's
Dudley, Sterling (Boo), (p), Charlottesville Squeeze-Ins
Durrette, Robert (Bobby), ss, Avon Twins
Durrette, Ernest, 1b, Avon Wrecking Crew
Durrette, George, Sr., c, Avon Wrecking Crew
Durrette, Wesley Dean, (p), Crozet Allstars (jr. team)
Durrette, Wilson, of, Avon Wrecking Crew
Dyer, Moses, Jr., Greenwood Hawks
Dyer, Moses, III, of, Greenwood, Covesville Astros
Easly, Howard, 1b, Roanoke Black Cardinals
Edwards, Steve, (p), Wilmington Eagles
Ellis, Charles, Grassland Sluggers
Ellis, Ernest, Grassland Sluggers
Ellis, George, Grassland Sluggers
Estes, John, Keswick Dodgers, Charlottesville Squeeze-Ins
Eubanks, Larry, Keene Colts
Falls, Lawrence, mgr., Elkton Bucks
Feggans, Ben, Esmont Giants
Feggans, Lloyd, (p), Esmont Giants
Fields, Welford, 2b, Madison Indians
Flippin, Harry (Buck), 3b, Avon Wrecking Crew
Fisher, Frankie, (p), Avon Wrecking Crew
Fitch, Joe, Wintergreen
Fitch, Randolph, Wintergreen
Fletcher, Hampton, (p), Little Washington Monarchs, Sperryville Tigers
Foster, Abe, Shipman Angels
Franklin, Edward, c, Wilmington Eagles
Franklin, George, Roanoke Black Cardinals
Franklin, Mel, Roanoke Black Cardinals
Franklin, Paul, Jr., 2b, Wilmington Eagles
Franklin, Paul, Sr., mgr., Wilmington Eagles
Franklin, Ralph, rf, cf, Wilmington Eagles
Freeman, Arthur, c, Little Washington Monarchs
Freeman, Jay (Meat Hook), lf, Sperryville Tigers
Frye, Bradley, lf, Madison Indians
Frye, Bradley, rf, Madison Orioles
Frye, Frank, Madison Orioles, Ivy Eagles
Frye, Fred, cf, mgr., Madison Orioles
Frye, Jesse, cf, Sperryville Tigers
Frye, Johnny, c, p, Madison Indians, Barboursville Giants, Madison Orioles
Frye, Lewis (Race Horse), cf, Kelly's Allstars, Madison Indians, Barboursville Giants, Ivy Eagles
Frye, Stoney, Sperryville Tigers
Gaines, Elmo, Massies Mill Cubs
Gaines, Fletcher, Jr., Massies Mill Cubs
Gaines, Fletcher, Sr., mgr., Massies Mill Cubs
Gardner, Bobby, Keene Colts
Gardner, Wayne, Keene Colts
Garrett, John, 1b, Buckingham Grays
Garrett, Moses, (p), Buckingham Grays
Gentry, Buck, (p), Covesville Astros
Gilbert, Theodore (Creeper), asst. mgr., Charlottesville Squeeze-Ins
Giles, Alex, 1b, Massies Mill Giants, Cubs
Giles, Jahosapha, (p), Massies Mill Giants
Giles, John (Buster), (p), Massies Mill Giants
Giles, Roger, (p), Massies Mill Giants
Giles, Wallace, (p), Massies Mill Giants
Glasgow, Arthur (Dolly), Little Washington Monarchs

Appendix 3: Virginia Player Register

Glasgow, Ellis, mgr., Little Washington Monarchs
Glover, Robert (Slick), rf, ss, Kelly's Allstars
Goodwin, Charley, Wintergreen
Gray, Donald, Esmont Giants, North Garden, South Garden Tigers
Gray, Willie, Esmont Giants, North Garden, South Garden Tigers
Green, Bernard, (D–Dot), Avon A's
Green, Forrest, Greenwood Hawks
Green, James (Itsy), Avon A's
Greene, John, Grassland Sluggers
Hackley, Leroy, Culpeper Dragons
Hall, Eulie, (p), B.B. Boosters
Hamilton, George, of, Roanoke Black Cardinals
Harper, Stanley, 2b, ss, Avon Wrecking Crew
Harris, Melvin, Shipman Angels
Harris, William, 2b, Madison Orioles
Hawkins, Montague, (p), Cismont Braves
Hearns, Sammy, c, Fork Union, Kelly's Allstars
Henderson, Albert, ss, Covesville Tigers
Henderson, Allen, Covesville Tigers, Covesville Astros
Henderson, Arthur, Covesville Astros
Henderson, Edward, c, Covesville Tigers, mgr., Cismont Braves, Covesville Astros
Henderson, Harold, Covesville Astros
Henderson, James, Jr., (Pee Wee), of, c, Covesville Astros
Henderson, James, Sr., Covesville Tigers
Henderson, Luther, (p), Covesville Tigers
Henderson, Robert, of, Covesville Tigers, Covesville Astros
Henderson, Samuel, Covesville Tigers
Hendricks, Bernard, mgr., Ivy Eagles
Hill, Eddie, (p), Crozet Allstars
Hill, Sammy, Crozet Allstars
Hogans, Francis, 1b, Little Washington Monarchs
Holland, Al, Sr., 1b-of, Roanoke Black Cardinals
Howard, Herman, 2b, of, Avon Allstars, Ivy Eagles
Howard, Pete, (p), Crozet Allstars
Howard, Randolph, (p), Orange Nats
Howard, Roger, c, Greenwood Hawks, Avon Twins
Hudson, Bobby, Massies Mill Cubs
Hudson, Don, Massies Mill Giants
Hudson, Eddie, (p), Massies Mill Cubs, Avon Allstars
Huggard, Raymond, Staunton Wild Cats
Hughes, Brian, Barboursville Giants
Hughes, Thomas, mgr., Amherst
Humes, Clarence, ss, 2b, Orange Nats
Humes, Moses, Orange Nats
Hutcherson, Lawrence, of, Sperryville Tigers
Inge, G. Roger, of, Covesville Astros
Ivory, Henry, Ivy Eagles, Crozet Allstars
Ivory, Johnny, 2b, Ivy Eagles
Ivory, Larry, cf, Ivy Eagles
Ivory, Louis, Ivy Eagles
Jackson, Alan, 1b, Staunton Wild Cats
Jackson, Alex, of, Avon Wrecking Crew
Jackson, Alvin, (p), Avon Wrecking Crew
Jackson, Archie, Keene Colts
Jackson, Donald, c, Avon Wrecking Crew
Jackson, General, 2b, Reva Aces
Jackson, Hugh, (p), Barboursville Giants
Jackson, John R. (Skeebo), lf, (p) Avon Wrecking Crew, Avon Twins, Avon A's
Jackson, Ray (Shotgun), (p), Sperryville Tigers
Jackson, Robert, (p), Avon Wrecking Crew, Avon Twins
Jackson, Roger, Orange Nats
Jackson, Roy, cf, Culpeper Dragons, Sperryville Tigers
Jackson, Strother, Jr., (Big Red), (p), Madison Orioles, Barboursville Giants
Jackson, Strother, Sr., Madison Indians
James, Freddie, Wilmington Eagles
Johnson, Butchy, Covesville Astros
Johnson, David, of, c, (p), Covesville Astros
Johnson, Garfield, Barboursville Giants
Johnson, Gilbert (Rabbit), cf, Covesville Astros
Johnson, James, Jr., of, Sperryville Tigers
Johnson, James, rf, Madison Orioles
Johnson, Lawrence L. (Puggy), (p), Covesville Astros
Johnson, Louis, Keswick Allstars
Johnson, Paul, Covesville Astros
Johnson, Robert, Culpeper Dragons
Johnson, Robert, rf, Madison Orioles
Johnson, William, (p), South Garden Tigers, Wilmington Eagles
Jones, Charlie, mgr., Kelly's Allstars
Jones, Frank, Ivy Eagles
Jones, James, Buckingham Grays
Jones, Jim, 2b, Roanoke Black Cardinals
Jones, John, Buckingham Grays
Jones, Junious, Buckingham Grays
Jones, Lewis, Buckingham Grays

Jones, Percell, (Rabbit), of, Charlottesville Squeeze-Ins
Jones, Powell, c, Buckingham Grays
Jones, Raymond, Ivy Eagles
Jones, Stanley, Buckingham Grays
Jones, Ted, Buckingham Grays
Jordan, George, Sperryville Yellow Jackets, Front Royal
Jordan, Henry, Sperryville Yellow Jackets, Front Royal
Kelly, Aaron, Kelly's Allstars
Kelly, Harry, rf,(p), Kelly's Allstars
Kelly, James, cf, Kelly's Allstars
Kelly, Leroy, Kelly's Allstars
Kelly, Levi, Kelly's Allstars
Kelly, Louis, Greenwood Hawks, Crozet Allstars
Kelly, Raleigh, 3b, Kelly's Allstars
Kelly, Riley, Kelly's Allstars
Kidd, Jerry, Wilmington Eagles
Kilby, Justin, c, Sperryville Tigers
Kilby, Otis, Jefferson Red Sox
Kirby, Rodney, 3b, c, South Garden Tigers, Covesville Astros
Koontz, Avis, Harrisonburg ACs
Lane, Charley, mgr., Culpeper Dragons
Lawson, Frederick, (p), Little Washington Monarchs
Lee, Bobby, Harrisonburg ACs
Lee, Jack, Wintergreen
Lewis, William (Little Willie), Charlottesville Dodgers, Charlottesville Squeeze-Ins
Lewis, Willy, Sr., c, Kelly's Allstars
Ligon, Alphonso, c, Massies Mill Giants
Ligon, Fulton, mgr., Massies Mill Giants
Lindsay, Curtis, c, (p), Madison
Lindsay, Russell, (p), Madison
Long, Roy, 2b, Orange Nats
Lynch, Clyde, (p), Avon Wrecking Crew
Mallory, Joe, lf, Madison Orioles
Mallory, John, c, Madison Orioles
Martin, Alfred, 1b, ss, (p), Charlottesville Dodgers, Charlottesville Squeeze-Ins, South Garden Tigers, Wilmington Eagles
Martin, Arthur, 3b, of, Wilmington Eagles
Martin, Joe, (p), Covesville Tigers
Martin, Lloyd, ss, Wilmington Eagles
Martin, Paul, cf, Wilmington Eagles
Maupin, William (Bill), Ivy Eagles
Mayo, George, (p), 1b, Ivy Eagles
Mayo, George, Jr., (Took), (p), 1b, c, Ivy Eagles, Covesville Astros, Greenwood
McCutcheon, Johnny, Staunton Wild Cats
Miles, Charles, Shipman Angels
Miles, James, Shipman Angels
Miller, Mason, c, Staunton Wild Cats
Mills, James (Jimmy), of, Charlottesville Squeeze-Ins
Minor, Bill, (p), Keswick Dodgers, Charlottesville Squeeze-Ins, Wilmington Eagles
Moore, Carlton, Elkton Bucks
Moore, Max (Doc), of, Keswick Dodgers, Barboursville Giants
Morris, Carlton, Elkton Bucks
Morton, Wilson, of, Barboursville Giants
Mosby, Isaiah, 1b, Covesville Tigers
Murray, Freddie (Flip), mgr., Charlottesville Squeeze-Ins
Murrill, Mettres, Orange Nats
Napier, Massie, c, of, Massies Mill Cubs
Nelson, Ivanhoe, of, c, (p), North Garden, South Garden, Covesville, Keene, Nellysford
Nelson, Powhatan, Culpeper Dragons, Orange Nats
Nelson, Warren, Culpeper Dragons, Orange Nats
Nickerson, Gary, (p), Keene Colts
Nickerson, Mick, Keene Colts
Nowell, Johnny, (p), of, South Garden, Charlottesville
Oliver, Herbert, Buckingham Grays
Page, Don, Esmont Giants
Page, Edgar, (p), Esmont Giants
Pannell, Creed, 1b, Staunton Wild Cats
Parker, William, ss, Sperryville Tigers
Payne, Alphonso, (p), Wilmington Eagles
Payne, Charles, (p), Wilmington Eagles
Payne, Clarence, 3b, Wilmington Eagles
Payne, Darnell, (p), Wilmington Eagles
Payne, Herman, Wilmington Eagles
Payne, James, 1b, c, Wilmington Eagles
Payne, Lawrence, Wilmington Eagles
Payne, Theodore (Buck), (p), Wilmington Eagles
Perkins, James, Jr., (Man), 1b, Ivy Eagles
Perkins, James, Sr., (p), Ivy Eagles
Perkins, Michael, c, Ivy Eagles
Perrow, Curtis, North Garden, Ivy Eagles, Shipman Angels, Massies Mill Cubs
Perrow, Mel, cf, North Garden, Ivy Eagles, Shipman Angels, Massies Mill Cubs
Porter, Jeff, of, if, Sperryville Tigers
Preston, William, Kelly's Allstars
Price, John Henry, (p), Culpeper Dragons
Ragland, James, Crozet Allstars
Rankin, "Pete," ss, Avon A's

Appendix 3: Virginia Player Register

Redd, William, Charlottesville Squeeze-Ins
Reed, George (Pop), cf, Cumberland Sluggers
Reid, Dan, c, lf, Kelly's Allstars
Rice, Fred, c, Roanoke Black Cardinals
Richardson, Scott, Grassland Sluggers
Robertson, Lawrence, 3b, Cumberland Sluggers
Robertson, William (Rabbit), lf, Cumberland Sluggers
Robinson, Bobby L., Orange Nats
Robinson, Charles, Orange Nats
Robinson, Clarence, lf, Orange
Robinson, Herbert, (Babe) 2b, (Babe), Staunton Wild Cats
Robinson, Ronald, ss, Orange Nats
Robinson, William, 2b, ss, Roanoke Black Cardinals
Ross, Rusty, (p), Wilmington Eagles
Scott, Albert (Buster), (p), Esmont Giants
Scott, Edward, 3b, Orange Nats
Scott, Herman (Lefty), (p), Tidewater Giants, Norfolk Black Tars, Birmingham Baron
Scott, Hugo, mgr., Barboursville, Sec. of Shen-Valley League
Scott, Larry, Shipman
Scott, Otis, Esmont
Shanks, Henry, Reva Aces, Culpeper Dragons, Sperryville Tigers
Shanks, Robert, ss, Reva Aces
Shanks, William, Sr., (Billy), (p), Reva Aces, Culpeper Dragons
Shelton, George (Chico), (p), Charlottesville Squeeze-Ins
Shelton, Nathaniel (Pat), if, Charlottesville Squeeze-Ins
Shelton, Tim, rf, (p), Wilmington Eagles
Sheridan, Steve, cf, Wilmington Eagles, Bridgewater College
Shifflett, Charles, (p), of, Crozet, Greenwood
Simmons, Bill, (p), Massies Mill
Simms, John (Chappie), mgr., Roanoke Black Cardinals
Simms, Newman, 3b, Madison
Sims, Arthur (Pop), c, (p), Greenwood
Sims, Bernard, (p), 1b, Greenwood
Sims, Charles, of, Avon
Sims, Edward (Dopey), 3b, rf, Greenwood, Charlottesville
Sims, Elgie B., Jr., ss, Avon
Sims, Elgie B., Sr., (p), ss, Greenwood
Sims, Esters (Preacher), (p), Greenwood Hawks-Twins, Avon A's, Staunton Braves, Waynesboro Generals
Sims, George, (p), Crozet, Greenwood
Sims, Harvey, of, c, Greenwood, Ivy
Sims, Leroy, Avon Twins
Sims, Lester, if, Greenwood
Sims, Stuart (Turkey), 3b Greenwood Hawks, Avon A's
Sims, William J., Jr., (Junie) ss, Greenwood
Sims, William J., Sr., (Winky), of, Greenwood
Slaughter, Bobby, rf, Sperryville Tigers
Slaughter, Richard, 1B, (p), c, of, Reva Aces, minor leagues—Batavia, Sperryville Tigers
Smith, Alexander, Jr., (Alec), 2b, Covesville
Smith, Clarence, Covesville
Smith, Clarence, Jr., Covesville
Smith, Earl, (p), Covesville
Smith, Eldridge, Kelly's Allstars
Smith, Elwood, c, Covesville
Smith, Herman O., Barboursville
Smith, Herman W., Barboursville
Smith, John, Covesville
Smith, Michael, of, Covesville, South Garden
Smith, Peyton, Covesville
Smith, Sidney, (p), Buckingham
Snead, Andrew, c, Orange
Snead, Clarence, ss, c, Orange
Snead "Ned," (p), Orange Black Sox, Orange Nats
Spears, Ernest, Crozet
Spears, Jackie (Moon), of, Charlottesville Dodgers, , Squeeze-Ins
Spottswood, Jack, ss, Madison Indians
Spottswood, Warren, 1b, Madison Indians
Spruill, Tony, (p), Belleville Grays, Portsmouth Senators
Staton, Curtis, (p), Buckingham
Staton, James, 2b, Buckingham
Steppe, Herman, c, Crozet Allstars, Greenwood Hawks
Stevens, John Emmit, of, Covesville
Stevens, Leroy, c, ss, Covesville Tigers, mgr., South Garden Tigers
Stevens, Wayne, South Garden
Stokey, Rufus, (p), Crozet Allstars
Stuart, George, mgr., Staunton Wild Cats
Swales, Herbert, (p), Madison Orioles
Taliaferro, Jackie, rf, Madison
Tate, Godfrey, (p) Staunton Wild Cats
Tate, Oliver, rf, Staunton Wild Cats
Taylor, Francis, Madison, Keene
Taylor, George, 1b, Little Washington Monarchs
Taylor, Roy, (p), Harrisonburg ACs
Temple, Theodore, Harrisonburg
Terrell, Robert (Red), rf, (p), Orange Nats
Thacker, Jerry (Junior), (p), Ivy

Thomas, Leroy, c, Esmont
Thompson, Edward, (p), Avon
Timberlake, Charles 1b, Crozet Allstars
Tolliver, Lewis (Ace, Dirty Red), (p), Kelly's Allstars
Trice, Lonnie, ss, Wilmington
Trice, Tudie, (p), Wilmington
Turner, John, Nellysford
Turner, Raymond, of, South Garden
Turpin, Philip, ss, Wilmington
Twyman, Nelson, c, (p), Madison Orioles
Vaughn, Ben, (p), Massies Mill Giants
Vaughn, Sidney, ss, Staunton Wild Cats
Venable, Charlie, LF, Staunton Wild Cats
Venable, Lewis, RF, Staunton Wild Cats
Vest, Carl Lee, Covesville Astros
Vest, James, (p), Covesville Tigers, South Garden Tigers
Vest, Robert, Shipman Pirates
Via, Wayne, Covesville Astros
Walker, Albert G., Crozet Allstars
Walker, Harry, Ivy
Walker, Robert T., (p), Little Washington, Homestead Grays
Walker, Zeke, ss, c, mgr., Orange
Wallace, David, Avon
Wallace, Henry, Avon
Wallace, John, cf, Avon
Wallace, Monk, Avon
Wallace, Russell, of, (p), Greenwood Avon
Waller, Alexander (Crow), c, Ivy Eagles
Waller, David, Ivy Eagles
Waller, Henry, Jr., (Bubba), (p), Ivy Eagles
Waller, Henry, Sr., mgr., Ivy Eagles
Waller, James (Boo), (p), ss, Ivy Eagles, Greenwood Hawks
Walton, Mike, 2b, (p), Wilmington, University of Richmond
Walton, Reno, (p), Wilmington, Manatee, Jr., College FL
Ward, Dick, c, Madison
Ward, Juicy, 1b, Madison
Ware, Chinn, 1b, Orange Nats, Grassland Sluggers
Ware, Howard, Orange
Ware, Robert (Butter), cf, Orange
Ware, Walter, Orange Nats
Washington, Bernard, North Garden, Covesville
Washington, James (J.E.), (p), mgr., Orange
Washington, Joseph Jr. (Pee Wee), of, Greenwood Twins, Ivy Eagles
Washington, Joseph L., of, Greenwood
Washington, Kenneth, Avon Twins
Washington, Leif, (p), Harrisonburg
Washington, Lester, Crozet
Washington, Lester, (Flash), Crozet
Washington, Russell, Crozet Allstars, Greenwood Hawks
Watkins, Vernon (Junior), (p), Orange Nats
Watts, Robert, Greenwood
Wells, Andrew, (p), of, Covesville Astros
Wells, Massie, asst. mgr., Avon Twins
Wheeler, Lawrence, Shipman
Whindelton, Meredith, (Butch), South Garden
White, Frank, 3b, Staunton Wild Cats, Greenwood Hawks, Greenfield
White, George, Greenwood Hawks
White, Robert, Jr., Staunton Wild Cats
White, Walter, Barboursville Giants
Whitelow, Clarency, Harrisonburg ACs
Whitelow, Junious (Junior) 1B, Mgr. Harrisonburg ACs
Whiting, Ricky, c, Ivy Eagles
Williams, Charles, Jr., ss, Little Washington Monarchs, of, mgr., Sperryville Tigers
Williams, Charles, Sr., Sperryville Yellow Jackets
Williams, George, Sperryville Tigers
Williams, Harold, Elkton Bucks
Williams, Howard, Grassland Sluggers
Williams, David, 3b, Madison Orioles
Williams, Frank, Covesville Tigers
Williams, John, Sperryville Yellow Jackets
Williams, Malcolm, 3b, Roanoke Black Cardinals
Williams, Thomas (Dootley), ss, Sperryville Tigers
Williams, Tom, (p) Sperryville Yellow Jackets
Wilson, Alfred, ss, Buckingham
Winkey, Charles, Gordonsville Eagles
Winkey, George, Gordonsville Eagles
Winston, Bradley, 1b, Keene
Winston, Claude, c, Wilmington Eagles
Winston, Robert, Jr., (Pogo), c, Wilmington Eagles
Winston, Robert, Sr., (Cool Papa), 1b, Wilmington Eagles
Wood, Lewis (Fat Daddy), c, Crozet Allstars
Woodfolk, Charles (Dinky) IF, Charlottesville Squeeze-Ins
Wright, Ray, Shipman
Wright, Roy, Grassland Sluggers
Wyant, David, (p) Barboursville Giants, Charlottesville Royals, University of Virginia
Yancey, Charlie, (p), Kelly's Allstars

Chapter Notes

Chapter II

1. *Washington* [D.C.] *Afro-American* 5-8-37, 7-17-37.
2. *Charlottesville Daily Progress*, 8-29-38, 9-6-38.
3. *Charlottesville Daily Progress* 6-29-36; *Baltimore Afro-American* 8-2-37.
4. *Charlottesville Daily Progress*, 8-12-35, 8-19-35.
5. *Charlottesville Daily Progress*, 6-15-36, 8-30-36, 7-16-38, 7-18-38.
6. *Charlottesville Daily Progress*, 7-24-37.
7. *Charlottesville Daily Progress*, 5-18-36.
8. *Charlottesville Daily Progress*, 7-21-37.
9. *Charlottesville Daily Progress*, 6-15-36.
10. *Charlottesville Daily Progress*, 7-1-37.
11. *Washington* [D.C.] *Afro-American*, 10-24-36.
12. *Washington* [D.C.] *Afro-American*, 7-17-37; *Charlottesville Daily Progress*, 9-6-37.
13. *Charlottesville Daily Progress*, 8-20-37.
14. *Charlottesville Daily Progress*, 9-10-38.
15. *Charlottesville Daily Progress*, 6-20-38.
16. *Charlottesville Daily Progress*, 6-12-39.
17. Riley, James, *Biographical Encyclopedia of the Negro Leagues*, 374.
18. Holway, John B., *Blackball Stars*, 382.
19. Peterson, Robert, *Only the Ball Was White*, 264.
20. Holway, John, *Black Ballstars*, 355, 367, 368.
21. *Baltimore Afro-American*, 8-24-35.
22. *Baltimore Afro-American*, 7-27-35.
23. *Norfolk Journal and Guide*, 7-13-46.
24. *Baltimore Afro-American*, 7-27-35.
25. *Norfolk Journal and Guide* 6-10-39.
26. Overmyer, James, *Queen of the Negro Leagues*, 179.
27. *Baltimore Afro-American*, 8-10-35, 6-10-36.
28. *Norfolk Journal and Guide*, 7-12-41.
29. *Richmond Afro-American*, 8-5-39, *Norfolk Journal and Guide*, 8-5-39.
30. Riley, James, *Biographical Encyclopedia of the Negro Baseball Leagues*, 414.
31. *Norfolk Journal and Guide*, 8-19-39.
32. Peterson, Robert, *Only the Ball Was White*, 377.
33. *Norfolk Journal and Guide*, 8-3-40, 8-31-40.
34. Peterson, Robert, *Only the Ball Was White*, 38, 39.
35. Peterson, Robert, *Only the Ball Was White*, 221, 262.
36. Peterson, Robert, *Only the Ball Was White*, 13, 14.
37. Riley James, *Biographical Encyclopedia of the Negro Baseball Leagues*, 684.
38. *Baltimore Afro-American*, 5-25-40; *Norfolk Journal and Guide*, 9-7-40.
39. Overmyer, James, *Queen of the Negro Leagues*, 85.
40. *Baltimore Afro-American*, 8-22-31.
41. *Baltimore Afro-American*, 8-3-35, 8-0-35, 8-24-35, 5-20-36, 6-6-36, 6-13-36.
42. *Norfolk Journal and Guide*, 6-17-39.
43. Riley, James, *Biographical Encyclopedia of the Negro Baseball Leagues*, 480, 481.
44. Kelly, Brent, *The Negro Leagues Revisited*, 109-112.
45. Riley, James, *Biographical Encyclopedia of the Negro Baseball Leagues*, 548, 692.
46. Riley, James, *Biographical Encyclopedia of the Negro Baseball Leagues*, 425.
47. Overmyer, James, *Queen of the Negro Leagues*, 179; Riley, James, *Biographical Encyclopedia of the Negro Baseball Leagues*, 663, 778.
48. Riley, James, *Biographical Encyclopedia of the Negro Baseball Leagues*, 221; *Norfolk Journal and Guide*, 5-6-39, 5-13-39.
49. Riley, James, *Biographical Encyclopedia of the Negro Baseball Leagues*, 761.
50. *Norfolk Journal and Guide*, 5-6-39, 5-13-39.
51. *Norfolk Journal and Guide*, 6-10-39, 7-29-39.
52. Riley, James, *Biographical Encyclopedia of the Negro Baseball Leagues*, 55, 56.
53. *Norfolk Journal and Guide*, 7-12-39.
54. *Norfolk Journal and Guide*, 5-27-39.
55. *Norfolk Journal and Guide*, 7-1-39.
56. *Norfolk Journal and Guide*, 7-8-39.
57. *Norfolk Journal and Guide*, 7-22-39; Riley, James, *Biographical Encyclopedia of the Negro Baseball Leagues*, 391, 392.
58. *Norfolk Journal and Guide*, 8-5-39.

59. *Norfolk Journal and Guide*, 9-2-39.
60. *Norfolk Journal and Guide*, 4-24-40, 7-6-40.
61. *Norfolk Journal and Guide*, 8-3-40, 8-10-40, 8-31-40.
62. *Norfolk Journal and Guide*, 8-24-40, 8-31-40.
63. *Norfolk Journal and Guide*, 8-31-40, 9-14-40.

Chapter III

1. *Richmond Afro-American* 4-13-40, 5-18-40.
2. Peterson, Robert, *Only the Ball Was White*, 259, 273; Riley, James, *Biographical Encyclopedia of the Negro Baseball Leagues*, 369, 761.
3. Riley, James, *Biographical Encyclopedia of the Negro Baseball Leagues*, 50.
4. *Baltimore Afro-American*, 9-15-34; *Washington [D.C.] Afro-American*, 4-10-37, 5-1-37.
5. *Norfolk Journal and Guide*, 7-15-39.
6. *Washington [D.C.] Afro-American*, 6-10-39.
7. Riley, James, *Biographical Encyclopedia of the Negro Baseball Leagues*, 409, 410.
8. Riley, James, *Biographical Encyclopedia of the Negro Baseball Leagues*, 42.
9. Riley, James, *Biographical Encyclopedia of the Negro Baseball Leagues*, 414.
10. *Baltimore Afro-American*, 5-6-33, 6-25-33, 6-23-34.
11. *Washington [D.C.] Afro-American*, 5-29-37.
12. *Washington [D.C.] Afro-American*, 4-24-37, 5-1-37, 5-8-37.
13. *Baltimore Afro-American*, 9-24-34.
14. *Washington [D.C.] Afro-American*, 8-20-38.
15. Riley, James, *Biographical Encyclopedia of the Negro Baseball Leagues*, 822, 889.
16. *Baltimore Afro-American*, 7-27-35.
17. *Richmond Afro-American*, 5-25-40.
18. *Richmond Afro-American*, 6-8-40; *Baltimore Afro-American*, 7-30-40.
19. *Richmond Afro-American*, 6-22-40.
20. *Richmond Afro-American*, 5-11-40, 5-18-40, 6-8-40.
21. *Baltimore Afro-American*, 7-13-40; 7-27-40.
22. *Baltimore Afro-American*, 7-6-40; *Richmond Afro-American*, 8-11-40; *Baltimore Afro-American*, 9-21-40.
23. *Norfolk Journal and Guide*, 5-31-41.
24. *Norfolk Journal and Guide*, 8-2-41, 7-18-42.
25. *Norfolk Journal and Guide*, 7-18-42, 7-25-42.
26. Riley, James, *Biographical Encyclopedia of the Negro Baseball Leagues*, 424, 425.
27. *Norfolk Journal and Guide*, 7-12-41, 8-2-41, 8-16-41.
28. *Norfolk Journal and Guide*, 4-19-41.
29. *Richmond Afro-American*, 6-10-39.
30. *Norfolk Journal and Guide*, 5-6-39; *Richmond Afro-American*, 7-15-39.
31. *Richmond Afro-American*, 7-29-39.
32. Peterson, Robert, *Only the Ball Was White*, 367.
33. Riley, James, *Biographical Encyclopedia of the Negro Baseball Leagues*, 108.
34. *Washington [D.C.] Afro-American*, 5-13-39, 5-20-39, 5-27-39, 6-10-39, 7-8-39.
35. *Norfolk Journal and Guide*, 7-5-47.
36. *Norfolk Journal and Guide*, 7-10-48, 9-4-48.
37. *Norfolk Journal and Guide*, 8-18-45, 7-10-48, 8-7-48.
38. Riley, James, *Biographical Encyclopedia of the Negro Baseball Leagues*, 88; *Richmond Afro-American*, 9-3-49, 9-24-49.
39. *Norfolk Journal and Guide*, 7-5-47, 7-12-47, 7-19-47, 8-16-47.
40. *Norfolk Journal and Guide*, 8-6-48, 8-28-48.
41. *Norfolk Journal and Guide*, 7-21-45.
42. *Norfolk Journal and Guide*, 8-2-47.
43. *Norfolk Journal and Guide*, 7-25-47, 8-16-47.
44. *Norfolk Journal and Guide*, 6-4-49, 6-18-49, 6-25-49.
45. *Richmond Afro-American*, 9-3-49, 9-10-49.
46. *Richmond Afro-American*, 9-24-49.
47. *Norfolk Journal and Guide*, 8-5-39, 8-12-39.
48. *Norfolk Journal and Guide*, 8-17-40.
49. *Norfolk Journal and Guide*, 4-26-41, 5-10-41, 7-5-41.
50. *Norfolk Journal and Guide*, 7-11-42.
51. *Baltimore Afro-American*, 8-31-40.

Chapter IV

1. *Roanoke Tribune*, 6-7-52.
2. *Roanoke Tribune*, 6-14-52.
3. *Roanoke Tribune*, 6-28-52.
4. *Charlottesville Albemarle Tribune*, 7-58, 9-58.
5. *Charlottesville Albemarle Tribune*, 6-59.
6. *Charlottesville Daily Progress*, 12-12-61.
7. *Baltimore Afro-American*, 7-8-33, 7-22-33.
8. *Baltimore Afro-American*, 6-8-35.
9. Riley, James, *Biographical Encyclopedia of the Negro Baseball Leagues*, 811.
10. *The Rappahannock News*, 7-23-59.

Chapter V

1. *Charlottesville Albemarle Tribune*, 8-4-60.
2. *Charlottesville Albemarle Tribune*, 8-60.
3. *Charlottesville Albemarle Tribune*, 8-18-60.
4. *Charlottesville Albemarle Tribune*, 6-29-61.
5. *Charlottesville Albemarle Tribune*, 8-10-61.
6. *Charlottesville Albemarle Tribune*, 8-31-61.
7. *Charlottesville Albemarle Tribune*, 7-13-61.
8. *Charlottesville Albemarle Tribune*, 7-61, 9-6-62; *Orange Review*, 8-14-66.

9. *Charlottesville Albemarle Tribune*, 8-31-61.
10. *Charlottesville Albemarle Tribune*, 7-27-61.
11. *Charlotteville Albemarle Tribune* 8-24-61.
12. *Charlottesville Albemarle Tribune*, 9-61.
13. *Charlottesville Albemarle Tribune*, 8-23-62, 9-27-62.
14. *Charlottesville Albemarle Tribune*, 8-30-62.
15. *Charlottesville Albemarle Tribune*, 9-6-62.
16. *Rappahannock News*, 7-9-61, 8-61.
17. *Rappahannock News*, 8-10-61.
18. *Orange Review*, 8-67.
19. *Orange Review*, 8-14-66.

Chapter VI

1. *Charlottesville Albemarle Tribune*, 5-12-77, 5-19-77, 5-26-77, 6-77, 6-2-77, 6-23-77, 8-77, 7-20-78, 7-79.
2. *Charlottesville Daily Progress*, 9-17-78.

Bibliography

Books

Adelson, Bruce. *Brushing Back Jim Crow*. Charlottesville: University Press of Virginia, 1999.

Holway, John. *Black Ball Stars, Negro League Pioneers*. New York: Carroll and Graf/Richard Gallen, 1992.

Kelly, Brent. *Voices from the Negro Leagues*. Jefferson, NC: McFarland, 1998.

Overmyer, James. *Queen of the Negro Leagues*. Lanham, MD: Scarecrow, 1998.

Peterson, Robert. *Only the Ball Was White*. New York: Gramercy, 1999.

Riley, James A. *Biographical Encyclopedia of the Negro Baseball Leagues*. New York: Carroll and Graf, 1994.

Newspapers

Baltimore Afro-American
Charlottesville Albemarle Tribune
Charlottesville Daily Progress
The News-Virginian
Norfolk Journal and Guide
Orange Review
Richmond Afro-American
Roanoke Tribune
Washington [D.C.] Afro-American

Interviews

Jim Dowell, 5-13-99, 12-99
Roger Bowles, 7-14-99
Linwood Awkard, 7-18-99
Alfred Martin, 7-18-99
Elgie B. Sims, George Sims, 7-18-99
Michael Smith, 7-18-99
Bob Winston, 7-22-99
R. Matthew Davis, Sr., 8-25-99
Roscoe Burgess, 9-25-99
Lenny Dowell, 10-99
John Armstead, 12-15-99
James "Boo" Waller, 12-21-99
Edward Henderson, 2-00
Doswell Diggs, Jr., 2-13-00
Buckingham Grays, Cumberland Sluggers, 3-00. Charles Agee, Willie Chambers, Frank Harris, George "Pop" Reed, Lawrence Robertson, William "Rabbit" Robertson, Charles White.
Leroy Stevens, 3-5-00
Jackie Spears, 3-8-00
Isaiah Mosby, 4-7-00
Ivanhoe Nelson, 7-00
Mel Perrow, 8-00, 1-30-01
Billy Shanks, Bobby Slaughter, 8-00
G. Rabbit Johnson, 8-12-00
Bobby Hudson, 10-5-00
Bobby Clanagan, David Clanagan, Will Carter, Arthur Freeman, 10-8-00
Kenny Diggs, 8-10-01
Al Holland, Sr., 8-21-01
Ralph Franklin, 9-01
Richard Slaughter, 9-01, 11-20-18
Michael Carey, 5-7-19
Robert Anthony, 6-19
Herman B. Awkard, Sr., 6-23-21
Phil Doyle, 4-03
James Becks, 4-21
Thomas Bibb, 7-19
David Wyant, 4-23

Index

Aaron, Henry "Hank" 31, 192
Abell, Clarence 121, 214
Agee, Jack 155, 214
Agee, Parkey 155, 214
Agee, Richard 155, 214
Akers, Herbert 77
Akers, John 114, 118, 214
Alabama Dodgers 25
Alco Flashes 45, 51
Alexander, Forrest 214
Alexander, Howard 141, 149, 161, 162, 214
Alexander, William 214
Alexandria Braves 120, 155, 210
Aylor, Bill 101
Allen, Melvin 101
Alston, Frank 47
Amelia 82, 83, 159, 210
Amelia Cubs 210
American Legion Baseball 75
Amherst 54, 55, 60, 61, 63, 71, 72, 100
Anacostia A.C. 39
Anderson, Early 155
Anderson, Ren 155
Apple Valley League 191, 198, 199
Appomattox VA 54, 71, 143
Arlington Athletics 120, 210
Arlington Black Sox 95
Armstead, John 122, 123 157, 158 177, 214
Armstead, Sterling 214
Armstead, William (Willie Wee) 122, 214
Armstead Hill (Ivy) VA 126
Arvonia VA 54
Asheville Black Tourist 45
Asheville Blues 34, 47, 48, 210
Ashland Tigers 27, 209, 213
Atlanta Black Crackers 25, 32, 47, 48, 191, 218
Atlanta White Sox 35
Atlantic City Bacharach Giants 46, 213
Avery, John 76, 214
Avon VA 76, 77, 78, 79, 184
Avon Allstars 184, 214, 215, 217
Avon A's 185, 200, 212

Avon Twins 155, 162, 177, 186, 212
Avon Wrecking Crew (A.W.C) 136, 150, 184, 211
Awkard, Herman Brad, Jr. 184
Awkard, Herman Brad, Sr. 161, 162, 163, 164, 165, 171, 173, 184, 185, 214, 225
Awkard, Kenneth 161, 214
Awkard, Linwood (Lin) 69, 70, 72, 139, 184, 214, 225
Awkard, Marshton 141, 184, 214
Awkard, Russell 40
Aylor, Bill (Big Bill) 93, 130, 214
Aylor, Reg 92
Aylor, Russell L. "Sam" 92, 102, 128, 129, 130, 131, 134, 142, 146, 148, 198
Aylor, William (Moody) 129, 132, 133, 214

Baltimore Afro-American 190, 221
Baltimore Black Sox 8, 24, 31, 33, 35, 41, 42, 45, 46, 194, 209, 213
Baltimore Elite Giants 24, 30, 34, 42, 45, 52, 213
Baltimore Stars 29, 33
Banks, Arthur 20, 23, 214
Banks, Norman 25, 26, 213
Bannister, James 149, 214
Barbee, Lamb (Bud) 26, 33
Barbee, Quincy 34
Barber, Jesse (Jess) 213
Barbour, Chris 157, 161, 214
Barbour, Frank "Frankie" 157, 158, 161, 214
Barbour, Kenneth "K.B." 214
Barbour, Stanley 214
Barboursville 72, 73, 138
Barboursville Giants 72–79, 136, 137, 141, 147, 152, 178, 182, 185, 210–212
Barratt, Doc 75, 214
Bartlett, Robert 27
Baseball Hall of Fame 8, 16
Bates, Carroll 78, 79, 147, 214

Beasley, Lawrence 214
Beasley, William "Willie" 75, 76, 214
Becks, James 61–63, 214
Beckwith, John 35
Bedford VA 22, 45, 71
Bell, Herman 174, 175, 200, 214
Belleville Grays (Portsmouth VA) 29, 31–37, 42, 44, 207
Berkley, Percell 106, 107, 109, 214
Berkley, Theodore "Teddy" 162, 165. 214
Berkley Braves 29, 35, 207
Better Business Boosters 26–28, 31, 36, 38, 46, 50, 209, 213
Bi-State League 40, 41, 213
Bing Crosby Stadium (Winchester VA) 95, 199
Birmingham Black Barons 31, 44
Black, Joesph "Joe" 44, 53
Blackstone VA 53, 54, 165, 208
Blair, Garnett 47, 49
Blair, G.G. 69, 214
Blakey, Wilson 148, 214
Boston ABCs 28, 30
Boston Royal Giants 27
Boswell, Vincent 168, 169, 173, 214
Bowles, Roger 159–161, 163, 165, 166, 171, 182, 200, 214, 225
Bowman, Lefty 30
Boyd, Frank 51–53, 214
Boze, (Pitcher, CCC) 21
Brackett, Tyrone 214
Brandy Station VA 97
Bridges, Arthur 93, 214
Bridgwater VA 100, 101, 201, 202, 206
Bridgewater College 159
Briery Branch VA (baseball) 100, 204, 205
Briggs, Otto 46
Brock, Lou 192, 193
Brock, Vance 148, 152, 200, 214
Brooklyn Cuban Giants 92
Brooklyn Dodgers 54, 89, 93, 192, 189

227

Index

Brooklyn Royal Giants 27, 28, 51
Brooks, David "Dave" 161–165, 182, 215
Brown, Lloyd 107, 109, 215
Brown, Raymond 39
Brown, Robert, Jr. 165, 166, 215
Brown, Robert, Sr. 165, 166, 215
Buckingham Grays 54
Buckner, Sam 74, 115, 215
Buena Vista VA 11, 28
Buhl, Bob 64
Bull Run Panthers 77
Burgess, Don 101, 102, 215
Burgess, Bernard 102
Burgess, Ronald 102, 205
Burgess, Roscoe, Jr. 102, 205
Burgess, Roscoe, Sr. 62, 63, 89, 100–103, 126, 134–140, 146, 147, 153, 180, 201, 203–206, 215, 225
Burley, Jackson P. 59, 67, 69, 104–107, 110, 123, 124, 144, 145, 147, 150, 155, 167, 179, 186
Burley Field 147, 155, 167, 186
Burley High School 69, 123, 150, 179
Burton, Gene 76, 105, 215
Burton, Harold 145, 215
Burton, Randall 76, 215
Butler, Lewis 102, 128, 129
Byers, Clinton 143, 215
Byers, Curtis 143, 179, 215
Byers, Donald 143, 145, 215

Cabell, Bud 20, 215
Cabell, Robert "Bobby" 175–177, 215
Calhoun, Leon "Lee" 38
Camden Giants 45, 46, 209
Camp Pickett Warriors 44, 53, 208
Capital City Elks 23, 25, 36, 38, 42, 43, 51, 208, 209, 213
Carey, Cornel 154
Carey, Cyril 159, 215
Carey, Michael 156, 159, 161, 166, 181–183, 215, 225
Carolina Semipro League 210
Carter, Art 38
Carter, Howard 58, 61, 85, 87, 88, 215
Carter, Jake 96, 215
Carter, Louis 68, 215
Carter, Mitchell 145, 202, 215
Carter, William 93, 95, 215
Cartersville VA 159
Cartledge, Menskie 47
Chambers, Willie 54, 55, 215
Charleston, Oscar 33, 41
Charlotte-Asheville Blues 49
Charlotte Black Hornets 33
Charlottesville Albemarle

Tribune 115, 181, 222, 223, 225
Charlottesville Cellar Dodgers 104, 105
Charlottesville Cubs 62
Charlottesville Elks 19, 111
Charlottesville Hornets 155, 170
Charlottesville Royals 178, 179
Charlottesville Squeeze-Ins 82, 104–106–110, 117, 135, 148
Charlottesville Tigers 5
Chase City VA 54, 211
Chesterfield Hornets 27
Chestnut Grove VA 60, 123
Chicago American Giants 3, 7, 8, 31, 32, 35
Chisholm, Chuck 20, 105, 109
Cincinnati Reds 107, 181, 191
Civilian Conservation Corp (CCC) 21
Clannagan, Bobby 92, 94, 215
Clannagan, David 198, 199, 215
Clark, Phillip 141, 215
Clark, Roger 162, 215
Clark, Sam (The Beast from the East DJ) 199
Clarke, Robert 24, 49, 213
Cleveland Buckeyes 28, 47
Cleveland Red Sox 40, 47
Clifton Forge C & O Nine 19
Clover Hill VA 100, 181
Coleman, Marcellus 79, 83, 200, 215
Coles, William 106, 215
Collins, George 66, 68, 69, 111, 123, 135, 215
Conn, Asher 106, 109, 215
Cooperstown NY (MLB Baseball Hall of Fame) 8, 11, 16, 17
Copeland, Otis 60
Covesville Astros 137, 145, 146, 150, 154, 155, 158, 163, 166–173, 176, 179, 198, 199, 211, 212
Covesville Tigers 4, 58, 63, 66, 69, 76, 78, 84, 86, 90, 91, 108
Covesville Yankees 52
Covington Red Sox 19
Crewe VA 54
Crozet Allstars 68, 69
Cuban X Giants 7
Culpeper A.C. 22, 95, 99
Culpeper Dragons 84, 95–98, 113, 115, 116
Cumberland Sluggers 52–55

Dandridge, Raymond "Ray" 25, 189, 194, 213
Danville Aces 47, 50, 51, 210, 213
Danville Allstars 191, 210, 213
Davis, Charles "Buddy" 73, 118, 215

Davis, Greg 152, 186, 187
Davis, Jimmy 76, 185, 215
Davis, Keith 152, 178, 183, 186, 187
Davis, Leewood 180, 181, 215
Davis, Matthew R., Jr. "Ricky" 152, 178, 186, 215
Davis, Matthew, Sr. "Mack" 73–77, 80, 113, 115, 118, 129, 138–142, 144–150, 152, 178, 180, 185, 187, 200–204, 215
Davis, Spencer 32, 49
Davis, Stanley 152, 202, 204, 215
Davis, Walker 76, 185, 215
Davis Brothers (Elkton) 180
Dawson, Richard 53, 216
Day, Leon 30
Deberry, C.I. 46
Debran, Roy 26, 49
Detroit Stars 8, 24, 25, 213
Diggs, Doswell 139, 140, 216, 225
Diggs, Elnorah 140
Diggs, Kenny 216
Diggs, Sidney 141, 216
Dixie Aces 45
Dixie Hill (Buckingham VA) 54
Douglas, Charles 106, 109, 216
Douglas, Dale 77
Douglas, William 106, 109, 216
Dowell, Curtis 154, 216
Dowell, Cyril 170
Dowell, Early 23, 58–61, 66, 70, 85, 86, 88, 216
Dowell, Haywood 56, 216
Dowell, Jim 73, 76, 84–91, 124, 137, 140, 145, 147, 150, 166–172, 198, 216, 225
Dowell, Joseph 216
Dowell, Lee 76, 86, 145, 172 216
Dowell, Rufus 57, 58, 73, 85, 86, 146, 172, 216
Dowell, William 169, 170, 216
Doyle, Curt 164, 216
Doyle, Phil 164, 183, 216
Dudley, Sterling 106–109, 216
Dupont Grays 23, 61, 69, 100, 208
Durham Athletic Park (Durham NC) 47
Durham Black Sox 26, 30, 31, 33, 34, 209
Durrette, Wesley Dean 123, 216

Easley, Howard 51, 216
East vs. West 1962 Allstar Game 95
Easter, Luke 49, 74
Eastern Colored League 6, 28, 31, 33, 39, 42, 45
Ebony and Ivory Field (Nelson Co. VA) 176

Index

Edgewater Giants 38, 41–43
Edinburg VA 198
Elam, Jim 26, 213
Elkton Bucks 180, 203, 211, 212
Ellis, Charles 202
Ellis, George 202
Ellis, Gus 22
Emporia Eagles 27, 44
Esmont Giants 60, 76, 80, 116, 136, 144
Esmont Rattlers 212
Ethiopian Clowns 51, 52, 207
Evans, George 92, 96

Fairview Lodge VA 54
Falls Church VA 117, 120, 121, 133, 134, 210
Farmers Park (Culpeper VA) 96
Farmville VA 44, 105, 108, 213
Federico, Sal 49
Fields, Wilmer 43, 49, 92, 213
Finney, Ed 47
Fischer, Frank 141, 216
Fletcher, Hampton 93, 216
Flippen, Harry 141, 216
Fluvanna Co. High School (Fluvanna Co. VA) 159, 165, 183
Fork Union VA 80, 181, 182
Fort Eustis Black Sox 30
Foster, A.R "Rube" 7
Foster, Willie 24
Four County League 75, 76, 134, 210
Franklin, George 51
Franklin, Melvin 51
Franklin, Morris 80
Franklin, Paul, Jr. 81
Franklin Paul, Sr. 80, 81, 83, 159–161, 163–166, 181, 216
Franklin, Ralph 83, 166, 216, 225
Franklin, Tommy 80
Franklin Elks 27, 29, 209
Freeman, Arthur 93, 225
Front Royal 23, 62, 66, 91, 94, 95, 98, 100, 117, 132, 199, 200
Frye, Frank 126, 216
Frye, Johnny 75, 76, 115, 118, 216
Frye, Lewis 75, 76, 216
Fulton Dodgers 82

Gaines, Elmo 175, 216
Gaines, Fletcher, Jr. 175, 216
Gaines, Fletcher, Sr. 68, 71, 72, 175, 216
Gardener, Bobby 155, 216
Gardener, Wayne 155, 216
Garner, Horace 47
Garrett, Moses 54, 55
Garys Grays 207
Gehrig, Lou 26
George Washington Carver High School (Culpeper Co. VA) 104, 112, 116, 179
Georgetown Athletics 38, 209
Gibson, Josh 30, 39, 52, 55, 190
Gilbert, Theodore 106, 109, 216
Giles, Alex 21, 22, 71
Giles, John "Jackie" 22
Giles, Roger 22
Giles, Wallace 22
Glasgow, Arthur 93, 216
Glasgow, Ellis 95, 117, 120, 217
Glover, Robert 20, 217
Gordonsville Bacharachs 19
Gordonsville Eagles 73, 75, 76, 115–117, 120, 148, 210
Graves, Whit 47
Gray, Donald 76, 136, 144, 217
Gray, Willie 76, 136, 144, 217
Green Valley VA 39
Greensboro Redwings 45, 46, 49, 50, 52, 209, 210
Greenwood A.C. 64
Greenwood Hawks 71, 78, 85, 86, 94, 95, 100, 108, 110, 111, 117, 121, 123, 125, 127, 135–139, 141–143, 145–149, 157, 162, 180, 201, 202, 211, 212
Greenwood Twins 211, 212
Griffith Stadium 33, 39, 40, 47, 49
Grottoes VA 100, 156, 185, 197, 212

Hackley, Leroy 94, 96, 217
Hall, Eulie 26, 217
Hanover Co. VA 82, 194, 208, 210
Harney, George 24
Harper, Stanley 141, 217
Harris, Frank 54
Harrisonburg ACs 62, 63, 100–103, 132, 148, 151, 153, 198, 204, 205
Harrisonburg Nationals 148
Harrisonburg Red Sox 62, 92, 100
Hartford Conn. Indians 48
Hawkins, Montague 78, 217
Hay Market VA 198
Hays, Burnalle 39
Haywood, Albert 42, 213
Hearns, Samuel 80, 217
Henderson, Albert 56, 58, 58, 66, 217
Henderson, Allen 90, 217
Henderson, Arthur 171, 217
Henderson, Edward 55, 59, 62, 64, 78, 79, 86, 92, 100, 217, 225
Henderson, Harold 168, 217
Henderson, James, Jr. 162, 166, 169–171, 217
Henderson, James, Sr. 56, 60, 217
Henderson, Luther 57, 217
Henderson, Ricky 91
Henderson, Robert 56, 217
Henderson, Samuel 56, 217
Heurich Brewers 43
High Point Red Sox 45, 46, 207, 209
High Rock Park (Norfolk VA) 47
Hill, Abraham 15
Hill, John Preston "Pete" 7–18, 213
Hill, Reuben 15
Hill, Ron 16
Hilldales (Darby PA) 7
Holland, Al, Sr. 51, 52, 225
Hollaway, Chris "Crush" 42
Homestead Grays 7
Honey Mooner's Park (Fluvanna Co VA) 80, 82
Hooker, Leniel "Len" 34, 50
Horseshoe Diamond (Sperryville VA) 116, 128, 131
House of David Nine 27, 43, 46, 207
Houston Astros 165, 193, 196
Howard, Herman 126, 217
Howard, Randolph 112–119, 217
Howard, Roger 11, 162, 217
Hudson, Bobby 58, 68–72, 86, 87, 217, 225
Hudson, Eddie 70–72, 86, 217
Hughes, Brian 73, 74, 217
Humes, Clarence 113, 217
Humes, Moses 113, 217
Huntsville Senators 40
Hyman, Isaiah 47

Idelson, Jeff 16
Indianapolis ABCs 32, 33
Indianapolis Clowns 31, 42, 44, 45, 48, 213
Inlet VA 117, 120
Intercounty League 153, 155, 160, 166, 169, 170, 175, 186, 206, 212
Interstate League 36, 38, 39, 42–45, 209
Irvin, Monte 24, 189
Israel, Clarence 40
Ivory, Henry 121, 217
Ivory, John Henry 157, 158, 217
Ivory, Larry 157, 158, 217
Ivory, Louis 217
Ivy Eagles 5, 73, 88, 121, 125, 137, 145, 148, 161, 211, 212

Jackson, Alex 140, 202, 217
Jackson, Alvin 140, 217
Jackson, Archie 155, 217
Jackson, Donald 140, 217
Jackson, General 98, 99, 217

Index

Jackson, John R. 140, 161, 162, 167, 217
Jackson, Lester 27, 28, 213
Jackson, Norman 40
Jackson, Ray 113, 130, 134, 148, 217
Jackson, Robert 139, 140, 141, 162, 217
Jackson, Roger 115, 118, 217
Jackson, Roy 99, 131, 217
Jackson, Strother, Jr. 150, 200, 217
Jacksonville Eagles 48, 191, 213
Jacksonville Red Caps 32
Jacobs, Eddie 45
Jenkins, James 44, 213
Jessup, Gentry 32, 42
Johnson, Brady 32, 47
Johnson, David 166, 170, 171, 173, 200, 217
Johnson, George 28
Johnson, Gilbert 167, 168, 217
Johnson, James 129, 217
Johnson, Judy 51
Johnson, Lawrence 168, 172–174, 217
Johnson, Louis 75, 217
Johnson, Walter 47
Johnson, William 44, 166, 217
Jones, Charles "Charlie" 19–21, 23, 80, 95, 217
Jones, Frank 121, 217
Jones, James 50–52, 218
Jones, Leroy 76
Jones, Percell 106, 107, 109, 218
Jones, Powell 54, 218
Jones, Raymond 121, 218
Jordan, George 92, 218
Jordan, Henry 92, 218

Kansas City Monarchs 28, 52, 213
Kate Collins Jr. High School 66
Keene Colts 183, 212
Kelly, Harry 19, 20, 218
Kelly, James 19, 20, 23, 218
Kelly, Leroy 19, 20, 218
Kelly, Levi 20, 218
Kelly, Lewis 58, 66, 69, 218
Kelly, Raleigh 19, 20, 218
Kelly, Walker 20, 218
Kelly's Allstars 19–24
Keswick Allstars 66, 71–76, 210
Keystone Giants 50, 52
Kidd, Jerry 166, 218
Kinston Grays 43, 44, 207
Kirby, Rodney 144, 154, 218
Knoxville Grays 47

Lacey, Sam 39
Lackawanna Black Sox 27
Lahore Indians 115
Lane, Charley 95–98, 218

Lawrenceville VA 165
Lawson, Frederick 93, 218
Leadbetter, Huddie (Lead Belly) 90
LeDroit Tigers 39
Lee, Bobby 102, 103
Leonard, Walter F. 29, 33, 39, 44, 49
Lewis, Joseph 31, 35, 36, 38, 41, 42, 44, 48
Lewis, Willie, Jr. 105, 106, 109
Lewis, Willie, Sr. 106
Lexington Cubs 28
Ligon, Fulton 21
Logan, Ralph 169
Louisa Eagles (Gordonsville VA) 61, 75, 76, 120
Love, George 84, 96, 113, 116
Luray, Virginia 94, 102, 147
Luray Eagles 66, 95, 117, 132
Lynch, Clyde 141, 218
Lynch, John 38
Lynchburg VA (Campbell Co. VA) 5, 50, 60
Lynchburg Bees 62, 210
Lynchburg City VA 68
Lynchburg Red Sox 28
Lyndhurst VA (Augusta Co. VA) 63, 136
Lyndhurst Wildcats 136, 211

Mackey, Raleigh 40
Madison Blue Jays 149, 151, 153, 191
Madison Heights VA 156, 212
Madison Indians 75, 76, 97, 210
Madison Orioles 136, 137, 186, 211, 212
Manassas Black Yankees 77
Mandak League (Canada) 32, 45
Manley, Abe 29, 207
Marichal, Juan 141
Marshall VA 94, 132, 199
Martin, Alfred 104–109, 144, 147, 148, 159, 200, 218, 225
Martin, Arthur 81, 218
Martin, Huneal "Neal" 144
Martin, Joseph 57, 218
Martinsburg WV 92, 100, 133, 134
Massies Mill Cubs 4, 58, 60, 61, 69, 71, 72, 137, 150, 152, 152, 156, 158, 169, 174–176, 198, 199, 211, 212
Massies Mill Giants 21–23, 54, 55, 71
Matthews, Junious 26, 46
Maupin, William, Sr. "Bill" 121, 218
Mayo, George, Jr. 158, 218
Mayo, George, Sr. 122, 218
Mayo Island VA 26, 28, 42

Mays, Willie 32, 71, 91, 184, 189, 192
Meadow MD 23
Memorial Field (Greensboro NC) 50
Memphis Tigers 48
Merrifield Giants 133, 210
Mickey, James 32
Middleburg VA 91, 120
Miles, Charles 174, 175, 218
Miles, Joseph 38, 208
Mills, James 106, 109, 218
Millwood VA 132
Minneapolis Millers 225, 190
Minor, Bill 75, 82, 83, 107, 123, 218
Minor, Southall 73, 74, 76, 218
Mitchells VA 13, 95, 96
Mobile Grays 47, 48
Mohawk Giants 28, 43, 51, 213
Moore, Max 75, 76, 218
Morris, F.B. 45, 46
Mosby, Isaiah 56, 57, 60, 61, 218, 225
Municipal Stadium (Salem VA) 50, 52
Murray, Freddy 106, 107, 109, 218
Murrill, Metress 77, 112, 113, 116, 218
Myrtle A.C. 23, 40

Negro American Association 26, 28, 32, 41–49, 191, 209, 210
Negro International League 33, 209
Negro Southern League 5, 25, 32, 34, 45, 47, 48, 189, 191
Nellysford VA 144, 155, 156, 175, 176, 212
Nelson, Ivanhoe 153, 154, 155, 156, 183, 218, 225
Nelson, Powhatan 98, 218
Nelson, Warren 98, 218
New York Black Yankees 24, 26, 27, 32, 34, 45, 51, 213
New York Cubans 29, 31, 32, 40, 44
New York Stars 35
Newark Eagles 40, 42, 47, 48, 189, 207
Newport News Black Swans 44
Newport News Giants 27, 29, 30, 31, 33, 35, 36, 37, 209, 210, 213
Niles A.C. 23
Norfolk All-Stars 44, 208
Norfolk Battling Palms 44, 208
Norfolk Black Tars 33, 34, 209
Norfolk County Giants 44, 213
Norfolk Cubs 35, 207, 209
Norfolk Journal and Guide 28, 29, 31, 33, 36, 45, 48, 50, 51, 207, 208, 221, 222, 225

Index

Norfolk-Newport News Royals 47, 48, 50
Norfolk-Portsmouth Virginians 44
Norfolk Red Stockings 28
Norfolk-Southern Giants 29
Norfolk Stars 28
Norfolk Tars 33
North Garden (Shen-Valley 1960s) 136, 211
North Garden All-Stars 75, 76, 134, 210
Nowell, Johnny 110, 144, 218

Oak Leaf Giants 44, 208
Orange, Black Sox 21, 22, 110
Orange Nats 77, 108, 110, 114, 115, 119, 120, 134, 135, 149, 204, 211, 212

Page's Semi-pros 27, 209
Paige, Satchel 34, 48, 52, 57, 65, 66
Paramount All-Stars 25
Payne, Alphonso 81, 218
Payne, Charles 81, 218
Payne, Clarence 81, 218
Payne, James 81, 159, 163, 165, 166, 181, 200, 218
Payne, Theodore 81, 218
Peanut Park (Suffolk VA) 47
Pearson's All-Stars 27, 28, 38, 207, 209
Pennsylvania Hilldales 7, 28, 46
Perkins, James, Jr. (Man) 157, 218
Perkins, James, Sr. 122, 125, 218
Perrow, Curtis 184, 185
Perrow, Melvin (Mel) 4, 150, 152, 156, 173–176, 218, 225
Petersburg Red Sox 27
Philadelphia Giants 7, 208, 213
Philadelphia Stars 28, 34, 40, 42, 207
Piedmont Association 49, 191
Piedmont League 213
Pine Grove All-Stars 117, 120
Pine Knott Inn (Washington VA) 94, 114, 128
Pittsburgh Crawfords 7, 29, 213
Pittsburgh Keystones 7, 213
Pittsburgh Pirates 51, 96, 123, 147
Plummer, Howard Z. 31, 35
Plymouth Tigers 29, 35, 207, 209
Point Pleasant New Jersey Nine 48
Porterfield Park (Orange VA) 77, 112, 114–119, 134, 136, 147, 186, 191
Portsmouth Black Revels 29

Portsmouth Dodgers 35, 207, 209
Portsmouth Fire Fighters 29, 31
Portsmouth Senators 29, 44, 208
Posey, Cumberland 8, 24, 49
Posey, S.H. 49
Powell, Leroy 150
Price A.C. (Richmond Cardinals) 27, 28, 209
Price, John Henry 98

Radcliffe, Alex 48
Radcliffe, Ted 48
Raleigh Grays 34, 44, 45, 50, 208, 210
Raleigh Tigers 34, 47–50, 208, 210
Red House VA 212
Red Robbins A.C. 66, 68
Redding, Richard "Dick" 33
Reed, George 53–55, 219
Remington VA 9, 212, 213
Reva Aces 94–99, 131, 132
Richmond All-Stars 23, 213
Richmond Black Sox 45, 61
Richmond City County League 27–29, 31, 209
Richmond City Stadium 47
Richmond Colts 26, 49
Richmond Giants 6, 24, 47, 49, 50, 210, 213; 1920s 24, 28
Richmond Hilldales 45, 46, 209
Richmond Rams 45
Richmond Royal Giants 27, 207, 209
Riddick, Vernon 32, 42, 213
Riddick, Willie 29, 30
Roanoke All-Stars 51
Roanoke Black Cardinals 28, 36, 45, 50, 52, 53, 63
Roanoke Tribune 75, 76, 222, 225
Robertson, Lawrence 53
Robertson, William 53, 219
Robinson, Bobby 113, 115, 219
Robinson, Charles 113, 219
Robinson, Clarence 113, 115, 117, 119, 219
Robinson, Dee 97
Robinson, Gilbert 117, 119
Robinson, Jackie 8, 58, 66, 81, 89, 91, 107, 188–190, 197
Robinson, Jerome 76
Robinson, Raymond 27
Robinson, Ronnie 113, 119
Robinson, Walker T. 92, 213, 220
Robinson, William 51
Rockingham County Baseball League 181, 204, 205
Roosevelt, Franklin D. 21
Ruffin, Leon 29, 213
Ruth, Babe 26

St. Julien Creek Tigers 29
Sampson, Tommy 31, 42
Scott, Albert 60, 80, 219
Scott, Edward 112, 115, 118, 119, 219
Scott, Eugene 175
Scott, Herman 28, 30, 35, 219
Scott, Hugo 74, 76, 134, 135, 153, 176, 180, 206, 219
Scott, James 175
Seals, Elizabeth "Lizzie" 10, 14–16
Seewanee Stadium (Portsmouth VA) 31, 33
Shanks, Billy 94, 97–99 219, 225
Shanks, Henry, Jr. 96, 219
Shanks, Robert 99, 131, 219
Shelton, George "Chico" 106, 109, 219
Shelton, Nathaniel "Pat" 106, 108, 109, 219
Shelton, Tim 160, 163, 166, 182, 219
Shenandoah Valley League 72, 79, 84, 95, 102, 110, 115, 126, 127, 134, 135, 145, 148, 150, 151, 180, 211, 212
Sheridan, Steve 159–161, 163, 165, 166, 181, 219
Shifflett, Charles 67, 68, 219
Shipman Angels 150, 152, 174, 212
Shipman Spiders 22, 55
Simms, John 36, 46, 50, 57, 207
Sims, Arthur 65, 66, 69, 87, 123, 124, 138, 139, 219
Sims, Bernard 64, 65
Sims, Edward 67, 70, 111, 138, 148, 201, 219, 225
Sims, Elgie, Jr. 162, 173, 219
Sims, Elgie B., Sr. 64–66, 68, 83, 86, 219
Sims, Esters 67, 108, 111, 117, 123, 138, 148, 201, 219
Sims, George 64, 68, 69, 72, 113, 157, 219, 225
Sims, Harvey 157, 219
Sims, Stuart 162, 164, 219
Sims, William J., Jr. 219
Sims, William J., Sr. 67, 219
Singleton, Albert 144
Skipper, George 50
Slaughter, Bobby 113, 131, 149, 219, 225
Slaughter, Richard 97–99, 121, 130–133, 148, 149, 191, 219, 225
Slav Fork Indians 50
Smith, Alexander, Jr. "Alec" 105, 167, 219
Smith, Bob 23, 59, 60, 104
Smith, Earl 76, 85, 86, 89, 219
Smith, Elwood 85, 219
Smith, Herman O. 76

Index

Smith, Herman W. 76
Smith, Lefty 30
Smith, Michael 144, 219, 225
Snead, Clarence, Jr. 112, 113, 117–119, 219
Snead, Clarence, Sr. 112, 219
Sons of Washington 77
South Boston A's 50
South Boston Blue Sox 51
South Garden Tigers 70, 89, 135–137, 140, 143–148, 150–155, 160, 169, 171, 172, 179, 179, 180, 202, 211, 212
South Hampton Prison (VA) 91
Southeast Atlantic League (Sally League) 40, 41
Southern League (MD) 40
Spears, John, Jr. 104–109, 219, 225
Spears, John, Sr. 104, 219
Sperryville Tigers 77, 78, 84, 96–99, 100, 113, 116, 117, 119, 120, 125, 128–137, 142, 145, 146, 148, 149, 151, 154, 177, 191, 198, 202, 211
Sperryville Yellow Jackets 22, 23, 62, 91, 92–95, 100
Spotsylvania Tigers 77, 114, 210
Spotsylvania Yellow Jackets 160, 210
Springwood Park VA 50–52
Spruill, Tony 32, 219
Starks, Harry 128
Staten Island Giants 48
Statesville Giants 30
Staunton VA 62
Staunton A.C. 62
Staunton Wild Cats 62, 63, 210
Stearns, Norman 48
Stephens, Bob 47
Steppe, Herman 69, 219
Stevens, Leroy 85, 87, 89, 90, 140, 143–150, 153, 154, 202, 225
Stevens, Wayne 144, 219
Stewart, Jim 46
Stewart, Lefty 30, 32, 34
Stewman 76
Strasburg VA 94, 95, 117
Stuarts Draft VA 123
Sturgeonville VA 54
Suffolk Aces 27, 35, 44, 207–209, 213
Suffolk Giants 44, 207, 209
Suttles, George (Mule) 20, 30, 34, 48

Tarboro Tigers 30
Taylor, Ben 29, 33, 39, 42
Taylor, C.I. 33
Taylor, George 93
Taylor, Jim 25
Taylor, Roy 102, 103, 219

Terrell, Robert 112, 113, 117, 118, 121, 149, 200, 220
Thomas, Charles 32
Thomas, Dave 27
Thomas, Joseph 38, 41
Thompson, Edward 70, 72, 77, 89, 139, 145, 220
Tiant, Luis 141
Tidewater Classic 36, 50
Tidewater Giants 27, 36, 50, 207, 209
Tolliver, Lewis 59, 80, 20–24
Treasure Island Park VA 27
Tri-County League 165, 176, 182, 212
Trice, Lonnie 152, 156, 160, 161, 164, 166, 182, 220
Trice, Tudie 83, 220
Turner, Raymond 145, 220
Turpin, Phillip 159, 220

University of Richmond 159, 162, 165, 200

Valley League (Rockingham Co. Amateur Baseball) 151, 169, 191
Vaughn, Alex 21, 22, 220
Vaughn, Ben 21, 22, 220
Vest, James 90, 144, 220
Victoria VA 53, 54, 165
Vienna VA 40, 133, 210
Virginia-Carolina League 29, 35, 46, 48, 209, 210
Vista MD Giants 40

Walker, Isaiah 112–116, 118, 119, 152, 200, 220
Walker, Robert (R.T.) 92, 213, 220
Wallace, John 141, 220
Waller, Alexander 125, 220
Waller, Henry, Sr. 122, 127, 220
Waller, James 121–127, 145, 156, 158, 220
Walton, Mike 162, 163, 165, 182, 220
Walton, Reno 162, 163, 165, 182, 220
Ware, Howard 112, 115, 118, 119, 202, 204, 220
Ware, Robert 112, 220
Ware, Walter 112, 115, 118, 119, 202, 204, 220
Warrenton VA 23, 91
Washington, Bernard 76, 85, 220
Washington, James, Sr. 77, 112–117, 135, 220
Washington, Joseph, Jr. 157, 220
Washington, Joseph, Sr. 220
Washington, Leif 101, 220

Washington, Lester 69, 220
Washington Aztecs 38–43, 63, 208, 209
Washington Black Senators 39, 41
Washington DC Afro-American 19, 38, 38, 63, 221, 222, 225
Washington DC (semipro) 133
Washington Eagles 42
Washington Elites 31, 33
Washington Hilldales 28, 30, 31, 35, 39, 41, 45
Washington Park (Charlottesville VA) 19, 59, 62, 106–109, 111, 169
Washington Pilots 39
Washington Potomacs 39
Washington-Rappahannock Monarchs 77, 91–96, 100, 114, 128, 130, 132, 133, 198, 199
Washington Royal Giants 33, 39, 40, 209
Washington Senators 39, 112, 114
Watkins, Abraham 145
Watkins, Maurice 42
Watkins, Vernon "Junior" 112–115, 118, 119, 226
Waverly VA 53, 54
Waynesboro Generals 143, 148, 149, 151
Wells, Andrew 167, 172, 220
Wells, Willie 34
West Indian Royals 51
West Norfolk Slides 44, 208
West Virginia Yellow Jackets 19
Whindleton, Merideth 144, 220
White, Charles 54, 225
White, Frank 87, 220
Whitelow, Clarence 220
Whitelow, Junious 100, 203, 205, 220
Wilder, Joseph 44, 208
Wilder, Pete 44, 208
Williams, Charles, Jr. 93, 113, 129, 130, 133, 148, 220
Williams, Charles, Sr. 92
Williams, Joe "Smokey Joe" 172
Williams, Thomas 129, 220
Williams, Tom 92
Williamsburg Black Sox 30, 45
Wilmington Eagles 57, 80, 87, 108, 148, 150, 155–59, 163, 165, 166, 179, 181, 183, 200, 212
Wilson, Hack 41
Wilson, Jud (Boojum) 8, 39, 213
Wilson NC Braves 30
Winchester VA 3, 91, 92, 95, 100, 117, 120, 132
Winchester Braves 91
Wine Cellar Field (Charlottesville VA) 19

Winston, Claude 166, 220
Winston, Robert, Jr. 166, 220
Winston, Robert, Sr. 158–160, 165, 166, 181, 220, 225
Winston-Salem Giants 32, 43, 45, 46, 49, 209, 210
Winston-Salem Tigers 51
Wintergreen VA 69
Winters, Jesse 28
Wolftown VA 136
Woodfolk, Charles 106, 109, 220
Woodliff, Ralph 50, 51
Woolfolk, Jay 197
Yancey, Charles 20, 23, 106, 220
Yellow Tavern All-Stars 27
Yokely, Laymon 41–43, 46
Yokely's All-Stars 41, 42

www.ingramcontent.com/pod-product-compliance
Lightning Source LLC
Chambersburg PA
CBHW060341010526
44117CB00017B/2913